Complete German

Jonas Langner and Heiner Schenke

First published by Teach Yourself in 2025

An imprint of John Murray Press

1

A CIP catalogue record for this title is available from the British Library

Paperback ISBN 9781399818650

ebook ISBN 9781399818674

Typeset in FS Albert Pro light 10.5/12 by Integra Software Services Pvt. Ltd. Pondicherry, India.

Printed and bound by Oriental Press, Dubai

John Murray Press policy is to use papers that are natural, renewable and recyclable products and made from wood grown in sustainable forests. The logging and manufacturing processes are expected to conform to the environmental regulations of the country of origin.

John Murray Press
Carmelite House
50 Victoria Embankment
London EC4Y 0DZ
www.teachyourself.com

Nicholas Brealey Publishing
Hachette Book Group
Market Place, Center 53, State Street
Boston, MA 02109, USA

John Murray Press, part of Hodder & Stoughton Limited

An Hachette UK company

The authorised representative in the EEA is Hachette Ireland, 8 Castlecourt Centre, Dublin 15, D15 XTP3, Ireland (email: info@hbgi.ie)

The QR codes in this book lead to external websites or content. The publisher has used its best endeavours to ensure that any website addresses are correct and active at the time of going to press. However, the publisher and the author have no responsibility for the websites and can make no guarantee that a site will remain live or that the content will remain relevant, decent or appropriate.

Contents

Resources available online at library.teachyourself.com:

- Audio
- My takeaway study guide
- Test your level: A1, A2, and B1
- German–English glossary
- English–German glossary
- Grammar summary
- In my own words (writing prompts)
- CEFR and ACTFL can-do statements

Meet the authors

Jonas and Heiner have extensive experience teaching German as a foreign language.

Jonas says:

I am passionate about languages and I am currently learning Swedish. In secondary school I started with French and then I also learned Latin, which helped me to understand grammatical concepts in all the languages I speak. However, it was English I fell in love with as soon as I started it in seventh grade. This led me to study English and German at university in order to become a secondary teacher for those subjects. After I finished my degree, I decided to come back to England (I had spent a year in Newcastle as part of an exchange program), where I have been teaching ever since. First, as a DAAD (German Academic Exchange Service) language assistant, then DAAD Lektor and Language Director for German, and now as Senior Lecturer in German Language Education and Team Leader for Germanic Languages and Modern Greek at King's College London.

Speaking other languages has allowed me to delve into other cultures and really get to know and understand the countries and their people, as well as finding out things about my own language and culture. This has been a wonderful experience. The learning process never ends: almost every day I still learn something new.

I wish you all the best on your language-learning journey!

Heiner says:

After more than 30 years of writing German language books and teaching German to students from a wide range of backgrounds and ages, I am still amazed by how fast and accurately beginners can learn and get a grasp of the language when equipped with the right materials and tools. The key for me is to understand the patterns and the little building blocks—getting to feel relaxed and confident about them so that you can apply them to new contexts and structures. Language learning should be stimulating and fun; by exploring a new language you will also learn so much about your own and may discover similarities and differences that could surprise you.

Writing and teaching have always been my passions, and after graduating from the University of Hannover and working in Hamburg, I moved to London where I started my career at City University and Morley College before coordinating the German section, and directing the Language Centre at the University of Westminster for many years. I now teach at Oxford University and City Lit and work as a private consultant.

I hope you will enjoy learning with this new edition of *Complete German* and that it will be a clear, supportive, and stimulating guide on your journey of learning this wonderful language. If things sometimes get a bit hard, there is a wise German proverb:
Übung macht den Meister! *Practice makes perfect!*

Acknowledgments

The authors would like to thank the team at Teach Yourself for their expertise, support and patience, in particular Chloe West, Emily Martyn, Frances Amrani, Emma Green and Ana Stojanovic, who was instrumental in developing the story line around Max. They are also grateful to Sabine Strobl, who shared her local knowledge about Vienna. A special thanks goes to Anna Miell for her invaluable comments, proofreading skills and encouragement.

How to use this book

Congratulations on deciding to learn (or relearn) German and thank you for choosing Teach Yourself. This book was designed specifically with the independent student in mind, offering features that provide as much motivation and support on your learning journey as possible. Join Max, a young blogger from the United States who has decided to spend a year in Germany. In the first part of the book, Max discovers various aspects of Berlin before traveling to Vienna in Austria, Basel in Switzerland, and up north to Hamburg. Finally, Max returns to Berlin where he explores more about the rich history and contemporary issues of Germany's capital. When Max rejoins Lisa, a songwriter he has met in Vienna, he will have to make some big decisions. What will he do?

In the company of Max, his flamboyant landlord Wally, and her extended family and friends, you will get an authentic glimpse into modern life and society in German-speaking countries, as you build and expand your knowledge of the language.

WARMING UP

This book begins with an introduction to the German alphabet and the basic sounds and rhythms of German. As you practice, you'll get a few **Key expressions** under your belt before you begin.

CORE UNITS

At the core of the book are **20 units**, designed to help you communicate in practical, everyday situations and steadily build your knowledge and facility with German. Each unit is structured in an easy-to-follow way and consists of two parts, each with the following features:

Culture point introduces the theme and provides a context for the unit. It presents practical information about the way things work in German speaking countries and introduces you to the rich tapestry of their culture—food, music, art, architecture, literature, social traditions, and more—and related words and phrases. Many Culture points also feature a QR code, which you can scan to learn more about the topic. This is a window into authentic sources and will let you explore the language and culture beyond the borders of the book.

Vocabulary builder introduces key unit vocabulary, accompanied by audio. Listen to the audio several times, repeating each word. Then do the **Vocabulary practice**, if available. Review the list as often as you can, covering up one side and then the other. Use the vocabulary builder for reference, as you work through the conversation that follows.

Conversations are the cornerstone of each unit. This is where you will follow the adventures of Max, his landlord Wally, her son Fabian, and others in Berlin, Vienna, Basel, and Hamburg. What will Max discover when visiting different parts of German-speaking countries? Will he be able to live on his blog writing or will he need to find another job? What will he do after the end of his 12-month stay? As the story unfolds, you will join our friends in common everyday situations and learn to participate in similar situations.

The conversations are recorded so that you can listen to them, practice your pronunciation, and even role play. Listen first and try to get the gist of the conversation; don't get hung up on understanding every word. Focusing questions and follow-up activities are there to guide you. Work with the conversations as much and as often as you can.

Language builders (four in each unit) introduce key language points you encounter in the conversation and explain how the language is used in practice. Each topic opens with a **Language discovery** activity, designed to help you notice patterns and usage on your own. Read more about the benefits of the **Discovery method** of learning later in **How to be a successful language learner**.

Throughout the units you will find **Tips** with study shortcuts, additional explanations, and cultural tidbits to enhance your learning.

Language practice offers a variety of exercises, including speaking opportunities, to give you a chance to see and use words and phrases in their context. The **Skill builder** section at the end of each unit provides additional practice, and you will have ample opportunity for **Speaking**, **Listening**, **Reading**, and **Writing practice**.

Test yourself puts together everything covered in the unit and helps you assess what you have learned. Try to do the tests without consulting the text and check your answers in the **Answer key**. If you are happy with your results, move ahead to the next unit. Otherwise, go back and review the unit once more before moving on. Three assessments, at A1, A2 and B1 CEFR levels (Intermediate Low, Mid and High ACTFL levels), are available online to help you gauge your overall progress at key stages.

The **Answer key** at the back of the book applies to all the exercises and tests in the book. You can look up the language topic you need in the **Index** to find the relevant units where it's covered. Additional resources are available online, including a two-way **English–German glossary**, a **Grammar summary**, **My takeaway** template, **In my own words** writing prompts, and a list of the **CEFR can-do statements and references** that map the book units to the CEFR and ACTFL proficiency comparison grid.

A LITTLE GOES A LONG WAY!

Try to use the book little and often, rather than for long stretches at a time (between 15 and 30 minutes, if possible, rather than two to three hours in one session). This will help you to create a study habit, much in the same way you would practice a sport or musical instrument. Leave the book somewhere handy so that you can pick it up for just a few minutes to refresh your memory on what you were looking at the time before. The book is structured so that you can work through one module (Culture point, Vocabulary builder, Conversation, Language builder) per sitting.

MAKE A PLAN, TRACK YOUR PROGRESS, AND REFLECT ON THE PROCESS!

Setting goals affects the programming of your brain, strengthening neural pathways and ultimately making it more likely that you will achieve those goals. Before you begin, think about how much time you want to devote to learning, which skills or areas you want to focus on, and identify specific ideas you want to be able to communicate or activities you want to engage in.

In this unit you will learn will help you identify what you should be able to do in German by the end of the unit and will help you set your personal goals for each unit. Each unit opens with a dashboard where you can note your personal goals.

Studies show that holding yourself accountable is another great way to stay motivated. Use **My progress tracker** at the beginning of each unit to help you keep track of your progress and the work you do.

You can use **My progress tracker** to keep track of the date or day, or you can enter an increment of time (15 minutes, 30 minutes ...). Add columns for culture, vocabulary, grammar, or any other area you wish to focus on. Give yourself a star when you feel you've done particularly well. Make it your own! Review your tracker regularly and see which areas could use more practice.

After you complete each unit, go back to the **Self check** and take stock of your progress. You will need to go back to the unit opener page to do this and to review your progress against your goals and the unit objectives. A **My takeaway** template page is available online. Here you can reflect on your process and record your impressions, questions and highlights. You will also find **In my own words**, a list of writing prompts that will give you further practice with your writing skills.

1

In this lesson you will learn how to:

» Say what your name is and where you are from
» Greet people and say goodbye
» Ask people where they come from and where they live
» Use the formal and informal way to address someone

Wilkommen in Berlin!

My study plan

I plan to work with Unit 1
○ Every day
○ Twice a week
○ Other _____
I plan to study for
○ 5–15 minutes
○ 15–30 minutes
○ 30–45+ minutes

My progress tracker

Day / Date	🎧	🎤	📖	✏️	💬
	○	○	○	○	○
	○	○	○	○	○
	○	○	○	○	○
	○	○	○	○	○
	○	○	○	○	○
	○	○	○	○	○
	○	○	○	○	○
	○	○	○	○	○

My goals

What do you want to be able to do or say in German when you complete this unit?

Done

1 .... ○
2 .... ○
3 .... ○

My review

SELF CHECK	
	I can ...
●	... say what my name is and where I am from.
●	... greet people and say goodbye.
●	... ask people where they come from and where they live.
●	... use the formal and informal way to address someone.

TRY TO PRACTICE EACH SKILL EVERY DAY

The icons in the progress tracker are used throughout the book to help you easily identify and locate the skills you want to practice:

 Listening skills

 Speaking—pronunciation skills

 Reading skills

 Writing skills

 Speaking—conversation skills

Remember, there are many ways to build your skills in addition to those provided in this book: use a language-learning app, listen to music or podcasts, watch TV shows or movies, go to a restaurant, follow social media accounts in German, read blogs, newspapers, or magazines, switch the language settings in your apps to German, or sign up for a language exchange or a tutor. And remember to keep a record of them in your notebook or use the **My takeaway** template provided online.

Above all, talk to other German speakers or learners, if at all possible; failing that, talk to yourself, to inanimate objects, to the imaginary characters in this book (warn your family and friends!). If you can find someone else to learn along with you, that is a great bonus. Do all the exercises and do them more than once. Make maximum use of the audio: play it as background, even when half your mind is on something else, as well as using it when you are actually studying. The main thing is to create a continuous German 'presence' so that what you are learning is always on your mind. Finally, enjoy yourself and celebrate your progress!

How to be a successful language learner

The Discovery method

There are lots of philosophies and approaches to language learning, some practical, some quite unconventional, and far too many to list here. In this book we have incorporated the Discovery method of learning, a sort of DIY approach to language learning. What this means is that you will be encouraged to engage your mind and figure out the language for yourself, through identifying patterns, understanding grammar concepts, noticing words that are similar to English, and more.

Simply put, if you figure something out for yourself, you are more likely to understand it. And when you use what you've learned, you're more likely to remember it. And because many of the essential features are introduced through the Discovery method, you'll have more fun while learning. Soon, the language will start to make sense and you'll be relying on your own intuition to construct original sentences independently, not just listening and repeating.

Everyone can succeed in learning a language—the key is to know how to learn it.

Learn to learn

There are many strategies that can help you become a successful language learner. Different people have different learning styles and some of these approaches will be more effective for you than others. Use this list as a point of inspiration when you want to find the most effective ways to advance your skills and begin your journey to fluency.

VOCABULARY

Words are the building blocks of language. The more you use the words you're introduced to, the more quickly they will lodge into your memory. These study tips will help you remember better:

- Say the words out loud as you read them. Listen to the audio several times.
- Write the words over and over again. Create flash cards, drawings, and mind maps.
- Group new words in categories, like food or furniture, or according to the situations, e.g. restaurant, hotel, sightseeing, or their functions, e.g. greetings, thanks, apologizing.
- Cover up the English side of the vocabulary list and see if you remember the meaning of the word. Then cover up the German side and see if you can remember the word itself.
- Use mnemonic tricks for words with similar sounding words in English, e.g. think of a dish served on a table to remember that Tisch means *table*.
- Write words for objects around your house and stick them to the objects.
- Pay attention to patterns in words, e.g. adding un- to an adjective often turns it into its opposite (as in English): freundlich > unfreundlich (*friendly > unfriendly*).

GRAMMAR

Grammar gives a language structure. It allows you to experiment with the vocabulary you learn because you will understand how they work together to create meaning. In other words, you will begin to develop a feel for the language. Here are some tips to help you study more effectively:

- Write your own grammar glossary and add new information and examples as you go.
- Experiment with grammar rules. Use old vocabulary to practice new grammar structures.
- Try to find examples of grammar in conversations or other articles.
- When you learn a new verb, review other verbs you know that follow the same pattern.
- Compare German structures with your own language or other languages you may speak. Try to find out some rules on your own and be ready to spot the exceptions.

PRONUNCIATION

The best way to improve your pronunciation is simply to practice as much as possible. Study individual sounds first, then full words and sentences. Don't forget, it's not just about pronouncing letters and words correctly, but using the right intonation. So, when practicing words and sentences, mimic the rising and falling intonation of German speakers.

- Repeat all the conversations, line by line. Listen to yourself and try to mimic what you hear.
- Record yourself and compare yourself to the audio.
- Make a list of words that give you trouble and practice them.

LISTENING AND READING

The conversations in this book include questions to help guide you in your understanding. But you can go further by following some of these tips:

- Imagine the situation. Try to imagine where the scene is taking place and who the main characters are. Let your experience of the world help you guess the meaning of the conversation, e.g. if a conversation takes place in a café, you can predict the kind of vocabulary that will be used.
- Concentrate on the main part. When watching a movie in another language, you usually get the meaning of the story from a few individual shots. Understanding a conversation or article is similar. Concentrate on the main message and don't worry about individual words.
- Learn to cope with uncertainty, don't overuse your dictionary! You don't have to look up every word you don't know, try to deduce the meaning from context. Concentrate on trying to get the gist of the passage and underline the words you don't understand. If after the third time there are still words which prevent you from getting the general meaning of the passage, look them up in the dictionary.

WRITING

You will have plenty of writing practice using this book. Creating vocabulary lists and grammar summaries and taking good notes as you study is another great opportunity to practice writing.

If you are keeping your lists or notes on your smartphone, computer, or tablet, remember to switch the keyboard language to be able to include all accents and special characters. Here are some other ways to practice writing:

- Write out the answers to all Practice and Test yourself questions.
- Create your own vocabulary lists and a grammar summary.
- Look up writing prompts for language learning or write a daily gratitude journal in German.
- Write out your to-do and shopping lists in German.
- Join online forums and discussion groups about or in German.

SPEAKING

The greatest obstacle to speaking a new language is the fear of making a mistake. Keep in mind that you make mistakes in your own language, it's simply part of the human condition. Accept it. Focus on the message. Most errors are not serious, and they will not affect the meaning; for example, if you use the wrong article, wrong pronoun, or wrong adjective ending. So, concentrate on getting your message across and use the mistakes as learning opportunities.

Here are some useful tips to help you practice speaking German:

- When you are going about your day, e.g. buying groceries, ordering food and drink, do it in German in your mind! Look at objects around you and try to name them in German. Look at people around you and try to describe them.
- Answer all of the questions in the book out loud. Say the conversations out loud, then try to replace sentences with ones that are true for you. Role play different situations in the book.
- Keep talking. The best way to improve your fluency in a language is to talk every time you have the opportunity to do so: keep the conversations flowing and don't worry about the mistakes. If you get stuck for a particular word, don't let the conversation stop; simplify what you want to say; paraphrase or replace the unknown word with one you do know.

Learning a language takes work. But the work can be a lot of fun. So, let's begin!

The German alphabet and pronunciation

The German alphabet has the same 26 letters found in the English alphabet: 21 consonants and 5 vowels (a, e, i, o, u). There are also four letters specific to German: the three Umlaute (umlauts)—ä, ö, ü—and ß, which is called scharfes s (sharp s) or eszett.

When spelling words out, the letters sound similar to the English sounds in the middle columns below. To clarify a letter, use the German spelling code in the right-hand column.

00.01

Listen and repeat.

Letter	Sound	Code	Letter	Sound	Code
A, a	ah	Anton	N, n	enn	Nordpol
B, b	beh	Berta	O, o	oh	Otto
C, c	tseh	Cäsar	P, p	peh	Paula
D, d	deh	Dora	Q, q	koo	Quelle
E, e	eh	Emil	R, r	err	Richard
F, f	eff	Friedrich	S, s	ess	Samuel
G, g	geh	Gustav	T, t	teh	Theodor
H, h	ha	Heinrich	U, u	oo	Ulrich
I, i	ih	Ida	V, v	fau	Viktor
J, j	yott	Julius	W, w	veh	Wilhelm
K, k	kah	Kaufmann	X, x	iks	Xanthippe
L, l	ell	Ludwig	Y, y	ipsilon	Ypsilon
M, m	emm	Martha	Z, z	tsett	Zacharias

Ä, ä a-Umlaut   Ö, ö o-Umlaut   Ü, ü u-Umlaut   ß, ß Esszett oder (*or*) scharfes S

Vowels

German vowels can have a short or long form, similar to *cat* or *car* in English. This often depends on the letters that follow. A vowel is usually pronounced long:

- when followed by h: fahren (*to drive*), wohnen (*to live*)
- when a double vowel occurs: Haar (*hair*), Boot (*boat*)

A vowel is normally pronounced short:

- when followed by a double consonant: Wasser (*water*), Bett (*bed*)
- when followed by more than one consonant: sechs (*six*), Mensch (*human being*)
- when appearing at the end of a word: habe (*have*), Liebe (*love*)

Diphthongs

A diphthong is a combination of two vowels that together produce a particular sound. The three main diphthongs in German are au (pronounced like the 'ow' in cow), ei (by/lie), and eu (coy/oyster).

Consonants

Most consonants sound very similar in German and English. However, there are a few exceptions, including:

j is pronounced as the English *y* (*yes*): ja (*yes*), Jahr (*year*)

s at the start of a word or syllable is pronounced as the English z: Sie (*you*), singen (*to sing*)

v is pronounced as the English *f*: Vater (*father*), viel (*a lot*)

w is pronounced as the English *v* in *van*: was (*what*), Volkswagen

z is pronounced as the English *ts* in *cats*: zwei (*two*), Zimmer (*room*)

Stress

As a general rule, most nouns in German are stressed on the first syllable:

Deutschland, Abend, Name, Hauptstadt, Willkommen.

Pronunciation sections

To help you with pronunciation there are **Pronunciation practice** sections throughout the book that will introduce you to the features mentioned in more detail and provide you with plenty of opportunity for practice.

Language practice 1

00.02

1 Which city is this? Listen and complete the names of these cities from German-speaking countries.

A a _ _ e n	K _ _ n	_ a _ _ b _ r _	B _ _ l i _	L _ _ p z _ g
_ _ e n	H _ _ b _ _ g	M ü _ c _ _ n	Z _ _ _ c h	

Which letters did you find difficult? Now listen again and check whether you were right.

00.03

2 Who has arrived? Listen to people attending a conference and put them in the order they arrive.

Clare Müller   Vivien Timmler   Gediz Yalman   Peter Brinkmann

3 How would you spell your name?

First things first

In this lesson you will learn how to:

» Use numbers
» Use days, months, and seasons
» Use key basic phrases
» Follow activity instructions

Zahlen 1–20 *Numbers 1–20*

German numbers are relatively easy to learn: 1–12 sound very similar to the English equivalents (e.g. vier *four*, sechs *six*, neun *nine*). From 12 to 19 you add zehn *ten*, just like *-teen* in English.

00.04

Listen and repeat.

1	eins	6	sechs	11	elf	16	sechzehn
2	zwei	7	sieben	12	zwölf	17	siebzehn
3	drei	8	acht	13	dreizehn	18	achtzehn
4	vier	9	neun	14	vierzehn	19	neunzehn
5	fünf	10	zehn	15	fünfzehn	20	zwanzig

The number for *zero* is null.

Notice that you drop the second s from sechzehn. You form siebzehn without the en used in sieben. You will learn higher numbers later in the book.

Language practice 1

1 Add the numbers.

a drei + vier = ...
b acht – fünf = ...
c vier + fünf = ...
d sechs + drei – sieben = ...
e sieben – drei – zwei = ...
f acht – drei – zwei = ...

g eins + drei + zwei = ...
h vier + sieben = ...
i elf + zwei = ...
j siebzehn – zwei = ...
k sechzehn + drei = ...
l zehn + neun – eins = ...

00.05

2 You are at a party and exchange phone numbers. Which numbers do you hear?

a	Paulina:	0 7 7 8 0 4 5 9 6 1 0	or	0 7 7 8 1 5 5 9 6 1 0
b	Markus:	0 7 4 5 8 8 2 3 5 6 6	or	0 7 4 5 8 8 2 3 5 5 6
c	Johann:	0 1 6 0 3 6 5 2 6 7 9	or	0 1 6 0 2 6 5 3 6 7 9
d	Asmaa:	0 7 5 3 6 6 5 9 1 9 1	or	0 7 5 3 6 6 5 9 1 0 1

Now have a go and say your phone number.

Wochentage *Days of the week*

00.06

Match the German with the English. Then listen and repeat.

1	Monday	**a**	Samstag / Sonnabend
2	Tuesday	**b**	Dienstag
3	Wednesday	**c**	Freitag
4	Thursday	**d**	Montag
5	Friday	**e**	Mittwoch
6	Saturday	**f**	Sonntag
7	Sunday	**g**	Donnerstag

Monate *Months*

00.07

Put the months in the correct order. Then listen and repeat.

Mai	November	Juni	April	Februar	Dezember
August	September	März	Juli	Oktober	Januar

....

....

Jahreszeiten *Seasons*

Frühling	*spring*	Herbst	*autumn / fall*
Sommer	*summer*	Winter	*winter*

00.08

Write out the names of the season in German. Then listen and repeat.

a ....   b ....   c ....   d ....

In German all nouns, not only proper nouns, need to be capitalized.

Mein Name ist Max.	*My name is Max.*
Berlin ist eine schöne Stadt.	*Berlin is a beautiful city.*
Am Wochenende geht meine Schwester ins Kino.	*On the weekend, my sister goes to the cinema.*

Key phrases

Look at the words and phrases. Listen and try to imitate the pronunciation of the speakers.

Hallo	*Hello*
Guten Morgen	*Good morning*
Guten Tag	*Good day*
Guten Abend	*Good evening*
Gute Nacht	*Good night*
Auf Wiedersehen (formal) / Tschüss (informal)	*Goodbye*
nein	*no*
ja	*yes*
bitte	*please*
Danke.	*Thank you.*
Bitte schön.	*You are welcome.*
Entschuldigung ...	*Excuse me ...*
Es tut mir leid.	*I am sorry.*
In Ordnung (formal) / OK (informal)	*OK*
Mein Name ist ...	*My name is ...*
Wie ist Ihr Name? (formal)	*What's your name?*
Wie ist dein Name? (informal)	*What's your name?*

Where German is spoken

German is the official language of both Germany and Austria and one of the official languages of Switzerland. But it is also spoken in Luxembourg, Liechtenstein, the South Tyrol province of Italy (German: Südtirol; Italian: Alto Adige) and in border regions of Belgium. German-speaking communities can also be found in Eastern Europe (particularly in Romania), in North America (e.g. the Pennsylvania Dutch), and in Namibia. With more than 90 million native speakers and at least 15 million people who use German as a second language, German is among the world's top ten most commonly spoken languages.

In this lesson you will learn how to:
» Say what your name is and where you are from
» Greet people and say goodbye
» Ask people where they come from and where they live
» Use the formal and informal way to address someone

Wilkommen in Berlin!

My study plan

I plan to work with Unit 1
○ Every day
○ Twice a week
○ Other _____
I plan to study for
○ 5–15 minutes
○ 15–30 minutes
○ 30–45+ minutes

My progress tracker

Day / Date	🎧	🎤	📖	✏️	💬
	○	○	○	○	○
	○	○	○	○	○
	○	○	○	○	○
	○	○	○	○	○
	○	○	○	○	○
	○	○	○	○	○
	○	○	○	○	○

My goals

What do you want to be able to do or say in German when you complete this unit?

Done

1 .... ○
2 .... ○
3 .... ○

My review

SELF CHECK

	I can ...
○	... say what my name is and where I am from.
○	... greet people and say goodbye.
○	... ask people where they come from and where they live.
○	... use the formal and informal way to address someone.

Berlin – Stadt des Wandels *Berlin – city of change*

With about 3.5 million inhabitants, Berlin, the capital city of Germany, is renowned for its wide range of landmarks, diverse cultural scene, and its liberal and relaxed outlook on life.

It is home to all the main government buildings, including the historical Reichstag, the seat of the German parliament. You can find more than 170 museums, with some of the most prominent ones on the Museumsinsel (*Museum Island*). Lovers of classical music can enjoy three opera houses or the well-known Berliner Philharmonie (*Berlin Philharmonic*).

Berlin is also a shopping destination. Besides luxury stores along the Kurfürstendamm or Friedrichstraße, the city has numerous independent boutiques and stores and is home to many startups.

During its almost 900-year history, Berlin has always attracted people from all over the world and set many trends in music, fashion, and art. It is a city of contrasts and change.

 What aspects of Berlin are you most interested in?
Look at the official tourist website and explore some of the things that interest you.

VOCABULARY BUILDER 1

01.01

Look at the words and phrases and complete the missing English words and expressions. Then listen and try to imitate the pronunciation of the speakers.

BEGRÜßUNGEN UND VERABSCHIEDUNGEN

Hallo.

Guten Morgen / Tag / Abend.

Gute Nacht!

Auf Wiedersehen (formal) / Tschüss! (informal)

SICH VORSTELLEN

Mein Name ist … / Ich heiße …

Wie heißen Sie?

Sind Sie nicht … ?

Schön, Sie kennenzulernen.

HÖFLICH SEIN

Danke schön. / Vielen Dank.

bitte

Kein Problem.

Das tut mir leid. / Entschuldigung.

NÜTZLICHE AUSDRÜCKE

Haus

ich habe

GREETINGS AND FAREWELLS

Hello.

Good .... / day / evening.

Good ....!

Goodbye.

INTRODUCTIONS

My name is …

What's your name? (lit. What are you called?)

Are you not … ?

Nice to meet you.

BEING POLITE

Thank you. / Thank you very much.

please

No ....

I am sorry. / Sorry.

USEFUL EXPRESSIONS

house

I have

Vocabulary practice 1

Practice some of the vocabulary from the list to describe your daily routine.

a It's 8 a.m. and you see your neighbors. You greet them with: ....

b You go to the coffee shop. The waiter brings you a coffee and you say: ....

c You spill the coffee and say: ....

d The waiter says .... and cleans it up.

e Your friend comes in to the coffee shop and says: ....

f They introduce you to their friend, and you introduce yourself saying: ....

g You leave for work and say goodbye to your friends: ....

CONVERSATION 1

Die falsche Adresse *The wrong address*

01.02

1 **Listen to the conversation without looking at the text. Play it a few times and see if you can make out a few new words and phrases each time. Then listen again and read the text. How do Max and the woman give their names?**

Max Peterson lives in the US. His mother is German. He grew up speaking German, and now he wants to spend a year in Berlin and write a blog about his experiences. Max has decided to rent a Zimmer (*room*) from Waltraud Hille, an old friend of his mother. He has found the Adresse (*address*) and sees the name HILLE on the intercom. Excited, he rings the buzzer.

Rita	Ja, bitte?
Max	Guten Morgen! Mein Name ist Max Peterson.
Rita	Hallo. Wie heißen Sie, bitte?
Max	Max Peterson. Ich miete ein Zimmer.
Rita	Ein Zimmer?
Max	Sind Sie nicht Waltraud Hille?
Rita	Nein, ich heiße Rita Hille.
Max	Oh, entschuldigung! Das tut mir leid. Ist das Hausnummer 2b?
Rita	Nein. Ich habe Hausnummer 2a.
Max	Oh. Wo ist Hausnummer 2b?
Rita	Im Hinterhaus.
Max	Ah, super. Vielen Dank!
Rita	Kein Problem! Auf Wiedersehen.

2 **Answer these questions.**

  a What time of the day does the conversation roughly take place? ....
  b What do Waltraud and Rita have in common? ....
  c Does Max actually speak to Waltraud? ....
  d What number does Waltraud live at? ....

In many German cities, like Berlin, houses are in two rows: one directly on the street—the Vorderhaus—and another behind it, accessible only through the courtyard—the Hinterhaus (literally 'behind house'). These Hinterhäuser were mostly built in the second half of the 19th century. In the past, you could often find tradesmen's workshops there or even restaurants and cinemas. A famous example of several Hinterhäuser together are the Hackeschen Höfe in Berlin.

LANGUAGE BUILDER 1

💡 Language discovery 1

1 Identify the words for *I* and *you* in these phrases from the conversation.

   a Wie heißen Sie? ....

   b Nein, ich heiße Rita Hille.
....

   c Ich miete ein Zimmer. ....

   d Sind Sie nicht Waltraud Hille? ....

2 Work out which of the two words always takes a capital letter. ....

Personal pronouns

The personal pronouns (words for *I*, *you*, etc.) in German are:

Singular (one person)		Plural (more than one person)	
ich	I	wir	we
du	you (informal)	ihr	you (informal)
Sie	you (formal)	Sie	you (formal)
er	he	sie	they
sie	she		
es	it		
xier	they (gender-neutral)		

So far you have seen ich and Sie (the formal *you*). Note that, unlike in English, Sie is always capitalized, while ich is not. You will learn about the various forms in the next few units.

Language practice 1

Complete with the appropriate word from the box.

> Sie   Sie   Ich   Ich

a Wie heißen .... ?

b .... miete ein Zimmer in Berlin.

c Sind .... nicht Frau Klump?

d .... heiße Xin.

Pronunciation practice

01.03

1 Listen to these words. Notice how ei and ie are pronounced.

  mein *my*   nein *no*   Wiedersehen *goodbye*

  heißen *to be called*   leid *sorry*   mieten *to rent*

01.04

2 Practice saying these words, then listen and repeat.

  ein   drei   vielen   zwei   kein   liebe

01.05

> ## 💡 Language discovery 2
>
> **Listen to the conversation again and repeat each line in the pauses provided. Try to imitate the phrasing and intonation you hear. Then look at the underlined endings. Which verb ending goes with Sie? Which verb ending goes with ich?**
>
> **a** Ich mie<u>te</u> ein Zimmer. ....
>
> **b** Ich hab<u>e</u> Hausnummer 2a. ....
>
> **c** Ich heiß<u>e</u> Rita Hille. ....
>
> **d** Wie heiß<u>en</u> Sie? ....

Verb endings (1) – Talking about you and me

Verbs are action words—they describe an action or state. In German, verbs change to reflect who is performing the action and when, similar to the verb *to be—I am, you are, she is...* . You know the verbs haben (*to have*), mieten (*to rent*), heißen (*to be called*) and sein (*to be*). This is the form of the verb that you find in a dictionary—the infinitive. The infinitive can be divided into two parts. Look at mieten as an example: miet- is the stem and -en is the ending. This ending changes according to the subject. This section looks at ich (*I*) and Sie (*you*, formal). For most verbs, the endings for ich and Sie are:

Subject	Ending	mieten	haben	heißen
ich	-e	miete	habe	heiße
Sie	-en	mieten	haben	heißen

Note that sein (*to be*), as in English, is an irregular verb: ich bin, Sie sind.

Ich bin Fadhel.   *I am Fadhel.*   Sind Sie aus Deutschland?   *Are you from Germany?*

Language practice 2

1 Complete with the correct endings.

    a Wie heiß ...... Sie? – Ich heiß ...... Max.

    b Miet ...... Sie ein Zimmer? – Ja, ich miet ...... ein Zimmer.

    c Welche Hausnummer hab ...... Sie? – Ich hab ...... Hausnummer 10b.

2 Complete with the appropriate forms for trinken (*to drink*) and lernen (*to learn*).

    a Was trink ...... Sie? – Ich trink ...... Kaffee.

    b Was lern ...... Sie? – Ich lern ...... Deutsch.

01.06

3 Now play Conversation 1 again and play Rita's role. Speak in the pauses. Try not to refer to the text.

CULTURE POINT 2

In Deutschland: du oder Sie verwenden? *When in Germany: using du or Sie?*

Unlike English, German has two different ways of addressing someone: du and Sie. Here are a few tips for when to use the informal and formal modes of address:

- Use du with a person you feel close to, and to a child or a pet; du is also used among young people and students.
- Use Sie with people you don't know well, in formal contexts or when you are unsure.

Following global trends, German is becoming less formal and you will often hear the informal du used in work settings, stores, and so on.

Germans often give only their Nachname (*surname*) when they introduce themselves. When addressing a person directly you would precede their Nachname with either Herr (*Mr.*) or Frau (*Mrs./Ms.*). The gender-neutral way of addressing someone is by dropping Herr or Frau and using the person's first and surname instead.

a Would you use du or Sie when meeting someone older for the first time?

b Would you use du or Sie when meeting your schoolfriends at a reunion?

 Explore more about du and Sie and watch this short video from Deutsche Welle.
In which two settings do people normally use du? And how can you switch from Sie to du?

01.07

Look at the words and phrases and complete the missing English words and expressions. Then listen and try to imitate the pronunciation of the speakers.

MEHR FRAGEN UND ANTWORTEN

Woher kommst du? (informal)	Where do you .... from?
Wo wohnst du? (informal)	Where do you live?
Wie findest du ...? (informal)	What do you think of ...? (lit. *How do you find ...?*)
Wie ist ...?	How is ...?
Was trinkst du? (informal)	What do you (want to) ....?
Ich komme aus ...	I come ....
Ich wohne in...	I live in ...
Ich finde ...	I think ... (lit. *I find ...*)
Ich liebe ...	I love ...
Ich schreibe ...	I write ...

MORE QUESTIONS AND ANSWERS

LÄNDER

Deutschland, Österreich	................, ...
die Schweiz	Switzerland
Frankreich, England	France, ...
Italien, Polen, Marokko	................, Poland, ...
Brasilien, Nigeria, Indien, China	................, Nigeria, ..., China

COUNTRIES

ADJEKTIVE

groß, klein	big / large, little / small
interessant, langweilig	................, boring
laut	....
chaotisch	chaotic
wunderbar	wonderful

ADJECTIVES

NÜTZLICHE AUSDRÜCKE

besser	better
eigentlich	actually
ein bisschen	a little
schon	already
Ich habe Material für ...	I have material for ...

USEFUL EXPRESSIONS

Vocabulary practice 2

Complete with the country corresponding to the Hauptstadt (*capital*).

a Berlin ist die Hauptstadt von ....

b Wien ist die Hauptstadt von ....

c Die Hauptstadt von .... ist Warschau.

d Neu-Delhi ist die Hauptstadt von ....

e Rabat ist die Hauptstadt von ....

f Die Hauptstadt von .... ist Peking.

Pronunciation practice 2

01.08

1 **In German, the stress often falls on the first syllable of a word. Listen to these country names. Notice where the words are stressed.**

Deutschland   Österreich   Spanien   Polen   Indien   China

01.09

2 **Practice saying these words, then listen and repeat.**

England   Irland   Amerika   Afrika   Asien   Griechenland

CONVERSATION 2

Sich kennenlernen *Getting to know each other*

01.10

1 **Here are a few words to help you understand the conversation.**

Kaffee	*coffee*
Tee	*tea*
Milch	*milk*
Zucker	*sugar*

01.11

2 **Listen to the conversation without looking at the text. Play it a few times and see if you can make out a few new words and phrases each time. Then listen again and read the text. Does Max drink tea or coffee? Which form of address do Wally and Max use?**

Max finally meets Waltraud. She shows him his room and then they have a chat in the kitchen. Max does not know whether to use du or Sie.

Wally	Max. Was trinkst du – Tee oder Kaffee?
Max	Kaffee, bitte. Kaffee ist super.
Wally	Mit Milch und Zucker?
Max	Ja, bitte. Mit Milch und Zucker.
Wally	Woher kommst du?
Max	Ich komme aus Portland, aus den USA. Und Sie, Waltraud? Woher kommen Sie?
Wally	Max, „du" ist besser. Und ich heiße Wally.
Max	Ok, Waltraud ... Äh, Wally. Woher kommst du?
Wally	Ich komme eigentlich aus Hamburg, aus Norddeutschland. Aber ich wohne lange in Berlin.
Max	Und wie findest du Berlin?
Wally	Berlin ist groß, laut und chaotisch, aber auch sehr interessant. Ich liebe Berlin. Und wie ist Portland?
Max	Ich finde, Portland ist ein bisschen klein und langweilig.
Wally	Und Berlin?
Max	Mmh, Hausnummer 2a und 2b, Hille und Hille, Berlin ist interessant. Ich habe schon Material für einen Blog.
Wally	Oh, du bist Blogger.
Max	Ja. Ich schreibe einen Blog.
Wally	Das ist wunderbar!

3 Decide if these statements are *true* (richtig) or *false* (falsch).

a Max drinks his coffee with milk only.   R   F
b He comes from Portland, USA.   R   F
c Waltraud's preferred name is Wally.   R   F
d She originally comes from Berlin.   R   F
e She thinks Berlin is loud and chaotic, but interesting.   R   F

LANGUAGE BUILDER 3

 Language discovery 3

You know that the common verb ending is **-e** for **ich** (*I*) and **-en** for the formal **Sie** (*you*). Look at the conversation again. Work out the typical ending for the **du** form (informal *you*).

a Was trink .... du – Kaffee oder Tee?

b Woher komm .... du?

c Wie finde .... du Berlin?

Verb endings (2)–Using **du** (informal *you*)

The typical ending for **du** (informal *you*, singular) is **-st**. Here are some verbs covered so far:

Subject	Verb ending	kommen	wohnen	finden	heißen	haben
ich	**-e**	komme	wohne	finde	heiße	habe
du	**-st**	kommst	wohnst	findest*	heißt*	hast*
Sie	**-en**	kommen	wohnen	finden	heißen	haben

Ich wohne in Mumbai in Indien.　　　　　*I live in Mumbai, in India.*

Wie findest du Deutsch?　　　　　　　　*How do you like German?*

Wie heißen Sie?　　　　　　　　　　　　*What's your name?*

Sein (*to be*) follows a different pattern: ich bin, du bist, Sie sind.

> * To ease pronunciation, when the stem (infinitive minus -en) ends in -d, there is an extra -e before the -st ending (finden – find-est). When the stem ends in -ß, the -s is dropped, leaving -t (heißen – heiß-t). Haben drops the -b in the du form: du hast.

Language practice 3

 While traveling you meet a young German. Complete the questions with the correct verb form.

a Hallo. Wie h .... du?

b Woher k .... du?

c Wo w .... du?

d Was t .... du – Kaffee oder Tee?

e Wie f .... du Berlin?

f Und wie f .... du Deutschland?

g Woher b .... du?

LANGUAGE BUILDER 4

01.12

💡 Language discovery 4

Listen to the conversation again and repeat each line in the pauses provided. Try to imitate the phrasing and intonation you hear. Then look at these questions. Identify the position of the verbs.

a Ich liebe Berlin.
b Ich komme eigentlich aus Hamburg.
c Wo wohnst du?

Basic word order in German

In general, the verb in German is in the second position. In **statements**, it often follows the subject:

Ich heiße Luca.   Ich komme aus Hamburg.   Ich wohne in Köln.

In **questions**, the verb follows the question word:

Wie heißen Sie?   Woher kommen Sie?   Wo wohnst du?

In **yes/no questions**, the verb moves to first position:

Trinkst du Kaffee oder Tee?   Sind Sie aus Deutschland?

Language practice 4

1 **Put the words in the correct order. Start with the underlined words. Then match the questions and answers.**

Example: Woher / du / kommst / ?   Woher kommst du?

                    komme / Ich / aus Hannover.   Ich komme aus Hannover.

Statements

a Magdalena. / Ich / heiße
b mit Zucker. / Tee / Ich / trinke
c ein Zimmer / miete / Ich
d bin / Ich / Blogger.
e Berlin / finde / international. / Ich

Questions

1 du / wohnst / Wo / ?
2 heißt / Wie / du / ?
3 Was / Sie / machen / ?
4 finden / Sie / Wie / Berlin / ?
5 du / Was / trinkst / ?

01.13

2 **Now play Conversation 2 again and play Max's role. Speak in the pauses and try not to refer to the text.**

SKILL BUILDER

1 Match the greetings with the photos.

1 .... 2 .... 3 .... 4 ....

   a Guten Morgen, Herr Fernandes.   **c** Gute Nacht, Susi.

   b Guten Abend, Frau Ramadan.   **d** Hallo. Guten Tag, Felix.

2 Complete the missing verb endings in the table.

Subject	Verb ending	kommen	wohnen	trinken	lieben	finden	heiß
ich	-e	komm ...	wohn ...	trink ...	lieb ...	find ...	heiß ...
du	-st	komm ...	wohn ...	trink ...	lieb ...	findest (!)	heißt (!)
Sie	-en	komm ...	wohn ...	trink ...	lieb ...	find ...	heiß ...

3 Complete with the forms for sein (*to be*) and haben (*to have*).

   sein: ich bin, du ...., Sie ....

   haben: ich ...., du hast, Sie ....

4 Use the question words you know to complete the questions and say them out loud.

   a .... ist Ihr Name?   **e** .... findest du Portland?

   b .... heißen Sie?   **f** .... trinkst du?

   c .... kommen Sie?   **g** .... lernst du?

   d .... wohnst du?

> Wo   Woher
>
> Was   Wie

5 Identify whether these adjectives are positive or negative and give the translation.

	chaotisch	interessant	laut	schön	langweilig	wunderbar
Positive						
Negative						
Translation						

6 Complete the information missing from Max's blog.

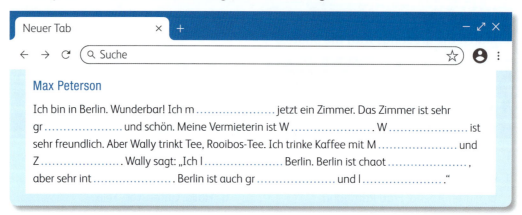

Max Peterson

Ich bin in Berlin. Wunderbar! Ich m . . . . jetzt ein Zimmer. Das Zimmer ist sehr
gr . . . . und schön. Meine Vermieterin ist W . . . . W . . . . ist
sehr freundlich. Aber Wally trinkt Tee, Rooibos-Tee. Ich trinke Kaffee mit M . . . . und
Z . . . . Wally sagt: „Ich l . . . . Berlin. Berlin ist chaot . . . . ,
aber sehr int . . . . Berlin ist auch gr . . . . und l . . . ."

TEST YOURSELF

In this unit you learned how to give some basic information about yourself. Prepare
the answers to the questions below. Then say them out loud until you feel confident.
Ihre Stadt means your *hometown*.

a Wie heißen Sie?
b Woher kommen Sie?
c Wo wohnen Sie?

d Wie finden Sie Ihre Stadt?
e Wie finden Sie Deutsch?

?

Wie geht's weiter? *What happens next?*

Wally takes a liking to Max, as he reminds her of her own son. She also
likes his idea of writing a blog about life in Berlin. She is thinking about
how she could best help him discover the city. Should she: 1) take him
on a tour, 2) introduce him to some friends, or 3) send him some links
for useful websites? Find out what she does in the next unit.

Before you move on to the next unit, assess your progress using the **My review**
section on the first page of the unit, and reflect on your learning experience with the
My takeaway section available online.

In this lesson you will learn how to:

» Talk about your job
» Say which languages you speak
» Describe people
» Ask people what they do

Wallys Freunde

My study plan

I plan to work with Unit 2

○ Every day
○ Twice a week
○ Other _____

I plan to study for

○ 5–15 minutes
○ 15–30 minutes
○ 30–45+ minutes

My progress tracker

Day / Date	🎧	🎤	📖	✏️	💬
	○	○	○	○	○
	○	○	○	○	○
	○	○	○	○	○
	○	○	○	○	○
	○	○	○	○	○
	○	○	○	○	○
	○	○	○	○	○

My goals

What do you want to be able to do or say in German when you complete this unit?

Done

1 .... ○
2 .... ○
3 .... ○

My review

SELF CHECK	
	I can ...
○	... talk about my job.
○	... say which languages I speak.
○	... describe people.
○	... ask people what they do.

CULTURE POINT 1

Die deutsche Sprache *The German language*

Deutsch (*German*) is the official Sprache (*language*) in Deutschland (*Germany*) and Österreich (Austria), and one of the official languages in Belgien (*Belgium*), Liechtenstein, Luxemburg, and die Schweiz (*Switzerland*). While most people in Deutschland speak Deutsch at home, about zwanzig (*20*) percent use (at least) one other language at home.

Wörterbücher (*dictionaries*) and grammar reference books will usually provide you with examples and rules from Standard German. However, there are many different Dialekte (*dialects*) in Germany, such as Berlinerisch (*Berlin dialect*), Kölsch (*Cologne dialect*) and Bairisch (*Bavarian*). Many Germans will speak in their local or regional dialect when at home or with their friends and family from the same area. Bairisch usually tops the list of the most popular Dialekte in Deutschland.

 Do you know what a Babbedeggel is? You can find out here and listen to examples of different dialects in the German language. Of the dialects mentioned in the text, which one is named after a region of Germany (not a city)?

VOCABULARY BUILDER 1

02.01

Look at the words and phrases and complete the missing English words and expressions. Then listen and try to imitate the pronunciation of the speakers.

ZAHLEN VON 20 BIS 100	***NUMBERS FROM 20 TO 100***
zwanzig, dreißig, vierzig	*twenty, thirty, forty*
fünfzig, sechzig, siebzig	*fifty, sixty, seventy*
achtzig, neunzig, (ein)hundert	*eighty, ninety, a hundred*
NATIONALITÄT UND BEZIEHUNGEN	***NATIONALITY AND RELATIONSHIPS***
Deutscher / Deutsche	*German person* (male / female)
Österreicher / Österreicherin	*Austrian person* (male / female)
Schweizer / Schweizerin	*Swiss person* (male / female)
Türke / Türkin	*Turkish person* (male / female)
Freund / Freundin	*friend* (male / female)
Partner / Partnerin	.... (male / female)
Sohn, Tochter	*son, daughter*
PERSÖNLICHKEIT	***PERSONALITY***
freundlich, lustig, intelligent	...................., *funny*, ...
direkt	*direct(ly)*
sympathisch	*likeable / nice*
hat Humor	*has* ....
FRAGEN	***QUESTIONS***
Was kochst du? (informal)	*What are you cooking?*
Wie alt sind Sie? (formal)	*How old are you?*
Kann ich dir helfen? (informal)	*Can I help you?*
Wer kommt heute?	*Who is coming today?*
NÜTZLICHE AUSDRÜCKE	***USEFUL EXPRESSIONS***
noch	*still*
echt	*real*
lecker	*yummy, delicious* (for food)
sprechen	*to speak / talk*
Das geht schon.	*It's OK. / No problem.*
Gemüse	*vegetable*
Jahr	*year*

Vocabulary practice 1

In German, numbers such as 24 or 48 start with the last number (the single units) and work backward. The word und is used to combine them, and they are written as one word.

24   vier + und + zwanzig = vierundzwanzig (lit. *four and twenty*)

33   drei + und + dreißig = dreiunddreißig (lit. *three and thirty*)

48   acht + und + vierzig = achtundvierzig (lit. *eight and forty*)

When you want to say 21, 31, etc., the s is dropped from eins: einundzwanzig, einunddreißig.

Write these numbers. Then say them out loud.

21   75   53   41   97   17   36   18   89

Pronunciation practice

02.02

1 Listen to these words, notice how the s and z are pronounced.

Sie   sind   sieben   siebenundsiebzig   zwei   zwölf

02.03

2 Practice saying these numbers, then listen and repeat.

zwanzig   zweiundzwanzig   sechs   siebzehn   sechsundsechzig   siebenundsechzig

3 Und Sie? Say: *How old you are.* **Write out your answer and then say it out loud.**

Wie alt sind Sie? — Ich bin .... Jahre alt.

> Note that for higher numbers a full stop or a space can be used to separate thousands where in English a comma or space would be used:
>
> 1.000 / 1 000 – eintausend
> 4.700 / 4 700 – viertausendsiebenhundert
> 10.100 / 10 100 – zehntausendeinhundert
>
> Unlike English, a comma is used instead of a decimal point:
>
> Berlin hat 3,5 Millionen Einwohner.
> *Berlin has 3.5 million inhabitants.*

CONVERSATION 1

Gäste zum Abendessen *Guests for dinner*

02.04

1 Listen to the conversation without looking at the text. Play it a few times and see if you can make out a few new words and phrases each time. Then listen again and read the text. Can you make out what Wally is cooking? How many guests has she invited?

> Max finds Wally in the Küche (*kitchen*). She wants to introduce Max to some of her friends and has invited them zum Abendessen (*for dinner*).
>
> **Max** Was kochst du, Wally?
>
> **Wally** Eine Gemüselasagne mit Salat.
>
> **Max** Oh, lecker. Kann ich dir helfen?
>
> **Wally** Nein, danke. Das geht schon.
>
> **Max** Und wer kommt heute?
>
> **Wally** Meine Freundin Nabi. Sie kommt aus Korea, aber sie wohnt schon seit 25 Jahren in Berlin. Sie ist sehr freundlich und lustig.
>
> **Max** Schön. Und wer kommt noch?
>
> **Wally** Dann kommt mein Sohn Fabian. Und Fabians Partnerin, Aylin. Aylin ist Türkin und Deutsche. Sie ist sehr sympathisch und intelligent.
>
> **Max** Und wie alt ist Fabian?
>
> **Wally** Er ist 34 Jahre alt. Und dann kommt noch Udo.
>
> **Max** Und wer ist Udo?
>
> **Wally** Udo ist ein echter Berliner. Er ist sehr direkt und hat Humor. Er spricht nicht Deutsch – er spricht Berlinerisch.

2 Answer these questions: Who is described here—Nabi, Fabian, Aylin or Udo?

a Hat Humor.   ....

b Ist 34 Jahre alt.   ....

c Ist sehr intelligent.   ....

d Ist freundlich und lustig.   ....

> To talk about actions that began in the past but continue in the present, German uses the present tense. The period of time is specified with seit (*for*):
>
> Ich lebe hier seit zwei Jahren. *I have been living here for two years.*

LANGUAGE BUILDER 1

Language discovery 1

You have learned the typical verb endings for **ich**, **du**, and **Sie**. Look at the conversation and find the typical ending for the third person (**er**, **sie**, **es**, **xier**). Complete with the missing letter.

a Nabi komm .... eigentlich aus Korea.

b Aber sie wohn .... schon seit 25 Jahren in Berlin.

c Dann komm .... mein Sohn Fabian.

d Er is .... ein echter Berliner.

Talking about another person

For the third-person singular (**er** = *he*, **sie** = *she*, **es** = *it*, **xier** = *they*, gender neutral), you normally add **-t** to the stem of the verb:

Subject	Ending	komme-en	wohn-en	heiß-en	find-en	hab-en	sein
er	-t	kommt	wohnt	heißt	findet*	hat	ist
sie	-t	kommt	wohnt	heißt	findet*	hat	ist
es	-t	kommt	wohnt	heißt	findet*	hat	ist
xier	-t	kommt	wohnt	heißt	findet*	hat	ist

* When the verb stem ends in **d** or **t**, you add **-et** rather than just **-t** to make pronunciation easier: **sie findet**, **er mietet**. Note that the verbs **haben** and **sein** are irregular, but they also end in **-t** in the third person.

Language practice 1

02.05

1 **Complete the sentences, using the verbs in parentheses. Then listen and repeat the sentences, focusing on pronunciation.**

   a Hannah .... aus Indien. (kommen)

   b Sie .... seit fünf Jahren in Montreal. (wohnen)

   c Wie .... er eigentlich? (heißen)

   d Wally .... Berlin. (lieben)

   e Max .... ein Zimmer. (mieten)

   f Xier .... gern grünen Tee. (trinken)

   g Er .... eine E-Mail. (schreiben)

   h Sabrina .... Technomusik laut und langweilig. (finden)

   i Xier .... 19 Jahre alt. (sein)

   j Udo .... viel Humor. (haben)

LANGUAGE BUILDER 2

02.06

💡 Language discovery 2

Listen to the conversation again and repeat each line in the pauses provided. Try to imitate the phrasing and intonation you hear. Then look at the four sentences. Identify the difference between the male and female forms.

Fabians Partnerin heißt Aylin.

Marias Partner heißt Leon.

Oskar ist Österreicher.

Christine ist Österreicherin.

Male and female forms

In German, all nouns have a gender, which is solely a grammatical feature (see Unit 4). When referring to people, such as for nationalities, professions or some relations, you use a different form of the word depending on the gender of the person. Most female forms add an -in to the masculine form. Here are some examples:

Freund > Freundin   Partner > Partnerin   Architekt > Architektin

Student > Studentin   Amerikaner > Amerikanerin   Koreaner > Koreanerin

If you would like to use a gender-neutral form or address nonbinary and diverse people, you can often insert a colon before -in.   Freund:in   Architekt:in

It is also possible to use an asterisk: Freund*in   Architekt*in

Language practice 2

1 Add the correct endings.

   a Stefan ist Student. Carmen ist Student . . . .

   b Gabriella ist Musiker . . . . Miles ist Musiker.

   c Ines ist Autor . . . . Robert ist Autor.

   d Udo ist Berliner. Nadja ist Berliner . . . .

   e Roger ist Schweizer. Silvana ist Schweizer . . . .

   f Nelson ist Südafrikaner. Charlize ist Südafrikaner . . . .

   g Mein Freund Tom ist sehr sympathisch. Meine Freund . . . . Chloe hat viel Humor.

02.07

2 Now play Conversation 1 again, and play Max's role. Speak in the pauses and try not to refer to the text.

3 Max has written a short introduction about one of his best friends from Portland. Following Max's example, introduce two of your best friends.

Susan kommt aus Portland und sie wohnt noch in Portland. Sie findet Portland schön und interessant. Sie ist 21 Jahre alt. Sie ist sehr freundlich und hat viel Humor. Ich finde, sie ist fantastisch.

Deutsche Staatsbürger und Menschen in Deutschland
German citizens and residents in Germany

Around fünfzehn (*fifteen*) percent of the residents in Germany do not hold a German Pass (*passport*) and over siebenundzwanzig (*twenty-seven*) percent of people living in Germany have a Migrationshintergrund (this term is used for people who either did not have German nationality when they were born or have at least one parent who was not German at birth). As mentioned before, this leads to about 20 percent of people living in Germany speaking either no German or (at least) one other language (in addition to German) zu Hause (*at home*).

You do not automatically get German Staatsbürgerschaft (*citizenship*) by being born in the country. It is also not always possible to have doppelte Staatsbürgerschaft (*dual citizenship*) as this depends on your age and what other Pass (*passport*) you hold. However, in recent years governments have been trying to simplify the process.

Latest figures suggest that there are more than five million people in Germany with doppelter Staatsbürgerschaft.

If you apply for Austrian citizenship you will most likely have to give up your other citizenship since doppelte Staatsbürgerschaft is usually not permitted in Austria.

Which other passport do most of the residents in Germany have? Use this website to find out and get more details about numbers of foreign nationals living in Germany.

02.08

Look at the words and phrases and complete the missing English words and expressions. Then listen and try to imitate the pronunciation of the speakers.

ICH SPRECHE ...	*I SPEAK ...*
Ich spreche fließend Deutsch.	*I speak German fluently.*
Ich spreche sehr gut Arabisch.	*..................... very well.*
Ich spreche ein bisschen Chinesisch / Mandarin.	*I speak a little Chinese / Mandarin.*
Englisch, Französisch	*....................., French*
Hindi, Urdu	*....................., ...*
Polnisch, Spanisch, Türkisch	*Polish, ..., ...*

EINIGE BERUFE	*SOME PROFESSIONS*
Arzt / Ärztin	*.....................*
Automechaniker / Automechanikerin	*car ....*
Elektriker / Elektrikerin	*electrician*
IT-Spezialist / IT-Spezialistin	*.....................*
Koch / Köchin	*chef*
Kundenberater / Kundenberaterin	*customer advisor*
Lehrer / Lehrerin	*teacher*
Stadtführer / Stadtführerin	*city guide*
Verkäufer / Verkäuferin	*sales assistant*

AKTIVITÄTEN	*ACTIVITIES*
reparieren	*.....................*
verkaufen	*to sell*

FRAGEN	*QUESTIONS*
Welche Sprachen sprecht ihr? (plural, inf.)	*Which languages do you speak?*
Was macht ihr? (plural, inf.)	*What do you do (for a living)?*

NÜTZLICHE AUSDRÜCKE	*USEFUL EXPRESSIONS*
Na klar!	*Of course!*
Kind	*child*
können	*to be able / can*
meistens	*most of the time*
zusammen	*together*

Vocabulary practice 2

Match these sentences about jobs.

a Carsten repariert Autos.

b Alika kocht in einem Restaurant.

c Marlene repariert Computer.

d Tobias verkauft Trainers und Shirts.

e Lou studiert an einer Universität.

f Hannah spricht mit Kunden.

1 Er ist Verkäufer.

2 Xier ist Student:in.

3 Sie ist Kundenberaterin.

4 Er ist Automechaniker.

5 Sie ist Köchin.

6 Sie ist IT-Spezialistin.

Pronunciation practice

02.09

Asking what languages another person can speak and talking about yours can be a bit of a tongue twister in German. Listen carefully and then repeat the sentences until you feel confident.

Und Sie? Welche Sprachen sprechen Sie? Now explain which language(s) you speak and how well.

CONVERSATION 2

Welche Sprache sprecht ihr zu Hause? *Which language do you speak at home?*

02.10

1 Listen to the conversation without looking at the text. Play it a few times and see if you can make out a few new words and phrases each time. Then listen again and read the text. What language(s) do Aylin and Fabian speak at home? And what professions do they have?

After the Abendessen, Max goes to the Balkon (*balcony*) with Aylin and Fabian and they start talking about where they live and which Sprachen they speak.

Max	Und wo wohnt ihr in Berlin?
Aylin	Wir wohnen in Steglitz, das ist in Südberlin.
Max	Und welche Sprache sprecht ihr zu Hause?
Aylin	Wir sprechen meistens Deutsch, aber Fabian spricht auch gut Türkisch.
Max	Und habt ihr Kinder?
Aylin	Ja, wir haben eine Tochter, Nuri. Sie lernt Türkisch und Deutsch. Und welche Sprachen sprichst du, Max?
Max	Ich spreche fließend Englisch und Deutsch und ein bisschen Chinesisch. Was macht ihr eigentlich?
Aylin	Fabian ist Elektriker und ich bin Ärztin. Und was machst du in Berlin?
Max	Ich schreibe einen Blog über Berlin. Ich bin Blogger.
Aylin	Das ist interessant! Ein Influencer ... Udo kann dir helfen. Er ist Stadtführer. Udo?
Udo	Na klar, Max. Wir machen eine Berlin-Tour zusammen.

2 Decide if these statements are *true* (richtig) or *false* (falsch).

a	Steglitz ist in Nordberlin.	R	F
b	Nuri lernt Türkisch und Deutsch.	R	F
c	Max spricht Englisch, Deutsch und Spanisch.	R	F
d	Udo ist Elektriker.	R	F

In Conversation 1 Max asks Wally: Kann ich dir helfen? (*Can I help you?*). Here, when Aylin talks to Max, she says: Udo kann dir helfen (*Udo can help you*). If you were in Germany and wanted to ask someone formally for help, you would say: Können Sie mir helfen? (*Can you help me?*).

LANGUAGE BUILDER 3

 Language discovery 3

Look at these four sentences. Identify which of the underlined pronouns correspond to *we*, *you* (plural formal), *you* (plural informal) and *they*.

a Was macht <u>ihr</u> eigentlich? ....
b <u>Wir</u> sprechen meistens Deutsch. ....
c Woher kommen <u>Sie</u>, Frau Peters and Herr Osel? ....
d Aylin und Fabian leben in Berlin und <u>sie</u> haben eine Tochter. ....

Talking about other people

If you want to talk about or address more than one person, the pronouns and verb forms are:

Wir wohnen in Berlin.	*We live in Berlin.*
Woher kommt ihr?	*Where do you come from?* (informal)
Woher kommen Sie?	*Where do you come from?* (formal)
Sie heißen Simone und Petra.	*They are called Simone and Petra.*

Apart from the ihr form, the verb ending for all plural forms is -en.

Here is a handy summary of verb endings in German.

Most verbs follow the regular pattern like kommen and wohnen. There are a few variations:

▷ Some verbs, like sprechen, have a vowel change in the du and the er/sie/es/xier forms.
▷ Verbs whose stem ends in -d or -t, such as arbeiten, add an extra -e in the du and ihr forms.

The irregular verbs sein (*to be*) and haben (*to have*) are also included because they occur so frequently.

Singular		kommen	wohnen	sprechen	arbeiten	sein	haben
ich	-e	komme	wohne	spreche	arbeite	bin	habe
du	-st	kommst	wohnst	sprichst	arbeitest	bist	hast
Sie	-en	kommen	wohnen	sprechen	arbeiten	sind	haben
er/sie/es/ xier	-t	kommt	wohnt	spricht	arbeitet	ist	hat
Plural							
wir	-en	kommen	wohnen	sprechen	arbeiten	sind	haben
ihr	-t	kommt	wohnt	sprecht	arbeitet	seid	habt
Sie/sie	-en	kommen	wohnen	sprechen	arbeiten	sind	haben

You might think it a little confusing that the word Sie/sie has so many different meanings. In practice there are several ways of distinguishing between them. Firstly, the formal Sie (*you*) always takes a capital initial letter; secondly, the ending of the verb for sie (*she*) is -t as opposed to -en for sie (*they*). Thirdly, and probably most importantly, the context almost always makes the meaning clear.

Language practice 3

1   Decide whether Sie / sie means *you*, *she*, or *they* in each of the sentences.

   a   Sie heißt Nadine.
   b   Guten Tag, heißen Sie Peter Roßmann?
   c   Jetzt wohnen sie in Edinburgh, in Schottland.
   d   Arbeitet sie jetzt in einem Restaurant?
   e   Entschuldigen Sie, Frau Salvati. Sprechen Sie Deutsch?
   f   Nele und James wohnen jetzt in Berlin und sie arbeiten als IT-Expert:innen.

2   While traveling in Germany you meet two groups of people. Complete with the correct verb endings in both formal and informal settings.

Formal

a   Wie heiß............... Sie?
   – Wir heiß............... Pia und Timo.
b   Woher komm............... Sie?
   – Wir komm............... aus Köln.
c   Wo wohn............... Sie?
   – Wir wohn............... noch in Köln.
d   Wie find............... Sie Köln?
   – Wir find............... Köln schön.
e   Und was mach............... Sie?
   – Wir arbeit................
f   Welche Sprachen sprech............... Sie?
   – Wir sprech............... Deutsch und Englisch.

Informal

g   Wie heiß............... ihr?
   – Wir heiß............... Thilo and Carl.
h   Woher komm............... ihr?
   – Wir komm............... aus Bern.
i   S............... ihr Schweizer?
   – Ja, wir s............... Schweizer.
j   Wie find............... ihr Bern?
   – Wir find............... es gut.
k   Was mach............... ihr?
   – Wir studier................
l   Welche Sprachen sprech............... ihr?
   – Wir sprech............... Deutsch und Französisch.

Language discovery 4

02.11

Listen to the conversation again and repeat each line in the pauses provided. Try to imitate the phrasing and intonation you hear. Then look at these sentences. Work out the pattern for the masculine and feminine forms. How do the names of languages normally end?

Thilo ist Schweizer. Maria ist Schweizerin. Sie sprechen Deutsch und Italienisch.

Chen ist Chinese und Xin ist Chinesin. Sie sprechen Chinesisch, sehr gut Englisch und lernen Deutsch.

Country, nationality, and language

As in English, there are some similarities between the name for the country, nationality, and language. Here are some examples:

Country	Nationality		Language
	masculine: -er/-e	feminine: -in	(i)sch
Deutschland	Deutscher	Deutsche (!)	Deutsch
Österreich	Österreicher	Österreicherin	Deutsch
England	Engländer	Engländerin	Englisch
Ägypten	Ägypter	Ägypterin	Arabisch
Indien	Inder	Inderin	Hindi (!)
Kolumbien	Kolumbianer	Kolumbianerin	Spanisch
USA	Amerikaner	Amerikanerin	Englisch
China	Chinese	Chinesin	Chinesisch
Polen	Pole	Polin	Polnisch
Türkei	Türke	Türkin	Türkisch

What do you notice? The nationality for men usually ends in -er or -e, and for women in -in (with the exception of Deutsche). Languages tend to add in (i)sch. Remember to insert a colon if you would like to use the gender-neutral form: Amerikaner:in, Chines:in.

You could also add an asterisk: Amerikaner*in, Chines*in.

Language practice 4

1 Add the nationality and the first language.

a Emma Watson kommt aus England. Sie ist Engländerin. Sie spricht perfekt ....

b Barak Obama kommt aus den .... Er ist .... Er spricht perfekt ....

c Shakira ist Sängerin und kommt aus Kolumbien. Sie ist .... Sie spricht perfekt ....

d Mohamed Salah kommt aus Ägypten. Er ist .... Er spricht super ....

e Donald Tusk ist Politiker und kommt aus Polen. Er ist .... Er spricht fließend ....

f Arnold Schwarzenegger kommt eigentlich aus Österreich. Er ist .... und .... Er spricht D .... und E ....

g Kajol Devgan kommt aus Indien. Sie ist Filmstar in Bollywood. Sie ist .... und spricht perfekt ....

02.12

2 Now play Conversation 2 again, and play Max's role. Speak in the pauses provided and try not to refer to the text.

SKILL BUILDER

02.13

1 Wie ist deine Handynummer? At the end of the Abendessen Max, Aylin, Nabi and Udo exchange their Handynummern (*mobile numbers*). Listen and write whose number it is.

a 01603655677: ....

b 01602656477: ....

c 01604656315: ....

d 01604646316: ....

2 Now, give your phone number. Say it out loud until you feel confident.

3 Complete the sentences with the correct form of the verbs in parentheses.

a Wie .... Sie? – Ich .... Aylin. (heißen)

b Woher .... Sie – Ich .... aus Berlin. (kommen)

c Woher .... du? – Ich .... aus Tokio. (kommen)

d Was .... du? – Ich .... (machen / arbeiten)

e Welche Sprachen .... ihr? – Wir .... Hindi, Englisch und ein bisschen Deutsch. (sprechen)

f Was .... ihr? – Wir .... (machen / studieren)

g Woher .... du? – Ich .... aus Istanbul. (sein)

h Woher .... Sie? – Ich .... aus Köln. (sein)

4 Introduce a famous person you admire. Use this text about the Schauspieler (*actor*) Christoph Waltz as a guide. Write your answers.

Christoph Waltz kommt aus Österreich. Er ist Österreicher und Deutscher. Er lebt in den USA und in Deutschland. Er ist Schauspieler. Er ist … Jahre alt. Er spricht Deutsch und ausgezeichnet Englisch. Er ist sehr intelligent und hat viel Humor.

02.14

5 You have learned how to give some basic information about yourself. Listen and answer the questions. You will also hear a model answer. If you don't want to give your age, just say: Kein Kommentar (*No comment*).

a Wie heißen Sie?
b Woher kommen Sie eigentlich?
c Wo wohnen Sie?
d Wie ist Ihre Handynummer?
e Wie alt sind Sie?
f Welche Sprachen sprechen Sie und wie gut?

6 You already know quite a lot about the main characters in this book. So that you keep on track with developments, summarize some of the main details below. You may need to look back at the story in the Conversation sections. The missing details (X) will be revealed in future units.

	Kommt woher?	Beruf	Sprachen
Max			
Wally		X	Deutsch, Englisch, Italienisch
Aylin	Berlin		
Fabian	Berlin		.... + Englisch
Udo			

1 Roger Federer introduces himself. Read the text and then rewrite the text to introduce him.

Ich heiße Roger Federer und bin Schweizer. Ich komme aus Basel. Ich spreche fließend Deutsch, Englisch und Französisch.

Er heißt ....

....

2 Now he talks about his family. Add the verb given in parentheses in the correct form. Here is a word to help you understand the text: Zwilling (*twin*).

Meine Mutter .... (kommen) aus Südafrika. Meine Frau .... (sein) auch Tennisspielerin. Sie .... (heißen) Mirka. Wir .... (haben) zwei Töchter und zwei Söhne. Sie .... (sein) Zwillinge. Wir .... (wohnen) zusammen in Valbella und Dubai.

Wie geht's weiter? *What happens next?*

So, Udo has agreed to show Max around Berlin. Where will he take him? And what will Max make of Berlin? Find out in the next unit.

Before you move on to the next unit, assess your progress using the **My review** section on the first page of the unit, and reflect on your learning experience with the **My takeaway** section available online.

3

In this lesson you will learn how to:
» Ask someone how they are and say how you are feeling
» Talk about buildings and sights in town
» Ask for and give directions
» Make requests and suggestions using the imperative

Erste Eindrücke von Berlin

My study plan

I plan to work with Unit 3
○ Every day
○ Twice a week
○ Other _____
I plan to study for
○ 5–15 minutes
○ 15–30 minutes
○ 30–45+ minutes

My progress tracker

Day / Date	🎧	🎤	📖	✏️	💬
	○	○	○	○	○
	○	○	○	○	○
	○	○	○	○	○
	○	○	○	○	○
	○	○	○	○	○
	○	○	○	○	○
	○	○	○	○	○

My goals

What do you want to be able to do or say in German when you complete this unit?

Done

1 .... ○
2 .... ○
3 .... ○

My review

SELF CHECK	
I can ...	
○	... ask someone how they are feeling and say how you are feeling.
○	... talk about buildings and sights in town.
○	... ask for and give directions.
○	... make requests and suggestions using the imperative.

Top- Sehenswürdigkeiten in Berlin *Top sights in Berlin*

Every year Berlin attracts more than 12 million visitors who come to see the Sehenswürdigkeiten (*sights*) it has to offer. Many of the main attractions are located in the Stadtzentrum (*city center*).

Top of the list for many is Berlin's Wahrzeichen (*landmark*), das Brandenburger Tor (*Brandenburg Gate*). Built between 1788 and 1791 as a Stadttor (*city gate*), it is now a symbol of national unity and peace. Not far away is der Reichstag, where the German parliament, der Bundestag, sits. It is well known for its Glaskuppel (*glass dome*).

Berlin's tallest building – which can be seen from all over the city – is der Fernsehturm (*TV tower*). From its top you have an impressive view of Berlin. Very popular also is the East Side Gallery, the longest remaining stretch of the Berliner Mauer (*Berlin Wall*).

Die Museumsinsel (*Museum Island*) is a unique collection of five museums and listed as a UNESCO World Heritage Site. Its collections range from prehistory to 19th-century art.

Find out more about the Die Museumsinsel.
What are the five museums?
Where can you find the world-famous Nefertiti Bust and what is it called in German?

03.01

Look at the words and phrases and complete the missing English words and expressions. Then listen and try to imitate the pronunciation of the speakers.

WIE GEHT ES DIR/IHNEN?	HOW ARE YOU?
Wie geht es dir? (informal)	How are you?
Wie geht es Ihnen? (formal)	How are you?
Mir geht es sehr gut / ganz gut / nicht so gut.	I am very well / well / not so well.

IN DER STADT	IN TOWN
der Bahnhof	train station
das Café	....
der Club	....
der Fernsehturm	TV tower
das Fitnessstudio	....
das Geschäft	shop
die Glaskuppel	glass dome
das Hotel	....
die Kneipe	bar / pub
das Museum	....
die Oper	....
der Platz	square
das Restaurant	....
die U-Bahnstation	metro/underground station

NÜTZLICHE AUSDRÜCKE	USEFUL EXPRESSIONS
links	left
rechts	right
oben	at the top / above
hier	here
da	there
hier vorne, da vorne	over here, over there
zum Beispiel	for example
die Kunst	art
grün	green
manchmal	sometimes
billig	cheap
nicht billig	not cheap

Vocabulary practice 1

Ask the following people how they are. Use the appropriate question from the box.

Wie geht es Ihnen? ~~Wie geht es dir?~~ Wie geht es Ihnen? Wie geht es dir?

a ....

c *Wie geht es dir?*

b ....

d ....

And you? How do you feel today?

Wie geht es Ihnen? Mir geht es ...

> Wie geht es dir? Asking how someone is literally translates as: *How does it go to you?* And the
> answer is something like: *It goes well to me.* Grammatically, this is a more complex structure.
> Learn these as set phrases. A simpler way to ask informally is: Wie geht's? Also, when you reply,
> you can simplify it: Wie geht es Ihnen? – Danke, gut. / Danke, ganz gut. / Danke, nicht so gut.

Pronunciation practice

03.02

1 **Listen to these words. Notice how the letter s is pronounced at the beginning and
at the end of a word.**

Sie   sehr   super   Haus   links   Glas

03.03

2 **Practice saying these words, then listen and repeat.**

sieben   Sehenswürdigkeit   so   sechs   rechts   Bus

Die Fahrt mit der Buslinie 100 *The journey on bus route 100*

03.04

1 Listen to the conversation without looking at the text. Play it a few times and see if you can make out a few new words and phrases each time. Then listen again and read the text. Where does the tour end?

The day after Wally's dinner party, Udo and Max meet at the train station Zoologischer Garten or Bahnhof Zoo, as Berliners say. Udo specializes in tours that rely on public transportation, and Buslinie 100 (*bus route 100*) passes by some of Berlin's most important Sehenswürdigkeiten (*sights*).

Udo	Hallo, Max. Wie geht es dir?
Max	Hallo, Udo. Ganz gut. Und dir?
Udo	Mir geht es sehr gut, Max. Danke. Also, nehmen wir die Buslinie 100.
	They board the bus. After a few minutes ...
Max	Oh, der Park ist sehr grün und schön.
Udo	Ja, das ist der Tiergarten. Ich jogge manchmal hier. Links ist das Schloss Bellevue. Hier wohnt der Bundespräsident.
Max	Und da vorne ist der Reichstag?
Udo	Genau. Hier tagt das Parlament, der Deutsche Bundestag. Die Glaskuppel ist großartig, finde ich.
Max	Und alles ist so zentral.
Udo	Ja, und hier ist die Straße „Unter den Linden". Rechts siehst du die Staatsoper.
Max	Und hier links?
Udo	Das ist die Museumsinsel. Dort findest du zum Beispiel das Pergamonmuseum mit alter Kunst aus Griechenland, Rom und Ägypten.
Max	Und wo endet die Tour?
Udo	Hier ist der Alexanderplatz und der Fernsehturm. Der Fernsehturm ist 368 Meter hoch. Oben ist ein Restaurant. Der Blick ist fantastisch. Aber es ist nicht billig.

2 Match these words and places.

- **a** Tiergarten
- **b** Schloss Bellevue
- **c** Bundestag
- **d** Straße „Unter den Linden"
- **e** Museumsinsel
- **f** Alexanderplatz

- **1** Pergamonmuseum
- **2** Glaskuppel
- **3** Fernsehturm
- **4** Bundespräsident
- **5** Jogging
- **6** Staatsoper

> The title of the German president is Bundespräsident (literally *federal president*). Bund(es) means *federal*. If the German president is female, she would be called Bundespräsidentin.

LANGUAGE BUILDER 1

💡 Language discovery 1

Look at Conversation 1 again. Write the article words der, die, das that appear before the nouns.

a .... Park, Bundespräsident   **c** .... Straße, Tour

b .... Parlament, Schloss

Nouns: gender and articles

All German nouns are capitalized and have a gender: masculine, feminine or neuter. The words for *the* and *a* (called *definite* and *indefinite articles*) must match the gender of the nouns:

	the	a
masculine	der Park (*the park*)	ein Park (*a park*)
feminine	die Straße (*the street*)	eine Straße (*a street*)
neuter	das Museum (*the museum*)	ein Museum (*a museum*)

Here are a few guidelines to help you recognize and remember the gender of nouns in German:

	Masculine nouns	Feminine nouns	Neuter nouns
Refer to:	males and male animals	females and female animals	names of hotels, cinemas, metals
Typical endings:	-ig (der Honig)	-e (die Straße)	-chen (das Brötchen)
	-mus (der Optimismus)	-ei (die Bäckerei)	-ing (das Meeting)
	-or (der Motor)	-heit (die Freiheit)	-ma (das Thema)
	-ling (der Liebling)	-ung (die Zeitung)	-o (das Kino)
		-tät (die Nationalität)	-um (das Museum)
		-ur (die Natur)	

Although there are some tips to identify gender, try to learn each new noun with its gender. From now on, we will indicate gender of nouns with der for *masculine*, die for *feminine* and das for *neuter* nouns.

> In the plural, die is used for all nouns. You will learn more about plural forms in the next unit.

Language practice 1

1 Complete the sentences with the appropriate article: der, die or das.

a Wie heißt d .... Mann?

b D .... Park ist sehr groß.

c D .... Frau kommt aus Neapel.

d D .... Kneipe ist sehr alt.

e Wo ist d .... Museum?

f Ich finde d .... Zentrum sehr schön.

2 Complete the sentences with the appropriate article: **ein** or **eine**.

a Wo ist hier .... Park?

b Er ist .... guter Arzt.

c Dort ist .... Bäckerei.

d Ich kenne .... Studentin aus Damaskus.

e Nico hat .... Katze.

f Wien hat .... Museum für Mathematik.

LANGUAGE BUILDER 2

💡 Language discovery 2

03.05

1 Listen to the conversation again and repeat each line in the pauses provided. Try to imitate the phrasing and intonation you hear. These nouns are made up of two components. Put them together. What is the meaning of the words?

a Telefon   **1** mechanikerin : ....

b Auto   **2** führer : ....

c Stadt   **3** kuppel : ....

d Glas   **4** nummer : ....

2 Find at least two more of these types of nouns in Conversation 1.

Compound nouns

If a noun is made up of two or more nouns, the last noun always determines the gender:

das Telefon + die Nummer: die Telefonnummer (*telephone number*)

das Auto + die Mechanikerin: die Automechanikerin (*car mechanic*, fem.)

To help with pronunciation, sometimes extra letters like **s** or **es** are added:

das Museum + die Insel: die Museumsinsel

der Bund + der Tag: der Bundestag

Language practice 2

1 Compound nouns appear quite frequently in German. Make a few, indicating the appropriate gender.

Example: das Handy + die Nummer: *die Handynummer*

a die Fitness + das Studio: ....

b das Haus + die Nummer: ....

c das Bier + der Garten: ....

d das Auto + der Mechaniker: ....

e der Altbau + die Wohnung: ....

f der Bus + die Linie: ....

g die U-Bahn + die Station: ....

2 Now play Conversation 1 again and play Max's role. Speak in the pauses provided and try not to refer to the text.

03.06

CULTURE POINT 2

Die geteilte Stadt *The divided city*

With the beginning of the Cold War in 1947, Germany was divided between the Western Bloc led by the United States, and the Eastern Bloc led by the Soviet Union. Two German states emerged: the Bundesrepublik Deutschland and the Deutsche Demokratische Republik. From 1952 a fortified border – 1378 km long – divided both countries, however, it was still possible for people to cross from the East to the West via Berlin. In August 1961 the East German authorities decided to close this loophole and to build the Berliner Mauer (*Berlin Wall*). It included guard towers placed along large concrete walls and a number of defenses.

From 1961 to 1989 Berlin was eine geteilte Stadt (*a divided city*) and the wall made it practically impossible for people from the East to go the West. After the end of the Cold War and the Mauerfall (*fall of the Wall*) large parts of the wall were destroyed. Today, there are only a few remains left, but dedicated places like the Gedenkstätte Berliner Mauer (*Berlin Wall Memorial*) stand as a reminder of this period. You can also walk or cycle the Mauerweg (*Berlin Wall Trail*) which traces the course of the former wall.

 Visit the Berlin Wall Trail website to explore more.

How long was the Mauer encircling the western part of Berlin? What is displayed on the info markers along the trail? How many sections of the trail are there? How can you complete any of the sections?

VOCABULARY BUILDER 2

Look at the words and phrases and complete the missing English words and expressions. Then listen and try to imitate the pronunciation of the speakers.

EINDRÜCKE VON BERLIN

Wie ist dein erster Eindruck?	*What are your first impressions?*
die Touristen (pl.)	....
die Geschichte	*history*
alte und neue Gebäude	*old and .... buildings*
die Führung	*guided tour*
die Passion	*passion*
typisch	*typical(ly)*
voll	*crowded, full*
müde	*tired*

IMPRESSIONS OF BERLIN

ORIENTIERUNGEN

Wo ist der / die / das ... ?	*Where is the ... ?*
Besuch ... / Geh ... / Benutz ... (imperative)	*Visit ... / Go ... / Use ...*
nahe, weit	*near, far*
geradeaus	*straight ahead*
immer geradeaus	(lit.) *always straight ahead*
die erste Straße links	*the first street on the ....*
die zweite Straße rechts	*the second street on the ....*
die dritte Straße	*the third street*

ORIENTATION

NÜTZLICHE AUSDRÜCKE

Es gibt ...	*There is / are ...*
Was möchtest du jetzt machen?	*What would you like to do now?*
Das klingt gut.	*That sounds good.*
Kein Problem.	*No ....*
Bis bald!	*See you soon!* (lit. *Until soon!*)

USEFUL EXPRESSIONS

In German, you can add 'oder' at the end of a sentence to turn it into a question.

Sie sind Frau Maier, oder?	*You are Mrs. Maier, aren't you?*
Du hast ja dein Handy dabei, oder?	*You have your phone on you, don't you?*

Vocabulary practice 2

Match the directions with the appropriate image.

a Gehen Sie die erste Straße links und dann die erste Straße rechts.
b Geh geradeaus und dann die erste Straße rechts und dann die zweite Straße links.
c Gehen Sie immer geradeaus. Dann nehmen Sie die zweite Straße links.

1

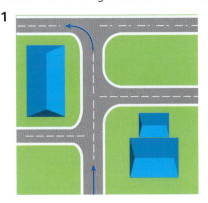

2

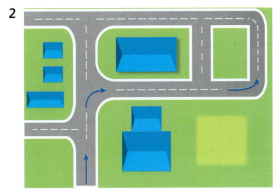

3

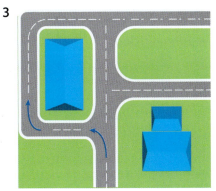

CONVERSATION 2

Benutz besser dein Handy *Better use your phone*

03.08

1 **Listen to the conversation without looking at the text. Play it a few times and see if you can make out a few new words and phrases each time. Then listen again and read the text. Where does Max want to go next? What is Udo's advice at the end?**

> At Alexanderplatz, Udo and Max go for a coffee in a Bäckerei (*bakery*) before Udo has to work and take a group of tourists on a tour. Udo is keen to hear Max's first impressions of Berlin. And Max is keen to discover more of Berlin.
>
> **Udo**   Und Max, wie findest du Berlin? Wie ist dein erster Eindruck?
>
> **Max**   Mein Eindruck? Berlin ist voll und es gibt viele Touristen. Aber das Zentrum ist schön und grün. Es hat viele alte und neue Gebäude.
>
> **Udo**   Ja, das ist typisch für Berlin. Was möchtest du jetzt machen?
>
> **Max**   Meine Passion ist deutsche Geschichte und auch die Mauer.
>
> **Udo**   Mmh. Besuch das Mauermuseum und Checkpoint Charlie. Es ist nicht weit.
>
> **Max**   Das klingt gut. Und wo ist das Museum?
>
> **Udo**   Geh hier vorne die erste Straße rechts in die Rathausstraße und dann immer geradeaus. Geh dann links in die Friedrichstraße und dann wieder geradeaus.
>
> **Max**   Mmh, also hier rechts, dann wieder rechts in die Friedrichstraße, dann geradeaus und äh ...
>
> **Udo**   Du hast ja dein Handy dabei, oder?
>
> **Max**   Ja, klar. Ich habe mein Handy dabei.
>
> **Udo**   Gut. Benutz besser dein Handy.
>
> **Max**   Ja, das glaube ich auch. Danke für die Führung, Udo.
>
> **Udo**   Kein Problem. Bis bald, Max.

2 **Decide if these statements are *true* (richtig) or *false* (falsch).**

     a   Max findet das Zentrum schön, aber nicht grün.   R   F

     b   Udo sagt, alte und neue Gebäude sind typisch für Berlin.   R   F

     c   Das Mauermuseum ist weit von Checkpoint Charlie.   R   F

     d   Udo sagt: Geh rechts, geradeaus, dann links und geradeaus.   R   F

LANGUAGE BUILDER 3

 Language discovery 3

Look at these sentences from Conversation 2. How does Udo tell Max to do something? What is unusual about the form of the verb?

Besuch das Mauermuseum und Checkpoint Charlie.

Geh dann links in die Friedrichstraße.

Benutz besser dein Handy.

Imperative

The *imperative* or *command* form is used when you ask or advise people to do something. There are different forms for du and Sie; however, the verb always comes first:

du: Besuch das Museum   Sie: Besuchen Sie das Museum.

In the Sie form the singular and plural forms are the same:

Gehen Sie geradeaus.   Warten Sie, bitte.

In the informal du (singular) and ihr (plural) the pronouns are dropped:

Geh geradeaus.   Geht geradeaus.

Warte bitte.   Wartet bitte.

> Some verbs are irregular and undergo a vowel change in the du form, e.g. sprechen — Sprich bitte Englisch.

Note that in the du and Sie form an extra -e is added after certain letters:

	Most verbs	Example	Stems ending in -d, -t or -n	Example
du	stem + no ending	geh- en > geh Geh die erste Straße links.	stem plus -e	wart-en > wart-e Warte!
Sie (sing. + pl.)	infinitive + **Sie**	Gehen Sie geradeaus.	infinitive + **Sie**	Warten Sie, bitte.
ihr	stem plus -t	geh- en > geht Geht nach rechts.	stem plus -et	öffn-en > öffnet Öffnet das Fenster!

Language practice 3

Which advice is the right one? Match the two sentences.

a Das Zimmer ist zu warm.

b Ich komme in fünf Minuten.

c Wo ist der Bahnhof, bitte?

d Ich bin müde.

e Der Bus kommt nicht.

f Paula kann kein Deutsch.

1 Nehmen Sie die U-Bahn.

2 Trink Kaffee.

3 Sprich bitte Englisch.

4 Warte bitte.

5 Öffnen Sie bitte das Fenster.

6 Geh hier links und dann geradeaus.

LANGUAGE BUILDER 4

03.09

💡 Language discovery 4

Listen to the conversation again and repeat each line in the pauses provided. Try to imitate the phrasing and intonation you hear. Here are three sentences from Conversation 2. Where do you have to add an -e to mein and why?

a Mein .... Eindruck?

b Mein .... Passion ist deutsche Geschichte und auch die Mauer.

c Ich habe mein .... Handy dabei.

Possessives (1): Require endings

Words like mein (my), dein (your, informal) and Ihr (your, formal) indicate who the object that follows belongs to. They also have masculine, feminine and neuter forms, which match the gender of the noun. In German these endings do not depend on the person who speaks but on the gender of the noun that comes after mein, dein, etc.:

masculine mein Name, mein Eindruck

feminine meine Handynummer, meine Passion

neuter mein Haus, mein Handy

plural meine Freunde, meine Kinder

> The endings of possessives follow the pattern of the indefinite articles. This may make it easier for you to apply them.

Wie ist dein Name? – Mein Name ist Stefanie.

Wie ist Ihre Handynummer? – Meine Handynummer ist 0049 3589745196.

Wo ist Ihr Haus? – Mein Haus ist dort.

Wie heißen deine Kinder? – Meine Kinder heißen Ana und Leon.

Language practice 4

1 Add the appropriate endings. Remember, an ending is needed only for feminine nouns. The gender is given in parentheses.

a Wie ist dein .... Name? – Mein .... Name ist Yasmin. (m)

b Wie ist dein .... Adresse? – Mein .... Adresse ist Kantweg 7. (f)

c Wie ist dein .... Hausnummer? – Mein .... Hausnummer ist 18b. (f)

d Ist das dein .... Handynummer? – Ja, das ist mein .... Handynummer. (f)

e Ist das Ihr .... Handy? – Ja, das ist mein .... Handy. (nt)

f Ist das Ihr .... Kaffee? – Ja, das ist mein .... Kaffee. (m)

g Wie heißt Ihr .... Partnerin? – Mein .... Partnerin heißt Rosa. (f)

2 Now play Conversation 2 again and play Udo's role. Speak in the pauses provided and try not to refer to the text.

03.10

SKILL BUILDER

1 Put these words together. They are all related to Berlin.

platz	museum	turm	garten	tag	station
kuppel	tag	museum	straße	oper	~~insel~~

Example: Museum*insel*

a Fernseh....................

b Bundes....................

c Glas....................

d Reichs....................

e Tier....................

f Alexander....................

g Staats....................

h Pergamon....................

i U-Bahn....................

j Mauer....................

k Friedrich....................

2 The nouns in each line all have the same gender. Decide if they are masculine (m), feminine (f) or neuter (nt). Identify the typical gender endings.

a Präsident, Kundenberater, Koch, Touristenführer   ....

b IT-Spezialistin, Autorin, Elektrikerin, Präsidentin   ....

c Sprache, Adresse, Straße, Kneipe   ....

d Museum, Zentrum, Auto, Foto   ....

e Nationalität, Universität, Kontinuität, Spontaneität   ....

3 Udo's friend often feels tired. Udo advises him to do the following. Rewrite all the advice using the formal imperative form.

Example: Trink mehr Wasser > *Trinken Sie mehr Wasser*

a Mach Pilates.

b Geh joggen.

c Besuch ein Wellnesscenter.

d Arbeite nicht so viel.

e Geh zu einem Tanzkurs.

f Finde ein neues Hobby.

g Denk positiv.

4 **Max's blog. Max has written his second blog. Read the text and answer the questions.**

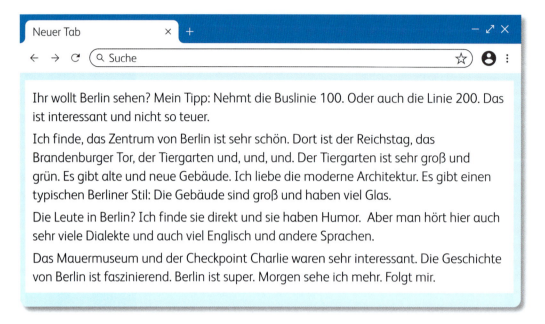

Ihr wollt Berlin sehen? Mein Tipp: Nehmt die Buslinie 100. Oder auch die Linie 200. Das ist interessant und nicht so teuer.

Ich finde, das Zentrum von Berlin ist sehr schön. Dort ist der Reichstag, das Brandenburger Tor, der Tiergarten und, und, und. Der Tiergarten ist sehr groß und grün. Es gibt alte und neue Gebäude. Ich liebe die moderne Architektur. Es gibt einen typischen Berliner Stil: Die Gebäude sind groß und haben viel Glas.

Die Leute in Berlin? Ich finde sie direkt und sie haben Humor. Aber man hört hier auch sehr viele Dialekte und auch viel Englisch und andere Sprachen.

Das Mauermuseum und der Checkpoint Charlie waren sehr interessant. Die Geschichte von Berlin ist faszinierend. Berlin ist super. Morgen sehe ich mehr. Folgt mir.

5 **Decide if these statements are *true* (richtig) or *false* (falsch).**

a	There are two bus routes that are interesting for tourists in Berlin.	R	F
b	Houses in Berlin are usually small.	R	F
c	Max does not like the local people in Berlin.	R	F
d	Berlin's history is interesting.	R	F

6 **Match the adjectives with the words as mentioned in the blog.**

a	groß und grün	**1**	Leute
b	direkt	**2**	Gebäude
c	nicht teuer	**3**	Tiergarten
d	alt und neu	**4**	Bus

TEST YOURSELF

03.11

You are meeting people from work in a restaurant. Your new colleague, Frau Amani, wants to join and calls you. Listen to the audio and say your responses out loud in the pauses.

Frau Amani	You
Hallo, hier ist Frau Amani.	*Say hello and give your name. Ask how she is.*
Danke, mir geht es super. Und Ihnen?	*Say many thanks and that you are very well.*
Ich nehme nachher die U-Bahn bis Hallerstraße. Wie gehe ich dann?	*Say OK. Then go left and straight.*
Also links und dann geradeaus.	*Say yes. And then take the second street to the left.*
Wunderbar. Und wie heißt das Restaurant?	*Say the restaurant is called Istanbul. Then say it's very nice und not so expensive.*
Ja, gut. Vielen Dank. Dann bis später.	*Say yes and see you later.*

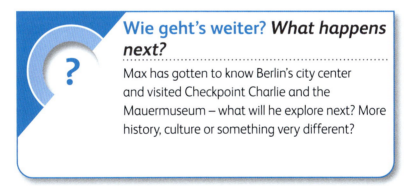

Wie geht's weiter? *What happens next?*

Max has gotten to know Berlin's city center and visited Checkpoint Charlie and the Mauermuseum – what will he explore next? More history, culture or something very different?

Before you move on to the next unit, assess your progress using the **My review** section on the first page of the unit, and reflect on your learning experience with the **My takeaway** section available online.

In this lesson you will learn how to:

» Order food and drinks at a street food stall and restaurant
» Ask for the price and say how much something costs
» Talk about some of your food preferences
» Form the plural of nouns

Einen Latte Macchiato, bitte!

My study plan

I plan to work with Unit 4
○ Every day
○ Twice a week
○ Other _____
I plan to study for
○ 5–15 minutes
○ 15–30 minutes
○ 30–45+ minutes

My progress tracker

Day / Date	🎧	🎤	📖	✏️	💬
	○	○	○	○	○
	○	○	○	○	○
	○	○	○	○	○
	○	○	○	○	○
	○	○	○	○	○
	○	○	○	○	○
	○	○	○	○	○

My goals

What do you want to be able to do or say in German when you complete this unit?

Done

1 .... ○

2 .... ○

3 .... ○

My review

SELF CHECK

	I can ...
●	... order food and drinks at a street food stall and restaurant.
●	... ask for the price and say how much something costs.
●	... talk about some of my food preferences.
●	... form the plural of nouns.

CULTURE POINT 1

Lokale Spezialitäten *Local specialties*

You might have heard of German Bier (*beer*), Würstchen (*sausages*) and Sauerkraut, but the cuisine in German-speaking countries is actually quite varied. Many dishes are associated with a specific area or city, which is sometimes reflected in their name, for example Wiener Schnitzel, Schwarzwälder Kirschtorte (*Black Forest Gateau*) and Lübecker Marzipan.

When you are in Germany, you might notice that there are a lot of bakeries offering a wide range of different types of Brot (*bread*) and Brötchen (*bread roll*). Germans love eating bread and appreciate the variety. Getting fresh rolls from the bakery around the corner for breakfast is something lots of Germans will do on a Saturday. Bread is such an important part of German culture that it was awarded World Heritage status in 2014.

You also find seasonal food such as Spargelzeit (*white asparagus season*) from April till Juni or Grünkohlzeit (*curly kale*), which is harvested in winter after the first frost.

Some dishes in Germany have a misleading name. Find out what dishes are Grünkohl mit Pinkel, Rollmops and Berliner. Which ones can be seen in the pictures below? And in which regions would you typically find them?

 Using the word Berliner to describe an item of food as well as a person from Berlin might be slightly confusing but there are also other words for this dish.

Find out here what they are and where they are used.

04.01

Look at the words and phrases and complete the missing English words and expressions. Then listen and try to imitate the pronunciation of the speakers.

KLEINE GERICHTE UND STREETFOOD	SNACKS AND STREETFOOD
die Currywurst	*fried sausage with ketchup and curry powder*
der Hamburger, der Veggieburger	*....................., ...*
die Pommes (plural)	*fries*
die Sauce, die Mayonnaise	*....................., ...*
der / das Ketchup	*...................*
der Holundersaft	*elderberry juice*
der Orangensaft	*.....................juice*
die / das Cola	*cola*
das Mineralwasser	*...................*
vegan	*...................*
scharf	*spicy*
erfrischend	*refreshing*

PREISE	PRICES
Was kostet / macht das (zusammen)?	*How much does this cost (in total)?*
Das kostet 4 Euro 10 Cent.	*This costs 4 Euros and 10 cents.*
Das macht zusammen 27,35 Euro.	*This comes to 27.35 Euros altogether.*

BEHÄLTER	CONTAINERS
die Dose, die Flasche	*can, bottle*
die Tasse	*cup*

NÜTZLICHE AUSDRÜCKE	USEFUL EXPRESSIONS
Was meinen Sie?	*What do you mean?*
Was möchten Sie?	*What would you like?*
Möchtest du etwas essen?	*Would you like to eat something?*
Ich möchte ... / Ich nehme ...	*I'd like ... / I'll have ...* (lit. *I'll take*)

The verb möchten is a very useful verb when asking for something: Ich möchte einen Kaffee (*I'd like a coffee*). When used with another verb, the other verb goes to the end, in the infinitive: Ich möchte eine Pizza essen (*I'd like to eat a pizza*).

Möchten is slightly irregular as the er/sie/es/xier form takes an -e: ich möchte, du möchtest, Sie möchten, er/sie/es/xier möchte, wir möchten, ihr möchtet, sie möchten.

Vocabulary practice 1

04.02

Listen to an announcement in a supermarket. Match the products in the box to the prices.

Bananen	Burger	Kaffee	Ketchup	Mineralwasser	Veggieburger

a 4,79 €: ....

b 1,39 €: ....

c 7,89 €: ....

d 6,99 €: ....

e 2,45 €: ....

f 0,77 €: ....

> Notice that, in the plural, Euro and Cent do not take an -s.

Pronunciation practice

04.03

1 Listen to these words. Notice how the /eu/ is pronounced.

Euro   heute   Leute   neun   teuer   Deutschland

04.04

2 Practice saying these words, then listen and repeat.

Europa   neu   Freunde   Freude (*joy*)

04.05

3 Say these prices out loud.

  a 2,50 Euro
  b 10,30 Euro
  c 7,25 Euro
  d 150,99 Euro
  e 70,59 Euro
  f 12,47 Euro

Die Kult-Currywurst *The legendary currywurst*

04.06

1 Listen to the conversation without looking at the text. Play it a few times and see if you can make out a few new words and phrases each time. Then listen again and read the text. What kind of currywurst does Max order? How much does it cost in total?

> Max has a craving for Currywurst, which he had loved to eat when he visited Germany before. He stops at a popular Imbiss (fast food stand) at a popular place in Berlin Kreuzberg.
>
> | **Max** | Ich möchte gern eine Currywurst. |
> |---|---|
> | **Verkäufer** | Da haben wir klassisch oder vegan. |
> | **Max** | Ah. Was kosten sie denn? |
> | **Verkäufer** | Klassisch 3,70 Euro, und vegan 4,10 Euro. |
> | **Max** | Mmh, ich glaube, dann nehme ich klassisch. |
> | **Verkäufer** | Scharf oder brutal? Möchten Sie die Sauce scharf oder sehr, sehr scharf? |
> | **Max** | Scharf ist okay. Und dann nehme ich noch Pommes mit Ketchup und Mayonnaise. |
> | **Verkäufer** | Und möchten Sie etwas trinken? |
> | **Max** | Ja, ich nehme eine Cola Zero und einen Kaffee. Was kostet das zusammen? |
> | **Verkäufer** | Das macht zusammen 12,70 Euro. |
>
> *As Max is enjoying his Currywurst, Wally passes by.*
>
> | **Wally** | Hallo, Max. Wie geht's? Isst du eine Currywurst? |
> |---|---|
> | **Max** | Ja, die Currywurst ist lecker. Das ist doch Kult in Berlin. Möchtest du auch etwas essen? |
> | **Wally** | Nein, danke. Aber ich denke, ich trinke etwas. |
> | **Max** | Was nimmst du? |
> | **Wally** | Ich nehme einen Holundersaft. Das ist erfrischend. |

> Kult in this context means *legend*.

2 Decide if these statements are *true* (richtig) or *false* (falsch).

   a The vegan currywurst costs 3,70 Euros.   R   F

   b Max also takes ketchup and mayonnaise.   R   F

   c He drinks a cola and a mineral water.   R   F

   d Wally thinks that elderflower juice is refreshing.   R   F

LANGUAGE BUILDER 1

Nominative and accusative case and articles

In the sentence Ich trinke einen Kaffee (*I drink a coffee*), ich is the subject of the sentence (the person doing the drinking) and einen Kaffee is the direct object (what the person is drinking).

In the previous unit, you learned the indefinite articles (ein, eine, ein) are used for nouns which function as the subject. When a masculine noun appears as the direct object, the article changes from ein to einen. Feminine and neuter articles do not change

Subject (Nominative)	Direct object (Accusative)
Das ist <u>ein</u> Kaffee. (m)	Ich nehme <u>einen</u> Kaffee. (m)
Das ist <u>eine</u> Currywurst. (f)	Ich möchte gern <u>eine</u> Currywurst. (f)
Das ist <u>ein</u> Wasser. (nt)	Ich nehme <u>ein</u> Wasser. (nt)

The same is true for definite articles (der, die, das). With masculine direct objects der changes to den:

Subject (Nominative)	Direct object (Accusative)
<u>Der</u> Kaffee ist gut. (m)	Ich nehme <u>den</u> Kaffee. (m)
<u>Die</u> Sauce ist scharf. (f)	Ich liebe <u>die</u> scharfe Sauce. (f)
<u>Das</u> Zimmer ist schön. (nt)	Er mietet <u>das</u> Zimmer. (nt)

These changes also apply to the possessives: mein > meinen, dein > deinen, Ihr > Ihren, etc.:

Das ist mein Kaffee. (m)   Du trinkst meinen Kaffee. (m)

In grammatical terms, the different roles of words are called cases. The role of the subject is referred to as the *nominative case* and the direct object as the *accusative case*. After most verbs in German, you will need to use the accusative forms, that is, einen or den for masculine nouns. Notice that with sein you use the nominative: Das ist ein Kaffee.

Language practice 1

Decide which accusative endings are correct. The genders of the nouns are given in parentheses.

1 Complete with einen, eine, or ein.

   a Ich möchte ein .... Cola, bitte. (f)

   b Ich nehme ein .... Limonade. (f)

   c Ich möchte ein .... Orangensaft. (m)

   d Ich nehme ein .... Kaffee. (m)

   e Er nimmt ein .... Cappucino. (m)

   f Karina nimmt ein .... Veggieburger. (m)

   g Wir kaufen ein .... Flasche Wasser. (f)

   h Ich nehme ein .... Tasse Kaffee. (f)

2 Complete with den, die, or das.

   a Tim trinkt d .... Limonade. (f)

   b Lucia trinkt d .... Cola. (f)

   c Heba bekommt d .... Saft. (m)

   d Ich trinke d .... Latte Macchiato. (m)

   e Patrick nimmt d .... Cheeseburger. (m)

   f Karina nimmt d .... Veggieburger. (m)

   g Wir trinken d .... Mineralwasser. (nt)

   h Wir möchten d .... Flasche Wasser. (f)

> When talking about containers, the gender of the container defines which article to use:
>
> *Ich möchte eine Tasse Kaffee. I'd like a cup of coffee.* (Tasse is feminine.)
>
> *Wir möchten eine Flasche Wasser. We'd like a bottle of water.* (Flasche is feminine.)
>
> *Xier kauft eine Dose Cola. They buy a can of cola.* (Dose is feminine.)

> Remember, nouns ending in -e are usually feminine: die Limonade. Sometimes you can also group nouns. For example all types of teas, coffees, and juices are masculine: der Pfefferminztee, der schwarze Tee, der Latte Macchiato, der Cappuccino, der Tomatensaft, der Orangensaft.

04.07

💡 Language discovery 2

Listen to the conversation again and repeat each line in the pauses provided. Try to imitate the pronunciation and intonation you hear. Then look at these sentences. What do you notice when you compare the verb form used in the sentence with the infinitive provided in parentheses?

a Isst du eine Currywurst? (essen)

c Kiara spricht gut Englisch. (sprechen)

b Was nimmst du? (nehmen)

d Er fährt nach Berlin. (fahren)

Verbs with a vowel change

Some verbs in German change their vowel in the du and er, sie, es, xier forms. The vowel change is either a > ä, e > i, or e > ie. An overview of the main verbs with vowel changes is in the list of irregular verbs in the online Grammar summary. Here are some examples. This change does not happen in the plural forms.

	essen	sprechen	lesen	fahren	nehmen		essen	sprechen	lesen	fahren	nehmen
ich	esse	spreche	lese	fahre	nehme	wir	essen	sprechen	lesen	fahren	nehmen
du	isst	sprichst	liest	fährst	nimmst*	ihr	esst	sprecht	lest	fahrt	nehmt
Sie	essen	sprechen	lesen	fahren	nehmen	Sie	essen	sprechen	lesen	fahren	nehmen
er*	isst	spricht	liest	fährt	nimmt*	sie	essen	sprechen	lesen	fahren	nehmen

*er, sie, es, xier

> * Note how the h in nehmen is also replaced with another m.

Welche Sprachen sprichst du? – Ich spreche Deutsch und Schwedisch.

Was liest sie? – Sie liest einen Artikel.

Wann fährst du? – Ich fahre morgen.

Language practice 2

1 Complete with the verb in parentheses in the correct form. They are all verbs with a vowel change.

Example: Er .... (schlafen). > *Er schläft.*

a Was .... (nehmen) du?

d Xier .... (sehen) einen Film.

b Du .... (sprechen) fließend Hindi.

e Er .... (fahren) Auto.

f Du .... (lesen) viel.

c Silvia .... (laufen) in den Park.

04.08

2 Now play Conversation 1 again and play Max's role. Speak in the pauses provided and try not to refer to the text.

Currywurst und anderes Streetfood *Currywurst and other street food*

As you know, Berlin is famous for its Currywurst. However, there is a rivalry between the cities of Berlin and Hamburg as to where Currywurst originates from. Both cities claim to have invented it. There is a novella by Uwe Timm called *Die Entdeckung der Currywurst* (*The Invention of Curried*

Sausage), which supports Hamburg's claim to be the home of the Currywurst. The plot is set during World War II and tells the story of Lena Brücker who accidentally meets Hermann Bremer, a soldier, during a bomb raid. Hermann deserts the army and hides in her apartment, but the novella also tells the story of how Lena invents the Currywurst.

The cult around Currywurst has made its way into popular culture and there is even a song about Currywurst by the German singer Herbert Grönemeyer who started his career as an actor in the film *Das Boot.*

How do you think that Lena invented Currywurst? Find the plot summary online and find out. If Currywurst was invented in Berlin, who invented it then? Can you find out?

These days you find a lot more than just Currywurst sold in the streets. On the various street food markets of Berlin, there is a range of different types of food available. Which one(s) do you find most interesting?

VOCABULARY BUILDER 2

04.09

Look at the words and phrases and complete the missing English words and expressions. Then listen and try to imitate the pronunciation of the speakers.

VORSPEISEN	STARTERS
die Kürbissuppe	pumpkin ....
die Tomatensuppe	tomato soup

HAUPTGERICHTE UND BEILAGEN	MAIN DISHES AND SIDES
das Fleisch	meat
das Hähnchen, das Schweinefleisch	chicken, pork
das Lammgulasch	.... goulash
die Boulette	meatball
der Fisch	....
die Bohne	bean
der Käse, der Feta	cheese, feta
der Salat	....
die Kartoffel, der Reis	potato, ...

NACHTISCH UND GETRÄNKE	DESSERT AND DRINKS
der Kuchen, der Apfelkuchen	cake, ... cake
das Stück	piece
der Wein, der Rotwein, der Weißwein	wine, ... wine, white wine
alkoholfrei	alcohol free

NÜTZLICHE AUSDRÜCKE	USEFUL EXPRESSIONS
Bio-Fleisch, Bio-Gemüse	organic meat, organic vegetables
vegetarisch, vegan	vegetarian, vegan
glutenfrei, laktosefrei, zuckerfrei	.................-free, lactose-free, sugar-.................
hungrig	hungry
Isst du gern ...?	Do you like to eat ...?
Ich trinke nicht gern ...	I don't like to drink ...
Wir möchten bestellen.	We would like to order.
Die Rechnung, bitte.	The bill, please.
Hat es geschmeckt?	Did you enjoy it? (lit. Did it taste?)

Vocabulary practice 2

Categorize the food into three categories:

vegan	vegetarisch	nicht-vegetarisch
die Bohne	der Feta	das Fleisch

CONVERSATION 2

Gut und Glücklich *Well and Happy*

04.10

1 Listen to the conversation without looking at the text. Play it a few times and see if you can make out a few new words and phrases each time. Then listen again and read the text. Who orders a vegetarian dish? Do they pay cash or by card?

> Wally shows Max the ufaFabrik, an alternative cultural center near Tempelhof. Afterwards, she invites him for dinner in a small nearby café called Gut und Glücklich.

Max	Ich bin jetzt sehr hungrig.
Wally	Dann nimm doch eine Vorspeise, Max. Vielleicht einen Anti-Pasti-Teller?
Max	Ich glaube, ich nehme die Tomatensuppe. Und du Wally?
Wally	Ich esse die Kürbissuppe. Und als Hauptgericht... Isst du gern Fleisch?
Max	Ja, ich esse sehr gern Fleisch.
Wally	Es gibt Bouletten aus Bio-Fleisch oder Lammgoulasch.
Max	Dann nehme ich das Lammgoulasch mit Kartoffeln und Bohnen als Hauptgericht. Und du?
Wally	Mmh, ich esse heute vegetarisch – die Fladenpizza mit Tomatensauce, Zucchini und Feta überbacken. Trinkst du auch ein Glas Wein?
Max	Nein, danke. Ich trinke nicht gern Wein. Ich trinke lieber ein Bier, alkoholfrei.
Wally	Hallo. Wir möchten bitte bestellen.
	A bit later, after they have eaten ...
Max	Das war lecker.
Kellner	Danke. Was möchten Sie als Nachtisch?
Max	Keinen Nachtisch für mich.
Wally	Ich nehme einen Latte Macchiato und ein Stück Apfelkuchen als Nachtisch. Und die Rechnung, bitte.
Kellner	Zahlen Sie bar oder mit Karte?
Wally	Mit Karte, bitte.
Kellner	Kein Problem!

> There are still a number of places in Germany where you can pay only by cash. Places that accept card/contactless payments might not accept all credit cards.

2 The waiter comes with the food and drinks. Who is which item for, Wally or Max?

a die Tomatensuppe ....

b die Fladenpizza ....

c das alkoholfreie Bier ....

d der Apfelkuchen ....

LANGUAGE BUILDER 3

 Language discovery 3

What letter is used to form the plural when the nouns end in -e?

die Bohne > die Bohnen

die Suppe > die Suppen

die Sache > die Sachen

die Sauce > die Saucen

Plural of nouns and articles

The definite article for the plural is die for all nouns regardless of their gender. There is no indefinite article for the plural. German has more ways to form the plural of nouns than English. Here are some tips which may make this easier. But you need to be careful, as these are only broad outlines and there are many exceptions in German:

- Nouns ending in -e, usually feminine, add -n: die Suppe > die Suppen.
- Feminine nouns not ending in -e often add -en: die U-Bahn > die U-Bahnen.
- Many masculine nouns add -e and often an umlaut: der Saft > die Säfte or -e with no umlaut: der Salat > die Salate.
- Neuter nouns often add -e: das Problem > die Probleme.
- Another common ending for neuter nouns is -er + umlaut: das Glas > die Gläser.
- Most nouns ending in -el, -en, or -er don't add an ending, but many add an umlaut: die Mutter > die Mütter.
- Nouns imported from English or a Romance language usually add -s: das Café > die Cafés.

> As there are many exceptions in German, try to learn the plural forms of new nouns as you meet them. From the next unit onward, the plural forms are indicated. You can find all plural endings of nouns covered so far in the Glossary.

Language practice 3

1 Identify the correct singular and plural forms of these nouns.

Singular	Plural	Singular	Plural
die Tomate	die	der Salat	die ....
die Vorspeise	die	der Fisch	die ....
die Sprache	die	das Problem	die ....
die Kneipe	die	das Geschäft	die ....
die Buslinie	die	das	die Restaurants
die	die U-Bahnen	das Hotel	die ....
die Station	die	der Park	die ....

04.11

💡 Language discovery 4

Listen to the conversation again and repeat each line in the pauses provided. Try to imitate the pronunciation and intonation you hear. Look at these sentences. Which two words are used to negate something?

Ich trinke nicht gern Wein.

Ich arbeite nicht.

Keinen Nachtisch für mich.

Kein Problem.

Negation – nicht, kein/keine/kein

There are two words which can be used to make a sentence a negative: nicht and kein.

Nicht is normally used in connection with verbs and adjectives:

Ich arbeite. > Ich arbeite nicht.   Das Essen ist lecker. > Das Essen ist nicht lecker.

In simple sentences, nicht usually follows the verb:

Ich komme nicht aus Deutschland.   Ich trinke nicht gern Wein.

Kein/keine/kein is normally linked to a noun and it translates as *no* or *any*: Kein Problem. It agrees with the noun in gender, number, and case.

Kein is the negative form of ein and takes the same endings as ein:

Ich trinke einen Kaffee. (m) > Ich trinke keinen Kaffee. (m)

Sie hat eine Schwester. (f) > Sie hat keine Schwester. (f)

Mo isst ein Stück Kuchen. (n) > Mo isst kein Stück Kuchen. (n)

Sie haben drei Kinder. (pl) > Sie haben keine Kinder. (pl)

Notice that *uncountable nouns* (that cannot be counted, such as rice, water, air) do not take an article in affirmative sentences. However, they need the proper form of kein in negative ones:

Er trinkt Alkohol. > Er trinkt keinen Alkohol. (m)   Ich habe Zeit. > Ich habe keine Zeit. (f)

Wir essen Fleisch. >Wir essen kein Fleisch. (n)

The same applies for nouns in the plural: Wir haben Kinder. > Wir haben keine Kinder. (pl)

Language practice 4

1 Add nicht in these sentences to make them negative.

Example: Tim isst gern Burger. > *Tim isst nicht gern Burger.*

a Er isst gern Fleisch.   **b** Die Suppe schmeckt gut.   **c** Die Bouletten sind vegetarisch.

d Sie ist satt.   **e** Xier kommt aus Kanada.   **f** Wir bestellen.

2 Reply to these questions in the negative, using the correct form of kein:

Example: Möchtest du ein Wasser? > *Nein, ich möchte kein Wasser.*

a Nimmst du einen Nachtisch?   **c** Trinken Sie Kaffee?   **e** Hast du heute Zeit?

b Möchten Sie ein Bier?   **d** Haben Sie Hunger?   **f** Ist das ein Witz?

04.12

3 Now play Conversation 2 again and play Wally's role. Speak in the pauses provided and try not to refer to the text.

SKILL BUILDER

1 Find the odd one out.

a Wasser   Kaffee   Wein   Tee

b Hähnchen   Lammfleisch   Schweinefleisch   Gemüse

c Rotwein   Weißwein   Bier   Orangensaft

d Salat   Tomate   Zucchini   Käse

e Dose   Flasche   Glas   Hauptgericht

f Vorspeise   Hauptgericht   Dessert   Rechnung

2 Look at the underlined masculine nouns and decide if they are the subject (nominative case) or direct object (accusative case) in the sentences.

a Der Salat schmeckt gut.

b Ich bekomme den Salat.

c Er hat einen Sohn.

d Das ist mein Sohn.

e Du trinkst meinen Kaffee.

f Der Kaffee kommt aus Peru und ist Fairtrade-Kaffee.

04.13

3 Say these sentences in German. Then check your pronunciation on the audio.

a I'd like a mineral water and an orange juice.

b I'll have a veggie burger and fries.

c Can we order, please?

d I'd like a tomato soup as a starter.

e I'll have the pizza, please.

f I'd like a coffee and a piece of cake.

g I'd like a beer, please.

h I'd like a beer, alcohol free.

i How much does it cost all together?

4 Add the food and drink Eduarda likes and doesn't like to the table.

> Eduarda: Ich esse gern Fisch und Salat. Das ist gesund. Ich esse nicht gern Lammfleisch. Ich trinke sehr gern Orangensaft und Mocktails. Ich trinke nicht so gern Cola. Cola ist zu süß. Mein Lieblingsessen ist Pancake, Pfannkuchen.

Eduarda isst und trinkt gerne:	Eduarda isst und trinkt nicht gerne:

5 Back home, Max looks at some reviews written about **Gut und Glücklich**. Read the three texts, then decide who says what:

Susi Klose
★ ★ ★ ★

Preis pro Person: €10–20 Essen: 5
Service: 4
Atmosphäre: 4
Super Café. Die Terrasse ist schön. Das Essen ist klasse! Die Salate sind frisch und das Bio-Fleisch kommt aus der Region. Die Bouletten sind fantastisch. Das Personal ist nett und freundlich. Wir waren glücklich hier und kommen wieder.

Viktor B
★

Preis pro Person: €10–20 Essen: 2
Service: 1
Atmosphäre: 2
Keine gute Erfahrung. Der Service war extrem schlecht und unfreundlich. Die Suppe war nicht warm, das Lammfleisch zu alt und die Portionen sind zu klein. Die anderen Gäste waren zu laut. Ich komme nicht wieder. „Gut und Glücklich"? Ein Witz!

Xin Weng
★ ★ ★ ★ ★

Preis pro Person: €10–20 Essen: 5
Service: 4
Atmosphäre: 5
Ein großes Angebot für Vegetarier und Veganer. Die Currywurst vegan war absolut lecker. 5 Sterne! Die Pommes waren auch fantastisch. Sehr guter Fairtrade-Kaffee. Und die Kuchen sind sehr lecker – mein Favorit ist der Bananenkuchen

a Who likes the choices for vegetarians and vegans? ....

b Who did not like the meat? ....

c Who likes the outdoor space? ....

d Who recommends the cakes? ....

e Who wants to come back? ....

6 Max decides to write a review himself. Help him complete the details.

Max Peterson
★ ★ ★ ★ ★

Das Gut und Glücklich ist ein kleines Café, nicht weit von der ufa-.................. Die Atmosphäre ist sehr freundlich. Meine Vorspeise, die T.................. , war ausgezeichnet. Auch die Kürbis.................. war lecker. Mein Haupt.................. war Lammgoulasch mit.................. und B.................. . Eine große Portion! Das Angebot für Vegetarier ist auch gut: die Fladen.................. mit F.................. war exzellent. Die Terrasse ist super: Hier kann man gut essen, trinken und mit Freunden sprechen.

Soham is in a restaurant. Play his role and order for him. Respond in the pauses.

Soham	*Say that you would like to order.*
Kellnerin	Ja, was möchten Sie?
Soham	*Say that you like a salad with feta as a starter.*
Kellnerin	Einen Salat mit Feta. Und als Hauptgericht?
Soham	*Say that you'll take the chicken with rice.*
Kellnerin	Das Hähnchen mit Reis. Und was möchten Sie trinken?
Soham	*Say that you'd like a glass of white wine and a mineral water.*
Kellnerin	Danke, wunderbar.
	Etwas später ...
Kellnerin	Hat es Ihnen geschmeckt?
Soham	*Say, yes, very good.*
Kellnerin	Und möchten Sie noch etwas?
Soham	*Say you will take a piece of apple cake and a tea. And ask for the bill.*
Kellnerin	Sehr gerne. Zahlen Sie bar oder mit Karte?
Soham	*Say by card, please.*

Wie geht's weiter? *What happens next?*

Although Wally and Max may differ in many ways, they seem to get on very well and enjoy each other's company. Where will their next adventure take them? Will they explore Berlin's foodie scene further? Will they try to find more alternative venues? Or will Wally take Max to a very different place?

Before you move on to the next unit, assess your progress using the **My review** section on the first page of the unit, and reflect on your learning experience with the **My takeaway** section available online.

5

In this lesson you will learn how to:

» Talk about your hobbies
» Say how often or regularly you do something
» Say where you are going
» Tell the time
» Describe a routine/daily schedule

Was sind deine Hobbys?

My study plan

I plan to work with Unit 5
○ Every day
○ Twice a week
○ Other _____
I plan to study for
○ 5–15 minutes
○ 15–30 minutes
○ 30–45+ minutes

My progress tracker

Day / Date	🎧	🎤	📖	✏️	💬
	○	○	○	○	○
	○	○	○	○	○
	○	○	○	○	○
	○	○	○	○	○
	○	○	○	○	○
	○	○	○	○	○
	○	○	○	○	○

My goals

What do you want to be able to do or say in German when you complete this unit?

Done

1 .... ○
2 .... ○
3 .... ○

My review

SELF CHECK

	I can ...
○	... talk about my hobbies.
○	... say how often or regularly I do something.
○	... say where I am going.
○	... tell the time.
○	... describe a routine/daily schedule.

CULTURE POINT

Freizeit und Vereine *Leisure time and clubs*

In their Freizeit (*leisure time*), many Germans like relaxing activities such as das Internet und soziale Netzwerke nutzen (*using the internet and social networks*), fernsehen und streamen (*watching TV and streaming*), Freunde treffen (*meeting friends*), or Musik hören (*listening to music*).

Statistics also show that most Germans work out at least once a week. Popular sports activities include ins Fitnessstudio gehen (*going to the gym*), Joggen (*running*), Nordic Walking (*Nordic walking*), Skaten (*skating*), Wandern (*hiking*), Radfahren (*cycling*), and Fußball (*soccer*).

There are more than 600,000 different Vereine (*clubs, associations*) in Germany, and about 30 million Germans are Mitglieder (*members*) of one club or another. Clubs cover a multitude of interests, from Gartenarbeit (*gardening*) to Münzen sammeln (*coin collecting*) or Singen (singing). Gesangsvereine (*singing clubs*) alone have over 2 million members and Sportvereine (*sports clubs*) manage to attract many more.

Find out more about sport and free-time activities.
How many sports clubs are there in Germany?
Which sport was invented in Germany?
What is special about FC Bayern München?
What does the word Sportmuffel mean?

05.01

Look at the words and phrases and complete the missing English words and phrases. Then listen and try to imitate the pronunciation of the speakers.

HOBBYS UND FREIZEIT	HOBBIES AND LEISURE TIME
Was sind deine Hobbys? (informal)	What are your hobbies?
Was ist Ihr Hobby? (formal)	What is your hobby?
hören	to hear, to listen
lesen	to read
malen	to paint
reisen	to travel
schwimmen	to ....
shoppen	to ....
spielen	to play
treffen	to meet
wandern	to go hiking
das Pilates (no pl.), das Yoga (no pl.)	.............., ...
der Fußball (-"e), Basketball (-"e)	soccer, ...
das Schach (no pl.), das Computerspiel (-e)	chess, computer game
die Leidenschaft (-en)	passion
das Lieblingsgenre (-s)	favorite genre
der Biergarten (¨)	.... garden
das Konzert (-e)	....
das Schwimmbad (-"er)	swimming pool

> For sports played with a ball, use the verb **spielen**: Ich spiele Fußball / Baseball / Tennis / Badminton etc. You also say: Ich spiele Schach.
>
> For many other activities, use machen (*to make*): Ich mache Yoga / Pilates / Musik.

WIE OFT?	HOW OFTEN?
einmal / zweimal die Woche	once / twice a week (lit. *the week*)
dreimal / viermal pro Monat	three / four times per month
jeden Tag	every day
regelmäßig	regular(*ly*)
selten	seldom / rare(*ly*)
nie	never

NÜTZLICHE AUSDRÜCKE	USEFUL EXPRESSIONS
Ich höre lieber ...	I prefer to listen to ...
Ich komme gerne mal mit.	I'd like to come with you sometimes.

Vocabulary practice 1

Complete the sentences with the appropriate verb.

| spielen | shoppen | trifft | malt | hört | reisen | liest | kocht |

a Paulina .... Reis und Gemüse.

b Xier .... einen Podcast.

c Anne .... ein Bild.

d Die Studenten .... nach Japan.

e Er .... Freunde.

f Robin .... ein Buch.

g Die Leute .... Fußball.

h Er geht ....

> Remember that some verbs like essen (*to eat*), lesen (*to read*), or treffen (*to meet*) have a vowel change in the du and er/sie/es/xier forms. For more information, see Unit 4.

Pronunciation practice

05.02

1 Listen to these words. The pronunciation of the ch sound usually depends on the vowel in front of it. Listen to the audio and spot the difference.

machen   kochen   Woche   Buch   ich   sprechen   dich   Bücher

05.03

2 Practice saying these words, then listen and repeat.

acht   Schach   Wochenende   nicht   München   richtig   Achtung   spricht

CONVERSATION 1

Ich schwimme 1500 Meter *I swim 1500 meters*

05.04

1 Listen to the conversation without looking at the text. Play it a few times and see if you can make out a few new words and phrases each time. Then listen again and read the text. What are Wally's two passions? What does Max offer at the end?

> Wally has invited Max to go swimming at the Badeschiff, an open-air harbored barge which functions as a floating swimming pool in the River Spree. From there you have a panoramic view of the river and the surrounding areas.
>
> | | |
> |---|---|
> | **Max** | Oh, ist das schön hier, Wally. Schwimmst du oft hier? |
> | **Wally** | Nein, meistens gehe ich ins Schwimmbad. |
> | **Max** | Und wie oft gehst du schwimmen? |
> | **Wally** | Zweimal die Woche. Und dann schwimme ich 1500 Meter. Und du? Machst du eigentlich Sport? |
> | **Max** | 1500 Meter?! Ich schwimme selten. Du weißt, ich gehe gerne in den Park und jogge. Manchmal gehe ich auch ins Fitnessstudio. Was hast du noch für Hobbys? |
> | **Wally** | Meine Hobbys sind Musik und Singen. Das sind meine Leidenschaften. Und dann koche ich auch gern und mache Yoga. |
> | **Max** | Und wie oft machst du Yoga? |
> | **Wally** | Einmal pro Woche. Und du, Max? Was sind deine Hobbys? |
> | **Max** | Musik ... Ich höre gern neue Bands und gehe zu Gigs. Und ich gehe auch gerne ins Kino oder streame Filme und Serien. Und ich reise gern. |
> | **Wally** | Hast du ein Lieblingsgenre? |
> | **Max** | Ich schaue gerne Musikfilme. Und du gehst ja auch oft in die Oper! |
> | **Wally** | Ja, ich liebe die Oper! Ich gehe regelmäßig in die Oper. Und du? |
> | **Max** | Äh, ich höre lieber moderne Musik. Aber ich komme gerne mal mit. |
> | **Wally** | Gute Idee! So, jetzt schwimmen wir. Aber vielleicht nur 1000 Meter. |

2 Identify who does these activities: Wally (W), Max (M), or both (W+M)?

a goes swimming ....

b works out in the gym ....

c goes jogging ....

d loves singing ....

e does yoga ....

f goes to the cinema ....

g goes to the opera ....

h likes modern music ....

LANGUAGE BUILDER 1

 Language discovery 1

Look at Conversation 1 again and complete the sentences with **in den**, **in die**, or **ins**. Notice which genders (masculine, feminine, neuter) the nouns are.

a Ich gehe gerne .... Park. (m)

b Ich gehe regelmäßig .... Oper. (f)

c Manchmal gehe ich auch .... Fitnessstudio. (nt)

Saying where you are going using **in**

When talking about going somewhere with **gehen** (*to go*), the preposition **in** is often used.

It is then followed by the accusative:

Ich gehe <u>in den</u> Park. (m)   Sie geht <u>in die</u> Kunstgalerie. (f)

Er geht <u>ins</u> Restaurant. (nt)   Sie gehen gern <u>in die</u> Museen in Berlin. (pl)

> Note that **in das** is shortened to **ins**: in das > ins.

Here is a short overview of some frequently used locations when using **ich gehe** + **in**:

ich gehe ... (m)	ich gehe ... (f)	ich gehe ... (nt)
in den Biergarten	in die Eisdiele (*ice cream shop*)	ins Café
in den Club	in die Kneipe	ins Fitnessstudio
in den Park	in die Kirche (*church*)	ins Kino, Theater
in den Zoo	in die Moschee (*mosque*)	ins Museum
	in die Oper	ins Restaurant
	in die Synagoge (*synagogue*)	ins Schwimmbad

Language practice 1

1 **Where do these people go? Complete the sentences with a suitable location/place.**

Example: Frau Ismar findet Kunst interessant und geht oft <u>ins Museum</u>.

a Peter und Hannah essen gern chinesisch und gehen einmal pro Woche ....

b Noah liebt die Natur und geht oft ....

c Kobe und Anissa tanzen gern und gehen zweimal die Woche ....

d Michiko macht viel Sport und geht regelmäßig ....

 2 **Use the sentences as a guide and write where you like going to and how often.**

....

....

LANGUAGE BUILDER 2

05.05

💡 Language discovery 2

Listen to the conversation again and repeat each line in the pauses provided. Try to imitate the phrasing and intonation you hear. Then look at these sentences. Identify when you usually use gern/gerne and when you use mögen to express likes.

Ich höre und spiele gerne klassische Musik.   Ich spiele und sehe gern Fußball.
Ich mag Musik.   Ich mag Fußball.

Expressing likes and dislikes with **gern** and **mögen**

When you want to say that you like something in general, use the verb mögen (*to like*):

Ich mag Fußball.   *I like soccer.*   Ich mag klassische Musik.   *I like classical music.*

In the negative, mögen requires the appropriate form of keinen/keine/kein:

Ich mag keine klassische Musik.   *I don't like classical music.*

You can also say that you like doing something, using the word gern/gerne (*with pleasure, gladly*) after the action you like. Note that gern and gerne are interchangeable, but gern is preferred in written language:

Ich spiele gern Fußball.   *I like playing soccer.*

Ich sehe gerne Fußball.   *I like watching soccer.*

With gern, the negative nicht comes between the verb and gern:

Ich spiele nicht gern Fußball.   *I don't like playing soccer.*

You have probably realized that mögen is an irregular verb:

ich mag	wir mögen
du magst	ihr mögt
Sie mögen	Sie mögen
er/sie/es/xier mag	sie mögen

Language practice 2

1 Rewrite these sentences in a different way, using **gern** together with a suitable verb.

   Example: Ich mag Hamburger >   *Ich esse gern Hamburger.*

   a Ich mag Kaffee.
   b Ich mag Schach.
   c Ich mag Musikfilme.
   d Wir mögen Computerspiele.

   e Anita mag Yoga.
   f Ich mag Krimis von Henning Mankell.
   g Wir mögen Tennis.
   h Corinna mag Reisen.

05.06

2 **Say three things you like or do not like doing.**

3 **Now play Conversation 1 again and play Wally's role. Speak in the pauses provided and try not to refer to the text.**

CULTURE POINT 2

Zoo Berlin – etwas für die Familie *Berlin Zoo—something for the family*

The Zoo Berlin is the oldest surviving and best-known zoo in Germany. It is also home to the largest variety of species of any zoo in the world—including the only Großen Pandas (*giant pandas*) in Germany.

Opened in 1844, Zoo Berlin covers 35 hectares (86.5 acres) and is located in Berlin's Tiergarten, right in the center of the city. The zoo and its Aquarium attract more than 5 million people per year, including many families from Berlin, and is the most-visited zoo in Europe.

Zoo Berlin collaborates with many research institutes, universities, and other zoos around the world and has its own species conservation program: Berlin World Wild. Its regular Fütterungen (*animal feedings*) are among its most famous attractions and especially loved by children.

Find out more about the Berlin Zoo.
What are the opening hours?
How much is a Tageskarte (*day ticket*) for a child and an adult?
Can you find a project the zoo supports in the area where you are from?

VOCABULARY BUILDER 2

05.07

Look at the words and phrases and complete the missing English words and expressions. Then listen and try to imitate the pronunciation of the speakers.

TAGESABLAUF – TÄTIGKEITEN	DAILY ROUTINE—ACTIVITIES
an/fangen, auf/hören	to begin, to stop
an/rufen	to call / ring
ab/holen	to pick up
auf/wachen, auf/stehen	to wake ...., to get up
aus/sehen	to look like
duschen	to have a shower
ein/kaufen	to do (food) shopping
fern/sehen	to watch TV
fertig/machen	to get (someone or something) ready
einen Ausflug machen	to take a day trip

BESCHREIBUNGEN	DESCRIPTIONS
zuerst	at first
dann, danach	then, then (after)
anstrengend, entspannend	exhausting, relaxing

ARBEITSPLATZ	WORKPLACE
die Schule (-n)	....
das Büro (-s)	office
die Mittagspause (-n)	lunch break
der Feierabend (-e)	after work (lit. *party evening*)

DIE UHRZEIT	THE TIME
Wie spät ist es?	What's the time? (lit. *How late is it?*)
Wie viel Uhr ist es?	What's the time?
Es ist zehn Uhr.	It's ten o'clock.
vor, nach	before, after
Es ist Viertel vor acht.	It is quarter to eight.
um 13 Uhr	at 1 p.m. (lit. *13.00 hours*)

> Verbs like anfangen (*to start*), aufstehen (*to get up*), or einkaufen (*to go shopping*) are so-called separable verbs. It means that the first part (the prefix or particle) is often split up from the core verb. You will learn more about them in Language Builder 3. In order to help you recognize these verbs we have added a slash in vocabulary lists an/fangen, auf/stehen, ein/kaufen.

Vocabulary practice 2

WIE SPÄT IST ES? *WHAT TIME IS IT?*

It is quite common in German to use the 24-hour clock when referring to time. State the hour followed by **Uhr** (hour) and the number of minutes. You can also add und Minuten instead of simply stating the number of minutes.

7:02   Es ist sieben Uhr zwei. / Es ist sieben Uhr und zwei Minuten.

12.30   Es ist zwölf Uhr dreißig. / Es ist zwölf Uhr und dreißig Minuten.

23:10   Es ist dreiundzwanzig Uhr zehn. / Es ist dreiundzwanzig Uhr und zehn Minuten.

For the 12-hour clock, you use nach (*after*), vor (*before*), Viertel (*quarter*) and halb (*half*).

14:10   Es ist zehn nach zwei. / Es ist zehn Minuten nach zwei.

16:40   Es ist zwanzig vor fünf. / Es ist zwanzig Minuten vor fünf.

9:15   Es ist Viertel nach neun.

13:30   Es ist halb zwei.

Be careful when using halb—in German you say *half to* the coming hour rather than *half past*. Es ist halb zwei. (*It is half past one*—literally: *It is half to two*).

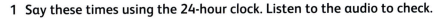

1 Say these times using the 24-hour clock. Listen to the audio to check.

05.08   **a** 8:45   **b** 14:30   **c** 17.20   **d** 21:00   **e** 04:17   **f** 18:00

2 Say these times using the 12-hour clock. Then check your answers on the audio.

05.09

   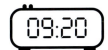      

> With the 12-hour clock, if you want to be specific you can add morgens (*in the morning*), vormittags (*before noon*), nachmittags (*in the afternoon*) or abends (*in the evening*).

Pronunciation practice

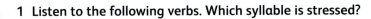

1 Listen to the following verbs. Which syllable is stressed?

05.10   aufstehen   aufwachen   fertigmachen   aufhören   anfangen

2 Notice that the stress falls on the first syllable. Practice saying these verbs, then listen and repeat.

05.11   einkaufen   abholen   fernsehen   aussehen

CONVERSATION 2

Ich stehe immer früh auf *I always get up early*

05.12

1 Listen to the conversation without looking at the text. Play it a few times and see if you can make out a few new words and phrases each time. Then listen again and read the text. What time does Fabian usually get up? When does he go to his workshop? When does he finish his work?

> Max wants to write about a typical workday in Berlin. He talks to Fabian, Wally's son, who runs a small Elektrofirma (*electrical company*). Here are a few of the words you'll hear in the conversation: die Werkstatt (*workshop*), der Kunde, die Kundin (*customer*). The gender-neutral plural form is Kund:innen.
>
> **Fabian**   Entschuldigung, ich bin etwas müde. Ich stehe immer sehr früh auf.
>
> **Max**   Wann stehst du denn normalerweise auf?
>
> **Fabian**   Ich stehe meistens um sechs Uhr auf. Ich dusche und dann mache ich Frühstück für Aylin und Nuri.
>
> **Max**   Und was machst du dann?
>
> **Fabian**   Ich mache Nuri für die Schule fertig. Die Schule fängt um acht Uhr an.
>
> **Max**   Und wann fängst du mit der Arbeit an?
>
> **Fabian**   Gegen halb acht gehe ich in die Werkstatt. Dann rufe ich Kund:innen an, lese und schreibe E-Mails. Ich arbeite gern im Büro und organisiere Sachen.
>
> **Max**   Und was machst du in der Mittagspause?
>
> **Fabian**   Normalerweise esse ich Mittag und lese die Nachrichten. Manchmal kaufe ich ein.
>
> **Max**   Und wann hast du Feierabend?
>
> **Fabian**   Ich höre um 17 Uhr auf. Dann hole ich Nuri von der Schule ab. Abends kochen Aylin und ich, und danach sehen wir oft fern.
>
> **Max**   Und am Wochenende?
>
> **Fabian**   Am Wochenende treffen wir oft Freunde und machen Ausflüge. Wir gehen auch gerne in den Zoo. Nuri liebt den Berliner Zoo, besonders die Pandabären. Wir haben eine Jahreskarte.

2 Decide if these statements are *true* (richtig) or *false* (falsch).

   a After he gets up, Fabian immediately prepares breakfast.   R   F
   b Nuri's school starts at 7.30 a.m.   R   F
   c At work, Fabian likes to organize things.   R   F
   d They don't watch much TV.   R   F
   e On the weekend, the family often goes to the zoo.   R   F

LANGUAGE BUILDER 3

 Language discovery 3

Look at Conversation 2 again and complete the sentences. Identify what happens to the verbs aufstehen, anfangen, anrufen, and einkaufen?

a Ich stehe meistens um sechs Uhr ....

b Die Schule fängt um acht Uhr ....

c Ich rufe Kund:innen ....

d Manchmal kaufe ich im Supermarkt ....

Activities: separable verbs

In English, there are verbs made up of two parts, such as *to get up*, *to pick up*, and *to come along*. In German, there are verbs called trennbare Verben (*separable verbs*), which look like one word but consist of two parts. In a sentence, the first part (the prefix) separates from the main part (the stem) and usually goes to the end of the sentence. For example:

ab/holen	Ich hole dich um acht Uhr ab.	*I'll pick you up at eight o'clock.*
auf/stehen	Wann stehst du auf?	*When do you get up?*
an/fangen	Die Arbeit fängt um neun Uhr an.	*Work starts at nine o'clock*
an/rufen	Sie ruft eine Kundin an.	*She phones a client.*
ein/kaufen	Sie kauft im Supermarkt ein.	*She shops at the supermarket.*
fertig/machen	Er macht sich fertig.	*He gets ready.*

Other frequently used separable verbs include:

ab/fahren	*to depart*	aus/gehen	*to go out*	ab/waschen	*to wash up*
ein/laden	*to invite*	an/kommen	*to arrive*	vor/bereiten	*to prepare*
auf/laden	*to charge (a battery/phone)*	statt/finden	*to take place*		

Wann kommt der Zug an?   *When does the train arrive?*

Language practice 3

Match the two sentence halves.

a Tina steht

b Dann macht sie sich

c Ihre Uni fängt um

d Am Nachmittag kauft sie

e Oh, das Handy geht nicht. Sie lädt

f Sie holt eine Freundin

g Am Abend sieht sie

h Um 23 Uhr ruft sie

1 die Batterie auf.

2 um neun Uhr auf.

3 im Supermarkt ein.

4 fern.

5 elf Uhr an.

6 einen Freund an.

7 ab.

8 fertig.

💡 Language discovery 4

05.13

Listen to the conversation again and repeat each line in the pauses provided. Try to imitate the pronunciation and intonation you hear. Then look at these sentences from Conversation 2. Identify the subject (S) and the verb (V).

Example: Ich *(S)* bin *(V)* etwas müde.

a Gegen halb acht gehe (......) ich (......) in die Werkstatt.
b Dann rufe (......) ich (......) Kund:innen an.
c Ich (......) arbeite (......) gern im Büro.
d Am Wochenende treffen (......) wir (......) oft Freunde.

Word order and verb position

The verb in a German sentence usually has to be the second idea or component:

Subject	Verb	Other elements
Ich	bin	oft am Morgen müde.
Ich	gehe	dann in die Werkstatt.

So, if the sentence starts with anything other than the subject, the verb and subject have to switch places. This swap is referred to as subject–verb inversion.

Position 1	Verb	Subject	Other elements
Am Morgen	bin	ich	oft müde.
Dann	gehe	ich	in die Werkstatt.
Am Freitag	mache	ich	Pilates.
Um 18 Uhr	gehen	wir	ins Kino.

It is quite common for expressions of time (am Morgen, am Freitag, um 18 Uhr) or sequencing adverbs (dann, danach) to start a sentence in German. In these cases, the subject needs to be placed after the verb.

Language practice 4

1 Put these words in the correct order. Start with the words or phrases in bold.

a um acht Uhr – **Sie** – steht – auf
b einen Tee – sie – **Dann** – trinkt
c um neun Uhr – **Ihre Arbeit** – fängt – an
d sie – **Um 13 Uhr** – trifft – eine Freundin
e Café – gehen – **Sie** – in ein
f macht – sie – **Um 18 Uhr** – Yoga
g sie – **Dann** – etwas zu Hause – kocht
h spielt – sie – Computerspiele – **Danach**

05.14

2 Now play Conversation 2 again and play Max's role. Speak in the pauses provided and try not to refer to the text.

SKILL BUILDER

1 Order the adverbs/words of frequency in ascending order from *never* to *always*.

immer selten regelmäßig manchmal oft nie

2 What time is it? Use the 24-hour and 12-hour systems.

a 22:11	Es ist	**d** 11:15	Es ist ....
b 17:34	Es ist	**e** 15:45	Es ist ....
c 5:00	Es ist	**f** 9:30	Es ist ....

3 Say if you like or dislike these things using gern.

Example: Fußball > *Ich spiele gern Fußball. / Ich spiele nicht gern Fußball.*

a Wein	**c** Yoga	**e** Pfefferminztee	**g** Fleisch
b Theater	**d** Musikfilme	**f** Oper	

4 Where are these people going? Complete the sentences using in den, in die, or ins.

a Maria geht .... Fitnessstudio.	**d** Heute gehen wir .... Park.
b Herr Fischer geht .... Kirche.	**e** Mohammed geht .... Café.
c Die Kinder gehen .... Schule.	**f** Um 11 Uhr gehen wir .... Zoo.

05.15

5 A German blogger wants to interview you about your routine. Answer the questions in the pauses. Then you will hear a sample answer.

a Wann stehst du auf? – Ich stehe um ....

b Was trinkst du am Morgen? – Am Morgen trinke ich ....

c Wann fängt deine Arbeit an? – Meine Arbeit ....

d Was machst du in der Mittagspause? – In der Mittagspause ....

e Wann hast du Feierabend? – Ich habe um ....

f Was machst du am Abend? – Am Abend ....

Max has written down his daily routine, but the sentences got all mixed up. Put them in the right order.

Dann gehe ich ins Bett. – Ich stehe um halb zehn auf. – Um 17 Uhr kaufe ich immer ein. – In der Mittagspause sehe ich fern. – Vor dem Abendessen gehe ich manchmal ins Fitnessstudio. – Nach dem Abendessen surfe ich im Internet. – Um 10 Uhr frühstücke ich. – Dann schreibe ich bis 16 Uhr weiter. – Dann mache ich mich fertig. – Um 23 Uhr höre ich auf. – Manchmal gehe ich auch in den Park und jogge. – Dann koche ich Abendessen. – Ich fange um 11 Uhr mit meinem Blog an. – Ich esse oft Pasta.

....

....

....

....

....

....

....

....

Wie geht's weiter? *What happens next?*

Max learns more about Wally and her family every day. What will they find out about each other next? How will they spend their time together? Will they do more exercise together? Perhaps they even go to the opera. Find out in Unit 6.

Before you move on to the next unit, assess your progress using the **My review** section on the first page of the unit, and reflect on your learning experience with the **My takeaway** section available online.

In this lesson you will learn how to:

» Talk about your family
» Provide more details about your job
» Express what belongs to someone: my, yours, his, her, etc.
» Say where you are located
» State what you can do and what you have to do

6

Arbeit und Familie

My study plan

I plan to work with Unit 6
○ Every day
○ Twice a week
○ Other _____
I plan to study for
○ 5–15 minutes
○ 15–30 minutes
○ 30–45+ minutes

My progress tracker

Day / Date	🎧	🎤	📖	✏️	💬
	○	○	○	○	○
	○	○	○	○	○
	○	○	○	○	○
	○	○	○	○	○
	○	○	○	○	○
	○	○	○	○	○
	○	○	○	○	○

My goals

What do you want to be able to do or say in German when you complete this unit?

Done

1 .... ○
2 .... ○
3 .... ○

My review

SELF CHECK

	I can ...
●	... talk about my family.
●	... provide more details about my job.
●	... express what belongs to someone: my, yours, his, her, etc.
●	... say where I am located.
●	... state what I can do and what I have to do.

CULTURE POINT 1

Familien heute *Families today*

Like in other countries, family structures are changing. In addition to the traditional Kernfamilie (*nuclear family*) there are now many different forms, such as eine Patchworkfamilie (*blended family*), eine Regenbogenfamiliie (*same-sex parent family,* lit. *rainbow family*), or eine Pflege- und Adoptivfamilie (*foster and adoptive family*). An increasing number of parents also bring up their children as alleinerziehend (*single parent*). About a third of Paare (*couples*) who have children live together but are unverheiratet (*unmarried*).

Since 2017 gleichgeschlechtliche Ehen (*same-sex marriages*) have been legal in Germany, followed by Austria two years later and Switzerland in 2022.

Despite demographic changes and shifts in societal norms, for about two-thirds of people in Germany, the family is still considered the most important thing in their list of personal priorities.

 What do you think are the five most popular baby names for boys and girls in Germany? Check out this website for the answer.
Were they what you expected?
Which of these names are popular in your country?
Do family models in your country follow a similar trend as in Germany?

VOCABULARY BUILDER 1

06.01

Look at the words and phrases and complete the missing English words and expressions. Then listen and try to imitate the pronunciation of the speakers.

DIE FAMILIE	FAMILY
die Eltern (plural only)	parents
die Mutter (¨), der Vater(¨)	mother, father
das Enkelkind (-er)	grandchild
die Geschwister (pural only)	siblings
die Schwester (-n), der Bruder (¨)	sister, brother
das Einzelkind (-er)	only child
die Tante (-n), der Onkel (-)	aunt, ...
der Cousin (-s), die Cousine (-n)	....
die Großeltern (pural only)	grand...................
der/die Verwandte (-n)	relative (male / female)

BEZIEHUNGEN	RELATIONSHIPS
verheiratet	married
geschieden	divorced
alleinerziehend	single parent
zusammenleben	to live together
mein Mann, meine Frau	my husband, my wife
das Verhältnis (-se)	relation, relationship
Hast du ein gutes Verhältnis zu ... ?	Do you have a good relationship with ... ?
unser kleiner Bruder	our little ....

NÜTZLICHE AUSDRÜCKE	USEFUL EXPRESSIONS
darum	therefore
kennen/lernen	to get to know
kreativ	....
übrigens	by the way / incidentally
zweisprachig	bilingual

> The official terms for Großeltern (*grandparents*) are Großmutter (*grandmother*) and Großvater (*grandfather*). However, it is much more common, especially for children, to use Oma and Opa or Omi and Opi.

Vocabulary practice 1

Here is the family tree of the Familie Klostermann. Work out the relationship between the family members.

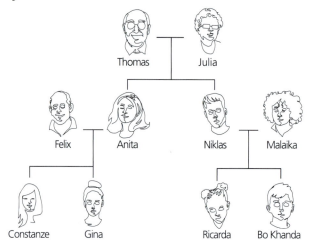

a Thomas ist der .... von Niklas.

b Julia ist die .... von Anita.

c Anita ist d .... von Niklas.

d Malaika ist d .... von Ricarda und Bo Khanda.

e Bo Khanda ist d .... von Gina.

f Bo Khanda ist d .... von Ricarda.

g Julia ist d .... von Ricarda.

h Gina, Ricarda und Bo Khanda sind d .... von Julia und Thomas.

Pronunciation practice

06.02

1 Umlaute are sometimes used to mark the difference between singular and plural forms. Listen to the following words, paying attention to how the Umlaut changes the pronunciation of the vowels (a > ä, o > ö, u > ü):

  a Vater > Väter, Apfel > Äpfel, Schwimmbad > Schwimmbäder

  b Sohn > Söhne, Tochter > Töchter

  c Mutter > Mütter, Bruder > Brüder, Currywurst > Currywürste

06.03

2 Practice saying these sentences, then listen and repeat.

  a Marco hat keinen Bruder. Frederike hat zwei Brüder.

  b Hast du eine Tochter? Ich habe zwei Töchter.

  c Sie haben einen Sohn. Sie haben drei Söhne und zwei Töchter.

CONVERSATION 1

Unsere Familien *Our families*

06.04

1 **Listen to the conversation a few times without looking at the text. Then listen again and read the text. How many siblings do Aylin and Max have?**

It is the 65th Geburtstag (*birthday*) of Aylin's father, Özkan. Max is invited to the Geburtstagsfeier (*birthday party*) and talks to Aylin about her family.

Aylin	Hallo, Max! Kommst du am Samstag zur Geburtstagsfeier? Dann kannst du meine Familie kennenlernen.
Max	Klar, Aylin. Ist eure Familie eigentlich groß?
Aylin	Na ja, ich habe noch eine Schwester, Dilara, und einen Bruder, Hakan. Dilara wohnt in Berlin, aber Hakan lebt und arbeitet in Frankfurt. So groß ist unsere Familie also nicht.
Max	Hast du ein gutes Verhältnis zu Dilara und Hakan?
Aylin	Ja, Dilara ist meine beste Freundin. Sie ist alleinerziehend und hat eine Tochter. Hakan ist unser kleiner Bruder. Er ist sehr kreativ und bloggt übrigens auch. Du musst beide kennenlernen.
Max	Oh, ja. Ich freue mich. Hast du noch andere Verwandte in Berlin?
Aylin	Ich habe noch einen Onkel. Sein Name ist Emre. Und du, Max? Hast du Geschwister?
Max	Nein, ich habe keine Geschwister. Ich bin Einzelkind. Aber ich habe drei Cousinen und vier Cousins.
Aylin	Das ist doch schön. Und deine Eltern?
Max	Meine Eltern wohnen beide in Portland. Mein Vater kommt aus Washington. Meine Mutter kommt eigentlich aus Deutschland, aus Hamburg. Ihr Vater, also mein Großvater, wohnt jetzt auch in den USA.
Aylin	Da hast du ja eine interessante Familie. Und darum kannst du auch so gut Deutsch sprechen! Wir sind auch zweisprachig.

2 **Match the names with the correct information.**

a	Aylin	**1**	ist alleinerziehend.
b	Max	**2**	kommt aus Washington.
c	Dilara	**3**	ist der Onkel von Aylin.
d	Hakan	**4**	hat zwei Geschwister.
e	Emre	**5**	hat drei Cousinen.
f	Der Vater von Max	**6**	wohnt in Frankfurt.

LANGUAGE BUILDER 1

 Language discovery 1

Look at Conversation 1 again. Notice the words preceding various family members and complete the sentences. Work out how to say *my*, *his*, *her*, and *our*.

a M .... Familie

b Un .... Familie

c S .... Name

d I .... Vater

Possessives – my, your, his, her, etc.

We have already seen the possessive mein, dein, Ihr and learned that the endings follow the pattern of the indefinite articles (ein, eine, ein). Here are the rest of the possessives:

	Masc. nouns	Fem. nouns	Neuter nouns
mein (my)	Das ist mein Sohn.	Das ist mein**e** Katze.	Das ist mein Handy.
dein (your, inf.)	Ist das dein Sohn?	Ist das dein**e** Katze?	Ist das dein Handy?
Ihr (your, form.)	Ist das Ihr Sohn?	Ist das Ihr**e** Katze?	Ist das Ihr Handy?
sein (his, its)	Das ist sein Sohn.	Das ist sein**e** Katze.	Das ist sein Handy.
ihr (her)	Das ist ihr Sohn.	Das ist ihr**e** Katze.	Das ist ihr Handy.
unser (our)	Das ist unser Sohn.	Das ist unser**e** Katze.	Das ist unser Handy.
euer (your, inf. pl.)	Ist das euer Sohn?	Ist das eur**e*** Katze?	Ist das euer Handy?
Ihr (your, form. pl.)	Ist das Ihr Sohn?	Ist das Ihr**e** Katze?	Ist das Ihr Handy?
ihr (their)	Das ist ihr Sohn.	Das ist ihr**e** Katze.	Das ist ihr Handy.

> * In the feminine and plural forms, euer drops the -e: Ist das eure Katze? Sind das eure Handys?

In the plural, all possessives take an -e ending:

Das sind meine Söhne. Das sind eure Töchter. Das sind unsere Kinder.

In the accusative, the masculine form ends in -en (feminine and neuter forms don't change):

Ich habe einen Sohn. Kennst du meinen Sohn?

Language practice 1

1 **Nina is welcoming an exchange student, and she writes a short description of her family. Complete the sentences, choosing from the possessives given.**

> ~~Meine~~ ihr ihre Meine sein Ihr Ihr sein Unsere Meine

Meine Familie ist relativ klein. Ich habe eine Schwester. .... Name ist Chloe. Sie ist 21 Jahre alt und .... Hobbys sind Reisen und Tanzen. .... Eltern heißen Steffi und Noah. Noah ist 42 und .... Beruf ist Physiotherapeut. Steffi ist Biologin. .... Hobby ist Indoor-Klettern. .... Großeltern wohnen nicht weit weg. Oma Hannah ist geschieden, aber .... neuer Partner ist sehr nett. Das Hobby von Opa Matthias ist .... Garten. Wir haben auch zwei Katzen: Cleopatra und Nofretete. .... Katzen sind sehr freundlich und individuell.

2 Now introduce your family. Use Nina's text as a guide.

LANGUAGE BUILDER 2

06.05

💡 Language discovery 2

Listen to the conversation again and repeat each line in the pauses provided. Then look at these sentences from the conversation. How many verbs are there in each sentence? Where do they go in the sentence?

a Er kann erst später kommen.

b Darum kannst du auch so gut Deutsch sprechen.

c Du musst beide kennenlernen.

d Er muss am Samstag leider arbeiten.

Expressing ability and obligation with **können** and **müssen**

Verbs like können or müssen, which express ability or obligation, are called *modal verbs*, and they do not take the usual endings in the ich and er/sie/es/xier forms:

können (*to be able to; can*)		müssen (*to have to; must*)	
ich **kann**	wir können	ich **muss**	wir müssen
du kannst	ihr könnt	du musst	ihr müsst
Sie können	Sie können	Sie müssen	Sie müssen
er/sie/es/xier **kann**	sie können	er/sie/es/xier **muss**	sie müssen

Modal verbs are usually used together with another verb. The second verb goes to the end of the sentence and is in the infinitive.

Er kann erst später kommen.   *He can only come later.*

Ich muss am Sonntag arbeiten.   *I have to work on Sunday.*

This also applies to separable verbs, which do not split in the infinitive form:

Ich muss heute Nachmittag einkaufen.   *I have to go shopping this afternoon.*

Language practice 2

1 Complete the sentences with the appropriate form of können and müssen.

können

a Er .... heute nicht kommen.

b .... du Jasmin von der Schule abholen?

c Was .... wir am Wochenende machen?

d .... Sie mir sagen, wie spät es ist?

e Ich .... sehr gut Klavier spielen.

müssen

f Ich .... Mittwoch nach Berlin fahren.

g .... du am Wochenende arbeiten?

h Claudia .... ihre Cousinen besuchen.

i Ihr .... mehr Wasser trinken.

j .... wir noch einkaufen?

06.06

2 Now play Conversation 1 again and play Aylin's role. Speak in the pauses. Try not to refer to the text.

Arbeiten in Deutschland *Working in Germany*

Germany is the largest Wirtschaft (*economy*) in Europe, and the third-largest by nominal GDP in the world, with more than 45 million people in employment. The majority works Vollzeit (*full time*), and about a quarter of employees work Teilzeit (*part time*).

The Arbeitstag (*workday*) in Germany tends to start earlier than in many other countries. Büros (*offices*) and Schulen (*schools*) often start at 8.00 a.m. The earlier start means that many people finish work earlier, too. Der Feierabend—the time when work is finished—is commonly regarded as a time to be enjoyed and to switch off from work. The average Wochenarbeitszeit (*workweek*) as a full-time employee is 36–40 hours.

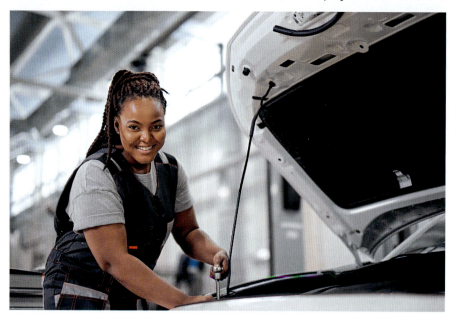

In many sectors, flexible Arbeitszeiten (*flexible working hours*) and the option to work from the Homeoffice (*working from home*) have helped to maintain a better work–life balance. The startup culture has stipulated innovation and development and has also helped to create new job opportunities.

Learn more about job opportunities in Germany.
Which jobs are currently in demand?
Can you find at least six professions?
Which jobs do you find interesting? Are there any jobs you had never heard of before?

VOCABULARY BUILDER 2

06.07

Look at the words and phrases and complete the missing English words and expressions. Then listen and try to imitate the pronunciation of the speakers.

WAS MACHEN SIE BEI DER ARBEIT?	WHAT DO YOU DO AT WORK?
behandeln	*to treat*
beraten	*to advise*
betreuen	*to look after, to care for*
ehrenamtlich / freiwillig arbeiten	*to volunteer*
entwickeln	*to develop*
leiten	*to lead*
schneiden	*to cut*
studieren	*to ....*
unterrichten	*to teach*
Ich bin pensioniert.	*I am retired.*
Vollzeit, Teilzeit	*full time, part ....*
die Arbeitsatmosphäre (-n)	*work environment*
die Bezahlung (-en)	*pay, salary*
der Nebenjob (-s)	*part-time job*
verschiedene Jobs	*different (types of) jobs*
das Engagement (-s)	*engagement, post, booking*
die Erfahrung (-en)	*experience*

BERUFE	PROFESSIONS
Was machen Sie beruflich?	*What do you do for a living?*
der Altenpfleger (-) / die Altenpflegerin (-nen)	*caregiver for the elderly*
der Anwalt (-"e) / die Anwältin (-nen)	*lawyer*
der Friseur (-e) / die Friseurin (-nen)	*hairdresser*
der Kellner (-) / die Kellnerin (-nen)	*server*
der Softwareentwickler (-) / die Softwareentwicklerin (-nen)	*.....................* *developer*

> Remember that female professions usually add an -in ending to the masculine form: der Kellner > die Kellnerin, der Friseur > die Friseurin
>
> In very rare cases, an umlaut is also added to the preceding vowel: der Arzt > die Ärztin, der Anwalt > die Anwältin
>
> For the gender-neutral form, you can normally insert a colon: Kellner:in, Lehrer:in

Vocabulary practice 2

1 **Say what you do for work. If you cannot find your profession in the list, look it up and find at least one activity associated with your job.**

CONVERSATION 2

Was machst du beruflich? *What work do you do?*

06.08

1 Listen to the conversation a few times. Then listen again and read the text. What does Hakan think of his job in Frankfurt? And what does Wally do?

> At Özkan's Geburtstagsfeier, Max starts talking to Hakan, Aylin's brother. Here are a few words you will hear: davor (*before*), der Chor (-"e) (*choir*), das Flüchtlingsheim (-e) (*home for refugees*).
>
> **Max** Hakan, was machst du eigentlich beruflich?
>
> **Hakan** Ich arbeite jetzt seit drei Jahren im Filmmuseum in Frankfurt. Ich arbeite in der Designabteilung. Davor war ich Designer in Berlin. Das war aber nur Teilzeit. Jetzt arbeite ich Vollzeit.
>
> **Max** Und gefällt dir deine Arbeit?
>
> **Hakan** Ja, die Arbeit ist interessant und die Arbeitsatmosphäre ist super. Hier in Berlin hatte ich mehr Stress. Und die Bezahlung war auch nicht so gut. Ah, da ist ja Wally.
>
> *Wally joins the conversation.*
>
> **Wally** Hallo, Hakan, schön, dich zu sehen.
>
> **Hakan** Dich auch, Wally. Singst du eigentlich noch in der Oper?
>
> **Wally** Nein, schon seit zwei Jahren nicht mehr. Jetzt bin ich pensioniert.
>
> **Max** Du warst Opernsängerin hier in Berlin? Das ist ja toll!
>
> **Hakan** Oh, ja. Wally war Sängerin an der Deutschen Oper und vorher in Hamburg. Und du hattest doch auch Engagements in London and Mailand, oder?
>
> **Wally** Ja, das waren fantastische Erfahrungen.
>
> **Hakan** Und was machst du jetzt?
>
> **Wally** Ich unterrichte und singe manchmal im Chor. Und ich arbeite ehrenamtlich in einem Flüchtlingsheim. Das macht mir viel Spaß.
>
> **Hakan** Und du, Max?
>
> **Max** Im Moment blogge ich nur. In den USA hatte ich aber verschiedene Jobs.

2 Decide if these statements are *true* (richtig) or *false* (falsch).

  a Hakan works part time.   R   F

  b Hakan's job in Frankfurt is better than the one he had in Berlin.   R   F

  c Wally was an opera singer in Berlin, London and Madrid.   R   F

  d She enjoys her voluntary work with refugees.   R   F

  e Max did not work in the USA.   R   F

LANGUAGE BUILDER 3

Saying where you are using **in** + dative

In German it makes a difference whether you are talking about movement to a certain location (Wir gehen ins Kino) versus being at the location (Wir sehen einen Film im Kino). Both can be expressed with the preposition in, but it is what comes next that changes. Look at these examples (Note that im is an abbreviation for in dem.):

	Movement to/into	**Position/Location**
masc.	Er geht **in den** Biergarten.	Er ist **im** Biergarten.
	Wir gehen **in den** Park.	Wir sitzen **im** Park.
fem.	Frauke geht **in die** Oper.	Frauke hört ein Konzert **in der** Oper.
	Ich gehe **in die** Bäckerei.	Ich kaufe Brot **in der** Bäckerei.
neut.	Yuko geht **ins** Restaurant.	Sie isst **im** Restaurant.
	Ich gehe heute früh **ins** Bett.	Ich lese gern **im** Bett.
pl.	Wir gehen **in die** Museen auf der Museumsinsel.	Wir schauen uns die Gemälde **in den** Museen an.

The examples under **Movement to/into** are in the accusative case and answer the question ask Wohin? (*Where to?*). Those under **Position/Location** are in the dative case and answer the question Wo? (*Where?*).

Language practice 3

For each pair, indicate whether **in** refers to movement (M) or position (P).

Example: Gehen wir heute ins Kino? (M) Es gibt einen neuen Film im Kino. (P)

1 a Sie arbeitet jeden Tag **im** Büro. ....
b Wann gehst du **ins** Büro? ....

2 a Ana kauft meistens **im** Supermarkt ein. ....
b Ich gehe noch **in den** Supermarkt. ....

3 a Kommst du mit **in den** Park? ....
b **Im** Park kann ich gut joggen. ....

4 a Treffen wir uns **in der** Oper? ....
b Morgen gehen wir **in die** Oper. ....

5 a Geht ihr oft **ins** Fitnesscenter? ....
b Jakob trainiert oft **im** Fitnesscenter. ....

LANGUAGE BUILDER 4

06.09

💡 Language discovery 4

Listen to the conversation again and repeat each line in the pauses provided. Then complete the sentences from the conversation with war (used twice) or **hatte. Is Hakan talking about his old or current job?**

a Hakan .... Designer in Berlin.

b Er .... in Berlin mehr Stress.

c Die Bezahlung .... auch nicht so gut.

Talking about the past—past tense of **haben** and **sein**

Hakan is talking about a job he had in the past, using the simple past of the verbs haben and sein, which allow you to say what you had and what you were in the past. As in the present tense, these two verbs are irregular in the simple past. Check the forms carefully and pay particular attention to the endings.

hatt + ending		war + ending	
ich hatte	wir hatten	ich war	wir waren
du hattest	ihr hattet	du warst	ihr wart
Sie hatten	Sie hatten	Sie waren	Sie waren
er/sie/es/xier hatte	sie hatten	er/sie/es/xier war	sie waren

Language practice 4

1 Complete the sentences with the correct form of haben und sein in the past tense.

a Wir w .... im Sommer in Polen.

b Du w .... nicht auf der Party.

c Priya w .... gestern im Homeoffice.

d Tim und Katja w .... im Theater.

e Ihr w .... heute nicht in der Schule.

f Ich h .... als Kind eine Katze.

g Markus h .... gestern frei.

h Du h .... früher mehr Zeit.

i Wir h .... im Winter viel Schnee.

j Ihr h .... als Student:innen kein Geld.

06.10

2 Now play Conversation 2 again and play Hakan's role. Speak in the pauses. Try not to refer to the text.

SKILL BUILDER

1 Match the questions with the appropriate answers.

a Wie ist dein Name?

b Sind das die Eltern von Simone?

c Frau Haller, ist das Ihr Handy?

d Ist das euer Auto?

e Sind das die Kinder von Liz und Ron?

f Kennst du den Partner von Tim?

g Sind die Getränke für uns?

1 Ja, das ist unser Auto.

2 Mein Name ist Felix Sanchez.

3 Ja, das sind ihre Kinder.

4 Nein, ich kenne seinen Partner nicht.

5 Ja, das ist mein Handy.

6 Ja, das sind eure.

7 Ja, das sind ihre Eltern.

2 Match the two parts to show where these people are or where they are going.

a Der Barista macht Kaffee

b Lara muss arbeiten und geht

c Der Mechaniker repariert Autos

d Die Kundenberaterin arbeitet

e Ich habe Hunger. Gehen wir

f Ich muss einkaufen. Ich gehe

g Die Opernsängerin singt

h Wir machen ein Picknick

1 in den Supermarkt.

2 im Büro.

3 ins Büro.

4 im Park.

5 in der Oper.

6 in der Werkstatt.

7 im Café.

8 ins Café.

3 Max tells Wally about his day yesterday. Complete with the correct forms of haben and sein in the past. Then listen and check your answers.

06.11

Gestern war ein toller Tag! Ich .... viel Zeit. Ich .... mit Aylin im Park. Das Wetter .... sehr schön. Dann .... wir beide hungrig. Aylin .... auch Durst. Wir .... in einem Restaurant im Park. Wir .... einen Antipasti-Teller. Zum Nachtisch .... ich noch ein Eis. Dann .... es schon vier Uhr. Wir .... ein bisschen müde, aber wir .... viel Spaß! Wo .... du gestern, Wally?

4 These people are very busy and have to do their work first before they can do what they really want to do. Complete with the correct forms of müssen and können. Then give at least two examples about yourself.

Example: Ich *muss* morgen früh aufstehen. Ich *kann* heute nicht tanzen gehen.

a Irina .... arbeiten. Sie .... leider nicht lesen.

b Du .... den Computer reparieren. Du .... nicht in die Oper gehen.

c Ihr .... Mittagessen kochen. Ihr .... nicht fernsehen.

d Ich .... noch einen Text schreiben. Ich .... nicht joggen gehen.

e Wir .... unsere Kinder abholen. Wir .... nicht ins Fitnessstudio gehen.

f Sie (*plural*) .... Englisch sprechen. Die Kund:innen .... kein Deutsch.

TEST YOURSELF

 1 Here are short portraits of Udo, Aylin, Fabian, Hakan, and Wally. But a few details are missing. Complete them with words from the box.

Opernsängerin	Elektriker	Alexanderplatz	Arbeitsatmosphäre	kreativ
Musik	verheiratet	Zoo	zweisprachig	Berlinerisch

a **Udo** ist ein echter Berliner. Er spricht viel und ist sehr humorvoll. In Unit 3 zeigt er Max das Zentrum von Berlin. Anschließend trinken beide Kaffee am .... Sein Beruf ist Touristenführer. Er sagt, er spricht Deutsch und ....

b **Aylin** ist Ärztin von Beruf. Sie ist mit Fabian .... und sie haben eine Tochter. In Kapitel 2 sagt Aylin, zu Hause sprechen sie meistens Deutsch, aber auch Türkisch. Sie sind .... In Kapitel 6 spricht sie über ihre Familie. Ihre Schwester heißt Dilara. Aylin und Dilara haben ein sehr gutes Verhältnis. Ihr Bruder ist Hakan.

c **Fabian** ist der Sohn von Wally. Er ist mit Aylin verheiratet. In Kapitel 5 spricht er über seinen Alltag. Er steht meistens sehr früh auf. Er ist .... von Beruf und er hat eine kleine Firma. Am Wochenende geht er oft in den Berliner ....

d **Hakan** ist der Bruder von Aylin. Er arbeitet als Designer im Filmmuseum in Frankfurt. Davor war er Designer in Berlin. Jetzt arbeitet er Vollzeit. Er mag die .... und die Kollegen. Aylin sagt, Hakan ist sehr ....

e **Wally** geht gerne schwimmen und kocht gern. In Kapitel 4 sagt sie, sie isst gern frische Salate, Gemüse, aber auch Fisch. Wally kann sehr gut singen und früher war sie .... Jetzt arbeitet sie aber noch ehrenamtlich in einem Flüchtlingsheim. Sie sagt, ... und Singen sind ihre Leidenschaften.

 **2** Now write a short text about Max. Say what he does and what you know about his family, hobbies, and so on.

?

Wie geht's weiter? *What happens next?*

Max gets to know Wally's family and her past better. Will he meet more of her friends and family? Or will he make friends of his own? Will he explore more of Berlin? Or does he have other plans?

Remember to use **My review** and **My takeaway** to assess your progress and reflect on your learning experience.

Congratulations on completing the first level of your studies! Now it's time to put your skills to the test—take the A1 Assessment online at library.teachyourself.com and see how much you've learned.

In this lesson you will learn how to:

» Talk about different means of transportation
» Say how you travel to work and travel around
» Ask how to get somewhere
» Discuss transportation issues in towns

Eine Reise nach Wien

My study plan

I plan to work with Unit 7

○ Every day
○ Twice a week
○ Other _____

I plan to study for

○ 5–15 minutes
○ 15–30 minutes
○ 30–45+ minutes

My progress tracker

Day / Date	🎧	🎤	📖	✏️	💬
	○	○	○	○	○
	○	○	○	○	○
	○	○	○	○	○
	○	○	○	○	○
	○	○	○	○	○
	○	○	○	○	○
	○	○	○	○	○

My goals

What do you want to be able to do or say in German when you complete this unit?   **Done**

1 .... ○
2 .... ○
3 .... ○

My review

SELF CHECK

	I can ...
○	... talk about different means of transportation.
○	... say how I travel to work and travel around.
○	... ask how to get somewhere.
○	... discuss transportation issues in towns.

CULTURE POINT 1

Willkommen in Wien *Welcome to Vienna*

With nearly two million inhabitants, Vienna is Austria's biggest city and the cultural, economic, and political center of the country. Until the beginning of the 20th century, Vienna was the largest German-speaking city in the world and the capital of the Austro-Hungarian Empire, one of Europe's major powers at the time.

Today, you can still experience a lot of the old Größe (*grandeur*) the city was famous for. However, Vienna is also a modern and forward-looking place and offers trendy stores, attractions like the popular MuseumsQuartier and an exciting Nachtleben (*nightlife*).

Vienna has a well-developed öffentliches Verkehrssystem (*public transportation network*). It is easy to travel by Bus (*bus*), Zug (*train*), Straßenbahn (*tram*), or U-Bahn (*metro*). Many lines run 24 Stunden (*24 hours*). When visiting Vienna, look out for offers like the 24, 48, or 72-hour passes, or the Vienna City Card.

 Find out more about the Vienna City Card:
Which ticket would you choose if you visited Vienna for two days?
What benefits are included? Where can you buy it? Is there a similar program where you live?

94

VOCABULARY BUILDER 1

Look at the words and phrases and complete the missing English words and expressions. Then listen and try to imitate the pronunciation of the speakers.

07.01

VERKEHRSMITTEL	MEANS OF TRANSPORTATION
das Auto (-s)	car
der Bus (-se)	....
der E-Scooter (-)	....
das Fahrrad (-"er), das E-Bike (-s)	bicycle, e-bike
das Flugzeug (-e)	airplane
das Motorrad (-"er)	motor.....................
das Schiff (-e)	ship
die Straßenbahn (-en) / die, das Tram (-s)	streetcar, tram
die Bahn (-en)	rail
die S-Bahn (-en)	suburban train
die U-Bahn (-en)	....
der Zug (-"e)	train
von A nach B ...	from A to B ...
fahren	to go (using a means of transportation), to drive
zu Fuß gehen	to go on foot
um/steigen	to transfer / to change transportation (bus, trains, etc.)
halten	to stop
die Fahrkarte (-n)	ticket
die Haltestelle (-n)	stop / station
der öffentliche Nahverkehr (no plural)	local public transportation
das öffentliche Verkehrsmittel (-)	public transportation
die Tageskarte (-n)	day ticket
die Wegbeschreibung (-en)	directions
Die Fahrt dauert...	The journey lasts ...
reisen	to travel
das Gepäck (no pl.)	baggage
der Koffer (-)	suitcase
der Rucksack (-"e)	backpack, rucksack

NÜTZLICHE AUSDRÜCKE	USEFUL EXPRESSIONS
die Ermäßigung (-en)	concession, discount

> The adjective öffentlich means *public* and, apart from transportation, can be used in many contexts, including: der öffentliche Dienst (*public service*), der öffentlich-rechtliche Rundfunk (*public service broadcasting*), die öffentliche Meinung (*public opinion*). The noun is die Öffentlichkeit (*public*).

das lohnt sich	it's worth it
Das war nur Spaß.	I'm only kidding.

Vocabulary practice 1

Identify these means of transportation. Don't forget to include the article.

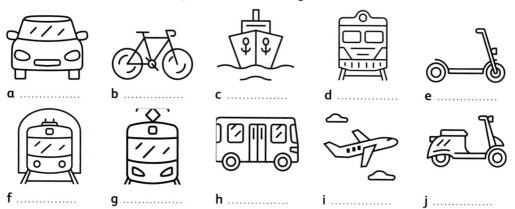

a ....   b ....   c ....   d ....   e ....

f ....   g ....   h ....   i ....   j ....

Pronunciation practice

07.02

1 Compound nouns—nouns that consist of more than one component—can sometimes be difficult to pronounce. Listen and practice saying them.

   a der Verkehr, das Verkehrsmittel, die öffentlichen Verkehrsmittel

   b die Karte, die Tageskarte, die Wochenkarte, die Monatskarte, die Jahreskarte

   c die Fahrkarte, der Fahrkartenverkauf, der Fahrkartenautomat

   d die Haltestelle, die Bushaltestelle, die Straßenbahnhaltestelle

   e die Ermäßigung, die Studentenermäßigung, die Seniorenermäßigung

2 Work out what all the words in Exercise 1 mean. Check to see if you're right in the answer key.

Remember that, with compound nouns, it is always the last noun which determines the gender:

Compound nouns ending with Zug are masculine: der Nachtzug, der Schnellzug.

Nouns ending with Auto or Rad are neuter: das E-Auto, das Motorrad.

Nouns ending with Bahn are feminine: die Straßenbahn, die U-Bahn.

Fahr mit den Öffis! *Go by public transportation!*

07.03

1 **Listen to the conversation a few times without looking at the text. Then listen again and read the text. Why is it better for Max to take public transportation?**

Max has just arrived at Hauptbahnhof Wien (*Vienna Central Station*). He calls Wally's friend Gustav who has invited Max to stay with him.

Gustav	Max, wo bist du?
Max	Vor dem Hauptbahnhof. Jetzt fahre ich am besten mit dem Taxi.
Gustav	Mit dem Taxi? Nein, das ist viel zu teuer.
Max	(*lacht*) Ich weiß. Das war nur Spaß. So viel Geld habe ich ja auch nicht.
Gustav	Fahr am besten mit den Öffis ... Mit den öffentlichen Verkehrsmitteln.
Max	Gut, ja, ich verstehe.
Gustav	Du bleibst ja ein paar Tage in Wien. Da kannst du eine Vienna City Card kaufen. Mit der Karte bekommst du auch Ermäßigungen für Museen, Restaurants und viele Sehenswürdigkeiten.
Max	Und du meinst, das lohnt sich?
Gustav	Das lohnt sich auf jeden Fall, Max. Also, fahr am besten mit der U1. Es ist nicht weit zur Station, etwa fünf Minuten zu Fuß.
Max	Ja, ich weiß. Ich habe die Wegbeschreibung auf meinem Handy.
Gustav	Du fährst Richtung Leopoldau bis ...
Max	... zum Stephansplatz.
Gustav	Genau! Vom Stephansplatz fährst du dann mit dem Bus, mit der Linie 1A. Der Bus hält direkt vor meinem Haus.
Max	Die Haltestelle heißt Teinfaltstraße.
Gustav	Richtig! Hast du viel Gepäck?
Max	Nein, nur meinen Rucksack und einen Koffer.
Gustav	Gut. Dann bis gleich.

2 **Decide if these statements are *true* (richtig) or *false* (falsch).**

a Gustav sagt, mit dem Taxi ist es zu langsam.   R   F

b Mit der Vienna City Card bekommt man Ermäßigungen für Museen, Restaurants und Sehenswürdigkeiten.   R   F

c Vom Bahnhof geht man zehn Minuten bis zur U-Bahnstation.   R   F

d Max muss zuerst mit dem Bus fahren und dann mit der U-Bahn.   R   F

e Die Buslinie 1A hält direkt vor dem Haus von Gustav.   R   F

LANGUAGE BUILDER 1

 Language discovery 1

Look at the conversation again. Add the missing articles.

a Vom Stephansplatz fährst du dann mit .... Bus. (m)

b Mit .... Taxi? (nt)

c Fahr am besten mit .... U1. (f)

d Mit .... öffentlichen Verkehrsmitteln. (pl)

How are these articles different from the definite articles you already know? Why do you think that is?

Ich fahre mit ... + dative

To say that you *go by car*, *by bus* etc., use the preposition mit (*with*): Ich fahre mit dem Auto, mit dem Bus, etc. Mit is always followed by the dative case. Compare the nominative and dative forms of the definite article *the*:

masc.	der Bus	Frau Krause fährt <u>mit dem</u> Bus.
neut.	das Auto	Herr Krause fährt <u>mit dem</u> Auto.
fem.	die U-Bahn	Rainer Krause fährt <u>mit der</u> U-Bahn.
plural	die Kinder	Er reist <u>mit den</u> Kindern.

In the dative plural, an extra -n is usually added to the noun:

Er reist mit den Kinder<u>n</u>. Sie fahren mit den Fahrräder<u>n</u>.

However, when the plural form ends in -s, there is no change:

Öffis: Fahr lieber mit den Öffis.

Language practice 1

Complete these sentences with dem, der, or den.

a In Amsterdam fahren viele Leute mit .... Fahrrad.

b Mit .... U-Bahn ist man in sieben Minuten in der Stadt.

c In Wien kann man mit .... Straßenbahn fahren.

d Er fährt mit .... E-Auto nach Österreich.

e Mit .... Zug kostet es 60 € bis nach Freiburg.

f Sie fahren viel mit .... öffentlichen Verkehrsmitteln.

LANGUAGE BUILDER 2

💡 Language discovery 2

Listen to the conversation again and repeat each line in the pauses provided. Then look at these sentences. Which of the underlined prepositions correspond to the English *to* and *from*? Which case do you think these prepositions require?

Es ist nicht weit <u>zur</u> Station.   <u>Vom</u> Stephansplatz fährst du dann mit dem Bus.
<u>Zum</u> Stephansplatz.

Prepositions indicating movement and direction

Apart from mit, other frequently used prepositions when talking about traveling are von (*from*) and zu (*to*). Both are followed by the dative case and combine to form a single word with the definite article when possible.

masc.	der Bahnhof	Ich fahre zum (= zu dem) Bahnhof.
neut.	das Stadion	Wie komme ich zum (= zu dem) Stadion?
fem.	die Universität	Sie fährt zur (= zu der) Universität.
masc.	der Park	Wie komme ich vom (= von dem) Park zum Supermarkt?
neut.	das Hotel	Ich möchte bitte vom (= von dem) Hotel zum Bahnhof fahren.
fem.	die Kirche	Wie komme ich von der Kirche zur Oper?

There are a few more common prepositions which are followed by the dative:

aus (*out [of]/from*)	gegenüber (*opposite*)	seit (*since*)
außer (*apart from, out of*)	bei (*with/at/in*)	nach (*after, to*)

Sie wohnen gegenüber dem Park.	*They live opposite the park.*
Nach der Arbeit gehe ich einkaufen.	*After work, I'll go shopping.*
Tim studiert seit einem Jahr.	*Tim has been studying for one year.*

Notice that bei can also be contracted when used with dem:

Ich war beim (= bei dem) Arzt.	*I was at the doctor's.*

Language practice 2

1   **Complete the questions. Note that Bahnhof is masculine, Touristeninformation feminine, and Hotel and Fußballstadion are neuter.**

   a Entschuldigen Sie bitte. Wie komme ich z .... Hauptbahnhof?

   b Entschuldigung, wie komme ich z .... Touristeninformation?

   c Entschuldigung, wie komme ich v .... Bahnhof z .... Hotel Meininger?

   d Entschuldigen Sie bitte. Wie komme ich z .... Fußballstadion?

2 Complete with the missing prepositions.

aus	beim	gegenüber	mit	nach	seit

a Sabine lebt .... fast zwanzig Jahren in Wien.

b Die Bushaltestelle liegt .... dem Supermarkt.

c Bianca geht um sieben Uhr .... dem Haus.

d Wir machen .... der Pause weiter.

e Tilo fährt immer .... dem Fahrrad zur Uni.

f Heute Morgen war ich .... Arzt.

07.05

3 Now play Conversation 1 again and play Max's role. Speak in the pauses. Try not to refer to the text.

CULTURE POINT 2

Die Wiener Ringstraße *Vienna Ring Road*

Created in the late 19th century to replace the old fortification walls, the Ringstraße was designed to accommodate some of Vienna's most spectacular works of architecture. It is a 5.3 km boulevard that also serves as a ringroad around the historic Innere Stadt (*Old Town*, lit. *inner town*) and has several sections, such as the Universitätsring (referring to the university area) and the Parkring (referring to Wiener Stadtpark). It took 50 years to complete the Ringstraße.

Apart from the Universität, other important buildings include die Wiener Staatsoper (*Vienna State Opera*), das Rathaus (*city hall*), das Kunsthistorische Museum (*Museum of Fine Arts*), das Parlament (*Parliament*) and das Burgtheater (*National Theater*). Here, the ceiling paintings above the staircase were created by Gustav Klimt, one of Vienna's most famous artists. On stage you will find some of the best German-speaking Schauspieler:innen (*actors*).

The Ringstraße has fulfilled a variety of purposes since its completion. Today, many different events and activities take place here—from the annual Rainbow Parade to the Vienna City Marathon.

 Find out more about the life and work of Gustav Klimt:
When did he live? What was his family background? What material did he use during his 'Golden Phase'? Can you find the titles of three of his major works?

VOCABULARY BUILDER 2

07.06

Look at the words and phrases and complete the missing English words and expressions. Then listen and try to imitate the pronunciation of the speakers.

VERKEHR IN DER STADT	TRAFFIC IN THE CITY
die Baustelle (-n)	construction site
der Fahrradabstellplatz (-"e)	bicycle parking space
der Fahrradständer (-)	bicycle stand
der Fahrradweg (-e)	cycle lane, bike path
die Innenstadt (-"e)	city center
der Parkplatz (-"e), der Parkschein (-e)	..................., parking ticket
der Stau (-s)	traffic jam
die Umwelt (-en)	environment
das Verkehrsnetz (-e)	transportation network
das Verkehrssystem (-e)	.... system
die Verspätung (-en)	delay
entlang/gehen	to go / walk along
überall hin/kommen	to get anywhere
ein Fahrrad aus/leihen	to rent a bike
außerhalb	outside

ATTRAKTIONEN IN WIEN	ATTRACTIONS IN VIENNA
das Atelier (-s)	studio
das Bild (-er), das Gemälde (-)	picture, painting
das traditionelle oder moderne Wien	the .... or modern Vienna
angenehm	pleasant
der Lieblingsmaler (-) / die Lieblingsmalerin (-nen)	favorite painter
der Kuss (-"e)	The Kiss (painting by Klimt)

Vocabulary practice 2

1 Sort the words into these categories: 1 Auto, 2 Bus, U-Bahn, 3 Fahrrad, E-Roller, etc.

Autobahn	Parkplatzprobleme	Baustelle	Haltestelle
um/steigen	Tageskarte	Parkplatz	Monatskarte
Bahnhof	Radfahrweg	Parkschein	Straßenbahn
U-Bahnstation	Wochenkarte	öffentlicher Nahverkehr	
Fahrradabstellplatz	man tut etwas für die Gesundheit		

CONVERSATION 2

Von A nach B *From A to B*

07.07

1 **Listen to the conversation a few times without looking at the text. Then listen again and read the text. What does Gustav think of public transportation in Vienna? Where is Klimt Villa?**

> After Max has unpacked, Gustav invites him to his local Kaffeehaus (*coffee house*). They start talking about Max's trip.
>
> | | |
> |---|---|
> | **Max** | Die Reise nach Wien war angenehm. Der Zug hatte nur ein bisschen Verspätung. Und dann war es ganz einfach, zu deiner Wohnung zu fahren. Das öffentliche Verkehrssystem in Wien ist gut, oder? |
> | **Gustav** | Ja, man kommt gut von A nach B, finde ich. Und es ist auch nicht zu teuer. Ich fahre aber meistens mit meinem Fahrrad. Da tue ich etwas für meine Gesundheit und es ist auch gut für die Umwelt. |
> | **Max** | Und wie lange brauchst du zum Beispiel in die Innenstadt? |
> | **Gustav** | In die Innenstadt sind es zehn bis fünfzehn Minuten, zur Arbeit fahre ich etwa dreißig Minuten. |
> | **Max** | Gibt es denn gute Radfahrwege? |
> | **Gustav** | Ja, es gibt ein gutes Verkehrsnetz für Radfahrer und auch viele Abstellplätze. Und ich fahre nicht gern mit dem Auto in die Stadt. Es gibt zu viele Baustellen und Staus, und mit dem Parken ist es schwierig. |
> | **Max** | Ich verstehe. Hast du noch Tipps für Wien? |
> | **Gustav** | Möchtest du das traditionelle oder moderne Wien sehen? |
> | **Max** | Eigentlich beides. Aber vor allem auch Originale von Gustav Klimt. Er ist mein Lieblingsmaler. |
> | **Gustav** | Die meisten Bilder hängen im Schloss Belvedere, zum Beispiel auch „Der Kuss". Aber fahr zuerst zur Klimt-Villa. Dort war sein Atelier. Da bekommst du einen guten Eindruck von seiner Arbeit und seiner Kunst. |
> | **Max** | Und liegt die Klimt-Villa in der Nähe von der Ringstraße? |
> | **Gustav** | Nein, es ist ein wenig außerhalb. Aber mit deiner Vienna City Card kommst du ja überall schnell hin. Oder du kannst auch ein Fahrrad ausleihen ... oder einen Scooter. |

2 **Answer the questions.**

a Was war das Problem mit dem Zug aus Berlin? ....

b Wie fährt Gustav meistens zur Arbeit? ....

c Was sind Probleme für Autofahrer in Wien? ....

d Wer ist der Lieblingsmaler von Max? ....

e Max hat eine Vienna City Card. Was kann er aber auch alternativ machen? ....

LANGUAGE BUILDER 3

 Language discovery 3

Complete these sentences from Conversation 2 by adding the correct endings. Which case do you think the missing words are in? And why?

a Mit dein .... Vienna City Card kommst du ja überall schnell hin.

b Ich fahre aber meistens mit mein .... Fahrrad.

c Da bekommst du einen guten Eindruck von sein .... Arbeit.

Pattern of endings in the dative

You saw how the definite articles change in the dative case. The indefinite articles and possessives follow the same -em, -er, -en pattern:

	Indefinite articles	Possessives
Masculine	Er fährt mit einem Bus nach Prag.	Der Rucksack ist von seinem Sohn.
Neuter	Sie haben den E-Scooter seit einem Jahr.	Benjamin fährt mit seinem Auto.
Feminine	Mit einer Tageskarte sparst du Geld.	Dunja war bei ihrer Schwester.
Plural	-	Sie reisen mit ihren Kindern nach Frankreich.

Do not forget to add the additional -n to the plural noun ending, whenever applicable.

> German is a very systematic language. If possible, try to learn the patterns—this will help you to remember and to apply certain features in German, like the dative endings.

Language practice 3

Match the two halves of the sentences.

a Mattheo fährt mit seinem

b Wie komme ich am besten zu deiner

c Tanja wohnt mit ihrer

d Ich war gestern bei meinem

e Sie arbeitet jetzt seit einem

f Morgen fahren wir mit unseren

1 Bruder in Salzburg.

2 Fahrrädern in die Umgebung von Wien.

3 Auto von Wien nach Prag.

4 Mutter zusammen.

5 Wohnung?

6 Jahr in der Secession.

LANGUAGE BUILDER 4

07.08

💡 Language discovery 4

Listen to the conversation again and repeat each line in the pauses provided. Then complete the sentences with the missing preposition. What do these prepositions mean in English? How are they different?

a Die Reise .... Wien war angenehm.

b Und wie lange brauchst du .... die Innenstadt?

c Und dann war es einfach, ... deiner Wohnung zu fahren.

d Aber fahr zuerst .... Klimt-Villa.

Use of prepositions and places

When referring to directions and places, there are a number of prepositions used in German. The most common are zu, in, or nach, which all translate as *to* in English, but are used in different contexts:

zu	in	nach
When focusing on direction toward a building or place: Wie komme ich *zum* Bahnhof? Wie komme ich *zur* Wohnung?	When the focus is on entering a building, an open space, and a part of town: Ich gehe jede Woche *ins* Kino. Sie gehen oft *in den* Park. Ich fahre *in die* Innenstadt.	In most cases with countries and towns/cities: Ich fahre *nach* Italien. Wir machen einen Ausflug *nach* Budapest.

> Remember zu and nach are always followed by the dative, while in takes the accusative with movement (see Unit 5) and dative with position (see Unit 6).

Language practice 4

1 Complete the sentences with in, zu, nach, or mit:

a Ich muss noch etwas einkaufen und fahre .... die Innenstadt.

b Ist das der Weg .... m Hauptbahnhof?

c .... dem Zug brauche ich nur zwei Stunden bis .... München.

d Kommst du mit .... s Museum?

e Wie komme ich .... m Sigmund-Freud-Museum?

2 Now play Conversation 2 again and play Gustav's role. Speak in the pauses. Try not to refer to the text.

07.09

SKILL BUILDER

1 Find the odd one out.

a Bus	Verkehr	Flugzeug	Straßenbahn
b Haltestelle	Verspätung	Stopp	Station
c Baustelle	Stau	Parkplatzprobleme	Umwelt
d Fahrkarte	Gepäck	Rucksack	Koffer
e Schloss	Ermäßigung	Dom	Museum

2 Practice the dative.

a Piotr lebt sehr gesund. Er fährt jeden Tag mit d .... Fahrrad z ....
Universität.

b In Berlin kann man schlecht parken. Frau Zeng fährt immer mit d ....
U-Bahn z .... Arbeit.

c Nina hat heute wenig Zeit und fährt mit d .... Taxi.

d Mit d .... Zug ist man in drei Stunden in Salzburg.

e In vielen deutschen Städten kann man noch mit d .... Straßenbahn fahren.

3 Choose the best answer.

a Fahre ich am besten mit dem Taxi?
   1 Du bleibst ja ein paar Tage in Wien.
   2 Fahr Richtung Stephansplatz.
   3 Nein, fahr mit den Öffis.

b Wie lange dauert die Fahrt mit dem
Bus?
   1 Etwa fünf Minuten zu Fuß.
   2 Das geht schnell.
   3 Das ist ja ziemlich einfach.

c Das öffentliche Verkehrssystem ist gut, oder?
   1 Ja, man kommt gut von A nach B.
   2 Ja, es gibt ein gutes Verkehrsnetz für
Radfahrer.
   3 Zur Arbeit fahre ich etwa dreißig Minuten.

d Möchtest du das traditionelle oder
moderne Wien sehen?
   1 Klimt ist mein Lieblingsmaler.
   2 Geh einmal die Ringstraße entlang. Da
gibt es viele wichtige Gebäude.
   3 Eigentlich beides.

4 Read the four texts about attractions in Vienna and answer the questions. Here are a few words to help you:

der Raum (-"e)	*rooms*		der Vergnügungspark (-s)	*amusement park*
die Glocke (-n)	*bell*		das Vorbild (-er)	*role model*
das Riesenrad (-"er)	*ferris wheel*		heiratete	*got married*

das Beethovenfries *Beethoven Frieze,* a wall painting by Klimt in the Secession Building
celebrating the famous German composer

Sehenswürdigkeiten in Wien

Schloss Schönbrunn
Das Schloss Schönbrunn ist ein Muss. Es war die Residenz von Joseph I. und ist über 300 Jahre alt. Das Vorbild war das Schloss von Versailles. Es gibt 1441 Räume. Besonders schön und beliebt ist der Garten. Hier gibt es im Sommer auch Konzerte. Der Garten hat auch ein Kindermuseum. Das Schloss Schönbrunn ist die Touristenattraktion Nr. 1 in Wien.

Wiener Secession
Die Wiener Secession gibt es seit 1897. Heute kann man hier moderne, avantgardistische Kunst sehen, aber es gibt auch Kunst des Jugendstils (Art Nouveau), zum Beispiel das Beethovenfries von Gustav Klimt. Die Secession zeigt Fotoausstellungen, Videoinstallationen etc. und präsentiert diverse Künstler:innen aus der ganzen Welt.

Prater und „Wurstelprater"
Der Prater ist ein großer Park in Wien. Im Park gibt es den „Wiener Wurstelprater". Der „Wurstelprater" ist ein Vergnügungspark – ideal für Familien mit Kindern. Berühmt ist das Riesenrad – dort kann man Wien von oben sehen. Es gibt das Riesenrad seit 1897. In anderen Städten gibt es moderne Riesenräder – aber das Riesenrad in Wien hat mehr Charme.

Stephansdom
Der Stephansdom ist das Zentrum von Wien und ein wichtiges Wahrzeichen. Das Gebäude ist 107 Meter lang und 136 Meter hoch. Der Dom ist über 800 Jahre alt. Es gibt 13 Glocken. Der Komponist Joseph Haydn war ein Chorsänger im Dom, und Mozart heiratete hier. Der Dom ist auch sehr wichtig für die Geschichte von Österreich. Von Januar bis Dezember gibt es viele Konzerte.

a What is Schloss Schönbrunn modeled on?
b What kind of art can you see in the Secession?
c Why is the ferris wheel in the Prater so special?
d Who got married in the Stephansdom?

5 Here are four international visitors. Look at their interests and then match each person with the most suitable attraction(s) in Vienna from exercise 4.

a Haruki kommt aus Japan. Er mag moderne Kunst. ....

b Sophie aus Kanada findet Kunst und Konzerte langweilig. ....

c Oluyemi kommt aus Tansania. Er liebt klassische Musik, besonders Joseph Haydn.

....

d Linda aus Schweden ist mit ihren zwei Kindern in Wien. Sie liebt Gärten und möchte gern etwas zusammen mit den Kindern machen. ....

TEST YOURSELF

07.10

Now talk about your commuting habits and preferences. Prepare your answers, then listen and say your answers out loud.

a Wie fahren Sie normalerweise zur Arbeit / zur Uni / in die Innenstadt?

b Wie lange fahren Sie?

c Müssen Sie umsteigen?

d Wie ist das öffentliche Verkehrssystem in Ihrer Stadt?

e Kommt man gut von A nach B?

f Sind die Fahrkarten teuer?

g Fahren Sie oft mit dem Fahrrad?

h Gibt es gute Fahrradwege in Ihrer Stadt?

i Wie ist Ihre Stadt für Autofahrer?

Wie geht's weiter? *What happens next?*

There are lots of things to do in Vienna, and Max is also trying to get an interview with an upcoming singer-songwriter. Will he succeed?

Remember to use **My review** and **My takeaway** to assess your progress and reflect on your learning experience.

In this lesson you will learn how to:
» Talk about what you did on the weekend
» Describe other events in the past
» Say what you have already done and what you still need to do
» Ask for the bill and give a tip

Was hast du am Wochenende gemacht?

My study plan

I plan to work with Unit 8
○ Every day
○ Twice a week
○ Other _____

I plan to study for
○ 5–15 minutes
○ 15–30 minutes
○ 30–45+ minutes

My progress tracker

Day / Date	🎧	🎤	📖	✏️	💬
	○	○	○	○	○
	○	○	○	○	○
	○	○	○	○	○
	○	○	○	○	○
	○	○	○	○	○
	○	○	○	○	○
	○	○	○	○	○

My goals

What do you want to be able to do or say in German when you complete this unit?

Done

1 .... ○
2 .... ○
3 .... ○

My review

SELF CHECK

	I can ...
○	... talk about what I did on the weekend.
○	... describe other events in the past.
○	... say what I have already done and what I still need to do.
○	... ask for the bill and give a tip.

CULTURE POINT 1

Ein typisches Wochenende *A typical weekend*

On Sundays, most people in der Schweiz, in Österreich und Deutschland don't have to work as Geschäfte (*stores*) and Büros (*offices*) are closed. While on Saturday, many are still occupied with chores like Aufräumen (*tidying up*), Staubsaugen (*vacuuming*), or Einkaufen (*shopping*), Sunday is usually regarded as a day of relaxation.

Traditionally, people would adhere to the Sonntagsruhe (lit. *Sunday rest*), which meant keeping noise to a minimum and avoiding certain activities, such as Rasenmähen (*mowing the lawn*) or Bohren (*drilling*). Instead, many people enjoy a Sonntagsbraten (*Sunday roast*) followed by a Sonntagsspaziergang (*Sunday walk*). Traditionally, you then have Kaffee und Kuchen (*coffee and cake*) in the afternoon. Taking an Ausflug (*excursion / day trip*) is another common activity.

After 20.15 Uhr it is best not to call anyone since they are most likely to be watching Tatort (lit. *crime scene*), a crime series that has been continuously running since 1970 and is set in different cities in Österreich, Deutschland, and der Schweiz.

 Take a look at the famous painting by German painter Carl Spitzweg (1808–1885) called Sonntagsspaziergang.
Who can you see in the picture? What are they doing? What is the weather like? What can you see in the background?

VOCABULARY BUILDER 1

08.01

Look at the words and phrases and complete the missing English words and expressions. Then listen and try to imitate the pronunciation of the speakers.

TÄTIGKEITEN	ACTIVITIES
an/machen, aus/machen	to switch on, to switch ....
auf/passen	to look after
auf/räumen	to tidy up
ein/packen, aus/packen	to pack, to unpack
entfernen	to remove
putzen	to clean
staubsaugen	to vacuum

VIDEOANRUF	VIDEO CALL
an/rufen	to call / ring
an/schalten, aus/schalten	to switch on, to switch ....
auf/legen	to hang up
der Breakout Room (-s)	....
der Chat (-s)	....
die Kamera (-s)	....
das Mikrofon (-e)	....
die Verbindung (-en)	connection

NÜTZLICHE AUSDRÜCKE	USEFUL EXPRESSIONS
früh	early
spät	late
leider	unfortunately
die Süßigkeit (-en)	sweets / candy
noch einmal	(once) again / another time
Die Zauberflöte	The Magic Flute (opera by Mozart)

Vocabulary practice 1

Describe what the people are doing.

a Martha ....

....

b Carsten ....

....

c Analisa ....

....

d Tim ....

....

e Ahmad ....

....

f Corinna ....

....

Pronunciation practice

St and sp in German are pronounced as sht and shp at the beginning of a word or syllable.

08.02

1 Listen and repeat these words.

Straße	studieren	Stunde	verstehen
Sport	spielen	Spanisch	versprechen

08.03

2 Practice saying these words, then listen and repeat.

staubsaugen	sprechen	spät	Spaß
stumm	bestellen	stehen	

Ein volles Wochenende! *A busy weekend!*

08.04

1 Listen to the conversation a few times without looking at the text. Then listen again and read the text. On what day did Wally meet Udo? And Nuri?

After a few days in Vienna, Max calls Wally to find out how she is doing and what she has been up to since he left.

Max	Hallo, Wally! Ich kann dich leider nicht sehen. Hast du deine Kamera angemacht?
Wally	Hallo, Max! Entschuldigung, einen Moment bitte! So, kannst du mich jetzt sehen?
Max	Ja! Wie geht es dir? Was hast du am Wochenende gemacht?
Wally	Oh, es war sehr viel los! Am Samstagmorgen habe ich erst schön mit Udo gefrühstückt und dann habe ich eingekauft. Am Nachmittag war ich mit Nuri im Zoo. Nuri hat alle Tiere fotografiert!
Max	Wie schön!
Wally	Danach hat Fabian für uns alle gekocht. Es hat wie immer sehr gut geschmeckt. Abends war ich noch in der Premiere von Mozarts *Die Zauberflöte*. Es war fantastisch, aber ich war dann sehr müde.
Max	Oh ja, das klingt nach einem langen Tag! Und was hast du gestern, am Sonntag, gemacht?
Wally	Morgens habe ich die Wohnung geputzt. Am Nachmittag habe ich dann für ein paar Stunden im Flüchtlingsheim gearbeitet.
Max	Und abends?
Wally	Abends habe ich auf Nuri aufgepasst. Fabian und Aylin waren im Theater. Aber genug von mir. Wie gefällt dir Wien, Max? Hast du schon viel besichtigt?
Max	Ja, Wien ist sehr schön. Gestern ...
Wally	Max? Hallo, Max? Ich kann dich nicht hören. Die Verbindung ist schlecht. Ich lege auf und versuche es noch einmal.

2 Who did what on the weekend? Match the activities with the right people.

	eingekauft	fotografiert	gekocht	geputzt	gearbeitet
Wally					
Fabian					
Nuri					

LANGUAGE BUILDER 1

💡 Language discovery 1

Look at the conversation again and complete the sentences. These sentences are examples of the present perfect tense. Which verb is used in all three examples? How do they compare to the simple past forms you are already familiar with?

a Es .... sehr gut geschmeckt.

b Morgens .... ich die Wohnung geputzt.

c Was .... du am Wochenende gemacht?

Using the present perfect tense to talk about the past

German has different tenses to refer to actions in the past. You have already encountered the simple past tense (ich hatte and ich war), which is mainly used in written language. However, when *talking* about past events, you mostly use the *present perfect tense*, which is formed by using two verbs:

● a form of haben (or sein; see Language Discovery 4) in the present tense and

● the *past participle* of the main verb.

The past participle of regular verbs is formed by adding ge- in front of the stem and a -t at the end (mach-en → ge-mach-t). Haben and sein show who performed the action and take second position in the sentence, while the past participle doesn't change and appears at the end of the sentence.

spielen: ge-spiel-t > Ich habe gestern Tennis gespielt.

machen: ge-mach-t > Er hat einen IT-Kurs gemacht.

schauen: ge-schaut-t > Wir haben eine Serie geschaut.

> Note that haben, sein and the modal verbs are commonly used in the simple past even in conversation.

If the stem ends in -d, -t or -n, add an -e- before the -t ending: reden > ge-red-e-t (*talk > talked*), warten > ge-wart-e-t (*wait > waited*), öffnen > ge-öffn-e-t (*open > opened*).

Language practice 1

Complete these sentences with the correct past participle of the verb in parentheses.

a Gestern haben wir Karten .... (spielen).

b Haben Mia und Carlos schon ihre Fahrkarten .... (kaufen)?

c Mozart hat im Stephansdom .... (heiraten).

d Du hast sehr gut .... (tanzen).

e Die Fahrt hat nicht lange .... (dauern).

f Wally hat eine schöne Wohnung in Berlin .... (mieten).

LANGUAGE BUILDER 2

08.05

💡 Language discovery 2

Listen to the conversation again and repeat each line in the pauses provided. Then look at these sentences from the conversation. Underline the past participles. Do you notice any differences to the ones we looked at before?

1 Dann habe ich eingekauft.
2 Abends habe ich auf Nuri aufgepasst.
3 Hast du schon viel besichtigt?

Past participles of separable and inseparable verbs

You have already learned about separable verbs in Unit 5. When forming the past participle of separable verbs, the ge is inserted between the prefix and the stem. For regular verbs, the -en ending of the infinitive is replaced by -t.

abholen: ab-**ge**-hol-**t** (*pick up: picked up*)

aufmachen: auf-**ge**-mach-**t** (*open: opened*)

aussuchen: aus-**ge**-such-**t** (*choose: chosen*)

Note that verbs starting with inseparable prefixes be-, ent-, er-, ge-, -ver-, and zer- don't add ge-:

Prefix	Infinitive	Past participle	
be-	bestellen	bestellt	order > ordered
ent-	entschuldigen	entschuldigt	excuse > excused
er-	erklären	erklärt	explain > explained
ver-	versuchen	versucht	try > tried
zer-	zerstören	zerstört	destroy > destroyed

> Verbs whose stems end in -ieren also do not use ge- to form the past participle, e.g. fotografiert (*photographed*) in the conversation. Their past participles are otherwise formed in the normal way by changing -en to -t: telefonieren: telefoniert (*phone > phoned*); trainieren: trainiert (*train > trained*)

Language practice 2

1 **Give the correct forms of the past participle.**

    a ausmachen...............
    d studieren...............
    g aufräumen...............

    b reservieren...............
    e einkaufen...............
    h auspacken...............

    c entfernen...............
    f verkaufen...............

08.06

2 **Now play Conversation 1 again and play Wally's role. Speak in the pauses. Try not to refer to the text.**

CULTURE POINT 2

Wiener Kaffeehauskultur *Viennese coffeehouse culture*

Vienna's Kaffeehäuser (*coffee houses*) have a long tradition and are part of Viennese culture. The first Kaffeehaus was opened in 1685 by Johannes Diodato, an Armenian merchant, who was familiar with the art of brewing Kaffee. Since 2011, Kaffeehäuser have been listed as intangible cultural heritage by UNESCO. Some of the most famous ones are Café Central, Café Landtmann, Café Sperl, Café Hawelka, and Café Alt-Wien.

Through the famous Thonet Stühle (*Thonet chairs*), Marmortische (*marble tables*), Parkettboden (*parquet flooring*), and Spiegel (*mirrors*) as well as a selection of complimentary Zeitungen (*newspapers*), you will immediately feel at home here, and you can easily spend hours in a Kaffeehaus. Expect to receive excellent service from the almost exclusively male waiting staff addressed as Herr Ober (literally: *Mister Head Waiter*).

Kaffeehäuser offer a range of different coffees, including the Melange (similar to a cappuccino, but made with milder coffee) and the Einspänner (espresso with whipped cream), both of which you will rarely find outside Austria, and a range of Torten (*gateaux/cakes*). Some specialties include Apfelstrudel (*apple strudel*), Guglhupf (*a ring-shaped cake*), and Buchteln mit Powidl (*a special bun with plum jam*). You can also enjoy breakfast here, and savoury snacks such as Würstel mit Senf (*sausages with mustard*) or Wiener Schnitzel are served until late in the evening.

Learn more about coffeehouse culture in Vienna on the website of the Café Central.
Why is coffee traditionally served with a glass of water?
What does the face-down coffee spoon on top of the glass signify?
What word do the Austrians use for cream?
Where does the Wiener Schnitzel actually come from?

VOCABULARY BUILDER 2

Look at the words and phrases and complete the missing English words and expressions. Then listen and try to imitate the pronunciation of the speakers.

VERBEN	VERBS
an/bieten	to offer
auf/nehmen	to record
aus/wandern	to emigrate
beeinflussen	to influence
ein/laden	to invite
hoch/laden	to upload
kommen	to ....
komponieren	to compose
laufen, rennen	to run
nennen	to name, to call
passieren	to happen
reiten	to ride
sich verlieben	to fall in ....
skaten	to ....
wachsen, werden	to grow, to become

NÜTZLICHE WÖRTER	USEFUL WORDS
der Besitzer (-), die Besitzerin (-nen)	owner
Ich würde gerne zahlen.	I would like to pay.
Stimmt so.	Keep the change.
begeistert	enthusiastic
tatsächlich	actually, indeed
unterwegs	on the way
der Plattenvertrag (-"e)	record deal
die Sendung (-en)	TV show, broadcast

Vocabulary practice 2

Complete with the best verb of movement.

fliegen	skaten	fahren	laufen	reiten

a mit dem Fahrrad: ....

b einen Marathon: ....

c auf einem Pferd: ....

d im Skatepark: ....

e mit dem Flugzeug: ....

CONVERSATION 2

Ich habe immer schon gern gesungen *I have always liked singing*

1 Listen to the conversation a few times without looking at the text. Then listen again and read the text. What influenced Lisa's music? Who composes her music?

Having followed Lisa's musical career for a while, Max is aufgeregt (*excited*) as well as slightly nervös (*nervous*) that he finally gets to treffen (*meet*) and interviewen (*interview*) her at the Café Hawelka, one of Vienna's famous Kaffeehäuser (*coffee houses*).

Max	Schön, dass es mit dem Interview geklappt hat! Und einen Einspänner habe ich auch noch nie getrunken.
Lisa	Aber du bist hier schon im Kaffeehaus gewesen, oder?
Max	Oh ja, ich habe schon viel Kaffee getrunken und viel Torte gegessen!
Lisa	Sehr gut! Ich brauche auch einen starken Kaffee. Ich habe schlecht geschlafen und bin heute Morgen früh aufgestanden.
Max	Danke, dass du trotzdem Zeit für das Interview gefunden hast.
Lisa	Kein Problem!
Max	Erzähl mir doch einfach etwas über dich und deine Musikkarriere.
Lisa	Okay, ich habe schon immer gern gesungen. Meine Mutter ist als Studentin aus Nigeria nach Wien gekommen. Sie hat sich dann in meinen Vater verliebt und ist hiergeblieben. Meine Eltern sind beide religiös und wir sind jeden Sonntag in die Kirche gegangen. Da habe ich im Chor gesungen. Ich habe es geliebt!
Max	Und diese Erfahrung hat auch deine Musik beeinflusst.
Lisa	Genau! Später habe ich dann meine eigenen Songs komponiert. Ich habe ein paar Songs auf YouTube hochgeladen. Dann hat mich tatsächlich ein Label angerufen und mir einen Plattenvertrag angeboten. Ich habe ein Album aufgenommen.
Max	Toll! Ich habe dich auf YouTube gefunden und war sofort total begeistert. Dein Album habe ich auch gleich gekauft. Es ist wirklich toll!
Lisa	Danke! Entschuldigung, aber ich muss gleich gehen. Wir können aber unterwegs noch weitersprechen. Herr Ober, wir würden gern zahlen!
Max	Ich lade dich natürlich ein. (to the waiter) Danke, stimmt so.

2 Answer the questions.

a What type of coffee is Max drinking?

b When did Lisa get up?

c Where is Lisa's mother from?

d What did Lisa do on Sundays?

e How did the record label discover Lisa?

f Who is paying?

LANGUAGE BUILDER 3

 Language discovery 3

Look at the conversation again. Underline the past participle in each sentence. What do you notice when you compare them to those discussed before?

a Ich habe schon viel Kaffee getrunken und viel Torte gegessen.
b Ich habe schlecht geschlafen.
c Ein Label hat mich angerufen.

Irregular verbs in the perfect tense

Some verbs do not add a -t at the end of the stem to form the past participle. Instead, they add -en. They are irregular. Some of them also change the vowel of the stem. However, they usually form their past participle by adding ge- at the front, unless they have an inseparable prefix like be or ver (see Language Discovery 2). They are sometimes also referred to as *strong verbs*.

bekommen	bekommen	to receive, get	schlafen	geschlafen	to sleep
essen	gegessen	to eat	sprechen	gesprochen	to speak
finden	gefunden	to find	trinken	getrunken	to drink

> The verb essen adds an extra g in the past participle.

Was hast du zum Geburtstag bekommen?	*What did you get for your birthday?*
Sie hat schlecht geschlafen.	*She slept badly.*
Sie haben viel Deutsch gesprochen.	*They spoke a lot of German.*

Because it may be difficult to know which verbs have irregular past participles, it is best to also learn the past tense form whenever you come across a new verb. You can find a list of irregular verbs in the Grammar summary online.

Language practice 3

Match the past participle with the correct infinitive. Guess what the verbs mean.

a gewinnen   **1** gesessen
b helfen   **2** genommen
c lesen   **3** gesprochen
d nehmen   **4** verstanden
e schreiben   **5** gewonnen
f sitzen   **6** gelesen
g sprechen   **7** geschrieben
h verstehen   **8** geholfen

LANGUAGE BUILDER 4

08.09

💡 Language discovery 4

Listen to the conversation again and repeat each line in the pauses provided. Then look at these sentences from the conversation. Complete them with the missing verb in its correct form. What do you notice? Which verb is used to form the present perfect here?

a Ich .... heute Morgen früh aufgestanden.
b Meine Mutter .... als Studentin aus Nigeria nach Wien gekommen.
c Wir .... jeden Sonntag in die Kirche gegangen.

The perfect tense with **sein**

Some verbs form the perfect tense with sein. These verbs fall broadly into two categories: verbs that express movement and verbs that describe a change in state. Most of them are irregular verbs.

Verbs that express movement			Verbs that describe a change in state		
fliegen	ist geflogen	*to fly*	aufwachen	ist aufgewacht	*to wake up*
gehen	ist gegangen	*to go*	einschlafen	ist eingeschlafen	*to fall asleep*
rennen	ist gerannt	*to run*	sterben	ist gestorben	*to die*

In addition to these, some other verbs also take sein in the perfect tense:

bleiben (*to stay*): du bist geblieben   gelingen (*to succeed*): es ist gelungen

geschehen (*to happen*): es ist geschehen   passieren (*to happen*): es ist passiert

sein (*to be*): du bist gewesen   werden (*to become*): ihr seid geworden

Language practice 4

1 Complete with the appropriate form of haben or sein.

   a Du .... mit der U-Bahn gefahren.
   b Naomi .... ein Buch geschrieben.
   c Wir .... eine Reise gemacht.
   d Unsere Kinder .... um acht Uhr aufgewacht.
   e Xier .... berühmt geworden.
   f Ihr .... alle Süßigkeiten gegessen.
   g Im Winter .... ich Eis gelaufen.
   f Er .... zwei Wochen in Salzburg geblieben.

08.10

2 Now play Conversation 2 again and play Lisa's role. Speak in the pauses. Try not to refer to the text.

SKILL BUILDER

1 Lisa's day. Lisa texts her housemate Ron about her meeting with Max. Complete with the correct form of haben or sein.

Hi Ron! Ich .... eben Max, den Blogger, getroffen. Er .... mich für seinen Blog interviewt. Er .... extra nach Wien gekommen. Er kommt eigentlich aus den USA, aber seine Mutter ist Deutsche. Sie .... nach Amerika ausgewandert. Er spricht also Deutsch. Wir .... ins Café Hawelka gegangen. Er .... schon in einigen Kaffeehäusern gewesen und er .... mich eingeladen. Es war wirklich nett. Wir .... uns sehr gut verstanden. Ich will ihn morgen wieder treffen.

 2 Read the descriptions of three famous coffee houses in Vienna and answer the questions.

Café Hawelka
Das Café Hawelka liegt im 1. Bezirk, nicht weit vom Stephansplatz und dem Stephansdom entfernt.
Man kann mit der U1 oder der U3 zum Café fahren.
Es war früher eine „American Bar". 1939 haben Leopold und Josefine Hawelka das Café Hawelka aufgemacht. Hier haben sich immer viele Schriftsteller:innen getroffen. Auch heute ist das Café für viele Autor:innen wie ein zweites Zuhause. Jetzt arbeitet die dritte Generation der Familie Hawelka hier. Es hat immer noch seinen alten Charme.

Café Landtmann
Du findest das Café Landtmann am Universitätsring (1. Bezirk). Die nächste U-Bahn-Haltestelle ist „Schottentor".
Die U2 hält hier.
Das Café liegt neben dem Burgtheater und gegenüber dem Rathaus.
Hier treffen sich deshalb viele Schauspieler:innen, Politiker:innen und Journalist:innen.
Franz Landtmann hat das Kaffeehaus 1873 gegründet. Aber die Besitzer:innen haben seitdem oft gewechselt. Die heutigen Besitzer:innen haben das Café mehrmals renoviert. Jetzt gibt es sogar ein kleines Café Landtmann in Tokio.

Café Central
Das Café Central liegt zwischen den beiden anderen Kaffeehäusern in der Herrengasse, auch im 1. Bezirk. Die Station „Herrengasse" ist nur wenige Minuten zu Fuß entfernt. Hier hält die Linie U3. Das Café Central hat 1876 seine Türen geöffnet. Es war vor allem bei Intellektuellen beliebt. Man hat das Café auch die Schachhochschule genannt. Denn hier haben viele Besucher:innen Schach gespielt. Von 1982 bis 1991 hat man hier eine Diskussionssendung für das österreichische Fernsehen gefilmt. Es ist auch der Kaffeehaus-Star auf Instagram.

a Welches Café kann man mit zwei U-Bahn-Linien erreichen?

b Wo haben Gäste oft Schach gespielt?

c Welches Kaffeehaus hat zuerst aufgemacht?

d Welches Café hat immer noch die gleiche Familie als Besitzer?

e Was kann man nach dem Café Hawelka schnell besichtigen?

f Welches Kaffeehaus gibt es auch im Ausland?

g Welches Café hat man früher im Fernsehen gesehen?

h Welches Kaffeehaus ist auf den sozialen Medien beliebt?

08.11

3 **So much to do! Max leaves a voicemail for Wally to tell her about his day and his plans for tomorrow. What has he already done? And what does he still have to do? Listen to the audio and make a list of the things he has done and those he still needs to do.**

Max hat/ist schon:	Max muss noch:
Lisa interviewt	einen Blog schreiben

4 **Talk about what you did yesterday/last weekend/on vacation. Here are some questions, but you can add other events in the past if you like.**

a Was hast du heute Morgen gemacht?

b Was hast du gestern gemacht?

c Was hast du am Nachmittag und am Abend getan?

d Was hast du am Samstagmorgen gemacht? Und am Sonntag?

e Was hast du im Urlaub gemacht?

f Was ist letztes Jahr passiert?

Transform these sentences into the present perfect tense.

Example: Ich stehe um acht Uhr auf. > *Ich bin um acht Uhr aufgestanden.*

a Zum Frühstück trinke ich Tee und esse ein Croissant. ....

b Ich fahre mit der U-Bahn zur Arbeit. ....

c Ich arbeite bis 17 Uhr. ....

d Ich treffe eine Freundin. ....

e Wir gehen ins Fitnesscenter. ....

f Zuhause mache ich einen Salat. ....

g Ich rufe meine Schwester an. ....

h Ich schaue eine Serie und die Nachrichten an. ....

i Um 23 gehe ich ins Bett. ....

j Ich lese noch ein bisschen und schlafe dann. ....

?

Wie geht's weiter? *What happens next?*

Max and Lisa got on really well together and they are seeing each other again tomorrow. What do you think they are going to do? Will Lisa show him her favorite parts of Vienna? Will she take him to a concert? Find out in Unit 9.

Remember to use **My review** and **My takeaway** to assess your progress and reflect on your learning experience.

In this lesson you will learn how to:

» Talk about different types of housing
» Name and describe rooms
» Describe the area you live in
» Make comparisons

9

Wohnen

My study plan

I plan to work with Unit 9

○ Every day
○ Twice a week
○ Other _____
I plan to study for
○ 5–15 minutes
○ 15–30 minutes
○ 30–45+ minutes

My progress tracker

Day / Date	🎧	🎤	📖	✏️	💬
	○	○	○	○	○
	○	○	○	○	○
	○	○	○	○	○
	○	○	○	○	○
	○	○	○	○	○
	○	○	○	○	○
	○	○	○	○	○

My goals

What do you want to be able to do or say in German when you complete this unit?

Done

1 .... ○

2 .... ○

3 .... ○

My review

SELF CHECK

	I can ...
○	... talk about different types of housing.
○	... name and describe rooms.
○	... describe the area I live in.
○	... make comparisons.

CULTURE POINT 1

Mieten oder Kaufen? *Buying or renting?*

Deutschland und Österreich are the two countries with the highest number of Mieter:innen (*renters*) in the European Union. More than half of the population in Deutschland wohnt zur Miete (*rents*); in Österreich, it is just under 50%. Your Miete depends on where you live. There is not enough affordable housing and, as a consequence, Mieten (*rents*) have been rising in recent years, especially in bigger cities.

The Kaltmiete (literally: *cold rent*), that is, rent without bills as opposed to the Warmmiete, which includes gas and electricity, starts from 7.50 Euros per Quadratmeter (*square meter*) in smaller cities but is much higher in big cities.

One of the reasons why many people still choose to rent is that Mieter:innen have a lot more legal protection than in many other countries. If there are any Mängel (*faults*) in your apartment, they need to be rectified by the Vermieter:in (*landlord*). Your Kaution (*deposit*) is normally held securely. The Kündigungsfrist (*notice period*) is at least three months, and this increases the longer you stay in your apartment. Some Germans stay in their rented apartment for decades.

When people in German-speaking countries talk about the number of rooms they have, they won't refer to Schlafzimmer (*bedrooms*) only but will say something like: Wir haben drei Zimmer, Küche und Bad. The size of an apartment or house is measured in Quadradmeter (*square meters*): Meine Wohnung hat 88 m².

Check out the website and find out where are the most expensive cities in Germany to rent.
Which city is the most expensive of all? Do you know where all the cities are? Look them up on a map. Can you work out any patterns? What is the situation like in your country? Do people usually rent or buy? What is the average rent? How does this compare to rents in Germany?

Look at the words and phrases and complete the missing English words and expressions. Then listen and try to imitate the pronunciation of the speakers.

WOHNUNGEN UND HÄUSER	APARTMENTS AND HOUSES
der Bungalow (-s)	....
das Einfamilienhaus (-"er)	*detached (family) house*
das Doppelhaus (-"er)	*semi-detached house*
das Hochhaus (-"er)	*tower block / skyscraper*
das Reihenhaus (-"er)	*row / terraced house*
das Studentenwohnheim (-e)	*student residence*
die Wohngemeinschaft (-en) / die WG (-s)	*apartment / house-share*
die Wohnung (-en)	*apartment*
die Hypothek (-en) / die Miete (-n)	*mortgage / rent*
die Nebenkosten (pl. only)	*utility bills*
die Stromrechnung (-en)	*electricity bill*

ZIMMER	ROOMS
das Arbeitszimmer (-)	*study*
das Badezimmer (-) / das Bad (-"er)	*bathroom*
der Balkon (-e/-s)	....
das Esszimmer (-)	*dining room*
der Flur (-e)	*corridor, hall*
der Keller (-)	*cellar / basement*
das Kinderzimmer (-)	*children's room*
die Küche (-n)	....
das Schlafzimmer (-)	*bedroom*
das Wohnzimmer (-)	*living room*
dunkel, hell	*dark, light*
gemütlich, ruhig	*cozy, quiet*

NÜTZLICHE AUSDRÜCKE	USEFUL EXPRESSIONS
teilen	*to share*
um die Ecke	*around the corner*
jeder	*everyone*
der Mitbewohner (-), die Mitbewohnerin (-nen)	*housemate*
Wir wohnen zu dritt.	*There are three of us living here.*
Ich fühle mich zu Hause.	*I feel at home.*

Vocabulary practice 1

1 Match the rooms with the descriptions.

> | Kinderzimmer | Badezimmer | Balkon | Esszimmer |
> | Wohnzimmer | Schlafzimmer | Arbeitszimmer | Küche |

a ....: dort schläft man.

b ....: ein Zimmer für Kinder.

c ....: dort kocht man, kann man essen, etc.

d ....: dort kann man sich waschen, duschen,

e ....: dort wohnt man, liest, sieht fern, etc.

f ....: dort kann man im Sommer sitzen.

g ....: dort kann man lernen, studieren, am Computer arbeiten, etc.

h ....: dort kann man essen.

2 Write out your answers and then say them out loud.

a Wo wohnen Sie? In einem Haus / einer Wohnung / einer WG?

b Wie viele Zimmer hat Ihr Haus / Ihre Wohnung?

> After Ich wohne in … , remember
> to use the dative forms:
>
> in einem Bungalow (m)
>
> in einem Haus (nt)
>
> in einer Wohnung (f)

Pronunciation practice

09.02

1 Listen and repeat to practice your pronunciation.

At the end of a word the letter g in German is pronounced like an English *k*:

genug　　Tag　　Ausflug　　mag

When g is not at the end of the word or syllable, it is pronounced more like a hard English *g*:

gern　　gut　　Ausflüge　　mögen

2 Practice saying these words, then listen and repeat.

09.03　　Tage　gemütlich　sagen　sag　Bungalow　Wohngemeinschaft

CONVERSATION 1

Lisas Wohnung *Lisa's apartment*

09.04

1 Listen to the conversation a few times without looking at the text. Then listen again and read the text. What are Lisa's housemates doing? Does she like the area where she lives?

> Lisa wants to show Max how she lives and has invited him for Brunch. They are sitting in the kitchen after she has shown him the apartment.

Max	Ihr habt eine wirklich große und schöne Wohnung.
Lisa	Ja, wir wohnen zu dritt. Jeder hat ein Zimmer. Dann haben wir noch ein gemütliches Wohnzimmer, ein Badezimmer und eine Küche. Und dann haben wir auch noch einen kleinen Balkon.
Max	Und was machen deine Mitbewohner?
Lisa	Marion studiert. Sie macht einen Master in Statistik. Ron ist auch Musiker.
Max	Aber die Wohnung ist doch bestimmt nicht billig. Wie hoch ist die Miete?
Lisa	Wir teilen die Nebenkosten und die Miete. Ich zahle 550 Euro pro Monat, plus Nebenkosten, also Strom, Wasser, etc.
Max	Das ist wirklich nicht teuer. Und die Lage ist doch auch ziemlich gut, oder?
Lisa	Ja, bis zum Supermarkt sind es zehn Minuten. Die Bushaltestelle ist gleich um die Ecke und zur U-Bahn gehe ich acht Minuten.
Max	Also lebst du gerne hier in deinem Stadtteil?
Lisa	Ja, hier im zweiten Bezirk fühle ich mich zu Hause. Hier kann man gut einkaufen, gut ausgehen und die Leute sind sehr freundlich. Und vor allem – der Prater ist nicht so weit. Das ist mein Lieblingsort in Wien. Hier kann ich wunderbar skaten. Und du? Hast du einen Lieblingsort in Berlin?
Max	Mmh, ich denke, den Tiergarten. Ich mag Parks in der Stadt.
Lisa	Super. Wir geben bald ein Konzert in Berlin. Da kannst du mir dann den Tiergarten zeigen.

2 Decide if these statements are *true* (richtig) or *false* (falsch).

  a Die Wohnung von Lisa hat drei Zimmer, ein Badezimmer und eine Küche.   R   F

  b Lisa wohnt mit zwei anderen Personen zusammen.   R   F

  c Die Miete ist 550 Euro pro Monat, inklusive Nebenkosten.   R   F

  d Bis zur Bushaltestelle ist es ziemlich weit.   R   F

  e Lisas Lieblingsort in Wien ist der Prater.   R   F

  f Lisa spielt bald mit ihrer Band in Berlin.   R   F

Language discovery 1

Here are three sentences from Conversation 1. Work out the meaning of the highlighted words: sehr, ziemlich, wirklich.

a Die Leute sind sehr freundlich.
b Und die Lage ist doch auch ziemlich gut, oder?
c Ihr habt eine wirklich große und schöne Wohnung.

Nuancing your language: using **sehr, ziemlich, wirklich, etc.**

If you want to modify your language, you can use words like sehr (*very*), ziemlich (*fairly*), or wirklich (*really*). These words are adverbs, and they can emphasize or soften the meaning of the adjective or adverb that follows. Here are some commonly used ones:

absolut	*absolutely*	ganz	*quite*	völlig	*completely*
besonders	*particularly*	kaum	*hardly*	ziemlich	*fairly*
bestimmt	*certainly*	total	*totally*	zu	*too*
etwa	*about*	ungefähr	*approximately*		

Du hast absolut recht.	*You are absolutely right.*
Die Serie war wirklich gut.	*The series was really good.*
Das ist viel zu teuer.	*That's much too expensive.*

Language practice 1

Choose the correct answer.

a Frau Akalay wohnt in der Nähe vom Hauptbahnhof.
  1 Sie wohnt nicht zentral.
  2 Sie wohnt nicht so zentral.
  3 Sie wohnt ziemlich zentral.

b Bis zur U-Bahnstation sind es 450 Meter.
  1 Das ist nicht so weit.
  2 Das ist sehr weit.
  3 Das ist relativ weit.

c Eine Vierzimmerwohnung in Salzburg kostet 600 Euro Miete im Monat.
  1 Das ist total teuer für Salzburg.
  2 Das ist relativ billig für Salzburg.
  3 Das ist nicht sehr billig.

d Das Haus hat 15 Zimmer, einen Swimmingpool und einen Golfplatz.
  1 Das Haus ist relativ groß.
  2 Das Haus ist ziemlich klein.
  3 Das Haus ist total groß.

09.05

💡 Language discovery 2

Listen to the conversation again and repeat each line in the pauses provided. Then complete the missing adjective endings. How and why are they different?

a Wir haben einen klein .... Balkon.

b Ihr habt eine schön .... und groß .... Wohnung.

c Wir haben ein gemütlich .... Wohnzimmer.

Adjectives and endings (1)

In German, if an adjective comes after the noun it is describing—often following sein (*to be*)—it does not take an ending: Die Wohnung ist groß. *The apartment is big.*

However, when the adjective appears before a noun, you need to add an ending. The endings for adjectives after the indefinite article in the accusative are:

masc. -en   Das Haus hat einen schönen Garten.

fem. -e   Die Wohnung hat eine gemütliche Küche.

neut. -es   Sie haben ein schönes Wohnzimmer.

plural -e   Die Wohnung hat helle und ruhige Zimmer.

Possessives (mein, dein, etc.) and the negative kein follow the same pattern in the singular. Notice the different endings in the plural:

masc. -en   Hast du seinen schönen Garten gesehen?

fem. -e   Kennst du ihre neue Wohnung?

neut. -es   Ich zeig dir mein neues Haus.

plural -en   Die Wohnung hat keine neuen Fenster.

> If a noun is modified by more than one adjective, they all take the same endings: Sie haben eine schöne, große und helle Wohnung.

Language practice

1 These people are describing their homes. Complete the missing endings.

a Wir haben endlich eine neu .... Wohnung gefunden. Jetzt haben wir ein gemütlich .... Wohnzimmer, ein groß .... Kinderzimmer, ein sehr ruhig .... Schlafzimmer, ein nett .... Badezimmer und eine hell .... Küche.

b Wir haben ein schön .... Einfamilienhaus gekauft – die Hypothek ist nicht so hoch. Wir haben einen groß .... Garten und eine modern .... Solaranlage. Um die Ecke gibt es einen gut .... Supermarkt und auch ein nett .... italienisch .... Restaurant.

c Ich bin in eine neu .... WG gezogen. Die WG liegt zentral. Es gibt viel .... Geschäfte und interessant .... Clubs in der Nähe. Wir haben auch einen klein .... Balkon.

2 Now play Conversation 1 again and play Lisa's role. Speak in the pauses. Try not to refer to the text.

09.06

Das Hundertwasserhaus in Wien *The Hundertwasserhaus in Vienna*

The Hundertwasserhaus is an iconic Wohnhaus (*apartment building*) which was opened in 1986 and is owned by the city of Wien. It offers 50 Wohnungen of social housing. Mieten are lower here than on average and Mieter:innen have also access to communal spaces, two playrooms for children and a conservatory. Apart from the restaurants and cafés it houses, the Haus is not open to the public.

The Hundertwasserhaus was designed by Austrian Künstler (*artist*) Friedensreich Hundertwasser. He initially started as a Maler (*painter*) but later shifted his focus to Architektur (*architecture*). In 1977, Wiens Bürgermeister (*Vienna's Mayor*) invited Hundertwasser to create a Wohnhaus following his own creative direction, and Architekt (*architect*) Josef Krawina joined him to bring his vision to life.

Hundertwasser challenged traditional norms in his design which includes undulating floors that defy conventional straight lines, a grass-covered Dachterasse (*rooftop terrace*), 'tree tenants' (actual trees growing from inside the rooms), and a colorful facade.

 Find out more about Hundertwasser and his work in the Museum Hundertwasser in the Kunst Haus Wien.
Who founded the museum? What types of art can be seen here? Do you like the artist's style?

VOCABULARY BUILDER 2

09.07

Look at the words and phrases and complete the missing English words and expressions. Then listen and try to imitate the pronunciation of the speakers.

UNTERKÜNFTE	ACCOMMODATIONS
der Aufenthalt (-e)	*stay*
der Bauernhof (-"e)	*farm*
das Ferienhaus (-"er)	*vacation house*
die Ferienwohnung (-en)	*vacation* ....
das Hostel (-s), das Hotel (-s)	........................, ...
das Einzelzimmer (-), das Doppelzimmer (-)	*single room,* .... *room*
das Mehrbettzimmer (-)	*dorm room, multi-bed room*
belegt, frei	*occupied,* ....
buchen	*to* ....
komfortabel	*comfortable*

AUSSTATTUNG	FACILITIES
der Fernseher (-)	*TV*
der Herd (-e)	*stove / cooker*
das Hochbett (-en)	*loft bed*
die Klimaanlage (-n)	*air-conditioning*
die Kochnische (-n)	*kitchenette*
der Kühlschrank (-"e)	*refrigerator*
der Schreibtisch (-e)	*desk*
der Trockner (-)	*tumble dryer*
die Waschmaschine (-n)	....
der Wasserkocher (-)	*kettle*
der Wintergarten (¨)	....
das WLAN (-s)	*Wi-Fi*

NÜTZLICHE AUSDRÜCKE	USEFUL EXPRESSIONS
einmal	*first(ly);* also: *once*
sogar	*even*
bewerten	*to rate, to assess*
um Rat fragen	*to ask for advice*
Dir wird es bestimmt gefallen.	*You'll definitely like it.*
Das macht Sinn.	*This makes sense.*

Vocabulary practice 2

 Read the description of this hotel in Basel.

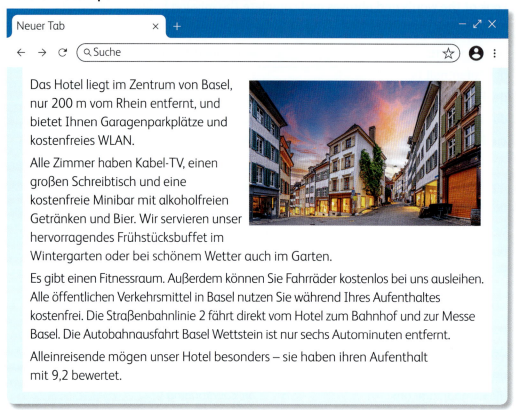

Das Hotel liegt im Zentrum von Basel, nur 200 m vom Rhein entfernt, und bietet Ihnen Garagenparkplätze und kostenfreies WLAN.

Alle Zimmer haben Kabel-TV, einen großen Schreibtisch und eine kostenfreie Minibar mit alkoholfreien Getränken und Bier. Wir servieren unser hervorragendes Frühstücksbuffet im Wintergarten oder bei schönem Wetter auch im Garten.

Es gibt einen Fitnessraum. Außerdem können Sie Fahrräder kostenlos bei uns ausleihen. Alle öffentlichen Verkehrsmittel in Basel nutzen Sie während Ihres Aufenthaltes kostenfrei. Die Straßenbahnlinie 2 fährt direkt vom Hotel zum Bahnhof und zur Messe Basel. Die Autobahnausfahrt Basel Wettstein ist nur sechs Autominuten entfernt.

Alleinreisende mögen unser Hotel besonders – sie haben ihren Aufenthalt mit 9,2 bewertet.

a Mark the facilities mentioned.

On-site parking

Minibar

Pets allowed

Good breakfast

Family rooms

Free bike rental

Free Wi-Fi

Air-conditioning

Fitness facilities

Good links to public transportation

b What information is given about public transportation?

c Why are solo travelers mentioned?

Welche Unterkunft ist am besten? *Which accommodation is the best?*

09.08

1 Listen to the conversation a few times without looking at the text. Then listen again and read the text. What are the three options Max has? Which accommodation does he take?

> After Vienna, Max wants to travel to Switzerland to see Basel and the world-famous Fasnacht (*Carnival*). He discusses accommodation options with Felix, a fellow blogger, from Basel.

Felix	Schön, dass du zur Fasnacht nach Basel kommst. Hast du denn schon eine Unterkunft gebucht?
Max	Ich schaue gerade und wollte dich um Rat fragen.
Felix	Klar. Was gibt es denn?
Max	Ich habe drei Optionen. Da ist einmal ein Hostel und dann ein günstiges Hotel. Das Hostel ist natürlich billiger, aber leider gibt es keine Einzelzimmer mehr. Aber es liegt zentraler als das Hotel.
Felix	Mmh, ein Mehrbettzimmer. Das ist vielleicht nicht so ideal. Was ist denn mit dem Budget Hotel?
Max	Das Hotel ist etwas teurer, aber bestimmt komfortabler. Bis in die Stadtmitte sind es 1,2 km.
Felix	Und die dritte Option?
Max	Ah, das ist ein Tiny House.
Felix	Ein Tiny House? Das klingt interessant.
Max	Ja, es sieht sehr gemütlich aus, mit Herd, WLAN, Hochbett und man kann sogar den Swimming-Pool im Garten benutzen.
Felix	Ja, aber in der Karnevalszeit im Februar ist es vielleicht ein bisschen zu kalt!
Max	(lacht) Da hast du recht. Und es ist auch am teuersten und liegt am weitesten vom Zentrum entfernt.
Felix	Dann nimm doch am besten das Budget Hotel.
Max	Gut, danke, Felix, das macht Sinn. Dann buche ich das jetzt gleich.

2 Answer the questions.

  a Has Max booked his accommodation?

  b What is the problem with the hostel?

  c How far is it from the hotel to the city center?

  d Where do guests sleep in the tiny house?

  e What can you use in the garden?

  f What is Max going to do now?

LANGUAGE BUILDER 3

 Language discovery 3

Complete these three sentences from Conversation 2. What ending do you use when you form the comparative in German?

a Das Hostel ist natürlich billig ....

b Es liegt zentral .... als das Hotel.

c Das Hotel ist etwas teur .... , aber bestimmt komfortabl ....

Making comparisons

When making comparisons, both with adverbs and adjectives, -er is normally added to the basic form. This corresponds to the English pattern *smaller, cheaper, nicer, bigger*, but in German it also works with longer adjectives:

klein > kleiner	*small > smaller*
billig > billiger	*cheap > cheap*
interessant > interessanter	*interesting > more interesting*
langweilig > langweiliger	*boring > more boring*

Most adjectives and adverbs of one syllable and containing a, o, or u add an umlaut:

alt > älter	*old > older*	groß > größer	*big > bigger*
jung > jünger	*young > younger*	kalt > kälter	*cold > colder*
lang > länger	*long > longer*	warm > wärmer	*warm > warmer*

There are also a few irregular forms and some spelling variations:

Irregular forms		**Spelling variations**	
gut > besser	*good > better*	hoch > höher	*high > higher*
viel > mehr	*a lot > more*	dunkel > dunkler	*dark > darker*
gern > lieber	*like doing it > prefer doing it*	komfortabel > komfortabler	*comfortable > more comfortable*
		teuer > teurer	*expensive > more expensive*

Remember that the German equivalent of *than* is als.

Berlin ist größer als München.	*Berlin is bigger than Munich.*
Heute ist es kälter als gestern.	*It's colder today than yesterday.*

> If a comparative form appears before a noun, it takes the same endings as any other adjective:
>
> Ich habe einen jüngeren Bruder. Sie haben ein besseres Hotel gebucht.

Language practice 3

Put the adjectives in parentheses in the appropriate comparative form.

Example: Lena ist .... als Maike. (jung) > *Lena ist jünger als Maike.*

a Ist der Rhein wirklich .... als die Donau? (lang)

b Mit dem Zug ist es .... als mit dem Flugzeug. (billig)

c Ich finde das Buch .... als den Film. (interessant)

d Das andere Hotel war viel .... (teuer)

e Auf dem Land ist es ...., aber auch .... als in der Stadt. (ruhig, langweilig)

f Es ist viel .... als letztes Jahr. (warm)

g Ich finde die Leute in München .... als in Berlin. (freundlich)

LANGUAGE BUILDER 4

09.09

💡 Language discovery 4

Listen to the conversation again and repeat each line in the pauses provided. When you form the superlative in German you normally add -sten to the adjective. Which other word do you use? Look at the conversation again and complete the sentences.

a Und es ist auch .... teuer**sten** und liegt .... weite**sten** vom Zentrum entfernt.

b Dann nimm doch .... be**sten** das Budget Hotel.

The superlative

The superlative is formed by adding -sten to the adjective or adverb. In addition, it is preceded by the word am:

klein > am kleinsten	*(the) smallest*
schnell > am schnellsten	*(the) fastest*
langweilig > am langweiligsten	*(the) most boring*
freundlich > am freundlichsten	*(the) most friendly*

As in the comparative, most monosyllabic adjectives with a, o, or u take an umlaut, including:

jung > am jüngsten	*(the) youngest*	stark > am stärksten	*(the) strongest*
lang > am längsten	*(the) longest*	warm > am wärmsten	*(the) warmest*

There are also a few irregular forms and spelling variations:

Irregular forms	Adjectives ending in -d, -t, -s, -z take an extra -e	Other variations
gut > am besten *(the) best* viel > am meisten *(the) most* gern > am liebsten *(the) best of all*	alt > am ältesten *(the) oldest* kurz > am kürzesten *(the shortest)* interessant > am interessantesten *(the) most interesting*	nah > am nächsten *(the) closest* groß > am größten *(the) biggest, tallest*

Language practice 4

1 Make comparisons using the prompts.

Example: Im Frühling ist es warm. > im Herbst / im Sommer

Im Herbst ist es wärmer als im Frühling. Im Sommer ist am wärmsten.

a München ist groß. > Hamburg / Berlin
b Ich finde Ria nett. > Hanna / Xia
c Die Donau ist lang. > die Elbe / der Rhein
d Mit dem Bus ist es schnell. > mit der Vespa / mit der U-Bahn
e Salat schmeckt gut. > Pasta / Pizza
f Portugiesisch ist kompliziert. > Ungarisch / Chinesisch
g Das 2-Sterne-Hotel ist komfortabel. > das 3-Sterne-Hotel / das Luxus-Hotel
h Das Hardcover kostet wenig. > das Taschenbuch / das E-Book

2 Now play Conversation 2 again and play Max's role. Speak in the pauses. Try not to refer to the text.

09.10

SKILL BUILDER

1 Complete the table with the missing forms of the adjectives and adverbs.

Adjective	Comparative	Superlative
klein	kleiner	am kleinsten
	langweiliger	
alt		
zentral		
groß		
	besser	
viel		
gern		

136

2 Find the odd one out.

a Reihenhaus	Doppelhaus	Hypothek	Einfamilienhaus
b Keller	Küche	Wohnzimmer	Schlafzimmer
c Miete	Nebenkosten	Hypothek	Wohngemeinschaft
d Aufenthalt	Hostel	Hotel	Ferienwohnung
e Kühlschrank	Hochbett	Waschmaschine	Wasserkocher
f zentral	günstig	billig	teuer

3 Put the words in the correct order.

Example: liegt / Die Wohnung / zentral / ziemlich > *Die Wohnung liegt ziemlich zentral.*

a wirklich / ist / Unser Stadtteil / nett

b Der lokale Park / besonders / ist / schön

c hier / gut / Man kann / einkaufen / relativ

d gehe / Ich / ungefähr / bis zur U-Bahnstation / 15 Minuten

e Da / absolut / du / hast / recht

09.11

4 Listen to these sentences and complete the adjective ending you hear.

a Das Kaufhaus hat ein interessant.......... Design.

b Habt ihr eine gut.......... Reise gehabt?

c Ich habe ein neu.......... Auto gekauft.

d Ich möchte einen stark.......... Kaffee, bitte.

e Tim besucht seine jünger.......... Schwester.

f Ich brauche einen schneller.......... Computer.

g Er hat nett.......... Freunde.

h Ich wünsche dir ein schön.......... Wochenende.

5 Your Austrian friend Karolina would like to know how you live and what you think about your area. Use the questions below as a guide and record a response.

a Wo wohnst du? (in einem Haus, in einer Wohnung, etc.)

b Wie viele Zimmer hat deine Wohnung / dein Haus?

c Wie sind deine Zimmer? (groß, klein, hell, ruhig, etc.)

d Hast du auch einen Garten? Wenn ja, ist dein Garten groß?

e Wie heißt dein Stadtteil und liegt er relativ zentral?

f Wie sind die Verkehrsverbindungen?

g Kann man dort gut einkaufen und ausgehen?

Translate these sentences into German.

a I have a small apartment in the center of Vienna.
b They have a big kitchen.
c We share the rent.
d The supermarket is around the corner.
e I need a new fridge and a new desk.
f What is your favorite place? (Use du.)
g I'd like a single room, please.
h Have you booked the accommodation? (Use du.)
i The hostel is much cheaper than the hotel.
j He finds the people in Berlin more friendly than in Vienna.

Wie geht's weiter? *What happens next?*

Now that the accommodation issue is solved, Max is ready to leave Vienna and look for new adventures. What is special about the Fasnacht in Basel? How does it differ from the ones in Germany, like in Köln (*Cologne*) or Düsseldorf (*Dusseldorf*)? Find out more in the next unit.

Remember to use **My review** and **My takeaway** to assess your progress and reflect on your learning experience.

In this lesson you will learn how to:

» Describe items of personal appearance
» Say what clothes you like wearing
» Express an opinion on fashion
» Say where you buy your clothes

Ist Mode wichtig?

My study plan

I plan to work with Unit 10

○ Every day
○ Twice a week
○ Other _____

I plan to study for

○ 5–15 minutes
○ 15–30 minutes
○ 30–45+ minutes

My progress tracker

Day / Date	🎧	🎤	📖	✏️	💬
	○	○	○	○	○
	○	○	○	○	○
	○	○	○	○	○
	○	○	○	○	○
	○	○	○	○	○
	○	○	○	○	○
	○	○	○	○	○
	○	○	○	○	○

My goals

What do you want to be able to do or say in German when you complete this unit?

Done

1 .... ○
2 .... ○
3 .... ○

My review

SELF CHECK

	I can ...
○	... describe items of personal appearance.
○	... say what clothes I like wearing.
○	... express an opinion on fashion.
○	... say where I buy my clothes.

CULTURE POINT 1

Die Schweiz *Switzerland*

Among the main German-speaking countries, die Schweiz (*Switzerland*) is the smallest, with about 8.7 million inhabitants. It is also a multilingual country with four national languages: Deutsch (*German*), Französisch (*French*), Italienisch (*Italian*) and Rätoromanisch (*Romansh*), a Romance language. German is the most widely used language, spoken by about 63 percent of the population, followed by French (23 percent) and Italian (8 percent). Romansh is spoken only by 0.5 percent in the southeastern part of the country.

The German dialect spoken in Switzerland is called Schwyzerdütsch or Schwizerdütsch (*Swiss German*) and is quite different from Standarddeutsch (*Standard German*). There are also a number of grammatical lexical, and spelling differences, including the use of ss instead of ß.

Switzerland is well known for its banking sector, and its chemical and pharmaceutical industry. Tourism also plays an important role in the economy, and the Karneval (*Carnival*) in Basel, also called Fasnacht, is one of the many tourist attractions Switzerland has to offer. Since 2017, Fasnacht has been included in UNESCO's list of intangible cultural heritage.

 Find out more about the Basler Fasnacht.
When does the Carnival in Basel take place? What happens at the 'Morgenstraich'? Are 'Schnitzelbanks' something to eat? How old is the Fasnacht? When was it first mentioned?

VOCABULARY BUILDER 1

Look at the words and phrases and complete the missing English words and expressions. Then listen and try to imitate the pronunciation of the speakers.

MODE UND KLEIDUNG	FASHION AND CLOTHES
das Hemd (-en), die Bluse (-n)	shirt, blouse
die Hose (-n), der Gürtel (-)	pants, belt
der Rock (-"e)	skirt
die Jeans (singular only)	jeans
das Kleid (-er)	dress
der Anzug (-"e), die Krawatte (-n)	suit, tie
die Jacke (-n), der Mantel (¨)	jacket, coat
das Kopftuch (-"er), die Mütze (-n)	headscarf, cap
die Socke (-n), die Strumpfhose (-n)	sock, tights
der Schuh (-)	....
der Pullover (-) / der Pulli (-s)	pullover
das T-Shirt (-s)	T-shirt
der Turnschuh (-e)	sneakers / trainers

> While in English, pants, trousers, tights, and jeans are used in the plural only, in German they are used in the singular when referring to one pair: Ich brauche eine neue Hose. Ist das deine Jeans?

FARBEN	COLORS
blau, gelb, grün	blue, yellow, ...
rot, lila, rosa	...................., purple, pink
schwarz, weiß, grau	black, white, ...
hellblau, hellrosa, hellgrau	light blue, light ...., light gray
dunkelrot, dunkelgrün, dunkelblau	.... red, dark green, dark ....

ADJEKTIVE	ADJECTIVES
bequem	comfortable
bunt	colorful
modisch	fashionable

NÜTZLICHE AUSDRÜCKE	USEFUL EXPRESSIONS
tragen, an/haben	to wear
passen	to fit
Es sieht gut aus.	It looks good.
Da habe ich Glück gehabt.	I was lucky.

Vocabulary practice 1

1 **Look at the description of these four people and decide if these statements are true (richtig) or false (falsch).**

a

Frau Meinhardt

c

Jennifer

b

Herr Hoeder

d

Herr Finn

a	Frau Meinhardt trägt eine graue Hose. Außerdem hat sie eine Bluse an.	R	F
b	Herr Hoeder hat einen Pullover an. Dazu trägt er eine schwarze Hose.	R	F
c	Jennifer trägt eine Jeans und ein graues T-Shirt.	R	F
d	Herr Finn hat einen Anzug an. Er trägt auch eine rote Krawatte.	R	F

2 **Use the examples above as a model and describe what you are wearing today. For more practice, describe a few people you know.**

Heute trage ich ...

Do you remember the adjective endings in the accusative case covered in the previous unit? This is how they work if you apply them to wearing clothes:

Sie trägt einen blauen Rock. (m)   Das Mädchen trägt eine blaue Mütze. (f)

Alex trägt ein dunkelgrünes T-Shirt. (n)   Leonie trägt weiße Turnschuhe. (pl.)

CONVERSATION 1

Was trägst du gerne? *What do you like to wear?*

10.02

1 Listen to the conversation a few times without looking at the text. Then listen again and read the text. How is Fasnacht in Basel different from the Karneval in Cologne?

> After Max has checked in to his hotel, he meets Felix, a lifestyle blogger from Basel. They talk about fashion and the upcoming Fasnacht.
>
> **Max**   Felix, du bloggst ja über Lifestyle-Themen wie Wellness, Design und Mode. Ist Mode sehr wichtig für dich?
>
> **Felix**   Ja, auf jeden Fall! Ich möchte gut aussehen. Ich fühle mich besser, wenn ich schöne Sachen trage.
>
> **Max**   Was trägst du denn gerne?
>
> **Felix**   Ich trage gern elegante, aber auch bequeme Kleidung, zum Beispiel ein blaues Hemd mit einer weißen Hose und leichten, braunen Schuhen.
>
> **Max**   Und trägst du auch manchmal einen Anzug?
>
> **Felix**   Ja, zum Beispiel bei einem offiziellen Termin. Oft trage ich meinen grauen Slim Fit Anzug mit einem roten Hemd oder einem schwarzen Pullover. Ich trage eigentlich ganz gern Anzüge. Und du, Max? Was trägst du gern?
>
> **Max**   Ich ziehe gern etwas Bequemes an, zum Beispiel eine Jeans mit einem T-Shirt, einem Pulli oder einem schwarzen Hoodie. Aber wenn ich ehrlich bin – Mode ist mir nicht wichtig.
>
> **Felix**   Und hast du eine Lieblingsfarbe?
>
> **Max**   Ja, meine Lieblingsfarbe ist schwarz. Aber zur Fasnacht will ich etwas Anderes, etwas Buntes anziehen. Ich habe eine Perücke und ein Clownskostüm gekauft.
>
> **Felix**   Eine Perücke und ein buntes Clownskostüm? Da siehst du bestimmt super aus, Max. Aber dann bist du morgen der einzige Clown! In Basel verkleiden sich die Zuschauer nicht.
>
> **Max**   Was? Oh, das ist nicht wie beim Karneval in Köln. Puh ... Da habe ich noch einmal Glück gehabt.

2 Identify who this applies to, Max (M), Felix (F), or both (M + F).

a Mode ist wichtig. ....

b Trägt gern bequeme Sachen. ....

c Mag Pullover. ....

d Schwarz ist die Lieblingsfarbe. ....

e Trägt gerne Anzüge. ....

> The Basler Fasnacht (*Basel Carnival*) usually takes place in February or March. It would, therefore, be good to wear Winterkleidung (*winter clothes*), such as Handschuhe (*gloves*), einen Schal (*scarf*), Stiefel (*boots*), and einen Hut (*hat*).

LANGUAGE BUILDER 1

 Language discovery 1

Look at the conversation again and find the missing words. Identify the meaning of the sentences.

a Ich ziehe gern .... Bequemes an.

b Aber zur Fasnacht will ich .... Anderes, ... Buntes anziehen.

Something special and nothing special

If you want to say *something comfortable*, *something good*, *something new*, etc., use etwas + adjective + -es:

bequem + -es	Er trägt gern etwas Bequemes.	*He likes wearing something comfortable.*
gut + -es	Kauf etwas Gutes.	*Buy something good.*
neu + -es	Das ist etwas Neues.	*That's something new.*

If an adjective ends in -s, you only need to insert an e: anders – etwas Anderes (*something different*), besonders – etwas Besonderes (*something special*).

The same pattern applies to nichts (*nothing/anything*).

neu + -es	Das ist nichts Neues.	*That's nothing new.*
besonders + e	Das ist nichts Besonderes.	*That's nothing special.*

Notice that you need a capital letter for the words after etwas and nichts.

Language practice 1

Use the adjectives in parentheses to express something/nothing interesting, new, etc.

Example: Hast du etwas Neues gekauft? (neu)

a Ich trage gern etwas .... (modisch)

b Max zieht oft etwas .... an. (schwarz)

c Nele trägt gern etwas .... (sportlich)

d Es ist nichts .... (wichtig)

e Die Serie war nichts .... (besonders)

f Hast du etwas .... gemacht? (interessant)

LANGUAGE BUILDER 2

10.03

💡 Language discovery 2

Listen to the conversation again and repeat each line in the pauses provided. Then add the missing endings to the adjectives.

a Oft trage ich meinen Anzug mit einem schwarz......... Pullover.

b Ich trage gern ein blaues Hemd mit einer weiß......... Hose.

c Oder ich trage meinen Anzug mit einem rot......... Hemd.

Adjective endings after **ein**, **eine**, etc. (2) – dative

You have learned the adjective endings after the indefinite articles (ein, etc.) for the accusative. In the dative, for instance after prepositions like mit and von, the adjective endings are all -en regardless of gender or number:

masc. -en   Er trägt ein Hemd mit einem schwarzen Hoodie.

fem.   -en   Carmen trägt eine Bluse mit einer roten Krawatte.

neut. -en   Florian hat eine blaue Jeans mit einem weißen T-Shirt an.

plural -en   Er trägt seinen Anzug mit leichten, braunen Schuhen.

> With more than one item, the preposition determines the case of all of the items: Martin trägt ein blaues Hemd mit einer blauen Hose, einem schwarzen Mantel und schwarzen Schuhen.

Remember to add an additional -n to the plural noun in the dative wherever possible.

Possessives (mein, dein, etc.) and the negative kein follow the same pattern:

Die Mütze hat er von seinem besten Freund. (m)

Language practice 2

1 What do you wear at work and at home? These people are describing what they normally wear. Complete the missing adjective endings in the dative:

a

Stephanie Otto
Bei der Arbeit trage ich gern eine Jacke mit ein................weiß.................Bluse, ein................schwarz................Hose und elegant................Schuhe................. Zu Hause trage ich gerne ein T-Shirt mit ein................bequem................Jeans.

b

Siggi Nikutta
Am liebsten trage ich Streetwear. Meistens trage ich eine schicke Jeans aus New York mit ein................modisch................ T-Shirt und ein................cool................ Mütze von Gucci. Dazu trage ich trendige Sneakers.

c

Tom Bauhaus
Auf der Arbeit trage ich einen grauen Anzug mit ein................blau................Hemd und ein................dunkelblau................ Krawatte. Zu Hause trage ich oft eine Jeans mit ein................alt................Hemd und bequem................Schuhen.................

d

Florbella Santoz
Im Winter trage ich meistens einen dicken Mantel mit ein................warm................ Pullover und warm............Stiefel.............. Im Sommer trage ich lieber ein schönes Kleid mit leicht............Sommerschuhe.............

10.04

2 Now play Conversation 1 again and play Felix's role. Speak in the pauses provided and try not to refer to the text.

CULTURE POINT 2

Mode aus Deutschland *Fashion from Germany*

Although German-speaking countries do not have the same reputation for fashion as France or Italy, it does lay claim to some internationally renowned Modedesigner (*fashion designers*), including Jil Sander, Wolfgang Joop, and Karl Lagerfeld, who died in 2019.

Germany is also home to a number of well-known Modemarken (*fashion labels*) such as Hugo Boss, Escada, Jack Wolfskin, and Gerry Weber. The two Sportartikelhersteller (*sports clothing manufacturers*) Adidas and Puma were founded by the Dassler brothers in Bayern (*Bavaria*) in the late 1940s. The fierce rivalry between the brothers is often credited with transforming the sports apparel industry. The feud was so deep that even employees of Adidas and Puma wouldn't speak to each other and avoided going to the same bars and shops. Because people looked down at shoes all the time to see whether someone was affiliated with Adidas or Puma, the town of Herzogenaurach, where both factories were located, got the nickname 'the town of bent necks'.

Die Modeindustrie (*fashion industry*) is important to the German Wirtschaft (*economy*), employing more than 100,000 people. The two main centers for fashion are Düsseldorf and Berlin. Berlin is known for its unconventional young designers and also hosts Germany's most important Modenshow (*fashion show*), Berlin Fashion Week.

 Find out more about Berlin Fashion Week:

When will the Berlin Fashion Week take place next time? Are there any brands or designers at the show you like? What is your favorite style?

VOCABULARY BUILDER 2

10.05

Look at the words and phrases and complete the missing English words and expressions. Then listen and try to imitate the pronunciation of the speakers.

DIE WELT DER MODE	*THE WORLD OF FASHION*
der Gründer (-) / die Gründerin (-nen)	*founder*
die Marke (-n), die Markenkleidung (-en)	*brand, brand(ed) clothing*
der Modedesigner (-), die Modedesignerin (-nen)	*fashion designer*
das Modegeschäft (-e)	*fashion store*
die Modekette (-n), das Modelabel (-s)	*fashion chain, fashion brand*
der Secondhandladen (¨)	*..................... / thrift store*
der Stil (-e)	*style*
designen, produzieren	*to design, to ....*

NÜTZLICHE AUSDRÜCKE	*USEFUL EXPRESSIONS*
allgemein	*general(ly)*
magisch	*magical*
nachhaltig	*sustainable*
unkonventionell, urban, traditionell	*unconventional, ..., traditional*
der Umzug (-"e), das Kostüm (-e)	*parade, costume*
die Dunkelheit (-en)	*darkness*
der Zuschauer (-), die Zuschauerin (-nen)	*spectator, viewer*
das Erlebnis (-se)	*experience*
Lieblings- (+ noun)	*favorite*
das Lieblingsgeschäft (-e)	*favorite shop / store*
die Lieblingsmarke (-n)	*favorite brand*

Vocabulary practice 1

Match the sentence beginnings and endings.

a H&M, Zara oder Uniqlo sind
b Alexander McQueen war ein bekannter
c Puma und Adidas sind wichtige Sport- und
d Für Fair Fashion ist
e Kleidung von bekannten Labels

1 Modelabels aus Deutschland.
2 nennt man Markenkleidung.
3 Modedesigner.
4 Modeketten.
5 Nachhaltigkeit wichtig.

CONVERSATION 2

Hast du eine Lieblingsmarke? *Do you have a favorite brand?*

10.06

1 Listen to the conversation a few times without looking at the text. Then listen again and read the text. Does Felix have a favorite designer? What is important to Max about fashion?

> It is 6 a.m. After witnessing the start of the Basler Fasnacht, the Morgenstreich in which all Cliquen (*groups*) parade their illuminated lanterns through the darkened city streets, Felix and Max are sitting in a typical Cliquenkeller (*cellar bar*).
>
> **Felix** Und Max. Hat dir der Umzug gefallen?
>
> **Max** Das war ein toller Morgen, wirklich toll. Die Laternen in der Dunkelheit – das hatte etwas Magisches. Dazu die Kostüme ... Und das geht jetzt drei Tage so?
>
> **Felix** Zweiundsiebzig Stunden, nonstop. Es ist eine wilde Zeit.
>
> **Max** Felix, hast du eigentlich einen Lieblingsdesigner oder eine Lieblingsdesignerin?
>
> **Felix** Eigentlich nicht. Aber allgemein mag ich elegante Designs mit einem modernen Twist.
>
> **Max** Und hast du eine Lieblingsmarke?
>
> **Felix** Ich finde Ottolinger sehr interessant. Das ist ein junges Label aus Berlin. Die zwei Gründerinnen, Christa Bösch und Cosima Gadient, haben zusammen hier in Basel studiert.
>
> **Max.** Und was machen sie für Mode?
>
> **Felix** Unkonventionell, urban, aber auch elegant. Sie haben auch Sneakers für andere Firmen designt. Und du, Max? Hast du eine Lieblingsmarke oder ein Lieblingsgeschäft?
>
> **Max** Markenkleidung ist nicht so wichtig für mich. Sie ist oft auch zu teuer. Ich habe auch kein Lieblingsgeschäft. Die Kleidung muss bequem und die Qualität gut sein. Das ist die Hauptsache. Ich gehe auch gern in Secondhandläden. Für mich ist wichtig, dass Mode nachhaltig ist.
>
> **Felix** Da hast du Recht, Max. In meinem Blog schreibe ich oft über nachhaltige Mode und Fair Fashion. Auch in der Schweiz gibt es immer mehr Modelabels, die fair produzieren.

2 Answer the questions.

a Wie lange dauert die Fasnacht in Basel?

b Welches Design mag Felix?

c Wo haben die zwei Gründerinnen von Ottolinger zusammen studiert?

d Wie findet Max Markenkleidung?

e Wo kauft Max gern seine Kleidung?

f Über welche Themen schreibt Felix oft in seinem Blog?

LANGUAGE BUILDER 3

 Language discovery 3

Notice the adjective endings in these three sentences from Conversation 2.
Two endings are the same as in the accusative, but one is different. Which one?

Das war ein toll<u>er</u> Morgen. (m)   Es ist eine wild<u>e</u> Zeit. (f)   Das war ein toll<u>es</u> Erlebnis. (n)

Adjective endings after **ein**, **eine**, etc. (3)—nominative

As you saw before, you need to add an ending if an adjective appears before a noun. With the indefinite articles (ein, etc.) in the nominative, the pattern is:

masc. -er   Das ist ein billig<u>er</u> Rock.

fem.   -e   Das ist eine modisch<u>e</u> Bluse.

neut. -es   Das ist ein interessant<u>es</u> Design.

plural -e   Das sind schön<u>e</u> Turnschuhe.

As you may expect, possessives and kein follow the same pattern:

Das ist kein billig<u>er</u> Rock.   This is not a cheap skirt.

Meine neu<u>e</u> Bluse war teuer.   My new blouse was expensive.

In the plural, the adjective ends in -en after a possessive or kein:

Meine neu<u>en</u>, cool<u>en</u> Schuhe sehen gut aus.   My new, cool shoes look good.

Ich habe keine sauber<u>en</u> Hemden.   I don't have any clean shirts.

Language practice 3

Pay some compliments. Put the adjective before the noun and add the correct ending.

Example: Das Outfit ist modern. > *Das ist ein modern<u>es</u> Outfit.*

a Der Anzug ist modisch.   Das ist ein .... Anzug.
b Die Krawatte ist farbig.   Das ist eine .... Krawatte.
c Die Jacke ist schön.   Das ist eine .... Jacke.
d Der Hoodie ist elegant.   Das ist ein .... Hoodie.
e Die Turnschuhe sind cool.   Das sind .... Turnschuhe.
f Die Schuhe sind bequem und schick.   Das sind .... und .... Schuhe.

> Lieblings means *favorite*, and you can combine it with many nouns to express what you like most:
> Lieblingsfarbe (*favorite color*), Lieblingsmarke (*favorite brand*), Lieblingsessen (*favorite dish*),
> Lieblingsmannschaft (*favorite team*), etc.

LANGUAGE BUILDER 4

10.07

💡 Language discovery 4

Listen to the conversation again and repeat each line in the pauses provided. Then add the correct adjective ending: -e, -er, -es, or -en.

a Das war ein toll .... Morgen.

b Das ist ein jung .... Label aus Berlin.

c Aber allgemein mag ich elegant .... Designs mit einem modern .... Twist.

Adjective endings: summary

Here is an overview of the different adjective endings after indefinite articles, possessives, and the negative kein.

	masculine	feminine	neuter	plural
nominative	ein neu**er** Rock	eine neu**e** Bluse	ein neu**es** T-Shirt	neu**e** T-Shirts
accusative	einen groß**en** Flur	ene groß**e** Küche	ein groß**es** Bad	groß**e** Zimmer
dative	meinem neu**en** Laptop	meiner neu**en** Kamera	meinem neu**en** Fahrrad	neu**en** Schuhen

With a possessive or kein in the nominative and accusative plural, the adjective takes -en:

Das sind meine neu**en** T-Shirts. Das Haus hat keine groß**en** Zimmer.

There are a few more details you should know:

● Adjectives ending in -a, like lila (*purple*), rosa (*pink*), and prima (*great*), don't take endings:
Er trägt ein rosa Hemd. Es war ein prima Abend.

There are also some spelling variations:

● Adjectives like sauer (*sour*) or teuer (*expensive*) drop the e before r:
Das ist ein saures Getränk.

● Adjectives ending in el loose the e before the l, and hoch drops the c:
Petra hat einen dunklen Mantel an. In der Schweiz gibt es hohe Berge.

In the comparative, the same endings are used:
Sie hat einen älter**en** Bruder. Österreich ist ein größer**es** Land als die Schweiz.

Language practice 4

1 Give the correct forms of the adjective in parentheses.

a Magst du meine .... Jacke? (lila)

b Moni trägt gern .... Socken. (rosa)

c Verena hat einen .... Rucksack gekauft. (teuer)

d Rob trägt gern einen .... Pullover. (schwarz)

e Das war ein .... Karneval. (prima)

2 Now play Conversation 2 again and play Max's role. Speak in the pauses provided and try not to refer to the text.

10.08

SKILL BUILDER

1 Match the German sentences with the English translations.

a Das ist etwas Neues.

b Das bedeutet nichts Gutes.

c Es ist nichts Gefährliches.

d Ist es etwas Wichtiges?

e Habt ihr etwas Schönes gemacht?

1 Is it something important?

2 Did you do something nice?

3 That's something new.

4 This doesn't mean anything good.

5 It's nothing dangerous.

2 Find the odd one out.

a die Jacke   der Mantel   der Gürtel   der Hoodie

b die Hose   das Hemd   die Leggings   die Jeans

c die Bluse   das Hemd   die Krawatte   das T-Shirt

d die Mütze   das Kopftuch   der Hut   der Schal

e die Schuhe   die Sportschuhe   der Anzug   die Sandalen

3 Isabel Santos has visited the Fasnacht in Basel and is interviewed by a local paper. Complete the missing adjective endings.

a Wie finden Sie die Schweiz?

Ich finde, die Schweiz ist ein schön.............. und reich.............. Land.

b Und wie finden Sie Basel?

Ich glaube, Basel ist eine interessant.............. Stadt mit viel..............
Sehenswürdigkeiten.

c Wie finden Sie eigentlich Karneval?

Karneval ist eine toll.............. Veranstaltung. Man kann viel.............. Menschen
kennerlernen.

d Feiert man Karneval auch in Ihrer Stadt?

Oh ja, ich komme aus Teneriffa. Da feiern wir jedes Jahr einen groß..............,
fantastisch.............. Karneval.

e Und wie finden Sie Schwyzerdütsch?

Es ist eine lustig.............. Sprache mit einer interessant.............. Intonation.

f Und wie finden Sie Hochdeutsch?

Ich finde, Deutsch ist eine sehr schön.............., aber auch schwierig............. Sprache.

4 Now answer the questions for yourself. Try to use plenty of adjectives.

5 Listen to Max's description of three costumes and match them with the pictures. Which is Carla, Frederike, and Lou?

a .... b .... c ....

6 Max has posted a blog about his time in Basel, but some details are missing. Complete with the appropriate word from the box.

Fasnacht	Zwiebelkuchen	Tage	Fashionblogger	dunkel
Modelabels	Laternen	Erlebnis	Fasnächtler:innen	Blog

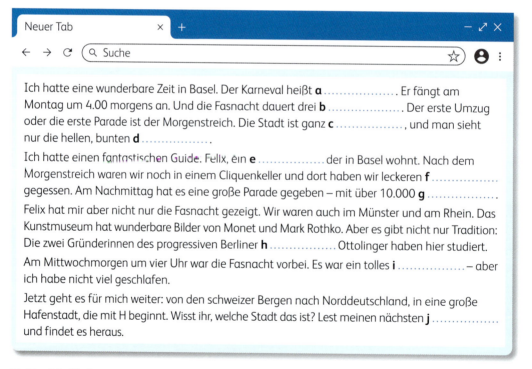

Neuer Tab ✕ +

Q Suche

Ich hatte eine wunderbare Zeit in Basel. Der Karneval heißt **a** .... Er fängt am Montag um 4.00 morgens an. Und die Fasnacht dauert drei **b** .... Der erste Umzug oder die erste Parade ist der Morgenstreich. Die Stadt ist ganz **c** ...., und man sieht nur die hellen, bunten **d** ....

Ich hatte einen fantastischen Guide. Felix, ein **e** .... der in Basel wohnt. Nach dem Morgenstreich waren wir noch in einem Cliquenkeller und dort haben wir leckeren **f** .... gegessen. Am Nachmittag hat es eine große Parade gegeben – mit über 10.000 **g** ....

Felix hat mir aber nicht nur die Fasnacht gezeigt. Wir waren auch im Münster und am Rhein. Das Kunstmuseum hat wunderbare Bilder von Monet und Mark Rothko. Aber es gibt nicht nur Tradition: Die zwei Gründerinnen des progressiven Berliner **h** .... Ottolinger haben hier studiert.

Am Mittwochmorgen um vier Uhr war die Fasnacht vorbei. Es war ein tolles **i** .... – aber ich habe nicht viel geschlafen.

Jetzt geht es für mich weiter: von den schweizer Bergen nach Norddeutschland, in eine große Hafenstadt, die mit H beginnt. Wisst ihr, welche Stadt das ist? Lest meinen nächsten **j** .... und findet es heraus.

7 Decide if these statements are *true* (richtig) or *false* (falsch).

a The Fasnacht starts at 4 p.m.   R   F
b A popular dish during the carnival is onion tart.   R   F
c Max thinks Basel is only about tradition.   R   F
d Next, Max is planning to visit a harbor town in Northern Germany. R   F

Now talk about what you like to wear. Prepare your answers, then listen to the audio and say your answers out loud.

a Was trägst du normalerweise bei der Arbeit / an der Uni?

b Was trägst du normalerweise zu Hause?

c Trägst du gern Markenkleidung?

d Was trägst du gern?

e Hast du eine Lieblingsmarke?

f Hast du eine Lieblingsfarbe?

g Wo kaufst du ein? Online oder in einem Geschäft? Hast du einen Lieblingsladen?

h Ist Mode wichtig für dich?

> **?** **Wie geht's weiter? *What happens next?***
>
> So, Max says that, next, he wants to go to a city in Northern Germany which starts with an H? Which city could this be? Find out in the next unit.

Remember to use **My review** and **My takeaway** to assess your progress and reflect on your learning experience.

11

In this lesson you will learn how to:
» Understand invitations to various events
» Name objects of everyday life
» Express what present to give to someone (him, her, etc.)
» Seek advice and ask for recommendations in a store

Einkaufen und Geschenke

My study plan

I plan to work with Unit 11
○ Every day
○ Twice a week
○ Other _____
I plan to study for
○ 5–15 minutes
○ 15–30 minutes
○ 30–45+ minutes

My progress tracker

Day / Date	🎧	🎙	📖	✏	💬
	○	○	○	○	○
	○	○	○	○	○
	○	○	○	○	○
	○	○	○	○	○
	○	○	○	○	○
	○	○	○	○	○
	○	○	○	○	○

My goals

What do you want to be able to do or say in German when you complete this unit?

Done

1 .... ○

2 .... ○

3 .... ○

My review

SELF CHECK

	I can ...
●	... understand invitations to various events.
●	... name objects of everyday life.
●	... express what present to give to someone (him, her, etc.).
●	... seek advice and ask for recommendations in a store.

CULTURE POINT 1

Hamburg – Das Tor zur Welt *Gateway to the world*

With about 1.9 million inhabitants, Hamburg is the second largest city in Germany. Like Berlin and Bremen, Hamburg is ein Stadtstaat, that is, a city which is also one of Germany's 16 Bundesländer (*federal states*). This special status stems from its participation in the Hanse (*Hanseatic League*), a customs union between Northern European port cities dating back to 1358.

Hamburg gained its economic prosperity from its history as a port city on the river Elbe, which flows into the Nordsee (*North Sea*), giving Hamburg its nickname Tor zur Welt (*gateway to the world*). Even today, the Hafen (*harbor*) plays an important role in Hamburg's Wirtschaft (*economy*) and is the third largest port in Europe.

Close to the harbor is the world-famous entertainment Stadtteil (*district*) St. Pauli, with its main thoroughfare die Reeperbahn. On the weekends, it draws thousands of partygoers and tourists to its lively bars, theaters, and nightclubs. In recent years, Hamburg has become a magnet for tourists who are attracted by the many Sehenswürdigkeiten (*sights*) it has to offer. Among them are das Rathaus (*city hall*), die Speicherstadt (*the world's largest warehouse complex*), die Landungsbrücken (*landing bridges* or *piers*), with a spectacular view on the harbor, and Hamburg's latest landmark, die Elbphilharmonie, which combines great music with architecture and a unique location.

Find out more about die Elbphilharmonie & Laeiszhalle.

What different kinds of events take place there?

Look at 'What's on' in the next few weeks. Is there a concert or other event you would like to see? How much is the ticket?

VOCABULARY BUILDER 1

11.01

Look at the words and phrases and complete the missing English words and expressions. Then listen and try to imitate the pronunciation of the speakers.

FEIERN	CELEBRATIONS
die Anmeldung (-en)	*application / registration*
die Einladung (-en)	*invitation*
der Geburtstag (-e)	*birthday*
die Grillparty (-s)	*barbecue*
die Hochzeit (-en)	*wedding*

KLEINE GESCHENKE	SMALL PRESENTS
das Abonnement (-s)	*subscription, season ticket*
die Blume (-n)	*flower*
die Fitnessuhr (-en)	.... *watch*
das Geschenk (-e)	*present*
der Gutschein (-e)	*voucher*
die Halskette (-n)	*necklace*
der Ohrring (-e)	....
der Schmuck (no plural)	*jewelry*
das Stofftier (-e)	*soft toy, stuffed animal*

ANDERE NOMEN	OTHER NOUNS
die Atemübung (-en)	*breathing exercise*
das Fischbrötchen (-)	*fish roll*
die Hafenrundfahrt (-en)	*harbor tour*
der Seehund (-e)	*seal*

> A Fischbrötchen (lit. *fish roll*) is a sandwich made with fish and fresh or dried onions and pickles. Typical varieties of fish used for Fischbrötchen are: Bismarck hering (*filleted salt herring*), Matjes (*soused herring*), Lachs (*salmon*).

VERBEN	VERBS
feiern	*to celebrate*
gehören	*to belong*
als Geschenk ein/packen	*to gift wrap*
heiraten	*to marry*
mit/bringen	*to bring (along)*
schenken	*to give (as a present)*
stärken	*to strengthen*

NÜTZLICHE AUSDRÜCKE	USEFUL EXPRESSIONS
auf den Link klicken	*to click on the* ....
Körper, Geist und Seele	*body, mind, and soul*
umgeben von (+ Dat.)	*surrounded (by)*

Vocabulary practice 1

Complete the four invitations with a word from the box. There are two extra words.

| Einladung | Hochzeit | Grillparty | Hafenrundfahrt | Geburtstagsparty | Geschenk |

a

Aisha

**wird am nächsten Samstag
8 Jahre alt!**

Das wollen wir natürlich mit einer
ganz tollen .... feiern,
mit Kuchen und vielen Spielen.

DIE ADRESSE:
Aisha, Rosa, Tobias KLAR
Willy-Brandt-Straße 4

b

BIANCA FRÖHLICH

und

GUSTAVO ROSSO

*Zu unserer .... laden
wir Sie/euch herzlichst ein.*

WIR HEIRATEN AM 8. MAI, UM 14.30
UHR IN DER ST. ELISABETH-KIRCHE,
STEPHANSTRASSE 12.

Bianca Fröhlich   *Gustavo Rosso*
Ahornweg 31 8   *Hauptstraße 48*
35043 Marburg   *35683 Dillenburg*

c

Wellness für Körper, Geist und Seele

.... ZUM
ME-TIME
YOGA RETREAT

24.–25. April | Blankenese/Hamburg

Finde Ruhe und Zeit für dich und
stärke deine Energie. Wir aktivieren
die Chakren (Energiekanäle) mit
Atemübungen, Hatha-Yoga und
Vinyasa-Yoga. Die Location liegt
direkt an der Elbe, umgeben von
wunderschöner Natur.

Für mehr Infos und zur Anmeldung,
einfach auf folgenden Link klicken:
Me-Time-Yoga

d

Ihr seid eingeladen.
ACHTUNG! ACHTUNG!

**Wir machen am Freitag,
dem 28. Mai, ab 17.00 Uhr
eine Grillparty in unserem Garten.**

Es gibt etwas für Fleischesser,
Vegetarier und Veganer.
Bringt einfach einen Salat mit.
Den Rest haben wir.
Wir freuen uns.
Eure Andreas und Mark

St. Pauli und zwei Seehunde *St. Pauli and two seals*

11.02

1 Listen to the conversation a few times without looking at the text. Then listen again and read the text. What does Wally want to show Max? Why is it easy to buy a present for Fabian?

Wally has invited Max to Hamburg, her hometown. She first takes him to the Landungsbrücken (*piers or landing bridges*), located in the St. Pauli area.

Max	Was für ein schöner Blick – und was für ein Kontrast zu den Bergen in der Schweiz, Wally. Und hier bist du aufgewachsen?
Wally	Ja, nicht weit von hier in Hamburg-Altona.
Max	Was wollen wir denn die nächsten Tage machen?
Wally	Ich möchte dir gern viel von Hamburg zeigen, zum Beispiel die Innenstadt, die Reeperbahn, die Parks und den Hafen ... Und dann habe ich auch zwei Karten für eine Gala in der Elbphilharmonie. Eine ehemalige Kollegin hat uns zu ihrer Geburtstagsfeier eingeladen.
Max	Apropos Geburtstag, hat Nuri nicht nächste Woche Geburtstag?
Wally	Ja. Das habe ich nicht vergessen. Du weißt, sie liebt Tiere, besonders Seehunde. Ich dachte, wir können ihr zwei Seehundstofftiere schenken.
Max	Gute Idee. Und Aylin und Fabian? Wir können ihnen doch auch etwas mitbringen, oder?
Wally	Bei Fabian ist das einfach. Er ist ein großer Fan vom FC St. Pauli, dem Fußballverein. Wir können ihm etwas aus dem Fanshop kaufen.
Max	Und Aylin mag Schmuck, besonders Halsketten und Ohrringe.
Wally	Gute Idee. Ich kenne hier in der Nähe einen kleinen Schmuckladen.
Max	Aber jetzt machen wir erstmal eine Hafenrundfahrt.
Wally	Und vorher essen wir noch ein Fischbrötchen. Das ist eine Spezialität hier in Hamburg.

2 Decide if these statements are *true* (richtig) or *false* (falsch). Correct the false ones.

a Wally ist in Hamburg-Altona aufgewachsen.   R   F

b Wally hat zwei Karten für ein Konzert in der Elbphilharmonie.   R   F

c Für Nuri möchte Wally Stofftiere kaufen.   R   F

d Aylin trägt gern Schmuck, besonders Halsketten und Ohrringe.   R   F

e Vor der Hafenrundfahrt möchten Wally und Max noch shoppen gehen.   R   F

LANGUAGE BUILDER 1

 Language discovery 1

Look at Conversation 1 again and find the missing pronoun. Identify which words expresses the meaning of *(to) you, (to) him, (to) her,* and *(to) them.*

a Ich möchte .... gern viel von Hamburg zeigen.

b Fabian – Wir können .... etwas aus dem Fanshop kaufen.

c Nuri – Wir können .... zwei Seehundstofftiere schenken

d Aylin und Fabian – Wir können .... doch auch etwas mitbringen, oder?

Indirect object pronouns (*to him, her, them .../ihm, ihr, ihnen...*)

To express that something is given to someone, you use what is called a *dative* or *indirect pronoun*. Here are all the dative pronouns:

Singular		Plural	
(to) me	mir	*(to) us*	uns
(to) you	dir, Ihnen	*(to) you*	euch, Ihnen
(to) him / it	ihm	*(to) them*	ihnen
(to) her	ihr		
(to) them (gender neutral)	xiem		

You have already seen some of these pronouns in expressions like:

Wie geht es Ihnen?   How are you? (lit. *How is it going to you?*)

Danke, es geht mir gut.   Thanks, I'm well. (lit. *It goes well to me.*)

Language practice 1

Complete the sentences using ihm, ihr, or ihnen?

a Lena hat Geburtstag. Lian schenkt .... ein Berlin-T-Shirt.

b Sebastian macht eine Party. Susi bringt .... eine Flasche Sekt mit.

c Maja und Ann heiraten. Wir schenken .... ein Abonnement fürs Theater.

d Alexa mag Schmuck. Ihr Partner kauft .... Ohrringe.

e Roberto mag Süßigkeiten. Man kann .... Pralinen schenken.

f Marion ist gestresst. Man kann .... einen Gutschein für ein Yogaretreat schenken.

g Leo und Oli gehen gern ins Fitnesscenter. Ihr Vater kauft .... zwei Fitnessuhren.

h Annalena hat vier Kinder. Sie lesen alle gerne. Wir wollen .... Bücher schenken.

LANGUAGE BUILDER 2

11.03

💡 Language discovery 2

Listen to the conversation again and repeat each line in the pauses provided. Then look at the following sentences. Complete with the appropriate article: den, dem, or der. Which case do the endings of these words indicate?

a Sie kauft .... Mann einen Kaffee.

b Er gibt .... Frau sein Handy.

c Florian kauft .... Kind ein Eis.

d Georg schenkt .... Kindern Spielzeuge.

Indirect objects take the dative case

In addition to the direct object, sentences can have an indirect object, i.e. a person or thing to/for whom or to which something is done.

Sie kauft <u>dem Mann</u> einen Kaffee.	*She buys <u>(for) the man</u> a coffee.*
Er gibt <u>der Frau</u> sein Handy.	*He gives <u>(to) the woman</u> his cell phone.*
Florian kauft <u>dem Kind</u> ein Eis.	*Florian buys <u>(for) the child</u> an ice cream.*
Sie erzählen <u>den Freunden</u> eine Geschichte.	*They tell <u>(to) their friends</u> a story.*

While the direct object is in the accusative, the indirect object requires the dative form. If the context is clear, you can substitute the indirect object with a pronoun. This goes before the direct object.

Sonja schreibt Florian eine Nachricht. > Sonja schreibt <u>ihm</u> eine Nachricht.

Er gibt der Frau ein Glas Wasser. > Er gibt <u>ihr</u> ein Glas Wasser.

> You can identify the indirect object by asking to/for whom or what something is done: *For whom does she buy the coffee? For the man.*

Language practice 2

1 Identify the direct object (DO) and indirect object (IO) in these sentences.

Example: Magda bringt ihrer Mutter Bumen mit.   Mutter = indirect object, Blumen = direct object

a Hast du dem Verkäufer schon das Geld gegeben?

b Kannst du mir bitte eine Flasche Olivenöl mitbringen?

c Sie haben ihrem Sohn einen E-Scooter gekauft.

d Leroy hat seinen Freunden seine neue Wohnung gezeigt.

e Wally möchte ihrer Schwiegertochter eine Halskette schenken.

f Kann Opa uns eine Geschichte vorlesen?

g Der Guide empfiehlt den Tourist:innen ein Restaurant.

11.04

2 Now play Conversation 1 again and play Wally's role. Speak in the pauses provided and try not to refer to the text.

CULTURE POINT 2

Einkaufen *Shopping*

Hamburg is also a well-known shopping destination. From international Luxusmarken (*luxury brands*) to charming Boutiquen (*boutiques*) in cozy neighborhoods, Hamburg offers a wide range of stores. Neuer Wall is a famous Einkaufsstraße (*shopping street*) in the

Innenstadt (*city center*), where you will find international top brands, whether for Mode (*fashion*), Schmuck (*jewelry*), Schuhe (*shoes*), or Möbel (*furniture*).

The biggest Kaufhaus (*department store*) in Hamburg is das Alsterhaus. If you prefer to shop at a Fachgeschäft (*specialized store*), you can go, for instance, to an Apotheke (*pharmacy*), Buchhandlung (*bookstore*), or Drogerie (*drugstore*). You will find that a lot of English words have crept into the shopping scene, such as Sale, Outlet, and of course Onlineshopping, written as one word.

Another popular way to do shopping is to visit the Wochenmärkte (*outdoor markets*). In Hamburg, every neighborhood has at least one market where locals can stock up on Lebensmittel (*groceries*) and more. The most famous market is the Hamburger Fischmarkt. It starts in the early hours on Sunday morning and is already closed by 9.30!

Öffnungszeiten (*opening hours*) have become more flexible in recent years, and in bigger cities Supermärkte are usually open until 22.00 from Monday to Saturday. However, on Sundays, stores generally remain closed. You would need to go to the nearest large Bahnhof to buy groceries or rise early and visit the Fischmarkt.

 Find out more about Hamburg's famous Fischmarkt.

How old is the market? What can you buy there? What is happening in the Fischauktionshalle *(Fish Auction Hall)?* What are the opening hours during summer and winter?

VOCABULARY BUILDER 2

11.05

Look at the words and phrases and complete the missing English words and expressions. Then listen and try to imitate the pronunciation of the speakers.

ALLTAGSGEGENSTÄNDE	EVERYDAY OBJECTS
die Bohrmaschine (-n)	drill, drilling machine
das Duschgel (-e oder -s)	shower ....
der Fahrradhelm (-e)	.... helmet
der Fön (-e)	hair dryer
die Handtasche (-n)	.... bag
die Handyhülle (-n)	phone case
die Kaffeemaschine (-n)	....
die Bürste (-n), der Kamm (-"e)	brush, comb
das Ladekabel (-)	charging ....
das Parfüm (-s oder -e), der Duft (-"e)	.... , scent
die Pflanze (-n)	plant
der Regenschirm (-e)	umbrella
der Trinkbecher (-)	drinking cup
die Zahnpasta (-pasten oder -s)	toothpaste

> Plural forms of imported nouns can sometimes vary. It is possible to say die Parfüme or die Parfüms, die Duschgele or die Duschgels.

IM GESCHÄFT	IN STORE
Können Sie mir helfen?	Can you help .... ?
Können Sie mir etwas empfehlen?	Can you recommend something (to me)?
Gefällt es Ihnen?	Do you like it?
Wo ist die Kasse, bitte?	Where is the checkout/till, please?

NÜTZLICHE AUSDRÜCKE	USEFUL EXPRESSIONS
aus/probieren	to try (out)
das passt zu mir	that suits me
erdig	earthy
irgendwie	somehow
süßlich	sweetish

Vocabulary practice 1

1 Where do these objects belong? Complete the table. Note that **Körperpflege** means *body care / personal hygiene* and **Kosmetika** *cosmetic products*.

Bürste	Bohrmaschine	Duschgel	Fahrradhelm	Fitnessuhr
Halskette	Handcreme	Handtasche	Fön	Handyhülle
Hemd	Hose	Jacke	Kaffeemaschine	Kamm
Ladekabel	Laptop	Ohrring	Parfüm	Pflanze
Regenschirm	Schal	Shampoo	Trinkbecher	Zahnpasta

Schmuck	Kleidung	Körperpflege / Kosmetika	Elektronisches	Anderes
		Handcreme		

CONVERSATION 2

Gefällt es Ihnen? *Do you like it?*

11.06

Listen to the conversation a few times without looking at the text. Then listen again and read the text. How does Max describe Wally? What does he think about the first perfume?

Max has decided to surprise Wally with a present to say Dankeschön. He goes to a well-known Parfümerie (*perfumery*) and approaches a Verkäuferin (*sales assistant*).

Max	Guten Tag. Ich suche ein Geschenk für eine sehr gute Freundin. Können Sie mir da vielleicht helfen?
Verkäuferin	Ja, gerne. Wie alt ist Ihre Bekannte denn? Und was für eine Person ist sie?
Max	Na, ja, sie ist so etwa um die Siebzig. Sie ist immer noch sehr aktiv. Sie war früher Opernsängerin.
Verkäuferin	Also, es muss schon etwas Besonderes sein. Für eine Opernsängerin... An was haben Sie denn gedacht? Ein Accessoire, Schmuck, eine besondere Creme oder ein Parfüm?
Max	Ein Parfüm ist am besten, denke ich. Sie trägt sehr gerne Parfüm. Können Sie mir etwas empfehlen?
Verkäuferin	Ja, natürlich. Ich zeige Ihnen gerne etwas. Hier haben wir zum Beispiel „Rosenparadies" aus Deutschland. Möchten Sie es einmal ausprobieren?
Max	Ja, sehr gerne ...
Verkäuferin	Und gefällt es Ihnen?
Max	Es ist ein bisschen zu süßlich. Mmh, ich bin mir nicht sicher. Haben Sie noch etwas Anderes?
Verkäuferin	Mmh. Hier haben wir „Ägyptischer Mond". Es ist erdig, aber auch exotisch.
Max	Oh, ja. Das hat einen wunderbaren Duft. Ich glaube, das passt zu ihr. Wie teuer ist es denn?
Verkäuferin	94 Euro. Es ist nicht ganz billig, aber es ist etwas Besonderes.
Max	Mmh. Gut, dann nehme ich das. Wo ist denn die Kasse?
Verkäuferin	Da vorne rechts. Da können Sie bezahlen.

2 Answer the questions.

a Wie alt, denkt Max, ist Wally?

b Was für ein Geschenk muss es sein?

c Wie ist der Duft von „Rosenparadies"?

d Wie beschreibt die Verkäuferin „Ägyptischer Mond"?

e Wo ist die Kasse?

LANGUAGE BUILDER 3

 Language discovery 3

Look at these sentences from Conversation 2. Identify what the verbs helfen, empfehlen, and gefallen have in common.

Können Sie mir da vielleicht helfen?

Können Sie mir etwas empfehlen?

Und gefällt es Ihnen?

The dative case after some verbs

Although most verbs are followed by the *accusative*, there are a few verbs which require the *dative case*. They include:

antworten	*to answer*	gehören	*to belong to*	schaden	*to harm*
danken	*to thank*	gratulieren	*to congratulate*	trauen	*to trust*
folgen	*to follow*	helfen	*to help*	wehtun	*to hurt*
gefallen	*to like*	sagen	*to say*		

Sie danken der Frau.	*They thank the woman.*
Er gratuliert dem Sieger.	*He congratulates the winner.*
Bitte antworte mir.	*Please answer me.*
Das T-Shirt gefällt mir sehr gut.	*I like the T-Shirt a lot.*

Language practice 3

Match the questions and sentences with the answers.

a Kannst du bitte dem Mann helfen?

b Zeig bitte den Gästen unseren Garten.

c Hast du der Frau gratuliert?

d Gefallen dir die Blumen?

e Kannst du mir ein interessantes Buch empfehlen?

f Gefällt euch eigentlich Berlin?

g Gehört dir der neue Scooter?

h Ich danke Ihnen für die Einladung.

1 Gerne. Folgen Sie mir, bitte.

2 Schön, dass Sie zur Party gekommen sind.

3 Nein, der gehört meiner Freundin.

4 Ja, die Stadt gefällt uns gut.

5 Ja, klar. Ich helfe ihm.

6 Ja, sehr. Sie haben einen wunderbaren Duft.

7 Ja, ich empfehle dir den neuen Roman von Haruki Murakami.

8 Ja, ich habe ihr eine E-Karte geschickt.

LANGUAGE BUILDER 4

💡 **Language discovery 4**

Listen to the conversation again and repeat each line in the pauses provided. Then look at these sentences, all containing dative structures. In the first sentence, dem Mann is the indirect object. What triggers the dative in sentences b–e?

a Sie kauft <u>dem Mann</u> einen Kaffee.

b Er fährt mit <u>dem E-Auto</u> nach Österreich.

c Sie gratulieren <u>der Siegerin</u>.

d Hakan hilft <u>seinen Großeltern</u>.

e Was machst du nach <u>der Schule</u>?

The dative—Summary

The three main uses of the dative case are:

1 After certain prepositions

  a always after aus, bei, mit, nach, seit, von, zu: Er fährt <u>mit dem</u> Auto.

  b after in and auf when the focus is on position: Sie waren gestern <u>im</u> Kino.

2 As the indirect object

  To indicate the indirect object, i.e. *to whom* something is being given, done, etc.:
  Sie kauft <u>dem</u> Mann einen Kaffee.

3 After certain verbs

  Verbs such as danken, gefallen, gratulieren, and helfen are followed by the dative:
  Sie helfen <u>der</u> Frau.

There are also a number of common expressions in which the dative case is used:

Wie geht es dir/Ihnen?	*How are you?* (lit. *How does it go for/to you?*)
Mir geht es gut.	*I am well.* (lit. *It goes well for/to me*)
Mir ist kalt/warm.	*I am cold/hot.*
Das tut mir leid.	*I am sorry (about this).*
Das macht mir Spaß.	*This is fun/enjoyable for me.*
Es gefällt mir gut.	*I like it.* (lit. *It's pleasing to me.*)

When the indirect object (dative) and direct object (accusative) appear together in a sentence, the indirect object goes first, whether it's a noun or a pronoun: mir, dir, ihm, etc.

Ich kaufe <u>meiner Schwester</u> einen Hoodie.   Ich kaufe <u>ihr</u> einen Hoodie.

> A number of verbs are frequently used with both a *direct* and an *indirect* object. You met a few in this unit: empfehlen (*to recommend*), kaufen (*to buy*), geben (*to give*), mitbringen (*to bring*), schenken (*to give as a present*), zeigen (*to show*).

Language practice 4

Complete the words with the dative endings.

1 a Sie fährt zu .... Arbeit.

   b Er ist Barrista i.......... Café.

   c Ich schenke mein.......... Bruder einen Fön.

   d Bitte danken Sie d.......... Ärztin.

   e Ich kaufe mein.......... Kindern ein Eis.

   f Sie hat eine Einladung zu ein.......... Yoga Retreat.

2 a Wie geht es d.......... ?

   b Können Sie m.......... etwas empfehlen?

   c Bitte hilf Leon. – Ja, ich helfe i........... .

   d Ich gratuliere d.......... zum Geburtstag.

   e Herr Xu, gefällt I.......... die Feier?

   f Das macht m.......... Spaß.

2 Now play Conversation 2 again and play Max's role. Speak in the pauses provided and try not to refer to the text.

11.08

SKILL BUILDER

1 Find the odd one out.

a Geburtstagsfeier	Schmuck	Grillparty	Hochzeit
b Halskette	Ohrring	Ring	Regenschirm
c Schmuck	Ladekabel	Handyhülle	Tablet
d Fön	Fahrradhelm	Bohrmaschine	Kaffeemaschine
e Duschgel	Zahnpasta	Handtasche	Shampoo
f exotisch	herzlich	erdig	süßlich

2 You are invited to a birthday party. Your friend Moritz was supposed to buy the presents, but something went wrong. Listen to his message and write down the main information.

11.09

   a Was passiert ist: ....

   b Was ich machen muss: ....

   c Was ich für Lea kaufen soll: ....

   d Was ich für Ahmed kaufen soll: ....

   e Was Moritz schon für Lea und Ahmed gekauft hat: ....

   f Wo und wann wir uns treffen: ....

3 Put these sentences in the right order. Start with the underlined word(s).

Example: der Frau / bringt / <u>Sie</u> / Pralinen mit. > *Sie bringt der Frau Pralinen mit.*

   a seiner Mutter / schenkt / ein Bild / <u>Pierre</u>

   b geschenkt / <u>Sie</u> / eine Flasche Champagner / ihren Freunden / haben

   c ein neues Handy / kaufen / unserem Sohn / <u>Wir</u>

   d ein Geschenk / <u>Hast</u> / zum Geburtstag / gekauft? / du / deiner Schwester

   e Sie / in Hamburg / ein Hotel / uns / <u>Können</u> / empfehlen?

   f helfen? / du / mir / <u>Kannst</u>

4 Read the text about Hamburg's new Wahrzeichen (*landmark*), die Elbphilharmonie.

Neuer Tab   ✕   +

← → C   Q Suche   ☆   🔵   ⋮

Die Elbphilharmonie – das neue Wahrzeichen von Hamburg

Die Elbphilharmonie ist das neue kulturelle Wahrzeichen von Hamburg. Viele nennen das Konzerthaus einfach „Elphi". Die „Elphi" liegt direkt an der Elbe und ist auf drei Seiten von Wasser umgeben. Seit 2017 kommen viele Besucher aus Hamburg, Deutschland und der ganzen Welt, um das Gebäude zu sehen oder ein Konzert zu hören.

Das Besondere ist die Architektur – die Elbphilharmonie ist ein Glasbau (*glass building*) und 110 Meter hoch. Und es gibt eine Plaza, eine öffentliche Aussichtsplattform (*public viewing platform*) mit einem wunderbaren 360-Grad-Blick auf den Hafen und Hamburg. Man kann die Aussichtsplattform auch benutzen, wenn man keine Karte für ein Konzert hat – ein Besuch ist kostenlos (*free (of charge)*).

Der *Große Saal* hat eine besondere Akustik. Es gibt Platz für 2100 Zuschauer und niemand sitzt mehr als 30 Meter vom Dirigenten oder der Dirigentin (*conductor*) entfernt. Das Gebäude hat aber noch zwei andere Säle: einen *Kleinen Saal* mit 550 Plätzen sowie einen dritten Saal (*hall*), das *Kaistudio 1*, mit 170 Sitzplätzen.

Das Musikprogramm ist sehr vielseitig (*diverse, varied*). Es gibt nicht nur klassische Musik, sondern auch Jazz, Elektro- oder Popmusik. Das Konzept von der Elbphilharmonie ist, ein Ort für Alle zu sein.

Decide if the statements are *true* (richtig) or *false* (falsch). Correct the false ones.

a Man nennt die Elbphilharmonie auch „Elphi".   R   F

b Die Elbphilharmonie liegt in der Innenstadt.   R   F

c Für die öffentliche Aussichtsplattform muss man bezahlen.   R   F

d Der Große Saal hat Sitzplätze für 2100 Zuschauer.   R   F

e In der Elbphilharmonie kann man nur klassische Musik hören.   R   F

TEST YOURSELF

11.10

Max wants to buy a book about Berlin for Lisa and goes to a bookstore. Use the prompts in the book and answer the questions in the pauses on the audio. Remember how to say *I like it* and *I don't like it*: Es gefällt mir and Es gefällt mir nicht.

Verkäufer	Sie
Guten Tag.	*Return his greetings and ask if he can help you.*
Ja, natürlich. Was kann ich denn für Sie tun?	*Say you are looking for a book about Berlin. Could he recommend something?*
Hier haben wir zum Beispiel ein neues Berlin-Magazin. Sehen Sie einmal. Gefällt Ihnen das Magazin?	*Say you are sorry. You don't like it.*
Ah, hier ist ein neues Buch über Berlin mit vielen kurzen Texten, zum Beispiel über die Geschichte, die Clubszene, die Musikszene ...	*Say that's interesting. You like that one. Ask how much it costs.*
14,99 Euro.	*Say thank you and ask where the checkout is.*

Wie geht's weiter? *What happens next?*

Having again spent some time with Wally, Max is astonished by her energy and fitness. What does she do to remain so active? What is her secret? Find out in the next unit.

Remember to use **My review** and **My takeaway** to assess your progress and reflect on your learning experience.

In this lesson you will learn how to:

» Name parts of the body
» Report on aches and pains
» Describe whether you live a healthy lifestyle
» Give reasons for your opinion

Gesundheit und Lifestyle

My study plan

I plan to work with Unit 12

○ Every day
○ Twice a week
○ Other _____

I plan to study for

○ 5–15 minutes
○ 15–30 minutes
○ 30–45+ minutes

My progress tracker

Day / Date	🎧	🎤	📖	✏️	💬
	○	○	○	○	○
	○	○	○	○	○
	○	○	○	○	○
	○	○	○	○	○
	○	○	○	○	○
	○	○	○	○	○
	○	○	○	○	○

My goals

What do you want to be able to do or say in German when you complete this unit?

Done

1 .... ○

2 .... ○

3 .... ○

My review

SELF CHECK

	I can ...
○	... name parts of the body.
○	... report on aches and pains.
○	... describe whether I live a healthy lifestyle.
○	... give reasons for my opinion.

CULTURE POINT 1

Ein gesunder Lebensstil *A healthy lifestyle*

In recent years, Germans are getting more conscious about how ein gesunder Lebensstil (*a healthy lifestyle*) can contribute to their overall wellbeing and that this is a factor well within their control. As in other countries, das Fitnessstudio (*the gym*) is a popular destination for many, not only for young people. Apart from offering a variety of Kurse (*courses*), they often serve as a social Treffpunkt (*meeting point*). A survey by Deutsche Welle revealed that 68 percent of the German population spends their leisure time outdoors, with activities like visiting forests, exercising, or simply relaxing in nature deeply embedded in the culture.

When it comes to food, 66 percent of the German population stated in a recent survey that they make an effort to consume healthy food and drinks. And despite the popular belief that Germany is a country run on Bratwurst and other Fleischprodukte (*meat products*), vegetarian or vegan alternatives are becoming increasingly popular 12 percent of Germans describing themselves as either Vegetarier:in (*vegetarian*) or Veganer:in (*vegan*) and more than 45 percent as Flexitarier:in (*flexitarian*), that is, they sometimes eat meat but often deliberately avoid it. Biolebensmittel (*organic foods*) also have a long tradition in Germany. You can buy organic foods in special stores called Bioläden, but they are also widely available in mainstream Supermärkten.

 Find out more about nutrition trends in Germany.
Do men or women eat more healthily? What are the main considerations for people to buy vegetarian or vegan? Which regional products do Germans like to buy? Did any of the findings surprise you?

VOCABULARY BUILDER 1

12.01

Look at the words and phrases and complete the missing English words and expressions. Then listen and try to imitate the pronunciation of the speakers.

DER LEBENSSTIL / DER LIFESTYLE

aktiv sein	to be ....
am Computer arbeiten	to work ....
genug für die Gesundheit machen / tun	to do enough for your health
fit sein, unfit sein	to be fit, to be ....
positiv denken	to .... positive(ly)
selbst kochen	to .... yourself
sich gesund ernähren	to eat a healthy diet
voller Energie sein	to be full of ....
vor dem Bildschirm sitzen	to sit in front of the screen
Sport machen / treiben	to do ....

LIFESTYLE

GESUNDHEIT

körperlich	physical(ly)
geistig / mental	mental(ly)
gesund, krank	healthy, sick
das Gesundheitsproblem (-e)	health ....
der Orthopäde (-n), die Orthopädin (-nen)	orthopedic doctor
das Rückenproblem (-e)	back problem
der Rückenschmerz (-en) (mostly plural)	.... pain

HEALTH

> You can say Ich mache Sport or Ich treibe Sport. The verb treiben is more formal.

EINE MEINUNG ÄUβERN

glauben	to believe
meinen	to mean, to think
wissen	to know
irgendwann	at some point
sollen	shall / should / ought
dass	that
weil	because
zwar ..., aber ...	although ... but ...

EXPRESSING AN OPINION

Vocabulary practice 1

Categorize these activities as *healthy* (gesund) or *unhealthy* (ungesund).

aktiv sein   oft Sport treiben   zu lange vor dem Bildschirm sitzen   Fastfood essen
sich gesund ernähren   Obst und Gemüse essen   viel Wasser trinken   schwimmen
acht Stunden ohne Pause am Computer arbeiten   regelmäßig Alkohol trinken   Yoga machen
positiv denken   zu viel Chips essen   viele Süßigkeiten essen   im Park spazieren gehen

CONVERSATION 1

Gesund bleiben! *Stay healthy!*

12.02

1 Listen to the conversation a few times without looking at the text. Then listen again and read the text. What health issue did Wally have in the past? What does Max agree to?

> Max has always been impressed by Wally's vitality, fitness, and positive attitude. He wants to find out whether she has any tips or advice about living healthily.
>
> **Max**   Wally, du bist immer so voller Energie. Wie machst du das eigentlich?
>
> **Wally**   Findest du, Max?
>
> **Max**   Ja, ich denke, dass du sehr fit bist.
>
> **Wally**   Danke. Na ja, du weißt ja, dass ich regelmäßig Sport treibe. Und ich glaube, dass ich mich auch gesund ernähre. Ich esse viel Obst und Gemüse und koche meistens selbst. Und ich trinke natürlich viel Wasser und Tee.
>
> **Max**   Hast du denn irgendwann einmal Gesundheitsprobleme gehabt?
>
> **Wally**   Ja, vor ein paar Jahren hatte ich Rückenprobleme. Meine Orthopädin hat mir dann gesagt, dass ich viel schwimmen soll. Sie hat mir auch empfohlen, Yoga zu machen. Yoga tut mir gut, körperlich und geistig. Und ich versuche, immer aktiv zu sein und positiv zu denken. Aber du lebst doch auch relativ gesund, Max, oder?
>
> **Max**   Na ja, manchmal esse ich zu viel Fastfood, wenn ich hungrig bin. Und auch zu viele süße Sachen.
>
> **Wally**   Aber du machst ja auch Sport und joggst gern im Park und du gehst ins Fitnesscenter.
>
> **Max**   Ja, manchmal habe ich Rückenschmerzen, weil ich zu lange am Computer sitze. Und dann hilft es mir, wenn ich ins Fitnesscenter gehe. Aber ich glaube, ich muss mehr Sport machen.
>
> **Wally**   Wir können ja auch wieder einmal zusammen schwimmen gehen ...
>
> **Max**   Mmh, ich schwimme nicht so besonders gern.
>
> **Wally**   Und wenn du einmal mit zum Yoga kommst?
>
> **Max**   Zum Yoga? Na gut. Ich kann es ja einmal versuchen.

2 Answer the questions.

  a Außer Sport, was macht Wally für ihre Gesundheit?

  b Was hat ihr die Orthopädin empfohlen?

  c Was versucht Wally auch?

  d Was für Gesundheitsprobleme hat Max?

  e Was glaubt Max, muss er mehr machen?

  f Wie findet er Schwimmen?

LANGUAGE BUILDER 1

Ich denke, dass ... *I think that ...*

The word dass can be useful when you want to voice an opinion in German. It is very similar to *that* in English, except that dass sends the verb to the end of the sentence or clause:

Ich denke, <u>dass</u> du sehr fit <u>bist</u>. Ich glaube, <u>dass</u> ich gesund <u>lebe</u>.

When you use dass with a modal verb or with the perfect tense, then the modal verb or haben/sein go to the last position. Note that dass-clauses start with a comma.

Meine Orthopädin hat mir gesagt, <u>dass</u> ich viel <u>schwimmen soll</u>.

Ich denke, <u>dass</u> Olivia gestern <u>gearbeitet hat</u>.

You can omit dass. The verb then comes earlier in the sentence: Ich denke, du bist sehr fit.

> When stating an opinion, people often say: ich denke ... (*I think*), ich finde ... (*I find / I think*), ich glaube ... (*I believe*), ich meine ... (*I think / I mean*) or ich weiß ... (*I know*).

Language practice 1

12.03

Rewrite the sentences using dass. Then listen to the audio and check your answers and repeat.

Example: Ich denke, ich lebe gesund. > *Ich denke, dass ich gesund lebe.*

a Jakob glaubt, er isst zu viele Süßigkeiten.
b Ich denke, Fitnessstudios sind oft zu teuer.
c Marlene findet, zu viel Sport ist nicht gut.
d Ganja meint, Kaffee ist gut für die Gesundheit.
e Nicolas findet, er ist topfit.
f Kazim glaubt, er muss mehr Sport machen.
g Ines denkt, sie tut genug für ihre Gesundheit.

LANGUAGE BUILDER 2

12.04

💡 Language discovery 2

Listen to the conversation again and repeat each line in the pauses provided. Then complete these sentences from the conversation. What role do the missing words play? Can you spot a difference between the sentences?

a Ich esse viel Obst und Gemüse .... koche meistens selbst.

b Dann hilft es mir, ... ich ins Fitnesscenter gehe.

c Manchmal habe ich Rückenschmerzen, ... ich zu lange am Computer sitze.

Conjunctions: joining words like und, aber, dass, weil, wenn

Conjunctions join two clauses into one sentence. There are two main groups of conjunctions:

1 Coordinating conjunctions

These conjunctions usually connect two main clauses: und (*and*), aber (*but*), oder (*or*), denn (*because*) and sondern (*but*, following a negative). They do not affect word order, and the verb stays in its usual (second) position in both clauses.

Jan ist Modedesigner und Carsten ist Arzt.
Jan is a fashion designer and Carsten is a doctor.

Emily hat ein Jahr in Berlin gelebt, aber sie spricht nicht viel Deutsch.
Emily lived for a year in Berlin but she does not speak much German.

Möchtest du einen Tee oder möchtest du einen Kaffee?
Would you like a tea or a coffee?

Basel liegt nicht in Österreich, sondern es liegt in der Schweiz.
Basel isn't in Austria, but is in Switzerland.

When the subject is the same in both clauses, it can be omitted in the second clause:

Ich esse viel Obst und Gemüse und (ich) koche meistens selbst.
I eat lots of fruit and vegetables and I mostly cook for myself.

2 Subordinating conjunctions

Subordinating conjunctions introduce a clause that adds information to the main clause. They send the main verb of the subordinate clause to the end. They are preceded by a comma. You have already seen how it works with dass (*that*). Other subordinating conjunctions are:

als	*when* (in the past)	ob	*if, whether*	weil	*because*
bevor	*before*	obwohl	*although*	wenn	*if, whenever*
nachdem	*after*	seit(dem)	*since*		

Sie gehen spazieren, obwohl es regnet.　　*They go for a walk although it is raining.*

Er kann nicht kommen, weil er krank ist.　　*He can't come because he is ill.*

When used with two verbs, the modal verb or haben / sein move to last position.

Sie lernt Deutsch,
weil sie in Berlin leben möchte.

She learns German,
because she would like to live in Berlin.

Language practice 2

1 Link the two clauses.

  a Nakissa geht joggen,

  b Mats fühlt sich besser,

  c Trink etwas,

  d Eduarda glaubt, sie ist topfit,

  e Wasch dir bitte die Hände,

  f Wir gehen in ein anderes Fitnesscenter,

  g Paul lernt Deutsch,

  1 obwohl es viel teurer ist.

  2 wenn du Durst hast.

  3 obwohl es stark regnet.

  4 bevor du zum Essen kommst.

  5 weil er in Wien arbeiten will.

  6 weil sie viel Sport macht und gesund isst.

  7 seitdem er ins Fitnesscenter geht.

12.05

2 Now play Conversation 1 again and play Max's role. Speak in the pauses provided and try not to refer to the text.

CULTURE POINT 2

Das deutsche Gesundheitswesen *German health care*

In some countries you go to a Hausarzt or Allgemeinarzt (*GP*) for almost any health-related Beschwerden (*complaints*) and then get referred to a Facharzt (*specialist*), such as a Chirurg/Chirurgin (*surgeon*), Hautarzt/Hautärztin (*dermatologist*), or a Kardiologe/Kardiologin (*cardiologist*).

In Germany you tend to choose a specialist appropriate for a given condition. You simply take along your elektronische Gesundheitskarte (eGK) (*electronic health insurance card*). Your Krankenkasse (*health insurance fund*) then makes payment on your behalf.

Die Öffentlichen Krankenkassen (*public health insurance*) offer statutory health care for a large number of people who are not privatversichert (*insured privately*). Private Krankenversicherungen offer additional treatments and extras, such as ein Einzelzimmer (*a room*) if you are im Krankenhaus (*in hospital*). However, preventative healthcare, such as eine Vorsorgeuntersuchung (*a health check*) are usually covered by all schemes.

To deal with an aging population and long-term care, Germany has introduced a compulsory Pflegeversicherung scheme. It is designed to help with the financial cost of home and residential care.

Find out more about the German health system: Why is health insurance obligatory in Germany? How is the scheme funded? What percentage of the population is insured through a public health insurance? How does health insurance work in your country and how is it different from that in Germany?

VOCABULARY BUILDER 2

12.06

Look at the words and phrases and complete the missing English words and expressions. Then listen and try to imitate the pronunciation of the speakers.

KÖRPERTEILE	PARTS OF THE BODY
der Kopf (-"e), das Gesicht (-er)	head, face
das Haar (-e)	....
das Auge (-n), die Nase (-n), das Ohr (-en)	eye, ..., ear
der Mund:(-"er), die Lippe (-n)	mouth, ...
der Zahn (-"e), die Zunge (-n)	tooth, tongue
der Hals (-"e)	neck / throat
der Rücken (-)	back
der Arm (-e), die Hand (-"e), der Finger (-)	....................., ..., ...
das Herz (-en)	heart
die Brust (-"e), der Busen (-)	breast/chest, bosom
der Bauch (-"e), der Magen (")	belly, stomach
das Bein (-e), das Knie (-)	leg, knee
der Fuß (-"e), der Zeh (-en), die Ferse (-n)	....................., toe, heel

BEIM ARZT	AT THE DOCTOR'S
Was fehlt Ihnen?	What is wrong?
Wo tut es weh?	Where does it hurt?
Ich habe Kopfschmerzen / Halsschmerzen / Magenschmerzen / Ohrenschmerzen.	I have a headache / a sore throat / stomach ache / ....
die Salbe (-n)	ointment / cream
die Tablette (-n)	....
die Schmerztablette (-n)	painkiller
die Zerrung (-en)	strain
vermeiden	to avoid
verschreiben	to prescribe
verspannt	tensed
weh/tun	to hurt
Gute Besserung!	Get well soon!
übertreiben	to exaggerate
die Übung (-en)	exercise

> When talking about pain, you normally use the plural form Schmerzen: Ich habe Herzschmerzen, Ohrenschmerzen, etc.
> An alternative is to use the verb weh/tun: Mein Herz tut weh (sing.). Meine Ohren tun weh (pl.).

Vocabulary practice 1

1 Complete with the correct body part.

   a Das Essen war schlecht. Jetzt habe ich .... schmerzen.

   b Nach dem Essen soll man sich die .... putzen.

   c Beim Fußball darf man den Ball nicht mit der .... spielen.

   d Ich habe etwas im .... Ich kann nicht richtig sehen.

   e Sie kann nicht richtig sprechen. Sie hat .... schmerzen.

   f Ich habe mir das linke .... gebrochen.

Pronunciation practice

When describing parts of the body, you may often need to use the plural forms. A number of Körperteile form the plural by adding an umlaut + e.

1 Listen and repeat.

die Hand	der Zahn	der Bauch	der Fuß
die Hände	die Zähne	die Bäuche	die Füße

Nouns ending in -e normally add an -n:

die Nase > die Nasen

die Lippe > die Lippen

die Ferse > die Fersen

2 How would you form the plural of these nouns and pronounce them? Listen to the audio and check your answers and pronunciation.

der Hals	der Kopf	das Auge
die Brust	der Arzt	die Zunge

CONVERSATION 2

Der Krieger *The Warrior*

1 Listen to the conversation a few times without looking at the text. Then listen again and read the text. Does Dr. Najab think Max has something serious? What does she prescribe?

Max joins Wally for a yoga class, but takes things a little too far and hurts his Schulter (*shoulder*) and Rücken doing the Krieger-Übung (*the Warrior exercise*). Wally insists he sees a doctor.

Dr. Najab	Guten Tag, Herr Peterson. Was kann ich für Sie tun? Was fehlt Ihnen?
Max	Guten Tag, Frau Doktor. Ich habe seit zwei Tagen ziemlich starke Schulter- und Rückenschmerzen.
Dr. Najab	Oh, das tut mir leid. Ist denn etwas Besonderes passiert?
Max	Na ja, ich war bei einem Yogakurs und ich glaube, dass ich es bei einer Übung, der Kriegerpose, ein bisschen übertrieben habe.
Dr. Najab	Darf ich einmal schauen?
Max	Ja, natürlich, danke.
Dr. Najab	Tut das weh?
Max	Nein, kein Problem. Oh, aua, doch ja ...
Dr. Najab	Also, Herr Peterson. Es ist eine Zerrung, nichts Schlimmes. Ich verschreibe Ihnen eine Salbe und ein paar Schmerztabletten. Sie müssen Ihren Rücken dreimal am Tag einreiben. Und nehmen Sie zweimal am Tag eine Tablette, morgens und abends.
Max	Darf ich ins Fitnesscenter gehen oder Sport machen?
Dr. Najab	Nein, in den nächsten sieben Tagen dürfen Sie keinen Sport machen. Ihr Rücken ist auch sehr verspannt. Ich verschreibe Ihnen auch zehn Massagen.
Max	Soll ich sonst noch etwas tun?
Dr. Najab	Vermeiden Sie zu viel Bewegung. In einer Woche ist alles wieder in Ordnung.
Max	Gut, denn eigentlich will ich ja aktiver und gesünder leben. Vielen Dank, Frau Najab.
Dr. Najab	Gern geschehen, Herr Peterson. Und gute Besserung!

2 Decide if these statements are *true* (richtig) or *false* (falsch). Correct the false ones.

a Max hat ziemlich starke Schulterschmerzen, aber keine Rückenschmerzen.   R   F
b Er glaubt, dass die Schmerzen von einer Yogaübung kommen.   R   F
c Dr. Najab denkt, dass es nichts Schlimmes ist.   R   F
d Max soll die Tabletten dreimal am Tag nehmen.   R   F
e In den nächsten sieben Tag darf er ein bisschen Sport machen.   R   F
f Er soll zu viel Bewegung vermeiden.   R   F

LANGUAGE BUILDER 3

💡 Language discovery 3

Look at these three sentences from Conversation 2. Translate them into English.

a Darf ich einmal schauen? ....

b Darf ich ins Fitnesscenter gehen oder Sport machen? ....

c In den nächsten sieben Tagen dürfen Sie keinen Sport machen. ....

You may, you must not—using dürfen

Dürfen is a modal verb. It conveys the idea of permission and can be translated with *may, can, to be allowed to*:

Darf ich ins Fitnesscenter gehen?   *Am I allowed to go to the fitness center?*

It often adds a sense of politeness and is used in formal situations:

Darf ich mal schauen?   *May I have a look?*

Darf ich Sie etwas fragen?   *May I ask you something?*

When used in the negative, dürfen expresses prohibition (*must not, not allowed*):

Sie dürfen keinen Sport machen.   *You must not do any sports.*

Sie dürfen hier nicht rauchen.   *Smoking is not permitted here.*

Notice that dürfen is irregular: ich darf, du darfst, Sie dürfen, er/sie/es/xier darf, wir dürfen, ihr dürft, sie/Sie dürfen.

Language practice 3

What may you or must not do? Match the sentences with the pictures.

1 Hier darf man Fahrrad fahren.

2 Hier darf man nicht Fahrrad fahren.

3 Hier darf man nicht fotografieren.

4 Hier darf man sein Handy nicht benutzen.

5 Hier darf man nicht parken.

6 Hier dürfen Kunden parken.

7 Hier darf man parken.

8 Hier darf man nicht rauchen.

a P Kunden

b 🚲

c 🚫P

d 🚫📷

e P

f 🚭

g 🚫📱

h 🚫🚲

LANGUAGE BUILDER 4

12.10

💡 Language discovery 4

Listen to the conversation again and repeat each line in the pauses provided. Then complete these sentences from the conversation. What do the missing verbs have in common?

a .... ich einmal schauen?

b Eigentlich .... ich aktiver und gesünder leben.

c Sie .... Ihren Rücken dreimal am Tag einreiben.

d .... ich sonst noch etwas tun?

Modal verbs—Overview

Modal verbs help you to express what you *may do*, *can do*, *must do*, *should do*, or *want to do*. Modal verbs are different from ordinary verbs: they undergo a vowel change (with the exception of sollen) and the ich and er/sie/es/xier forms have different endings.

	dürfen (*may*)	können (*can*)	müssen (*must*)	sollen (*should*)	wollen (*want [to]*)
ich	darf	kann	muss	soll	will
du	darfst	kannst	musst	sollst	willst
Sie	dürfen	können	müssen	sollen	wollen
er/sie/es/xier	darf	kann	muss	soll	will
wir	dürfen	können	müssen	sollen	wollen
ihr	dürft	könnt	müsst	sollt	wollt
Sie/sie	dürfen	können	müssen	sollen	wollen

Modal verbs are usually used with a second verb which is at the end of the sentence in the infinitive.

Soll ich sonst noch etwas *tun*?   *Should I do something else?*

Ich muss morgen früh *aufstehen*.   *I have to get up early tomorrow.*

In a subordinate clause, the modal verb goes to the last position:

Ich denke, dass ich mehr Sport machen <u>soll</u>.   *I think I should do more sports.*

Remember, to say *must not*, use dürfen + nicht/kein:

Hier dürfen Sie Ihr Handy nicht benutzen.   *You are not allowed to use your phone here.*

Occasionally, modal verbs are used on their own:

Ich kann sehr gut Chinesisch.   *I can (speak) Chinese very well.*

Ich will nachher zum Arzt.   *I want (to go) to the doctor later.*

> Careful! Ich will means *I want*. *I will* (used to form the future tense) is **ich werde**.

Language practice 4

1 Complete with the correct form of the verb in parentheses.

Example: Mein Arzt sagt, ich <u>soll</u> mehr schwimmen gehen. (sollen)

a Was .... ich machen? (sollen)

b Nächsten Monat .... er mit einem Tanzkurs anfangen. (wollen)

c Stefan und Andrea .... im Sommer heiraten. (wollen)

d .... du eigentlich wieder Volleyball spielen? (dürfen)

e Hier .... man nicht rauchen. (dürfen)

f Kinder unter 16 Jahren .... den Film nicht sehen. (dürfen)

g Ich denke, dass ich mehr joggen .... (müssen)

2 Now play Conversation 2 again and play Max's role. Speak in the pauses provided and try not to refer to the text.

12.11

SKILL BUILDER

12.12

1 Three people explain whether they think they do enough for their health. Listen to the audio and complete with the missing words.

 Julia Volkmer

Seit zwei Jahren esse ich mehr ....
und Obst und weniger .... Das ist gut für mich. Seitdem fühle ich mich ....
Ich gehe nicht gern ins ...., aber ich gehe gern spazieren und mag auch Nordic Walking. Ich glaube eigentlich, ...
ich genug für meine Gesundheit tue.

 Michael Nowak

Ich habe .... mit dem Herzen. Der Arzt sagt, ich darf nicht mehr rauchen und ....
auch weniger Fett essen.
.... soll ich auch mehr Sport treiben, weil ich den ganzen Tag am Computer ....
Im Moment jogge ich abends, aber am Wochenende ....
ich auch mehr mit dem Rad fahren.

 Lydia Schmidt-Joyner

Ich .... viel Sport, spiele Fußball, Handball, ein bisschen Tennis. Ich .... nicht, trinke sehr wenig ....
Außerdem esse ich viel .... und Obst.
Ja, ich denke, dass ich genug tue. Ich fühle mich fit und bin nur selten ....
Nächstes Jahr .... ich einen Fitnessurlaub machen.

2 Combine the two sentences by using the conjunction in parentheses.

Example: Ich esse ein Sandwich. Ich habe Hunger. (wenn)
> *Ich esse ein Sandwich, wenn ich Hunger habe.*

a Ich gehe gern ins Fitnesscenter. Ich habe Zeit. (wenn)
b Ich bin topfit. Ich mache dreimal pro Woche Sport. (weil)
c Ich habe Herzprobleme. Ich habe Stress. (weil)
d Ich glaube. Berlin ist eine interessante Stadt. (dass)
e Ich bin mehr gejoggt. Ich war jünger. (als)
f Meine Augen tun weh. Ich habe zehn Stunden an meinem Laptop gearbeitet. (weil)

> **machen / tun**
> In various contexts, machen and tun are synonyms, e.g. Was machst/tust du für deine Gesundheit? However, with a direct object you can use only machen: Ich mache einen Kaffee. Some fixed expressions can be used with only one of the verbs: e.g. Das tut mir leid (*I am sorry*); Das macht Spaß (*This is fun*).

3 Read this short text about yoga for beginners and answer the questions.

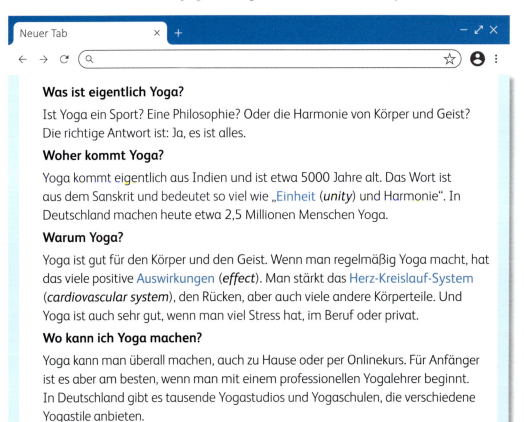

Was ist eigentlich Yoga?

Ist Yoga ein Sport? Eine Philosophie? Oder die Harmonie von Körper und Geist? Die richtige Antwort ist: Ja, es ist alles.

Woher kommt Yoga?

Yoga kommt eigentlich aus Indien und ist etwa 5000 Jahre alt. Das Wort ist aus dem Sanskrit und bedeutet so viel wie „Einheit (*unity*) und Harmonie". In Deutschland machen heute etwa 2,5 Millionen Menschen Yoga.

Warum Yoga?

Yoga ist gut für den Körper und den Geist. Wenn man regelmäßig Yoga macht, hat das viele positive Auswirkungen (*effect*). Man stärkt das Herz-Kreislauf-System (*cardiovascular system*), den Rücken, aber auch viele andere Körperteile. Und Yoga ist auch sehr gut, wenn man viel Stress hat, im Beruf oder privat.

Wo kann ich Yoga machen?

Yoga kann man überall machen, auch zu Hause oder per Onlinekurs. Für Anfänger ist es aber am besten, wenn man mit einem professionellen Yogalehrer beginnt. In Deutschland gibt es tausende Yogastudios und Yogaschulen, die verschiedene Yogastile anbieten.

a What aspects does yoga combine?
b How old is it?
c How many people in Germany practice yoga?

d Which positive effects are mentioned?
e What should beginners do?

4 **While visiting Hamburg, you have developed a sore throat and decide to see a Allgemeinarzt (*general practitioner / family physician*). Use the prompts and respond in the pauses.**

Der Arzt	Sie
Guten Tag. Was kann ich für Sie tun? Was fehlt Ihnen?	*Say that you have got a sore throat.*
Oh, das tur mit leid. Wie lange haben Sie die Schmerzen?	*Tell him for two days.*
Darf ich einmal schauen?	*Say, yes, of course, thank you.*
Tut es hier weh?	*Yes, it hurts here.*
Also, es ist nichts Schlimmes. Ich verschreibe Ihnen Tabletten. Nehmen Sie eine Tablette dreimal am Tag, bitte.	*Ask whether you should do anything else.*
Trinken Sie viel Wasser und versuchen Sie, nicht zu viel zu sprechen.	*Say thank you.*

TEST YOURSELF

Meine Notizen *My notes—the story so far*

Max had an adventurous trip in the last six units, visiting Vienna, Basel, and Hamburg. Can you remember some of the details and complete these sentences?

Wien

a Öffentliche Verkehrsmittel in Wien nennt man auch die Ö _ _ _ _ .
b Die Straße in Wien, wo man viele berühmte Gebäude findet, heißt die

   R _ _ _ _ _ _ _ _ .
c Der Lieblingsmaler von Max ist G _ _ _ _ _ K _ _ _ _ .
d Als Kind hat Lisa in einem G _ _ _ _ _ c h _ _ gesungen.
e Sie wohnt mit zwei anderen Personen in einer W _ _ _ g _ _ _ _ _ _ _ _ _ _ _ _ im
   zweiten Bezirk.
f Ihr Lieblingsort in Wien ist ein Park: der P _ _ t _ _ .

Basel

a Der Karneval in Basel heißt die F _ _ _ _ _ _ _ .
b Der Karneval dauert d _ _ _ Tage oder _ _ Stunden.
c Die Zuschauer ver _ _ e i _ _ _ sich nicht.

d Der Morgenstreich beginnt um vier Uhr nachts. Max denkt, es hat etwas
M _ g _ _ _ _ _ _ .

e Traditionelle Gerichte sind M e h l _ _ _ _ _ und Zw _ _ _ _ _ k _ _ _ _ _ _ .

Hamburg

a Der Fluss in Hamburg heißt die _ _ b _ .

b Ein beliebtes Essen in Hamburg sind Fischbr _ _ _ _ _ _ .

c Das große Konzerthaus heißt die _ _ _ phi _ _ _ _ _ _ _ ie.

d Als Geschenk kauft Max eine Flasche _ _ _ f _ _ für Wally.

e Wally macht gern Yoga, weil es gut für sie ist, körperlich und gei _ _ _ _ .

f Max sagt, dass er aktiv _ _ und gesünd _ _ leben möchte.

Wie geht's weiter? *What happens next?*

Even after his setback at yoga, inspired by his trip, Max is determined to make changes to his lifestyle. Will he succeed once he is back in Berlin? And will he see Lisa again?

Find out in the next few units.

Remember to use **My review** and **My takeaway** to assess your progress and reflect on your learning experience.

Congratulations, you have now completed the second level of your studies! Put your skills to the test—take the A2 Assessment online at library.teachyourself.com and see how much you've learned.

In this lesson you will learn how to:

» Describe your morning routine
» Talk in more detail about your current life situation
» Talk about your interests, dislikes and plans
» Ask others about their interests, dislikes, and plans

Alltag in Berlin

My study plan

I plan to work with Unit 13

○ Every day
○ Twice a week
○ Other _____

I plan to study for

○ 5–15 minutes
○ 15–30 minutes
○ 30–45+ minutes

My progress tracker

Day / Date	🎧	🎤	📖	✏️	💬
	○	○	○	○	○
	○	○	○	○	○
	○	○	○	○	○
	○	○	○	○	○
	○	○	○	○	○
	○	○	○	○	○
	○	○	○	○	○

My goals

What do you want to be able to do or say in German when you complete this unit?

Done

1 .... ○
2 .... ○
3 .... ○

My review

SELF CHECK

	I can ...
○	... describe my morning routine.
○	... talk in more detail about my current life situation.
○	... talk about my interests, dislikes and plans.
○	... ask others about their interests, dislikes and plans.

CULTURE POINT 1

Ein paar Fakten über Berlin

Berlin ist nicht nur die Stadt mit den meisten Einwohnern in Kontinentaleuropa, auch von der Fläche (*area*) her ist sie die Nummer eins und mit etwa 900 km² fast neunmal so groß wie Paris. Berlin ist – wie Hamburg und Bremen – auch ein Stadtstaat, das heißt, es ist eine Stadt und ein Bundesland. Der/

Die Regierende Bürgermeister:in (*Governing Mayor*) und das Parlament, der Berliner Senat, tagen (*sit*) im Roten Rathaus (*Red Town Hall*) im Zentrum von Berlin.

Berlin besteht aus zwölf Bezirken (*districts*), wie zum Beispiel Mitte, Pankow oder Neukölln. Außerdem gibt es siebenundneunzig Ortsteile (*neighborhoods*). Bekannt sind beispielsweise Kreuzberg und Tempelhof.

Das Wappentier (*heraldic animal*) von Berlin ist der Berliner Bär. Man glaubt, dass der Bär seit 1280 das Wappentier von Berlin ist. Man sieht ihn überall in Berlin: auf Fahnen, Souvenirartikeln, auf Produkten aus Berlin. Es gibt ihn auch als Skulptur, als sogenannten (*so-called*) Buddy Bär. Hunderte von ihnen stehen in der Stadt. Jeder Bär ist anders und individuell. Doch die Buddy Bären gibt es nicht nur in Berlin. Man kann sie unter anderem in Shanghai, Buenos Aires, Istanbul, Paris oder Neu-Delhi sehen. Vielleicht gibt es ja auch einen Buddy Bären in Ihrer Stadt?

Hier ist ein ABC von 26 Fun Facts über Berlin*.
Wer sagte: Ich bin ein Berliner? (siehe unter I)
Was ist das Lieblingstier von den Menschen in Berlin? (siehe unter L)
Welche Stadt hat mehr Brücken: Venedig oder Berlin? (siehe unter P)
Wie viele Spätis gibt es in Berlin? (siehe unter S)

*Try to read the text on the website in German. However, if you get stuck, just switch to the English version of the site.

VOCABULARY BUILDER 1

Look at the words and phrases and complete the missing English words and expressions. Then listen and try to imitate the pronunciation of the speakers.

13.01

MEINE MORGENROUTINE	*MY MORNING ROUTINE*
sich rasieren	*to shave*
sich schminken	*to apply makeup*
sich waschen, sich duschen	*to wash, to take a shower*
sich kämmen	*to comb your hair*
sich an/ziehen, sich um/ziehen	*to get dressed, to get changed*
sich ab/trocknen	*to dry off*
sich ein/cremen	*to apply moisturizer*

AKTIVITÄTEN	*ACTIVITIES*
sich bewegen, sich entspannen	*to move, to relax*
sich konzentrieren, sich fühlen	*to ...., to feel*
sich verspäten, sich erholen	*to be late, to recuperate*
sich freuen, sich langweilen	*to be happy, to feel bored*
sich vorstellen, sich merken	*to imagine, to memorize*
sich sehen	*to .... each other*
sich Sorgen machen	*to be worried*
sich wünschen	*to wish*

NÜTZLICHE WÖRTER	*USEFUL EXPRESSIONS*
der Bart (-"e)	*beard*
das Gedächtnis (-se)	*memory*
der Pförtner (-) / die Pförtnerin (-nen)	*door supervisor (male / female)*
der Wachdienst (-e)	*security firm*

Vocabulary practice 1

1 Describe Greta's morning routine using the words in the box. Do not forget that some verbs are separable. They are marked with '/'.

> sich schminken   sich kämmen   sich ein/cremen
> sich ab/trocknen   sich duschen   sich an/ziehen

a Nach dem Duschen .... sie sich mit einem Handtuch ....

b Danach .... sie sich .... Sie hat trockene Haut.

c Anschließend .... sie sich .... Heute trägt sie leichte Kleidung, denn es ist warm.

d Danach .... sie sich die Haare.

e Zum Schluss .... sie sich mit ihrem neuen Make-up.

CONVERSATION 1

Nach dem Sport fühle ich mich besser

13.02

1 Listen to the conversation a few times without looking at the text. Then listen again and read the text. Why is Rainer at the gym so early? How does he describe the gym at this time of the day? What does Max do next?

On their return from Hamburg, a nasty Überraschung (*surprise*) was awaiting Wally and Max: a Rohrbruch (*burst pipe*) in the bathroom. While waiting for the Klempner (*plumber*) to repair the damage, Max has been using the showers in his gym, going very early to avoid the busy times. While he is shaving, another person turns up.

Rainer	Du bist aber auch schon früh unterwegs.
Max	Ja, zu Hause haben wir einen Rohrbruch und wir können das Bad nicht benutzen. Aber ich kann mich ja hier duschen. Und deshalb rasiere ich mich jetzt auch hier. (lacht) Das würde ich normalerweise nicht im Fitnessstudio tun. Ich hoffe, das stört dich nicht.
Rainer	Und hast du auch schon so früh trainiert?
Max	Nein, leider nicht. Ich war ein paar Tage in Hamburg und habe mich an der Schulter und am Rücken verletzt. Da muss ich mich jetzt erst einmal erholen.
Rainer	Oh je, ich hoffe, das geht schnell. Ich hatte heute Nachtschicht. Ich bin Pförtner bei einem Wachdienst. Da sitze ich die ganze Zeit und langweile mich oft.
Max	Das kann ich mir gut vorstellen. Wie lange arbeitest du denn normalerweise?
Rainer	Die Nachtschicht ist immer von 19 Uhr bis 6 Uhr morgens. Ich freue mich, dass ich mich jetzt etwas bewegen kann. Danach fühle ich mich immer besser.
Max	Ja, das verstehe ich gut.
Rainer	Und morgens ist es hier immer so schön ruhig. Das ist angenehmer als am Tag.
Max	Allerdings. Das muss ich mir merken.
Rainer	Vielleicht sehen wir uns ja mal wieder hier. Jetzt gehe ich erst einmal trainieren.
Max	Ja, ja, ich hoffe doch. Viel Spaß beim Trainieren. Ich gehe jetzt erst einmal frühstücken.

2 Decide if these statements are *true* (richtig) or *false* (falsch). Correct the false ones.

a	Max rasiert sich oft im Fitnessstudio.	R	F
b	Er kann schon wieder normal trainieren.	R	F
c	Rainer findet seine Arbeit interessant.	R	F
d	Seine Nachtschicht fängt abends um sieben Uhr an.	R	F
e	Mittags sind mehr Menschen im Fitnessstudio als am Morgen.	R	F
f	Rainer geht jetzt trainieren, aber Max geht wieder ins Bett.	R	F

LANGUAGE BUILDER 1

Language discovery 1

Complete these sentences from Conversation 1. What do you think the missing words indicate?

a Aber ich kann .... ja hier duschen.
b Und deshalb rasiere ich .... jetzt auch hier.
c Danach fühle ich .... immer besser.
d Vielleicht sehen wir .... ja mal wieder hier.

Reflexive verbs with accusative reflexive pronouns

Reflexive verbs refer to an action that the subject does to themself. Reflexive verbs are more common in German than in English. Their meaning is not always literally, 'reflexive', but grammatically, they use a reflexive pronoun, usually in the accusative (mich, sich, etc.).

Ich erhole mich. (*I recuperate.*) Ich freue mich. (*I am happy.*)

Here are the reflexive pronouns:

Personal pronouns + reflexive pronouns (accusative)

ich	mich	wir	uns
du	dich	ihr	euch
Sie	sich	Sie	sich
er, sie, es, xier	sich	sie	sich

> Gender-neutral pronouns are still relatively new in the German language. There is no commonly accepted gender-neutral reflexive pronoun, but it is OK to use sich since it is not marked for gender and is used for both sie and er.

Many reflexive verbs can also be used in a non-reflexive way when they have a direct object (i.e. in the accusative):

Ich wasche mich.	*I wash myself.*
Ich wasche das Auto.	*I wash the car.*
Ich ziehe mich an.	*I get dressed.*
Ich ziehe das neue Kleid an.	*I put on the new dress.*

In most sentences, the *reflexive pronoun* appears directly after the conjugated verb:

Ich erinnere *mich* gerne an unseren Urlaub.   *I like thinking back to our vacation.*

If, however, the conjugated verb precedes the personal pronoun, the reflexive pronoun comes after the personal pronoun.

An unseren Urlaub erinnere ich mich gerne.   *Our vacation (which) I like to think back on.*
For a list of reflexive verbs, please see the online Grammar summary.

Language practice 1

What are these people doing? Complete with the appropriate reflexive pronoun.

a Es ist spät. Ihr müsst .... beeilen.
b Ich kann nicht mehr stehen. Ich muss .... setzen.
c Sein Hemd ist schmutzig. Er zieht .... um.
d Die Aufgabe ist schwer. Die Schüler:innen müssen .... konzentrieren.
e Du hast ganz trockene Haut. Du musst .... täglich eincremen.
f Schön, dass ihr zu Besuch kommt. Wir freuen .... auf euch.

Pronunciation practice

13.03

1 **Listen to how these reflexive pronouns are pronounced. They all end in -ch. Then read them out loud.**

mich   dich   sich   euch

13.04

2 **Practice saying these words, then listen and repeat.**

ich   sprechen   freundlich   richtig   schlecht   Technik

13.05

3 **Note that there are also other ways of pronouncing ch. Listen and repeat how ch sounds after a, o, u.**

acht   doch   kochen   Buch

13.06

4 **Practice saying these words, then listen and repeat.**

Nacht   Achtung   noch   nach   Tochter   Kochbuch

LANGUAGE BUILDER 2

13.07

💡 **Language discovery 2**

Listen to the conversation again and repeat each line in the pauses provided. Then complete the sentences from the conversation. What do you notice about these pronouns? How are they different from the reflexive pronouns you already know?

a Das kann ich .... gut vorstellen.
b Das muss ich .... merken.

Reflexive verbs with dative reflexive pronouns

There is also a group of reflexive verbs that require a reflexive pronoun in the dative. These include: sich etwas merken (*to memorize, retain*), sich etwas vornehmen (*to intend to do something*), sich etwas vorstellen (*to imagine*):

Ich stelle mir das lustig vor.

I imagine that must be funny.

Ich kann mir das sehr gut merken.

I can memorize/retain this very well.

Only the reflexive pronouns for ich and du differ from the reflexive pronouns in the accusative:

> Sich vorstellen is one of the rare verbs which can have either an accusative or dative reflexive pronoun depending on its meaning: Ich stelle mich vor. *I introduce myself.* Ich stelle mir etwas vor. *I imagine something.*

Personal pronouns + reflexive pronouns (dative)

ich	mir	wir	uns
du	dir	ihr	euch
Sie	sich	Sie	sich
er, sie, es, xier	sich	sie	sich

Some reflexive verbs that usually use a reflexive pronoun in the accusative need to use a reflexive pronoun in the dative when used with a direct object:

Ich wasche mich. *I wash myself.*

Ich wasche mir die Haare. *I wash my hair.*

Du wäschst dich. *You wash yourself.*

Du wäschst dir die Hände. *You wash your hands.*

Er kämmt sich. *He combs himself.*

Er kämmt sich die Haare. *He combs his hair.*

Sie zieht sich an. *She gets dressed.*

Sie zieht sich eine Bluse an. *She puts on a blouse.*

The online grammar summary has a list of common reflexive verbs always taking the dative.

Language practice 2

1 Akkusativ or Dativ? Complete with the missing reflexive pronoun.

   a Paolo hat lange Haare und kämmt .... jeden Morgen.

   b Ich kämme .... nicht gerne die Haare.

   c Wasch .... bitte die Hände vor dem Essen.

   d Du hast ein gutes Gedächtnis. Du merkst .... einfach alles.

   e Ich rasiere .... selten und jetzt habe ich einen Bart, aber heute rasiere ich .... den Bart.

   f Ich fühle .... wieder besser. Du kannst .... vorstellen, dass ich .... freue.

   g Zieh .... lieber Handschuhe an. Es ist kalt draußen.

2 Your German friend Sabrina thinks she spends too much time getting ready in the morning. She wants to know about your morning routine. Listen to her message and then reply to her. Take a few notes before you record yourself.

13.08

Waschsalons – ein sozialer Treffpunkt

Waschsalons gibt es seit den 1950er Jahren. Damals hatten viele Menschen keine Waschmaschine, weil sie noch ganz neu und deshalb sehr teuer waren. Heute haben die meisten Haushalte eine Waschmaschine, aber nicht alle. Es gibt immer noch Menschen, die sich keine Waschmaschine leisten können (*to be able to afford*) oder die keinen Platz für eine Waschmaschine in ihrer Wohnung haben. Für einen Ein-Personen-Haushalt lohnt sich (*to be worth it*) eine Waschmaschine vielleicht auch nicht.

Aber es gibt auch noch einen anderen Grund: Waschsalons sind zu einem sozialen Treffpunkt geworden. Viele Waschsalons sind nämlich gleichzeitig (*at the same time*) auch ein Café. Man kann hier also einen Kaffee trinken und Freund:innen treffen, während man seine Wäsche wäscht. Man kommt in einem Waschcafé auch leicht ins Gespräch mit anderen und lernt so neue Menschen kennen. Oder man nutzt die Wartezeit zum Lesen oder das WLAN zum Arbeiten. Deshalb kann man auch in ein Waschcafé gehen, wenn man gar keine Wäsche waschen (*to do the laundry*) will.

Man findet diese Waschcafés vor allem in größeren Städten, und die meisten sind in Berlin. Es gibt sogar ein Comedy-Programm im Fernsehen, das in einem Waschsalon gefilmt wird. Es heißt *NightWash*.

 Finden Sie mehr über eines der Waschcafés in Berlin heraus. Wo liegt das Waschcafé? Wo kann man sitzen? Was können Kinder machen? Wie ist die Speiseauswahl? Gibt es in Ihrem Land auch Waschcafés? Sind Sie anders als in Deutschland?

VOCABULARY BUILDER 2

13.09

Look at the words and phrases and complete the missing English words and expressions. Then listen and try to imitate the pronunciation of the speakers.

MIT ANDEREN KOMMUNIZIEREN	COMMUNICATING WITH OTHERS
sich bedanken bei	*to thank someone*
sich ärgern, beschweren über	*to be annoyed, complain about*
sich einigen auf	*to agree on*
sich entschuldigen bei / für	*to apologize to / for*
sich unterhalten mit / über	*to have a conversation with / about*

NÜTZLICHE VERBEN	USEFUL VERBS
sich ändern	*to change*
sich ein/setzen für	*to advocate for*
sich entscheiden für	*to decide on*
sich erinnern an	*to remember*
sich gewöhnen an	*to get used to*
sich informieren über	*to .... oneself about*
sich konzentrieren auf	*to focus on*
sich kümmern um	*to look after*
die Meinung ändern	*to change your mind*
sich Mühe geben mit	*to make an effort*
sich überlegen	*to think about / ponder*
sich beeilen	*to hurry*
kennen/lernen	*to get to know*
schaffen	*to manage*
sich setzen	*to sit down*
sich verlieben in	*to fall in .... with*

NÜTZLICHE AUSDRÜCKE	USEFUL EXPRESSIONS
das Gefühl (-e)	*feeling*
der Grund (-"e)	*reason*
die Möglichkeit (-en)	*possibility*
nämlich	*you see, that is to say, namely*

Vocabulary practice 2

1 Put the verbs into the table according to the preposition they take. Please note that some verbs can go in more than one group.

an	auf	bei	für

in	mit	über	um
		sich ärgern	

CONVERSATION 2

Ich habe mich verliebt

13.10

1 Listen to the conversation a few times without looking at the text. Then listen again and read the text. Why does Max want to stay in Berlin?

> Max meets Wally in a Waschsalon (*laundromat*) as they can't use the Waschmaschine at their apartment. Max is thinking about staying in Germany and talks to Wally. They order a coffee and sit down at a table in a corner.

Wally	Also, was ist so dringend? Worüber willst du dich mit mir unterhalten?
Max	Ich möchte mit dir über meine Zukunftspläne sprechen. Ich kann mir nämlich gut vorstellen, länger in Berlin oder Deutschland zu bleiben.
Wally	Das freut mich! Gibt es einen bestimmten Grund?
Max	Ich finde Berlin so schön und interessant und ich habe mich an den Lebensstil gewöhnt. Aber jetzt muss ich mir überlegen, was ich hier mache. Ich kann ja nicht mein Leben lang nur bloggen. Ich muss einen richtigen Job finden.
Wally	Hast du dich schon über deine Möglichkeiten informiert? Wofür interessierst du dich denn?
Max	Na, das ist eine gute Frage! Ich bin mir nicht sicher.
Wally	Du hast doch Marketing studiert und es macht dir Spaß, zu bloggen und Texte zu schreiben.
Max	Ja, sicher.
Wally	Also würde ich etwas im Marketingbereich oder als Texter suchen. In Berlin gibt es so viele Start-Up-Unternehmen, da findest du bestimmt etwas. Du kannst dich doch einfach bewerben.
Max	Gut, Wally, das ist ein guter Tipp. Das mache ich.
Wally	Und gibt es vielleicht noch einen anderen Grund?
Max	Was meinst du?
Wally	Na, ja, ich kenne dich ja ein bisschen ...
Max	Mmh, nun ja ... Ich glaube, ich habe mich auch ein bisschen verliebt ...
Wally	Oh, wie schön! In wen hast du dich verliebt? Ist es Lisa? Du erzählst doch so oft von ihr.
Max	Ja, und sie kommt bald mit ihrer Band nach Berlin. Dann kannst du sie auch kennenlernen.
Wally	Schön, ich freue mich auf unser Treffen. Jetzt muss ich mich aber beeilen, denn ich kümmere mich heute um Nuri.

2 Decide if these statements are *true* (richtig) or *false* (falsch). Correct the false ones.

a	Max denkt, dass er den Rest seines Lebens bloggen kann.	R	F
b	Max hat schon einen Plan für seine Zukunft.	R	F
c	Wally denkt, dass Max leicht einen Job findet.	R	F
d	Wally möchte Lisa gerne kennenlernen.	R	F
e	Wally muss am Ende des Gesprächs schnell gehen.	R	F

LANGUAGE BUILDER 3

Language discovery 3

Complete these three sentences from Conversation 2 with the missing word.

a Ich habe mich .... den Lebensstil gewöhnt.

b Ich freue mich .... unser Treffen.

c Ich kümmere mich heute .... Nuri.

Verbs with prepositions

As in English, some verbs in German are always followed by a preposition.

Nele ärgert sich über das Wetter. *Nele complains about the weather.*

Ella konzentriert sich auf die Hausaufgaben. *Ella is focusing on her homework.*

1 Some of these prepositions, such as für and um, always take the accusative:

Max interessiert sich für Musik. *Max is interested in music.*

Enrico bewirbt sich um einen Job. *Enrico applies for a job.*

2 Other prepositions, such as bei and nach, always take the dative:

Elisa bedankt sich bei ihrer Ärztin. *Elisa thanks her doctor.*

Per sucht nach seiner Kreditkarte. *Per is looking for his credit card.*

3 You may remember that certain prepositions, such as an, in, auf, über, can take either the accusative or the dative. In verb + preposition structures an, in, auf, über, normally take the accusative:

Paolo wartet auf den Bus. *Paolo is waiting for the bus.*

Andrea freut sich über das Geschenk. *Andrea is pleased about the present.*

A few are followed by the dative:

Ich leide an einer chronischen Krankheit. *I suffer from a chronic disease.*

4 A few verbs can be used with different prepositions and change their meaning according to the preposition used:

Ich freue mich <u>auf</u> das Konzert. *I am looking forward to the concert.*

Ich freue mich <u>über</u> das Geschenk. *I am pleased about the present.*

As a reminder, here is an overview of the different prepositions and the cases they take:

Prepositions taking the accusative	Prepositions taking the dative	Prepositions taking the accusative or dative
bis, durch, für, gegen, ohne, um	aus, außer, bei, gegenüber, mit, nach, seit, von, zu	an, auf, hinter, in, neben, über, unter, vor, zwischen

Language practice 3

Give the missing preposition.

a Meine Mutter unterhält sich .... Leo.

b Frida beschwert sich oft .... das Wetter.

c Ich möchte mich .... dir bedanken.

d Haben Sie sich schon .... einen Wein entschieden?

e Die Schüler:innen freuen sich .... die Ferien.

f Antonio kümmert sich jeden Samstag .... seine Enkeltochter.

g Hast du .... Ulrikes Geburtstag gedacht?

h Amir hat sich sehr viel Mühe .... dem Kuchen gegeben.

LANGUAGE BUILDER 4

💡 Language discovery 4

13.11

Listen to the conversation again and repeat each line in the pauses provided. Then complete the questions with the missing question words. How are these question words formed?

a .... willst du dich mit mir unterhalten?

b .... interessierst du dich denn?

Asking questions with verbs with prepositions

When asking questions with verbs and prepositions, the preposition moves to the beginning of the sentence. If the question refers to an object or a concept, it starts with wo- plus the preposition. If the preposition starts with a vowel, an -r- is added in the middle (wo + (r) + preposition):

suchen nach:	Wonach suchst du?	*What are you looking for?*
reden über:	Worüber willst du reden?	*What do you want to talk about?*
sich freuen auf:	Worauf freust du dich?	*What are you looking forward to?*

If the question refers to a person or people, the preposition precedes the question word (preposition + question word). Note that the question word wer (*who*) in the accusative is wen and in the dative wem.

In wen hast du dich verliebt?	*Who have you fallen in love with?*
Mit wem hast du dich unterhalten?	*Who have you talked to?*

Language practice 4

1 Add the missing question word.

Example: Wofür interessiert sich Pia? > *Sie interessiert sich moderne Kunst.*

a .... beschwert sich Malou?   Sie beschwert sich über den Service.

b .... freut ihr euch?   Wir freuen uns auf unseren Urlaub.

c .... kümmert sich Philipp.   Philipp kümmert sich um die Wäsche.

d .... konzentriert sich Matthias?   Er konzentriert sich auf seine Hausaufgaben.

e .... ärgert sich Yevgeni?   Er ärgert sich über die hohen Preise.

f .... setzt sich Georgia ein?   Sie setzt sich für Toleranz ein.

2 Now play Conversation 2 again and play Max's role. Speak in the pauses provided and try not to refer to the text.

13.12

SKILL BUILDER

1 Read the text and answer the questions.

Lisa hat in ihren sozialen Netzwerken ein Update zu ihrem neuen Album und Informationen zu ihrer Tournee gepostet.

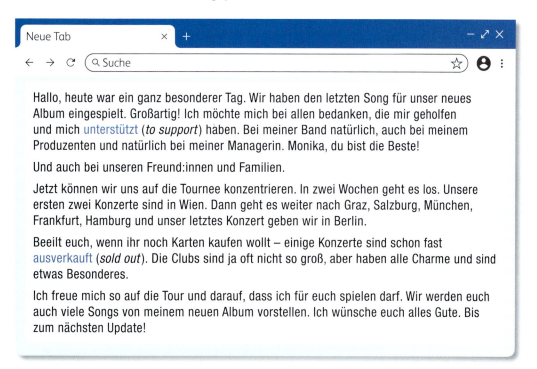

Neue Tab   ✕   +   — ↗ ✕

← → C   🔍 Suche   ☆ 😊 ⋮

Hallo, heute war ein ganz besonderer Tag. Wir haben den letzten Song für unser neues Album eingespielt. Großartig! Ich möchte mich bei allen bedanken, die mir geholfen und mich unterstützt (*to support*) haben. Bei meiner Band natürlich, auch bei meinem Produzenten und natürlich bei meiner Managerin. Monika, du bist die Beste!

Und auch bei unseren Freund:innen und Familien.

Jetzt können wir uns auf die Tournee konzentrieren. In zwei Wochen geht es los. Unsere ersten zwei Konzerte sind in Wien. Dann geht es weiter nach Graz, Salzburg, München, Frankfurt, Hamburg und unser letztes Konzert geben wir in Berlin.

Beeilt euch, wenn ihr noch Karten kaufen wollt – einige Konzerte sind schon fast ausverkauft (*sold out*). Die Clubs sind ja oft nicht so groß, aber haben alle Charme und sind etwas Besonderes.

Ich freue mich so auf die Tour und darauf, dass ich für euch spielen darf. Wir werden euch auch viele Songs von meinem neuen Album vorstellen. Ich wünsche euch alles Gute. Bis zum nächsten Update!

Which answer is correct?

a Es ist ein besonderer Tag für Lisa,
    1 weil ihre Tournee beginnt.
    2 weil ihr neues Album fertig ist.

b Ihre Tournee startet
    1 in Wien und endet in Wien.
    2 startet in Wien und endet in Berlin.

c Für einige Konzerte gibt es
    1 nur noch wenige Karten.
    2 keine Karten mehr.

d Lisa will
    1 viele von ihren neuen Liedern spielen.
    2 viele von ihren Lieblingsliedern spielen.

2 Complete with the correct question word Wen or Wem.

a An .... denkst du?

b Über .... redet ihr?

c Bei .... hast du dich bedankt?

d Mit .... hast du dich unterhalten?

e In .... hat sich Max verliebt?

f Bei .... soll ich mich entschuldigen?

3 Complete the sentences with the correct reflexive verb from the box.

sich erholen	~~sich freuen~~	sich um/ziehen
sich wünschen	sich konzentrieren	sich überlegen

Example: Die Spielerinnen freuen sich.

a Die Woche war sehr anstrengend. Am Wochenende will ich ....

b Bald ist Weihnachten. Nuri .... ein Fahrrad.

c Ich weiß nicht, was ich machen soll. Das muss ich .... noch ....

d Die Schüler:innen schreiben einen Test. Sie sollen ....

e Mein Hemd ist schmutzig. Ich muss .... schnell ....

4 Complete with the correct preposition.

a sich ärgern, sich informieren, sich beschweren: ....

b sich erinnern, sich gewöhnen, glauben: ....

c sich bedanken, sich entschuldigen: ....

d sich interessieren, sich einsetzen, sich entscheiden: ....

e sich einigen, sich freuen, sich konzentrieren: ....

5 Answer the questions using the information given in parentheses. Check your answers and pronunciation on the audio.

13.13

Example: Worüber beschwerst du dich? (über das Wetter)
> *Ich beschwere mich über das Wetter.*

a Wofür interessierst du dich? (für Fußball)
b Wofür bedankst du dich? (für die Hilfe)
c Worüber äußerst du dich? (über die politische Situation)
d Worauf konzentrierst du dich? (auf die Arbeit)
e Womit gibst du dir Mühe? (mit der Aufgabe)
f Wofür entschuldigst du dich? (für den Lärm)
g Worüber informierst du dich? (über die Schweiz)
h Worauf habt ihr euch geeinigt? (auf einen Kompromiss)
i Worüber ärgerst du dich in deiner Stadt? (über den vielen Verkehr)
j Worauf freust du dich? (auf die Ferien)

6 And now you. Answer the questions from Exercise 5, giving reasons for your answers.

TEST YOURSELF

Form questions using verb and preposition constructions.

Example: Marco freut sich auf die Ferien. > Worauf freut sich Marco?
Vivian spricht mit ihrer Schwester. > Mit wem spricht Vivian?

a Alberto wartet auf den Bus. ....
b Er wartet auf seine Freundin. ....
c Angela bedankt sich bei ihren Nachbarn. ....
d Sie bedankt sich für ihre Hilfe. ....
e Herr Schneider informiert sich über die Abfahrtszeiten der Züge. ....
f Benjamin konzentriert sich auf die Hausaufgaben. ....
g Xier setzt sich für Immigrant:innen ein. ....
h Freddie kümmert sich um seine Mutter. ....

Wie geht's weiter? *What happens next?*

It is decision time for Max. Will he really stay in Berlin for longer and what will he do to earn some money? Will he find a job? Find out more in Unit 14.

Remember to use **My review** and **My takeaway** to assess your progress and reflect on your learning experience.

In this lesson you will learn how to:
» Describe jobs and activities
» Express abilities and skills needed for certain jobs
» Scan job adverts
» Understand a basic job interview
» Write a text about yourself for a professional network

Start-Ups und die Arbeitswelt

My study plan

I plan to work with Unit 14
○ Every day
○ Twice a week
○ Other _____
I plan to study for
○ 5–15 minutes
○ 15–30 minutes
○ 30–45+ minutes

My progress tracker

Day / Date	🎧	🎤	📖	✏️	💬
	○	○	○	○	○
	○	○	○	○	○
	○	○	○	○	○
	○	○	○	○	○
	○	○	○	○	○
	○	○	○	○	○
	○	○	○	○	○

My goals

What do you want to be able to do or say in German when you complete this unit?

Done

1 .... ○

2 .... ○

3 .... ○

My review

SELF CHECK	
	I can ...
●	... describe jobs and activities.
●	... express abilities and skills needed for certain jobs.
●	... scan job adverts.
●	... understand a basic job interview.
●	... write a text about myself for a professional network.

Das deutsche Ausbildungssystem

Viele junge Menschen machen in Deutschland nach der Schule eine Ausbildung (*apprenticeship*). Das deutsche Ausbildungssystem hat weltweit einen sehr guten Ruf. Eine Ausbildung ist eine gute Möglichkeit, einen Beruf zu lernen. Dafür braucht man kein Abitur und auch kein Studium. Eine Ausbildung bietet Auszubildenden (kurz: Azubis) (*apprentices*) gute Berufschancen und Karrieremöglichkeiten. Sie dauert zwischen zwei und dreieinhalb Jahren. Die Azubis verdienen in der Ausbildung auch schon ein bisschen Geld.

Schon vor der Industrialisierung haben viele Lehrlinge, ein alter Name für Azubis, bei einem Meister in der Werkstatt eine Ausbildung gemacht. Seit 1969 gibt es die duale Ausbildung in Deutschland. Das bedeutet, dass die Azubis einen Teil ihrer Ausbildung in einem Betrieb (*business/company/workshop*) und den anderen Teil in einer Berufsschule verbringen. Im Betrieb lernen sie die praktischen Fähigkeiten und in der Berufsschule die theoretischen. Nach einer Ausbildung und ein paar Jahren Berufserfahrung kann man auch noch eine Weiterbildung machen oder sogar an einer Fachhochschule (*university of applied sciences*) studieren.

Es gibt Ausbildungsberufe beispielsweise im sozialen (z.B. Erzieher:in *kindergarten/preschool*), kaufmännischen (z.B. Bankkauffrau/-mann), medizinischen (z.B. Physiotherapeut:in) und handwerklichen (z.B. Bäcker:in) Bereich. Aber man kann auch eine Ausbildung zum/zur Game-Designer:in machen.

 Hier finden Sie andere Ausbildungsberufe.
Was für Bereiche gibt es? Finden Sie mindestens sechs. Wie heißen diese Bereiche auf Englisch?
Klicken Sie sich durch. Welche Berufe finden Sie interessant?
Unter dem Tab „Berufe" können Sie auch einen Test machen.
Welcher Beruf passt zu Ihnen?
Gibt es in Ihrem Land auch ein Ausbildungssystem? Wie funktioniert es?

VOCABULARY BUILDER 1

14.01

Look at the words and phrases and complete the missing English words and expressions. Then listen and try to imitate the pronunciation of the speakers.

BERUFSLEBEN	*WORK LIFE*
die Arbeitszeit (-en)	*working hours*
die flexiblen Arbeitszeiten (pl. only)	*flexible working hours*
die Arztpraxis (-praxen)	*medical practice*
das Gehalt (-"er)	*salary, pay*
die Prüfung (-en)	*exam*
die Stelle (-n)	*position / post*
die Teilzeitstelle (-n)	*part-time job*
die Vollzeitstelle (-n)	*full-time job*
das Vorstellungsgespräch (-e)	*job interview*
MEHR BERUFE	*MORE PROFESSIONS*
der Bauarbeiter (-) / die Bauarbeiterin (-nen)	*construction worker / builder*
der Busfahrer (-) / die Busfahrerin (-nen)	*bus driver*
der/die Comedian (-s)	*comedian*
der Designer (-) / die Designerin (-nen)	....
der Mechatroniker (-) / die Mechatronikerin (-nen)	*mechatronics engineer*
der Programmierer (-) / die Progammiererin (-nen)	*computer* ....
der Techniker (-) / die Technikerin (-nen)	*technician*
EIGENSCHAFTEN	*QUALITIES*
Geduld haben	*to have patience*
ein gutes Gefühl für Zahlen haben	*to have a good understanding of numbers*
gut kommunizieren können	*to be able to communicate well*
körperlich fit sein	*to be physically fit*
sich nicht aus der Ruhe bringen lassen	*to not let oneself get worked up*
ruhig bleiben	*to stay calm*
Sinn für Humor haben	*to have a sense of humor*
NÜTZLICHE WÖRTER	*USEFUL WORDS*
der Vorteil (-e), der Nachteil (-e)	*advantage, disadvantage*
sich bewerben (+ um + Akk.)	*to apply (for)*
erzählen	*to tell, recount*
schauspielern	*to act*
sich verstehen	*to get on with someone*
gegenseitig	*each other, mutual(ly)*
übermorgen	*day after tomorrow*

Vocabulary practice 1

Sort these sentences into positive or negative statements.

> ~~Es kann sehr stressig sein.~~
> Man kann viel reisen.
> Die Arbeitszeiten sind lang.
> Das Gehalt ist nicht so hoch.
> Ich muss oft länger arbeiten.
> Die Kolleg:innen sind freundlich.
>
> Wir helfen uns gegenseitig.
> Ich arbeite gern mit Patient:innen.
> Ich habe flexible Arbeitszeiten.
> Die Arbeitsatmosphäre ist nicht besonders gut.
> Man kann zwei Tage im Homeoffice arbeiten.
> Ich kann kreativ sein.

positiv	negativ
	Es kann sehr stressig sein.

Pronunciation practice

14.02

1 Listen to these words, notice how the letter g is pronounced at the beginning, in the middle, and at the end of a word.

Gehalt	morgen	stressig
Geduld	Tag	richtig
gegen	genug	

Did you notice that when g appears at the end of a word it is usually pronounced as k. However, after the letter i (-ig) it is pronounced just like ich.

14.03

2 Practice saying these words, then listen and repeat.

gut	Eigenschaft	ruhig
Gefühl	gegenseitig	wichtig

CONVERSATION 1

Vorteile und Nachteile im Beruf

14.04

Listen to the conversation a few times without looking at the text. Then listen again and read the text. What were Aylin's and Max's dream jobs? What is the exciting news?

Aylin wants to catch up with Max and has invited him for dinner in one of her favorite restaurants. Max meets her in the Arztpraxis where she works.

Max   Was für eine schöne Praxis, Aylin. Seit wann arbeitest du denn hier?

Aylin   Seit acht Jahren. Ich konnte damals nach meiner Prüfung gleich hier anfangen.

Max   Und macht dir die Arbeit immer noch Spaß?

Aylin   Ich arbeite sehr gern mit Patienten, obwohl es manchmal natürlich auch stressig sein kann.

Max   Aber du lässt dich ja auch nicht so leicht aus der Ruhe bringen. Wenn man als Ärztin arbeitet, ist das bestimmt eine gute Eigenschaft.

Aylin   Findest du, dass ich immer ruhig bleibe? Ich weiß nicht, ob Fabian das auch so sieht.

Max   Und wie ist die Arbeitsatmosphäre? Verstehst du dich gut mit deinen Kolleg:innen?

Aylin   Ja, wir sind ein kleines Team. Alle sind sehr freundlich und wir helfen uns gegenseitig. Ein Problem sind die Arbeitszeiten. Obwohl ich im Moment nur eine Teilzeitstelle habe, arbeite ich oft länger, als ich sollte.

Max   Und wolltest du schon immer Ärztin werden?

Aylin   Nein, als ich ein Kind war, wollte ich Schauspielerin werden. Aber na ja, ich glaube, ich konnte nicht besonders gut schauspielern. Meine Eltern meinten, ich sollte Medizin studieren. Und du?

Max   Als ich ein Kind war, wollte ich Basketballprofi werden.

Aylin   Und jetzt, Max? Willst du weiter als Blogger arbeiten oder hast du andere Pläne?

Max   Ach, das habe ich dir noch gar nicht erzählt. Ich habe mich um einige Jobs beworben und habe übermorgen ein Vorstellungsgespräch. Vielleicht kannst du mir noch ein paar Tipps geben.

Aylin   Na klar. Komm, lass uns etwas essen gehen und dann erzähl' mir mehr.

2   Answer the questions.

    a   Wie lange arbeitet Aylin schon in der Arztpraxis?

    b   Was findet Aylin positiv bei ihrer Arbeit?

    c   Welche Nachteile gibt es?

    d   Warum ist Aylin nicht Schauspielerin geworden?

    e   Was hat Max ihr noch nicht erzählt?

LANGUAGE BUILDER 1

Language discovery 1

Complete these sentences from Conversation 1 with the appropriate modal verb. Which ending is used to refer to past events?

a Als ich ein Kind war, ... ich Schauspielerin werden.

b Ich .... damals nach meiner Prüfung gleich hier anfangen.

c Meine Eltern meinten, ich .... Medizin studieren.

d Ich glaube, ich .... nicht besonders gut schauspielern.

Using modal verbs in the past

When *talking* about the past, you normally use the *perfect tense*. However, there are a few exceptions, including modal verbs which are commonly used in the *simple past* (Präteritum). To form the simple past, add the endings below (in bold) to the stem. The umlaut- in dürfen, können, and müssen are dropped.

	dürfen (*may*)	können (*can*)	müssen (*must*)	sollen (*should*)	wollen (*want*)
ich	dur**fte**	kon**nte**	mus**ste**	sol**lte**	wol**lte**
du	duf**test**	kon**ntest**	mus**stest**	sol**ltest**	wol**ltest**
Sie	dur**ften**	kon**nten**	mus**sten**	sol**lten**	wol**lten**
er/sie/es/xier	dur**fte**	kon**nte**	mus**se**	sol**lte**	wol**lte**
wir	dur**ften**	kon**nten**	mus**sten**	sol**lten**	wol**lten**
ihr	dur**ftet**	kon**ntet**	mus**stet**	sol**ltet**	wol**ltet**
Sie/sie	dur**ften**	kon**nten**	mus**sten**	sol**lten**	wol**lten**

Ich durfte leider nicht zur Party gehen.   *I was not allowed to go to the party.*

Daniel konnte fantastisch singen.   *Daniel could sing fantastically.*

Wir mussten länger arbeiten.   *We had to work longer.*

Sollten Sie nicht nach Rom fliegen?   *Weren't you supposed to fly to Rome.*

Wolltest du etwas fragen?   *Did you want to ask something?*

Language practice 1

Complete with the correct simple past form.

a Zuerst .... ich Busfahrer werden, später .... ich Popstar werden. (wollen)

b Ich .... gut Skateboard fahren und ich .... gut singen. (können, können)

c .... ihr in eurem früheren Job im Homeoffice arbeiten? (dürfen)

d .... du letztes Wochenende arbeiten? (müssen)

e Ja, erst .... meine Kollegin arbeiten, aber dann .... sie nicht. (sollen, können)

LANGUAGE BUILDER 2

14.05

💡 Language discovery 2

Listen to the conversation again and repeat each line in the pauses provided. Look at these three sentences from Conversation 1. Can you identify the main clause and the subordinate clause in each?

a Als ich ein Kind war, wollte ich Basketballprofi werden.
b Wenn man als Ärztin arbeitet, ist das bestimmt eine gute Eigenschaft.
c Obwohl ich nur eine Teilzeitstelle habe, arbeite ich oft länger.

What do you notice about word order in the main clause?

Conjunctions and word order (Wortstellung)

You have learned to use words like dass, weil, obwohl, or als (called *subordinating conjunctions*) which introduce a subordinate clause and send the verb(s) to the end:

Ich jogge, obwohl es regnet.
I go running although it's raining.

Leon lernt Deutsch, weil er in Berlin leben möchte.
Leon is learning German because he would like to live in Berlin.

It is not uncommon to start a sentence with the subordinate clause. In this case, the main clause starts with the verb, followed by the subject:

Obwohl es regnet, jogge ich.

Weil er in Berlin leben möchte, lernt Leon Deutsch.

If there are two verbs in the main clause, the second verb goes to the end:

Als Yasmin ein Kind war, hat sie in Berlin gelebt.
When Yasmin was a child, she lived in Berlin.

Using als
Als has three different meanings. As a conjunction, it means *when*, referring to past events:
Als ich ein Kind war, ... *When I was a child ...*
But it can also be used as an adverb, meaning *as*:
Als Teenager lebte ich in ... *As a teenager I lived in ...*
And it is needed when making comparisons:
Hamburg ist größer als München. *Hamburg is bigger than Munich.*

Language practice 2

1 Jobs and skills. Match the sentence halves.

a Wenn man Technik mag,	**1** muss man körperlich sehr fit sein.
b Wenn man in einer Bank arbeitet,	**2** muss man gut kommunizieren können.
c Wenn man Bauarbeiter ist,	**3** brauchst du viel Geduld.
d Wenn man Comedian werden möchte,	**4** braucht man ein gutes Gefühl für Zahlen.
e Wenn man als Kundenberaterin arbeitet,	**5** ist Mechatroniker ein interessanter Beruf.
f Wenn du gern kreativ bist,	**6** braucht man viel Sinn für Humor.
g Wenn du als Altenpfleger arbeitest,	**7** ist Designer/in vielleicht ein guter Beruf.

2 Put the words after the comma in the correct order.

Example: *Weil die Kollegen nett sind, Laura / mag / ihren Beruf /. > Weil die Kollegen nett sind, mag Laura ihren Beruf.*

a Wenn ich Hunger habe, ich / ein Sandwich / esse

b Wenn es morgen einen Bahnstreik gibt, ich / arbeite / im Homeoffice

c Weil sie viel lernt, mit ihrem Beruf / Svetlana / ist / zufrieden

d Obwohl das Gehalt nicht so hoch ist, als Altenpfleger / arbeitet / Ronny / gern

e Als ich ein Kind war, Eisverkäufer / wollte / ich / werden

f Obwohl es viele freie Stellen gibt, Andreas / findet / keinen Job

3 Answer the questions and talk about your work experience in as much detail as possible.

a Was sind Sie von Beruf? Arbeiten Sie im Moment Vollzeit oder Teilzeit?

b Wie viele Stunden arbeiten Sie pro Woche?

c Welche Vorteile hat Ihre Arbeit?

d Welche Nachteile gibt es?

e Welche Fähigkeiten braucht man, wenn man in Ihrem Job arbeitet?

f Was wollten Sie werden, als Sie ein Kind waren?

Now play Conversation 2 again and play Max's role. Speak in the pauses provided and try not to refer to the text.

CULTURE POINT 2

Wirtschaft und Arbeit

Die deutsche Wirtschaft ist die größte Volkswirtschaft (*national economy*) in Europa und die viertgrößte Volkswirtschaft in der Welt. Die wichtigsten Branchen (*sectors*) sind die Autoindustrie (*car industry*), der  Maschinenbau (*mechanical engeneering*), die chemische Industrie (*chemical industry*) und die Elektrotechnik (*electrical industry*). Weltbekannte Firmen sind Volkswagen, Daimler, BMW, BASF, SAP und Siemens.

Der Grund, warum die deutsche Wirtschaft so erfolgreich ist, sind aber nicht nur die großen Konzerne (*corporations*). In ganz Deutschland verteilt, gibt es tausende von kleineren oder mittelständischen Unternehmen (*medium-size businesses*). Oft sind sie in ihrem Bereich weltführend (*world-leading*). Man nennt diese Art von Firmen den Mittelstand. Die meisten dieser Firmen sind Familienunternehmen (*family-owned businesses*).

In den letzten Jahren hat sich in Deutschland auch eine sehr innovative Start-up-Szene entwickelt. Das Zentrum dieser Szene – das ist wahrscheinlich keine Überraschung – ist Berlin. Jedes Jahr gibt es hier mehr als 500 Start-up-Gründungen (*foundations*).

Fragt man die Deutschen nach ihren Traumjobs, so sind die Topberufe: 1. Arzt / Ärztin; 2. Schauspieler / Schauspielerin; 3. Software-Entwickler / Software-Entwicklerin; 4. Fotograf / Fotografin; 5. Tierpfleger / Tierpflegerin; 6. Reiseführer / Reiseführerin; 7. Anwalt / Anwältin; 8. Manager / Managerin.

 Finden Sie mehr Informationen über den Mittelstand.

Wie nennt man kleine und mittelständische Unternehmen auch?
Wie viel Prozent der deutschen Unternehmen gehören dem Mittelstand an?
Wie viele Beschäftigte (*employees*) hat eine mittelständische Firma?
Wie viele Menschen mit Migrationshintergrund besitzen eine eigene Firma?

VOCABULARY BUILDER 2

14.07

Look at the words and phrases and complete the missing English words and expressions. Then listen and try to imitate the pronunciation of the speakers.

STELLENANGEBOTE	JOB OFFERS
der Ansprechpartner (-), die Ansprechpartnerin (-en)	contact / contact person
der Einsatzort (-e)	job site
das Honorar (-e)	fee / honorarium
der Kinderbetreuer (-) / die Kinderbetreuerin (-nen)	childcare provider / nanny
die Kundenanfrage (-n)	customer inquiry
der / das Kundenservice (-s)	....
das Produktsortiment (-e)	product line
die Stellenbeschreibung (-en)	job description
das Unternehmen (-)	company, business
betreuen	to look after
m/w/d = männlich, weiblich, divers	male, female, gender neutral
der Lebenslauf (-"e)	resumé / CV
der Gründer (-) / die Gründerin (-nen)	founder
die Hochschule (-n)	university, higher education institution
der Hochschulabschluss (-"e)	.... degree
die Personalabteilung (-en)	HR department
die Schwäche (-n)	weakness, shortcoming
die Stärke (-n)	strength
bearbeiten	to work (on sth.), to process, to edit
um/setzen	to put into practice, to implement
sich weiter/entwickeln	to develop / to improve oneself

CHARAKTEREIGENSCHAFTEN	CHARACTER TRAITS
flexibel	....
kommunikativ	....
zuverlässig	reliable
unter Druck arbeiten	to work under pressure
den Fokus verlieren	to lose focus

NÜTZLICHE AUSDRÜCKE	USEFUL EXPRESSIONS
idealerweise	ideally
liebevoll	caring / affectionate
teilweise	partly
Ich arbeite daran.	I am working on it.

> Hochschule refers to institutions of higher education, corresponding to universities and colleges in English. It is different from the concept of high school.

Vocabulary practice 2

1 Look at the job descriptions A–D and match with the best person (1 or 2) for each.

a 1 Piotr arbeitet seit drei Jahren im Kundenservice. Er hat zwei Jahre in Kanada gelebt.

    2 Lukas hat Erfahrung im Kundenservice. Sein Englisch ist nicht gut.

b 1 Ellie unterrichtet Englisch, will aber nur im Homeoffice arbeiten.

    2 Ron arbeitet gern flexibel.

c 1 Steffi ist Köchin und sucht einen Teilzeitjob.

    2 Shahzad ist Koch und möchte Vollzeit arbeiten.

d 1 Marita ist kinderlieb. An drei Nachmittagen muss sie zur Uni.

    2 Ria hat am Vormittag Uni.

a

Customer Care Specialist (m/w/d)

Wir sind *Schnell und Frisch* – dein Online-Supermarkt. Wir machen das Einkaufen einfach.

Stellenbeschreibung

- **Du bearbeitest Kundenanfragen meistens per Chat / WhatsApp.**
- **Du bist Ansprechpartner/in bei Fragen zu unserem Produktsortiment.**

Qualifikationen

- **Idealerweise hast du schon Erfahrungen im Kundenservice.**
- **Du hast starke Kommunikationsfähigkeiten in Deutsch, gute Englischkenntnisse sind wichtig.**
- **Du bringst positive Energie mit, bist zuverlässig.**

b

Englisch-Lehrer (m/w/d)

Die EasyEnglish Sprachenschule sucht einen freiberuflichen Englisch-Trainer für Erwachsene, teilweise berufsspezifisch, z. B. Business, Tourismus. Der Einsatzort ist Berlin und Umgebung, aber teilweise unterrichten Sie auch online im Homeoffice.

Ihr Profil: exzellente Englischkenntnisse, Unterrichtserfahrung, Freude mit Menschen zu arbeiten, zeitliche Flexibilität, idealerweise einen Hochschulabschluss, gern aber auch Studierende.

Honorar: 24–30 Euro pro Unterrichtsstunde (45 Minuten)

c

Café-Restaurant „Zur Linde" in Zeesen bei Berlin sucht **Koch (m/w/d)** für vegetarische und vegane Küche zum 1. Oktober. Vollzeitstelle (40 Stunden), freundliche Atmosphäre, nette Kolleg:innen. Interesse? Ansprechpartnerin Sybille Oser beantwortet gern deine Fragen: 0176-34975563, s.oser@zurlindeos.de

d

Familie sucht liebevolle **Kinderbetreuerin**, die an 3–4 Nachmittagen unsere zwei Kinder betreuen kann. Bilge ist neun und Asmaa ist sieben Jahre alt. Beide gehen in die Grundschule und brauchen auch etwas Hilfe bei den Hausaufgaben. Wir wohnen in Steglitz. Familie Can, 0176-21897422

Das erste Vorstellungsgespräch

14.08

Listen to the conversation a few times without looking at the text. Then listen again and read the text. Who conducts the interview? What questions is Max asked?

Max has applied for a job as a Content & Marketing Assistent at a Start-Up-Unternehmen and—to his surprise—has been invited to an interview.

Celine   Guten Tag, Max. Es freut mich sehr, Sie kennenzulernen. Mein Name ist Celine Großmann. Ich bin die Start-Up Gründerin. Und das ist Malik von der Personalabteilung.

Max   Es freut mich auch sehr, Sie kennen zu lernen. Danke für die Einladung.

Celine   Max, können Sie ein bisschen über sich und Ihren Lebenslauf erzählen?

Max   Ich bin in Portland, in den USA, geboren und wuchs dort auch auf. Meine Mutter ist Deutsche und deshalb bin ich zweisprachig. Nach der Schule habe ich dann an der University of Michigan Marketing studiert und dort einen Master gemacht. Seit ein paar Monaten lebe ich in Berlin.

Celine   Und warum haben Sie sich um die Stelle beworben?

Max   Nun, ich fand Marketing schon immer interessant, vor allem den digitalen Bereich. Und dann schreibe ich auch gerne Texte. Nachdem ich jetzt eine kleine Pause gemacht habe, würde ich gern mein Wissen in die Praxis umsetzen und mich auch weiterentwickeln. Außerdem gefällt mir das Profil von Ihrer Firma sehr gut.

Celine   Was, glauben Sie denn, sind Ihre Stärken?

Max   Tja, ich denke, dass ich sehr kreativ bin und dass ich auch gut schreibe. Ich bin sehr offen für neue Dinge und auch sehr kommunikativ und arbeite gut im Team. Ich bin auch sehr zuverlässig und kann unter Druck arbeiten.

Celine   Und Ihre Schwächen?

Max   Nun, ich interessiere mich für viele Dinge und ich kann manchmal den Fokus verlieren. Aber ich arbeite daran ...

Celine   Vielen Dank, Max. Jetzt möchte Malik Ihnen gerne noch ein paar Fragen stellen ...

2   Decide if these statements are *true* (richtig) or *false* (falsch) ones.

   a Celine und Malik haben das Start-Up-Unternehmen gegründet.   R   F

   b Max hat in Portland Marketing studiert.   R   F

   c Er möchte jetzt sein Wissen umsetzen und sich weiterentwickeln.   R   F

   d Max meint, dass er kommunikativ ist, aber nicht so gern im Team arbeitet.   R   F

   e Er glaubt, dass er gut unter Druck arbeitet.   R   F

Language discovery 3

For his application, Max wrote a short cover letter. Compare the verbs in these sentences to similar sentences in the conversation. What is the difference?

a Als Kind lebte ich in Portland, in den USA.
b Nach der Schule studierte ich an der Universität von Michigan.
c Dort machte ich auch einen Master.

Regular verbs in the simple past

The Präteritum (*simple past*) is commonly used in German when people write about the past, especially in formal texts, reports, articles, novels, etc.

Regular verbs form the Präteritum by adding a t and the relevant ending to the stem. If the stem ends in -d, -n, -t, or -m, an extra e is added:

	besuch-en	mach-en	arbeit-en		besuch-en	mach-en	arbeit-en
ich	besuchte	machte	arbeitete	wir	besuchten	machten	arbeiteten
du	besuchtest	machtest	arbeitetest	ihr	besuchtet	machtet	arbeitetet
Sie	besuchten	machten	arbeiteten	Sie	besuchten	machten	arbeiteten
er/sie/ es /xier	besuchte	machte	arbeitete	sie	besuchten	machten	arbeiteten

These are the same endings as for the modal verbs you learned earlier in the unit.

Er wollte die Stelle unbedingt haben.	*He really wanted to have the job.*
Gestern besuchte ich meine Eltern.	*Yesterday I visited my parents.*
Saskia arbeitete bis Mitternacht.	*Saskia worked until midnight.*

Language practice 3

1 Complete the missing endings.

a Früher wohn.................... ich auf dem Land.
b Als Kind spiel.................... ich viel Fußball.
c Sabrina studier.................... in Heidelberg.
d Interessier.................... du dich früher für Physik?
e Nach dem Konzert post.................... Miriam ein Foto.
f Gestern regn.................... es den ganzen Tag.
g Wir verabred.................... uns im Café.
h Wir diskutier.................... die ganze Nacht.

LANGUAGE BUILDER 4

14.09

💡 Language discovery 4

Listen to the conversation again and repeat each line in the pauses provided. Although you normally use the perfect tense when speaking about the past, Max uses the simple past for aufwachsen and finden. Look at the conversation again and find the correct forms.

a **aufwachsen:** Ich bin in Portland geboren und .... dort auch ....

b **finden:** Ich .... Marketing schon immer interessant.

Irregular and mixed verbs in the simple past

Similar to English, irregular verbs in German often have a vowel change or sometimes change the whole stem in the simple past tense: finden > fand (*to find* > *found*); sehen > sah (*to see* > *saw*); kommen > kam (*to come* > came); gehen > ging (*to go* > *went*).

You need to add the following endings to the modified stem. Note that the ich and er/sie/es/xier forms only undergo the vowel change and do not take an ending.

	fahren	sprechen	gehen		fahren	sprechen	gehen
ich	fuhr	sprach	ging	wir	fuhren	sprachen	gingen
du	fuhrst	sprachst	gingst	ihr	fuhrt	spracht	gingt
Sie	fuhren	sprachen	gingen	Sie	fuhren	sprachen	gingen
er/sie/es/xier	fuhr	sprach	ging	sie	fuhren	sprachen	gingen

For the du-form only: If the stem of the past tense form ends in -s, -ß, -x, or -z, the -st ending becomes -t: lesen: du last; heißen: du hießt; sitzen: du saßt.

There are also verbs called mixed verbs—including denken (*to think*), kennen (*to know*), and wissen (*to know*)—which have a vowel change but take the **regular** endings: denken > dachte; kennen > kannte; wissen > wusste.

Many irregular and mixed verbs follow certain patterns when changing their stem in the simple fast. For a list of irregular and mixed verbs, see the online grammar summary.

e > a	i > a	ei > ie	a > u
bewerben > bewarb	finden > fand	bleiben > blieb	fahren > fuhr
essen > aß	singen > sang	heißen > hieß	waschen > wusch
helfen > half	sitzen > saß	scheinen > schien	wachsen > wuchs
stehen > stand	trinken > trank	schreiben > schrieb	tragen > trug

Language practice 4

1 Complete Verena's diary with verbs from the box.

las	stand	aß	aßen	ging	ging
gingen	fuhr	trank	~~duschte~~	hatten	dauerte
sprach	traf	schrieb			

Heute Morgen .... ich um 8 Uhr auf und duschte mich. Zum Frühstück .... ich einen grünen Tee und .... ein Toastbrot mit Marmelade. Um Viertel vor neun .... ich aus dem Haus und .... mit dem Fahrrad zur Arbeit. Am Vormittag .... ich einen längeren Bericht über das letzte Quartal.

Nach dem Mittagessen .... wir ein Meeting. Carsten, unser Chef, ... wieder viel zu viel. Gut, dass das Meeting nicht so lange .... Um 17 Uhr .... ich meine Kollegin Sonja. Wie jeden Donnerstag .... wir zusammen ins Fitnessstudio. Danach .... wir noch etwas in einem thailändischen Restaurant. Später .... ich noch ein Buch. Gegen 23 Uhr .... ich ins Bett. Morgen ist Freitag, dann kommt das Wochenende.

2 Now play Conversation 2 again and play Max's role. Speak in the pauses provided and try not to refer to the text.

14.10

SKILL BUILDER

1 Find the odd one out.

a	Kundenservice	Bauarbeiter	Kinderbetreuer	Mechatroniker
b	das Unternehmen	die Firma	die Praxis	das Gehalt
c	die Prüfung	die Hochschule	das Examen	der Test
d	Geduld haben	gut kommunizieren können	ruhig bleiben	den Fokus verlieren
e	zuverlässig	kreativ	teilweise	kommunikativ

2 Answer the questions and talk about your childhood.

a Was wollten Sie als Kind werden?

b Was konnten Sie als Kind gut? Was konnten Sie nicht so gut?

c Was durften Sie als Kind tun? Was durften Sie nicht machen?

d Was sollten Sie als Kind (in der Schule, zu Hause) machen? Was haben Sie aber nicht (immer) gemacht?

e Was mussten Sie als Kind tun? Was mussten Sie nicht tun?

> nicht müssen means *not having to*. To say that *you mustn't do* or *are not allowed to do* something, you have to say nicht dürfen.
> Rita muss heute nicht arbeiten.
> *Rita does not have to work today.*
>
> Im Büro darf man nicht rauchen.
> *You are not allowed to smoke in the office.*

3 Complete with the prepositions from the box.

als	bevor	obwohl	obwohl	~~weil~~	weil	wenn

Example: Susanne ist mit ihrem Job zufrieden, <u>weil</u> die Kollegen nett sind.

a Ronja wollte Astronautin werden, ... sie ein Kind war.

b Zac ist gern Kfz-Mechatroniker, ... die Arbeit körperlich anstrengend ist.

c Sie hat noch ein Meeting um 16.00 Uhr, ... sie um 17.00 Uhr Feierabend hat.

d Yasmin mag ihren Job, ... sie immer etwas Neues lernt.

e Man muss sehr kreativ sein, ... man als Designer arbeitet.

f Ole blieb im Bewerbungsgespräch ganz ruhig, ... er sehr nervös war.

4 Rewrite the sentences in Exercise 3 starting with the second clause.

Example: Weil die Kollegen nett sind, ist Susanne mit ihrem Job zufrieden.

5 Complete with the simple past or infinitive for each verb.

a bekommen > ....

f fahren > ....

k schreiben > ....

b .... > bewarb

g .... > fand

l tragen > ....

c bleiben > ....

h gehen > ....

m .... > saß

d essen > ....

i kommen > ....

n trinken > ....

e helfen > ....

j .... > stand

o .... > wuchs

14.11

6 Listen to Selima's job interview and answer the following questions.

a Um welche Stelle hat sich Selima beworben?

b Wer stellt die Fragen? Welche Funktion hat die Person?

c Was und wo hat Selima studiert?

d Warum will sie die Stelle unbedingt haben?

e Was sind Selimas Stärken?

f Was sind ihre Schwächen?

Complete the short text about Max's career with the verbs in parentheses in the simple past.

Ich bin in Portland, in den USA, geboren. Dort ging (gehen) ich auch in die Schule. Als Kind .... (wollen) ich eigentlich Basketballprofi werden, aber ich .... (sein) zu klein. Meine Mutter ist Deutsche und deshalb .... (wachsen) ich zweisprachig auf.

Nach meinem Highschool-Abschluss .... (beginnen) ich gleich ein Marketing-Studium an der Universität in Michigan. Für meinen Master .... (spezialisieren) ich mich auf digitales Marketing. Meine Thesis .... (schreiben) ich über Online-Marketing in den USA und Deutschland.

Neben dem Studium .... (arbeiten) ich als Kellner und auch für das Hochschulmagazin. Außerdem .... (machen) ich zwei Praktika. Nach dem Master .... (gehen) ich nach Berlin, weil ich Deutschland und Europa besser kennenlernen .... (wollen). Ich .... (reisen) nach Österreich und in die Schweiz und .... (schreiben) viel für meinen Blog. Jetzt bin ich wieder in Berlin und suche idealerweise einen Vollzeitjob.

?

Wie geht's weiter? *What happens next?*

Will Max get the job?

And there is other exciting news. Lisa is coming to Berlin with her band to give a concert. Will they have enough time to meet? And will they get on? Find out in Unit 15.

Remember to use **My review** and **My takeaway** to assess your progress and reflect on your learning experience.

In this lesson you will learn how to:

» Express likes and dislikes
» Describe your favorite cultural activities
» Agree to and decline suggestions
» Refer to the future

Musik, Clubbing, Kunst

My study plan

I plan to work with Unit 15

○ Every day
○ Twice a week
○ Other _____

I plan to study for

○ 5–15 minutes
○ 15–30 minutes
○ 30–45+ minutes

My progress tracker

Day / Date	🎧	🎤	📖	✏️	💬
	○	○	○	○	○
	○	○	○	○	○
	○	○	○	○	○
	○	○	○	○	○
	○	○	○	○	○
	○	○	○	○	○
	○	○	○	○	○

My goals

What do you want to be able to do or say in German when you complete this unit?

Done

1 .... ○

2 .... ○

3 .... ○

My review

SELF CHECK

	I can ...
○	... express likes and dislikes.
○	... describe my favorite cultural activities.
○	... agree to and decline suggestions.
●	... refer to the future.

CULTURE POINT 1

Die Partyhauptstadt

Seit einigen Jahren nennt man Berlin auch die „inoffizielle" Partyhauptstadt der Welt. Menschen aus der ganzen Welt sind von der besonderen Clublandschaft Berlins begeistert. Hier spielen die angesagtesten (*hippest*, *hottest*) DJs ihre Musik, und hier gibt es einige der bekanntesten Clubs, wie das Berghain oder den Tresor.

Die Anfänge dieses Phänomens liegen im Jahre 1989. Nach dem Fall der Mauer gab es in Berlin viele leerstehende (*disused*, *vacant*) Gebäude, wo sich junge Leute zu illegalen Raves trafen und DJs einen besonderen Berliner Techno-Sound entwickelten. Seitdem ist Berlin ein, wenn nicht, das Zentrum der Technomusik.

Die Clubkultur ist aber auch ein wichtiger wirtschaftlicher (*economic*) Faktor für Berlin. Etwa ein Drittel (*a third*) der Tourist:innen – vor allem junge Leute – sagen, dass sie wegen des Nachtlebens nach Berlin kommen. Und über 9000 Menschen arbeiten in Clubs.

Wenn Sie kein Technofan sind – Berlin bietet für jeden Musikgeschmack (*musical taste*) etwas und hat wunderbare Veranstaltungsorte (*venues*) für Livemusik – von Konzerthallen, drei Opernhäusern, der Waldbühne, einer Freilichtbühne (*open-air stage*), bis hin zu mittleren und kleinen Clubs, wo man neue und unterschiedliche Musik hören und dazu tanzen kann.

 Nicht nur Berlin, auch andere deutsche Städte wie Hamburg, Düsseldorf und Köln waren wichtig für die Entwicklung der deutschen Musikszene. Lesen Sie den Text und entscheiden Sie, was passt.

a Düsseldorf   **1** Hier entstand der Krautrock.

b Köln   **2** Extravagante Bands, viele Technoclubs.

c Hamburg   **3** Heimat von elektronischer Musik (Kraftwerk) und Punk.

d Berlin   **4** Die Musik ist handgemacht, das Bandkonzept ist wichtig.

Kennen Sie Musiker:innen oder Bands aus Deutschland, Österreich, der Schweiz?

VOCABULARY BUILDER 1

15.01

Look at the words and phrases and complete the missing English words and expressions. Then listen and try to imitate the pronunciation of the speakers.

MUSIKER, BAND, TOURNEE

das Album (Alben)
der Applaus (no plural)
der Gig (-s)
der Ort (-e)
die Probe (-n)
das Publikum (no plural)
die Reaktion (-en)
die Stimme (-n)
der Text (-e)
die Tour (-en) / die Tournee (-n)
die Zugabe (-n)
live vor Publikum spielen

MUSICIAN, BAND, TOUR

....
applause
....
place, spot
rehearsal
audience
....
voice
text, lyrics
tour
encore
to play live in front of an audience

> In the world of popular music, many German words are either very similar or directly loaned from English. This also applies to music genres: der Hiphop (*hip-hop*), der Jazz (*jazz*), die Countrymusik (*country music*), der R&B (*R&B*), die Rockmusik (*rock music*), der/das Techno (*techno*), etc.

VERBEN

clubben gehen
fertig/stellen
sich etwas überlegen
verzaubern

VERBS

to go ....
to complete, finalize
to think about something
to enchant

ADJEKTIVE

emotional
zufrieden

ADJECTIVES

....
content, satisfied

VORSCHLÄGE UND ANTWORTEN

Hast du Lust, ...?
Hast du Zeit, ...?
Ich schlage vor, ...
Ich habe (keine) Lust, ...
Es macht mir (keinen) Spaß, ...

SUGGESTIONS AND RESPONSES

Do you fancy ...?
Do you have time ...?
I suggest ...
I (don't) fancy ...
I (don't) enjoy ...

NÜTZLICHE AUSDRÜCKE

sicherlich
rechtzeitig
wahrscheinlich
es kommt mir vor ...

USEFUL EXPRESSIONS

certainly, surely
in time
probably, likely
it seems to me ...

Vocabulary practice 1

Read the four posts and answer the questions.

 Tolle Lieder, tolle Texte, tolle Band, und was für eine tolle Stimme – ein wunderbarer, emotionaler Abend. Danke Lisa. Du warst großartig! Marie

 5 Minuten Applaus, drei Zugaben – wir Zuschauer waren begeistert. Wir vermissen dich jetzt schon, Lisa. Komm bald wieder nach Salzburg. Piotr

 Die neuen Lieder haben mir gut gefallen, aber ich hätte gern auch mehr von den alten Songs gehört. Gabriel

 Was für ein fantastisches neues Album. Die Musik ist komplexer als früher und die Texte sind wie immer emotional, aber auch kritischer. Gestern hast du Hamburg verzaubert. Matze

a Who wants Lisa to come back soon? ....

b Who wanted to hear more of the old songs? ....

c Which two people mention the lyrics? ....

d Who was fascinated by her voice? ....

Pronunciation practice

15.02

15.03

1 Listen to these words, which are very similar in English. Notice the difference in pronunciation between German and English. Repeat the words in the pauses.

Konzert   Szene   Album   Reaktion   Applaus   Lisa

2 Practice saying these words, then listen and repeat.

Generation   emotional   Berlin   Zoo   Information   Ball

> Compound nouns are common in German. If two compound nouns with an identical element appear close together, you normally omit the identical part to avoid repetition: Musikszene und Clubszene > Musik- und Clubszene; Technomusik und Housemusik > Techno- und Housemusik.

Wie läuft die Tour?

15.04

1 **Listen to the conversation a few times without looking at the text. Then listen again and read the text. What does Lisa say about her first two concerts in Vienna? What are her plans for the next days?**

> Although he was in close contention, Max didn't get the job. However, there is some good news—Lisa is in Berlin with her band. Their gig is tonight, and she meets Max before their final rehearsal.

Lisa	Ah, Max. Es ist wirklich schön, dich zu sehen. Wie lange ist das jetzt her, dass du in Wien warst?
Max	Über sechs Monate. Es kommt mir aber gar nicht so lange vor. Wie war denn die Tournee bislang? Bist du zufrieden?
Lisa	Sehr zufrieden, aber auch ein bisschen müde. Es macht einfach Spaß, auf Tour zu sein und live vor Publikum zu spielen. Die ersten beiden Konzerte in Wien waren schon sehr emotional, weil so viele Freunde unter den Zuschauern waren.
Max	Und die neuen Songs, Lisa?
Lisa	Die Reaktionen waren sehr positiv. Aber wie du wahrscheinlich weißt, war es ganz schön stressig, das Album vor der Tournee fertigzustellen.
Max	Das freut mich total für dich. Aber dann fährst du sicherlich morgen nach dem Konzert mit der Band nach Wien zurück?
Lisa	Nein, es ist ja der letzte Gig. Ich möchte gern noch ein paar Tage in Berlin bleiben, um eine alte Schulfreundin zu treffen. Und dann möchte ich natürlich auch die Berliner Club- und Musikszene kennenlernen. Da hast du ja bestimmt ein paar Tipps!
Max	Ja, aber ich wusste gar nicht, dass du auch gerne clubben gehst. Berlin ist natürlich der ideale Ort, um Techno- und Housemusik zu hören.
Lisa	Das sagt man in Wien auch. Hast du Lust, mir ein paar Clubs zu zeigen?
Max	Aber natürlich, Lisa. Ich überlege mir etwas.
Lisa	Oh. Ich muss los, um rechtzeitig bei der Probe zu sein.

2 **Complete the sentences.**

Example: Bislang ist Lisa mit der Tournee <u>sehr zufrieden</u>.

a Es macht Lisa Spaß, ...

b Es war stressig für Lisa, ...

c Die Reaktionen auf ihre neuen Songs ....

d In Berlin möchte Lisa eine alte Schulfreundin treffen und ....

e Sie muss gehen, um pünktlich ....

LANGUAGE BUILDER 1

 Language discovery 1

Complete these sentences from Conversation 1. Identify which form the verb following zu takes.

a Es ist wirklich schön, dich zu ....
b Es macht einfach Spaß, auf Tour zu .... und live vor Publikum zu ....
c Hast du Lust, mir ein paar Clubs zu .... ?

Making suggestions and plans

Zu + infinitive clauses are often used to make or reply to suggestions, say how you feel about something, or talk about plans. The zu + infinitive clause finishes the sentence and is introduced by a comma:

Ich habe (keine) Lust, clubben zu gehen.	I (don't) feel like going clubbing.
Ich finde es entspannend, ein Buch zu lesen.	I find it relaxing to read a book.
Er plant, ein neues Tablet zu kaufen.	He is planning to buy a new tablet.

With separable verbs, zu is placed between the prefix and the main verb:

Ich habe versucht, das Album fertigzustellen.	I tried to finish the album.

Zu + infinitive clauses are used after the following structures:

1. verb + noun structures	2. verb + adjectives	3. verbs
Hast du Interesse, ...?	Ist es möglich, ...?	an/fangen *to start*
Hast du Zeit, ...?	Findest du es schwierig, ...?	planen *to plan*
Ich habe (keine) Lust, ...	Es ist (nicht) schön, ...	versuchen *to try*
Es macht (keinen) Sinn, ...	Es ist (nicht) teuer, ...	sich vor/nehmen *to intend*
Es macht (keinen) Spaß, ...	Ich finde es (nicht) stressig, ...	vor/schlagen *to suggest*

> As an alternative zu + infinitive, you can often use dass or wenn clauses:
> Es ist wichtig für mich, häufig zu trainieren. > Es ist wichtig für mich, dass ich häufig trainiere.
> Es ist billiger, ein Jahresticket zu kaufen. > Es ist billiger, wenn man ein Jahresticket kauft.

Language practice 1

Match the questions with the answers.

a Hast du Zeit, noch etwas zu trinken?
b Hast du Lust, morgen clubben zu gehen?
c Ist es möglich, uns später zu treffen?
d War es einfach, die Fotos hochzuladen?
e Was sind deine Pläne für den Sommer?

1 Ja, es war nicht schwer, das zu machen.
2 Ich plane, Urlaub in Spanien zu machen.
3 Es tut mir leid, aber ich muss jetzt los.
4 Nein. Ich tanze nicht gern und es ist zu laut.
5 Ja, natürlich. Passt dir 17 Uhr?

LANGUAGE BUILDER 2

15.05

💡 Language discovery 2

Listen to the conversation again and repeat each line in the pauses provided. Look at these sentences from the conversation. How would you say um ... zu in English? Where are um and zu placed in a clause?

Ich möchte noch ein paar Tage in Berlin bleiben, um eine alte Schulfreundin zu treffen.

Berlin ist ja der ideale Ort, um Techno und House zu hören.

Ich muss los, um rechtzeitig bei der Probe zu sein.

Expressing purpose

To express the purpose of an action in German, use um ... zu + infinitive. It corresponds to the English *in order to*:

Er joggt jeden Morgen, um fitter zu werden.	*He goes for a run every morning (in order) to get fitter.*
Sie macht ein Praktikum, um Erfahrungen zu sammeln.	*She is doing a work placement. (in order) to gain experience.*

Notice that um is placed at the beginning of the clause, while zu + infinitive is at the end. There is a comma before um.

Language practice 2

1 **Put the words in the correct order after the comma.**

   Example: Er geht nachher in die Stadt, seine Freunde / um / zu treffen/.

   Er geht nachher in die Stadt, um seine Freunde zu treffen.

   a Wir gehen ins Museum, eine Ausstellung / zu sehen / um / über Pop-Art /.
   b Sie macht Jiu-Jitsu, zu können / um / sich besser / verteidigen /.
   c Sie lernt ein Instrument, um / zu spielen / in einem / Orchester /.
   d Er steht früh auf, seinen Flug / zu verpassen / nicht / um /.
   e Ich bleibe heute Abend zu Hause, zu schauen / eine Serie / um / auf Netflix /.
   f Berlin ist der ideale Ort, um / zu gehen / und clubben / Ausstellungen zu sehen /.

2 **Answer the questions. Give as much detail as possible.**

   a Hast du Interesse, für ein paar Tage nach Berlin zu fahren?
   b Hast du Lust, einen Salsakurs mit mir zu machen?
   c Hast du Zeit, am Wochenende zu einem Konzert zu gehen?
   d Ich versuche, eine Familienfeier zu organisieren. Passt dir Ende April?
   e Ist es möglich, uns nächste Woche zu treffen?
   f Ich schlage vor, heute Abend etwas zusammen zu kochen. Hast du Lust?

3 Now play Conversation 2 again and play Lisa's role. Speak in the pauses provided and try not to refer to the text.

15.06

CULTURE POINT 2

Mehr Museen als Regentage

Man sagt, Berlin hat mehr Museen als Regentage. In der Tat hat die Stadt mehr als 170 Museen mit einer riesigen Bandbreite (*range*). Das Angebot reicht von weltberühmten Kunstschätzen (*art treasures*) wie der Büste der Königin Nofretete im Neuen Museum, über Museen,

die sich mit geschichtlichen Ereignissen (*events*) beschäftigen, wie dem Deutschen Historischen Museum oder dem DDR Museum, bis hin zu Kindermuseen, einem Computerspielmuseum oder dem Berliner S-Bahn-Museum.

Die meistbesuchten Kunstmuseen befinden sich auf der Museumsinsel. In der Alten Nationalgalerie kann man, neben den Werken französischer Impressionisten, Gemälde (*paintings*) der Romantik von Caspar David Friedrich und Karl Friedrich Schinkel sehen. Die Neue Nationalgalerie – die etwas entfernt liegt – zeigt Kunst aus dem 20. Jahrhundert, unter anderem von Pablo Picasso, Paul Klee, Max Ernst und Andy Warhol.

Für zeitgenössische (*contemporary*) Kunst besucht man am besten den Hamburger Bahnhof. Dort gibt es auch Arbeiten der bekanntesten zeitgenössischen deutschen Künstler, Anselm Kiefer und Gerhard Richter. Gerhard Richter wurde zuerst mit großen fotorealistischen Bildern bekannt. Anselm Kiefer benutzt unkonventionelle Materialen wie Blei (*lead*) oder Stroh (*straw*) in seinen Arbeiten. Beide beschäftigen sich mit Themen aus der deutschen Geschichte.

Finden Sie ein Museum in Berlin, das Sie interessiert.
Wofür interessieren Sie sich? Für traditionelle oder moderne Kunst? Oder vielleicht eher für Geschichte, Fotografie, Sport, Technik oder etwas anders?
Was zeigt man dort? Welche aktuelle Austellung(en) gibt es? Gibt es ein besonderes Highlight? Wie sind die Öffnungszeiten?

15.07

Look at the words and phrases and complete the missing English words and expressions. Then listen and try to imitate the pronunciation of the speakers.

KUNST	ART
die Fotografie (no plural)	*photography, photographic art*
das Gemälde (-)	*painting* (object)
der Impressionismus (no plural)	....
der Künstler (-) / die Künstlerin (-nen)	*artist*
das Museum (Museen)	....
die Malerei (no plural)	*painting* (the art form)
die Romantik (no plural)	*Romanticism*
der Ticketpreis (-e)	....
die Videoinstallation (-en)	....
abstrakte Kunst / moderne Kunst	*abstract* .... / ....
zeitgenössische Kunst, Musik	*contemporary* ....

VORLIEBEN UND PLÄNE MACHEN	PREFERENCES AND PLANNING
bevorzugen	*to prefer*
bewundern	*to admire*
dar/stellen	*to represent*
sich beschäftigen mit	*to engage with, to deal with*
etwas vor/haben	*to plan, intend*
um/legen	*to reschedule*
der Termin (-e)	*appointment*

NÜTZLICHE AUSDRÜCKE	USEFUL EXPRESSIONS
das Festland (-"er)	*mainland*
die Insel (-n), die Küste (-n)	*island, coast*
der Schwimmwettbewerb (-e)	*swimming competition*
atmosphärisch	....
unglaublich	*incredible, unbelievable*
Mir gefällt das (nicht).	*I (don't) like this.*
nicht wirklich	.... *really*
Das ist nicht mein Ding.	*That's not my thing.*

Vocabulary practice 1

Identify if these statements about art are positive or negative.

Das ist mir zu traditionell. – Ich liebe zeitgenössische Kunst. – Museen sind nicht mein Ding, – Videoinstallationen sind mir zu langweilig. – Ich mag die Bilder von van Gogh. – Ich bevorzuge Fotografien. – Ich interessiere mich nicht für Malerei. – Abstrakte Kunst gefällt mir nicht wirklich.

CONVERSATION 2

Interessen und Vorlieben

1 **Listen to the conversation a few times without looking at the text. Then listen again and read the text. How did Lisa's concert go last night? What topics do Wally and Lisa discuss?**

The day after the concert, Lisa, Max, and Wally meet up at the East Side Gallery, the open-air art gallery on the Ufer (*bank*) of the Spree where the longest remaining section of the Berlin Wall is. While Max goes to get coffee for everyone, Wally and Lisa start talking.

Wally	Es freut mich wirklich, dich endlich kennenzulernen. Max hat schon so viel von dir erzählt.
Lisa	Es freut mich auch sehr, Wally.
Wally	Wie war dein Konzert gestern? Hat alles gut geklappt?
Lisa	Ja, es war ausverkauft. Und am Ende haben wir vier Zugaben gegeben.
Wally	Schön, du weißt ja, dass ich früher Opernsängerin war.
Lisa	Ja, natürlich. Interessierst du dich auch für moderne Musik?
Wally	Wenn ich ehrlich bin, nicht so richtig. Ich glaube ich bin da eher traditionell. Ich bevorzuge klassische Musik. Aber jede Generation ist da wahrscheinlich auch anders.
Lisa	Und Kunst, Wally? Beschäftigst du dich auch mit Kunst? Es gibt ja hier so viele Museen.
Wally	Ja, ich mag die Impressionisten, van Gogh, aber auch bekannte moderne deutsche Künstler wie Anselm Kiefer und Gerhard Richter. Mein Lieblingsmuseum ist die Neue Nationalgalerie.
Lisa	Ja, die wollte ich mir auch noch ansehen. Und auch den Hamburger Bahnhof. Ich liebe zeitgenössische Kunst – Fotografie und auch Videoinstallationen.
Wally	Weißt du denn schon, wie lange du noch in Berlin bleiben wirst?
Lisa	Ich werde bis nächsten Mittwoch bleiben. Dann muss ich zurück nach Wien.
Wally	Wenn du noch etwas anderes sehen möchtest, Lisa – wir fahren am Samstag an die Küste. Da werde ich an einem Schwimmwettbewerb teilnehmen, von der Insel Rügen ans Festland. Komm doch mit.
Lisa	Sport machst du auch, Wally? Unglaublich. Ich hatte eigentlich schon etwas anderes vor, aber das klingt toll. Ich werde versuchen, den Termin umzulegen.

2 Decide if these statements are *true* (richtig) or *false* (falsch). Correct the false ones.

a	Max hat nicht viel über Lisa erzählt.	R	F
b	Wally interessiert sich auch für moderne Musik.	R	F
c	Wally mag van Gogh, aber auch moderne deutsche Künstler.	R	F
d	Lisa findet zeitgenössische Kunst sehr gut.	R	F
e	Lisa kann noch zwei Wochen bleiben.	R	F
f	Wally möchte, dass Lisa mit zum Schwimmwettbewerb kommt.	R	F

LANGUAGE BUILDER

💡 Language discovery 3

Look at these two questions from Conversation 2 and find the missing verbs.

a .... du dich auch für moderne Musik?

b .... du dich auch mit Kunst?

Verbs and prepositions (3)

In Unit 13, you learned how to form questions with verbs + prepositions. When referring to people, start with the preposition:

Mit wem hast du dich unterhalten?   *Who have you talked to?*

When referring to a concept, with an open question, you use Wo(r) + *preposition*:

Worüber habt ihr geredet?   *What did you talk about?*

In yes/no questions, put the verb in first position:

Interessierst du dich für Fußball?   *Are you interested in soccer?*

Begeisterst du dich für Techno?   *Do you get excited about techno?*

Informierst du dich über Ausstellungen?   *Do you keep yourself informed about exhibitons?*

Beschäftigen Sie sich mit Kunst?   *Do you engage with art?*

The reflexive pronoun (mich, sich, etc.) comes straight after the verb. In a negative statement, nicht follows the pronoun:

Ja, ich interessiere **mich** für Fußball. >

Nein, ich interessiere **mich** nicht für Fußball.

Ja, ich beschäftige **mich** mit Kunst. >

Nein, ich beschäftige **mich** nicht mit Kunst.

> It is possible to replace the object with a da(r) + preposition, when the context is clear:
> Ich interessiere mich **für Fußball**.
> > Ich interessiere mich **dafür**.
> Ich beschäftige mich **mit Kunst**.
> > Ich beschäftige **mich damit**.

Language practice 3

Answer the questions about your interests and give reasons.

Example: Interessieren Sie sich für Fußball?

Ja, ich interessiere mich sehr für Fußball. Ich bin ein großer Fußballfan. Mein Lieblingsverein ist Mainz 05.

Nein, ich interessiere mich nicht für Fußball. Ich finde, Fußball ist zu kommerziell.

a Interessieren Sie sich für Fußball?
b Interessieren Sie sich für Musik?
c Beschäftigen Sie sich viel mit sozialen Medien?
d Begeistern Sie sich für Mode?
e Beschäftigen Sie sich mit Kunst?
f Ärgern Sie sich manchmal über hohe Ticketpreise?
g Informieren Sie sich über neue Ausstellungen?

LANGUAGE BUILDER 4

15.09

 Language discovery 4

Listen to the conversation again and repeat each line in the pauses provided.
Look at these sentences from the conversation. What time period do they refer to
(past/present/future)? Which element do they have in common?

a Ich werde bis nächsten Mittwoch bleiben.
b Da werde ich an einem Schwimmwettbewerb teilnehmen.
c Ich werde versuchen, den Termin umzulegen.

Expressing the future: Futur I

In German, as in English, the present tense is often used to refer to the future, as long as the context makes it clear.

Ich gehe morgen ins Museum.	*I am going to the museum tomorrow.*

The future can also be expressed with the future tense known as Futur I. This is formed with werden + infinitive:

Ich werde bis nächsten Mittwoch bleiben.	*I will stay until next Wednesday.*
Wirst du zur Party kommen?	*Will you come to the party?*

As a general rule, Futur I is used for emphasis, to state intentions, or to make a prediction:

Ich werde an dem Wettbewerb teilnehmen.	*I will take part in the competition.*
Morgen wird es wohl regnen.	*It's probably going to rain tomorrow.*

As you can see, in main clauses werden is in second position while the infinitive of the main verb goes to the end. In subordinating clauses, werden moves into last position:

Ich bin mir sicher, dass ich einen interessanten Job finden werde.	*I am sure that I will find an interesting job.*

> Remember that werden is an irregular verb: ich werde, du wirst, Sie werden, er/sie/es/xier wird, wir werden, ihr werdet, Sie/sie werden.

Language practice 4

1 **Put these sentences in Futur I.**

a Er geht nachher ins Fitnesscenter.

b Naomi schreibt nächste Woche ihre Prüfung.

c Wir ziehen im September um.

d Das Museum öffnet in 15 Minuten.

e Wann fängt Tim seinen neuen Job an?

f Ich muss ein neues Handy kaufen.

15.10

2 **Now play Conversation 2 again and play Wally's role. Speak in the pauses provided and try not to refer to the text.**

SKILL BUILDER

1 **Give creative reasons for doing these things, using um ... zu.**

Example: Ich fahre in die Stadt, um .... >
Ich fahre in die Stadt, um ein paar Sachen zu kaufen.

a Ich fahre in die Stadt, um ....

b Ich lerne Deutsch, um ....

c Ich gehe nachher in den Park, um ....

d Ich bleibe heute Abend zu Hause, um ....

e Wir fahren im Sommer in die Alpen, um ....

f Du trinkst keinen Alkohol, um ....

2 **Complete with the correct form of werden.**

a Morgen .... es regnen.

b Ich .... den Kindern bei den Hausaufgaben helfen.

c Sabrina kann nicht kommen, weil sie nach Hamburg fahren ....

d Ich glaube, dass die Zuschauer gegen 19.00 Uhr kommen ....

e .... du heute Abend zur Party gehen?

15.11

3 **Listen to three people from Berlin talking about their cultural interests. Complete the missing information.**

	Mag am liebsten	Warum	Zusätzliche Info
Marlene			Spielt selbst
Mirja			Lieblingsmaler:
Lars			Geht manchmal ...

4 **Listen again and complete the sentences.**

a Museen sind nicht mein ....

b Es macht einfach .... , immer wieder neue Musik zu ....

c Ich finde es faszinierend, wie er ....

d Wenn ich .... bin.

5 Describe your favorite cultural activities.

   a Interessieren Sie sich für Musik? Haben Sie ein Lieblingsgenre?

   b Hören Sie verschiedene Stile? Was sind Ihre Lieblingsmusiker / Lieblingsmusikerinnen?

   c Gehen Sie gern in Museen? Haben Sie einen Lieblingskünstler oder eine Lieblingskünstlerin?

   d Gehen Sie gerne ins Theater? Oder gehen Sie lieber ins Kino?

   e Welche Comedians finden Sie lustig?

TEST YOURSELF

1 Read the text about Berlin and techno music and match the headings a–d with paragraphs 1–4.

   a Bekannte Techno-Clubs in Berlin

   b Entwicklung des Techno in Berlin

   c Besonderheiten der Clubszene in Berlin

   d Entstehung des Techno

Berlin – Hauptstadt der Technomusik

Techno, Deephouse, Trance – ohne diese Musik kann man sich Clubs und Partys nicht mehr vorstellen. Und ein Zentrum des Techno, wenn nicht sogar das Zentrum, ist Berlin.

1 ....

Die Geschichte der elektronischen Tanzmusik in Berlin begann 1989 nach der Wiedervereinigung (*reunification*). Die Mauer war weg, und es entwickelte sich eine neue Clubszene mit einem neuen Sound. Junge Künstler:innen und Musiker:innen aus Ost- und Westberlin begannen damit, in verlassenen (*disused, derelict*) Häusern und Fabrikgebäuden (*factory building*) Raves und Techno-Partys zu organisieren und die Nacht durchzutanzen. Die ersten bekannten Clubs waren das „E-Werk", der „Tresor" und das „Ufo". Mit der Zeit reisten immer mehr Anhänger:innen (*fans, supporters*) aus Europa an, um Techno in Berlin hautnah zu erleben.

2 ....

Entstanden ist Techno allerdings nicht in Berlin, sondern ein paar Jahre früher in Detroit. Die Urväter sind aber die Musiker der deutschen Band „Kraftwerk" aus Düsseldorf. Seit den 1970er Jahren machte die Gruppe rein elektronische Musik. Ihr Album *Autobahn* war ein internationaler Hit und inspirierte Musiker:innen und Produzenten:innen weltweit.

3 ....

Heutzutage findet man die beliebtesten Spots für Techno in Berlin zwischen dem Alexanderplatz und der Revaler Straße. Einer der bekanntesten Clubs der Stadt ist das „Berghain". Es befindet sich in einem ehemaligen Kraftwerk in Friedrichshain. Andere populäre Institutionen sind der „Tresor" und „Kater Blau".

4 ....

Was Clubbing in Berlin so besonders macht: Am Wochenende gibt es keine Sperrstunde (*closing time*). Das heißt, dass manche Partys am Freitag beginnen und erst am Montag enden. In den meisten Clubs gibt es auch keine Kleiderordnung. Man kann also anziehen, was man möchte, und solange bleiben, wie die Energie reicht.

2 Summarize the text in English.

Wie geht's weiter? *What happens next?*

Wally has set herself quite a challenge by taking part in the Sundschwimmen competition to swim from the island of Rügen to the mainland. Will she succeed and if so, how long will it take her? And what about Lisa? Will she be able to join and travel with Wally and Max? Find out in Unit 16.

Remember to use **My review** and **My takeaway** to assess your progress and reflect on your learning experience.

In this lesson you will learn how to:
» Name objects in nature
» Describe various landscapes
» Discuss different types of vacation
» Describe your ideal trip

Ein Ausflug an die Küste

My study plan

I plan to work with Unit 16
○ Every day
○ Twice a week
○ Other _____
I plan to study for
○ 5–15 minutes
○ 15–30 minutes
○ 30–45+ minutes

My progress tracker

Day / Date	🎧	🎤	📖	✏️	💬
	○	○	○	○	○
	○	○	○	○	○
	○	○	○	○	○
	○	○	○	○	○
	○	○	○	○	○
	○	○	○	○	○
	○	○	○	○	○

My goals

What do you want to be able to do or say in German when you complete this unit?

Done

1 .... ○

2 .... ○

3 .... ○

My review

SELF CHECK	
	I can ...
●	... name objects of nature.
●	... describe various types of landscape.
●	... discuss different types of vacation.
●	... describe my ideal trip.

CULTURE POINT 1

Endlich Urlaub

Die Deutschen, Österreicher:innen und Schweizer:innen haben zwischen 26 und 30 Tage Urlaub (*annual leave*) im Jahr. Viele Menschen machen Urlaub auf Balkonien (*staycation*), aber viele nutzen die freie Zeit zum Verreisen. Die beliebtesten Reiseziele der Deutschen im Ausland sind dabei Spanien und Italien. Auch das Nachbarland Österreich gehört zu den Top 10 der beliebtesten Reiseziele. Allerdings machen die meisten Deutschen innerhalb Deutschlands Urlaub.

Die abwechslungsreiche (*varied*) Landschaft in Deutschland bietet für jeden Geschmack (*taste*) etwas. Wer die Berge liebt und gerne wandert, kann in den bayerischen Alpen oder auch im Schwarzwald Urlaub machen. Die meisten Deutschen verbringen (*spend*) ihren Urlaub aber am Meer. Deutschland liegt sowohl an der Nordsee (*North Sea*) als auch an der Ostsee (*Baltic Sea*). Die langen Sandstrände laden hier zum Sonnenbaden (*sunbathing*) und Schwimmen ein. Mecklenburg-Vorpommern und die Insel Rügen sind hierbei Spitzenreiter (*number one, frontrunner*).

Auch die Schweizer verbringen ihren Urlaub am liebsten im eigenen Land, gefolgt von Italien und Frankeich. Top-Reiseziel (*holiday destination*) für die Österreicher ist Italien, danach folgt Kroatien. Das eigene Land liegt auf Rang 3.

 Hier finden Sie weitere Urlaubsregionen in Deutschland.

Welche Ziele bieten Ihnen Berge?

Wo können Sie schwimmen gehen?

Welche Ziele laden zum Wandern ein?

Welches Ziel gefällt Ihnen am besten? Warum?

VOCABULARY BUILDER 1

16.01

Look at the words and phrases and complete the missing English words and expressions. Then listen and try to imitate the pronunciation of the speakers.

NATUR UND LANDSCHAFTEN	*NATURE AND LANDSCAPES*
der Baum (-"e)	*tree*
der Berg (-e), bergig	*mountain, mountainous*
die Erhebung (-en)	*elevation*
das Feld (-er)	....
der Fels (-en), der Kreidefels (-en)	*cliff / rock, chalk* ....
das Gebiet (-e), die Gegend (-en)	*area, region*
das Gebirge (-)	*mountain range*
der Hügel (-), hügelig	*hill, hilly*
das Meer (-e)	*sea*
das Mittelgebirge (-)	*low mountain range*
der Ozean (-e)	*ocean*
der See (-n), die See (-n)	*lake, sea*
der Strand (-"e)	*beach*
das Tal (-"er)	*valley*
der Wald (-"er), waldig, waldreich	*forest, forested, densely forested*
der Dreitausender (-)	*mountain higher than 3000 m*
flach	*flat*
flächenmäßig	*by area*
sandig	....
sonnig	....

NÜTZLICHE AUSDRÜCKE	*USEFUL EXPRESSIONS*
überall	*everywhere*
insgesamt	*in total*
mir fällt auf	*I notice*
der Tagesausflug (-"e)	.... *trip*
Kaum zu glauben, aber wahr.	*Hard to believe but true.*

> There a few nouns which have two different genders and change their meaning according to the gender. Apart from der See (*lake*) and die See (*sea*), they include: der Leiter (*leader*), die Leiter (*ladder*); die Steuer (*tax*), das Steuer (*steering wheel*); der Stift (*pen*), das Stift (*foundation*, e.g. home for elderly); der Tor (*fool*), das Tor (*gate, goal*, e.g. soccer).

Vocabulary practice 1

Label the two images using the words provided.

| der Baum (-ˮe)   der Berg (-e)   das Gebirge (-) |
| der See (-n)   der Strand (-ˮe)   der Wald (-ˮer) |

a .... b .... c ....

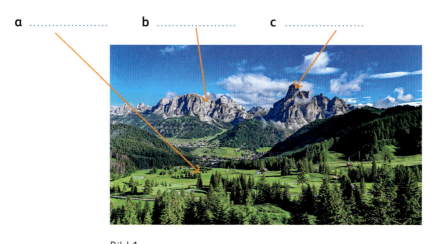

Bild 1

d .... e .... f ....

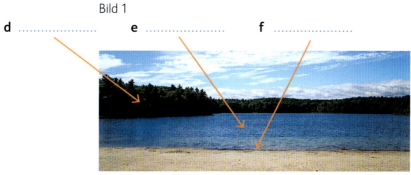

Bild 2

Pronunciation practice

16.02

1 **Listen to these words. They are all places in German-speaking countries and have many consonants, as is quite common in German. Repeat the words in the pauses.**

Norddeutsche Tiefebene   Innsbruck   Helpter Berg

Mecklenburg-Vorpommern   Dortmund

16.03

2 **Practice saying these words. Listen to the audio to check.**

Stuttgart   Zugspitze   Schwarzwald

Baden-Württemberg   Großglockner

Kaum zu glauben, aber wahr!

16.04

1 Listen to the conversation a few times without looking at the text. Then listen again and read the text. What does Lisa say about the landscapes in Germany? Can you name the two things Wally finds special about Rügen?

It is Wally's big day. She will take part in the Sundschwimmen, Germany's oldest long-distance swimming competition. The race starts in Altefähr, on the island of Rügen, and ends in Stralsund. It is 2,315 m long.

Lisa	Die Gegend hier ist aber wirklich grün, allerdings auch extrem flach.
Wally	Ja, das ist die sogenannte Norddeutsche Tiefebene. Weißt du, was die höchste Erhebung in Mecklenburg-Vorpommern ist?
Lisa	Mmh, keine Ahnung, aber so hoch wird es wohl nicht sein.
Wally	Der Helpter Berg mit 179 Metern.
Lisa	Wahnsinn! Der höchste Berg in Österreich ist der Großglockner mit etwa 3800 Metern. Insgesamt haben wir fast 700 Dreitausender.
Wally	Tja, hier im Norden ist die Landschaft ganz anders. Ich liebe diese Gegend – besonders die vielen schönen Seen.
Lisa	Auf unserer Tour ist mir aufgefallen, wie unterschiedlich die Landschaften in Deutschland sind. Im Süden ist es sehr bergig. Auch die Mittelgebirge wie der Schwarzwald haben mir gut gefallen. Und der Norden ist wieder ganz anders. Aber überall war es sehr waldig.
Wally	Ja, wir haben in Deutschland über 30 Prozent Waldfläche – wir sind das waldreichste Land in Mitteleuropa. Kaum zu glauben, aber wahr.
Lisa	Und kennst du die Ostseeküste gut?
Wally	Ja, es ist ja nicht weit von Berlin, und wenn ich Zeit habe und mich entspannen will, komme ich ein paar Tage hierher. Manchmal auch nur für einen Tagesausflug.
Lisa	Ich habe gehört, dass Rügen die größte deutsche Insel ist.
Wally	Ja, und was die Insel noch besonders macht, sind die Kreidefelsen und die langen, sandigen Strände. Aber ihr werdet sie ja bald selber sehen.
Lisa	Und, Wally, wie fühlst du dich? Bist du nervös?
Wally	Nein, nervös bin ich nicht. Ich fühle mich gut. Es ist sonnig und ich freue mich auf das Rennen.

2 Match a–g with 1–7.

a Norddeutsche Tiefebene

b Helpter Berg

c Großglockner

d Mittelgebirge

e Süddeutschland

f Waldfläche in Deutschland

g Rügen

1 der Schwarzwald

2 über 30 Prozent

3 179 Meter hoch

4 extrem flach

5 bergige Landschaft

6 Kreidefelsen, Sandstrände

7 der höchste Berg in Österreich

LANGUAGE BUILDER 1

 Language discovery 1

Look at Conversation 1 again. Find the adjective forms for these nouns. What do they have in common?

a der Berg .... **b** der Wald .... **c** die Sonne ....

Word formation: adjectives

Some adjectives, often in landscapes and nature, can be formed by adding -ig to the noun:

Berg > bergig   Sand > sandig   Hügel > hügelig   Moor > moorig

Wind > windig   Wald > waldig   Durst > durstig   Salz > salzig

If the noun ends in -e, you normally drop the -e before adding -ig:

Sonne > sonnig   Wolke > wolkig   Freude > freudig   Langeweile > langweilig

Another common adjective ending is -isch:

der Sturm > stürmisch   der Regen > regnerisch   der Alkohol > alkoholisch

Language practice 1

1 Say it another way. Use an adjective.

Example: Die Landschaft hat viele Berge. > *Die Landschaft ist bergig.*

a Die Gegend hat viele Hügel. > Die Gegend ist sehr ....

b Die Mitte von Deutschland hat viele Wälder. > Die Mitte von Deutschland ist ....

c Heute gibt es viele Wolken > Heute ist es ....

d Er arbeitet viel. Er zeigt viel Fleiß. > Er ist sehr ....

e Nach dem Training haben sie viel Durst. > Nach dem Training sind sie sehr ....

f Das Chili con Carne hat zu viel Salz. > Das Chili con Carne ist zu ....

g Die Sonne scheint. > Es ist ....

h Die Stadt bietet eine große Vielfalt. > Die Stadt ist sehr ....

LANGUAGE BUILDER 2

💡 Language discovery 2

Listen to the conversation again and repeat each line in the pauses provided. Add the correct adjective endings. Check your answers in Conversation 1.

a Der höchst .... Berg in Österreich ist der Großglockner.

b Ich liebe diese Gegend – besonders die viel .... schön .... Seen.

c Wir sind das waldreichst .... Land in Mitteleuropa.

d Ich habe gehört, dass Rügen die größt .... deutsch .... Insel ist.

Adjective endings after definite articles

In Units 9 and 10, you saw how adjective endings work after the *indefinite article* (ein, eine, etc.). Here is an overview of endings after the definite article (der, die, das, etc.).

	masculine	feminine	neuter	plural
nominative	der hoh**e** Berg	die groß**e** Insel	das schön**e** Land	die alt**en** Bäume
accusative	den hoh**en** Berg	die groß**e** Insel	das schön**e** Land	die alt**en** Bäume
dative	dem hoh**en** Berg	der groß**en** Insel	dem schön**en** Land	den alt**en** Bäumen

There are only two endings after the definite article:

● -e is used for all singular forms in the nominative and accusative case, with the exception of masculine nouns when you use -en in the accusative.

● -en is used for all plural forms, for all forms in the dative case, and for the masculine accusative form. Remember that plural nouns add **-n** in the dative.

Note the definite articles frequently appear with adjectives in the superlative, which take the same endings: der höchste Berg, das größte Land, etc.

Language practice 2

1 Complete with the correct adjective ending.

a Im Reichstag tagt der deutsch .... Bundestag.

b Die klein .... Insel gefällt mir gut.

c Die Alpen sind das höchst .... Gebirge in Europa.

d In den letzt .... Jahrzehnten hat sich die Region stark verändert.

e Der Schwarzwald ist das bekanntest .... Mittelgebirge und hat auch die meist .... Besucher.

f An der polnisch .... Ostseeküste gibt es sehr schöne Badeorte.

g Ich mag die sandig .... Strände und das warm .... Klima in Portugal.

h Der Sihlwald ist der größt .... Wald in der Schweiz.

2 Now listen to Conversation 1 again and play Wally's role. Speak in the pauses provided and try not to refer to the text.

Die Insel Rügen

Rügen ist mit 926 Quadratkilometern die größte Insel Deutschlands. Sie liegt in der Ostsee und gehört zum Bundesland Mecklenburg-Vorpommern. Mit 56 Kilometern Sandstrand und rund 2.000 Sonnenstunden im Jahr ist Rügen ein sehr beliebtes Urlaubsziel der Deutschen.

Bei einem Besuch sollte man man auf jeden Fall eines der Seebäder (*seaside resorts*) besichtigen (Binz, Baabe, Göhren und Sellin) und ihre Bäderarchitektur (*spa-style architecture*) bewundern. Nur zu Fuß kann man das idyllische Fischerdörfchen Vitt erreichen, das mit seinen reetgedeckten (*thatched roof*) Häusern unter Denkmalschutz steht (*is listed as a national monument*). Wenn man es ruhig mag, sollte man die Fähre (*ferry*) zur Nachbarinsel Hiddensee nehmen, wo es gar keine Autos gibt.

Historisch interessant ist Prora. Hier hatten die Nazis eine 4,5 km lange Ferienanlage (*vacation resort*) geplant. Heute gibt es hier Wohnungen, ein Hotel, eine Jugendherberge (*hostel*) und auch ein Dokumentationszentrum. Eine kulinarische Besonderheit auf Rügen ist der Sanddorn (*sea buckthorn*). Man nennt ihn auch die „Zitrone des Nordens", weil er zehnmal mehr Vitamin C als Zitronen enthält. Man trinkt ihn zum Beispiel als Saft.

Am bekanntesten sind aber wahrscheinlich die Kreidefelsen auf Rügen, die viele auch durch das Gemälde von Caspar David Friedrich kennen.

 Jedes Jahr finden auf Rügen die Störtebeker-Festspiele statt. Sie sind nach dem Piraten Störtebeker benannt. Wann finden die Festspiele statt? Wo auf der Insel finden sie statt? Was kosten die Karten? Welches Stück kann man sehen? Hätten Sie Lust, sich das Stück anzusehen?

VOCABULARY BUILDER 2

16.07

Look at the words and phrases and complete the missing English words and expressions. Then listen and try to imitate the pronunciation of the speakers.

MEIN TRAUMURLAUB	MY DREAM VACATION
der Abenteuerurlaub (-e)	adventure travel
die Badekappe (-n)	bathing cap
der Campingurlaub (-e)	.... vacation
die Fernreise (-n)	long-distance travel
die Freiwilligenarbeit (-en)	volunteering
der Heimaturlaub (-e)	domestic vacation / staycation
der Kontinent (-e)	....
die Kreuzfahrt (-en)	cruise
der Partyurlaub (-e)	.... vacation
der Pauschalurlaub (-e)	package vacation
die Rundreise (-n)	.... trip
die Sprachreise (-n)	language vacation
die Städtereise (-n)	.... break
der Strandurlaub (-e)	beach vacation
der Wellnessurlaub (-e)	.... vacation, wellness / spa vacation
die Weltreise (-n)	.... trip

AKTIVITÄTEN	ACTIVITIES
ab/steigen	to stay (at a hotel, hostel, etc.)
belasten	to harm, burden, pollute
faulenzen	to idle, to laze
rasen	to race
sich leisten	to afford
sich sonnen	to ....
spenden	to donate
etwas unternehmen	to undertake, to do something

VERBEN	VERBS
ich hätte, ich wäre	I would have, I would be / I were
ich könnte, ich würde	I could, I would

NÜTZLICHE AUSDRÜCKE	USEFUL EXPRESSIONS
abenteuerlustig	adventurous
von einem Termin zum nächsten	from one appointment to the next
Wenn ich du / Sie wäre, ...	If I were you ...
An deiner / Ihrer Stelle ...	In your position ...

240

Vocabulary practice 2

1 **Five people say what they like to do on vacation. Match the activity with each person. There are two extra choices.**

> Abenteuerurlaub   Heimaturlaub   Pauschalurlaub   Partyurlaub
> Städtereise   Strandurlaub   Wellnessurlaub

a Im Urlaub habe ich endlich einmal Zeit, mich mehr zu bewegen. Wenn ich kann, buche ich mich in ein Wellnesshotel ein, wo es ein gutes Angebot an Kursen und Anwendungen gibt. Im Winter fahre ich am liebsten in den Bergen Ski.

b Das Jahr über gibt es viel Stress und man muss viel planen. Ich mag es, wenn ich mich um nichts kümmern muss, und Flug, Unterbringung, Essen usw. für mich organisiert sind. Dann am Pool liegen oder an der Bar sitzen – so sieht mein perfekter Urlaub aus. Das bedeutet pure Entspannung für mich.

c Im Urlaub möchte ich viel feiern und Spaß haben – schlafen kann ich ja, wenn ich wieder zu Hause bin. Letztes Jahr war ich auf Ibiza und dieses Jahr möchte ich mit ein paar Freunden nach Lloret de Mar fahren.

d Warum weit verreisen und die Umwelt belasten, wenn es doch auch im eigenen Land so viele schöne Orte und Landschaften gibt? Seit ein paar Jahren mieten wir eine Ferienwohnung im Schwarzwald, und mich überrascht immer wieder, wie viel Neues man dort entdecken kann.

e Urlaub an einem Ort – das ist nichts für mich. Am liebsten bin ich mit dem Rucksack unterwegs und steige in kleinen Hostels ab oder mache Couchsurfing. Ich finde, so kann man am besten Land und Leute kennenlernen.

> When referring to rivers, lakes, oceans, etc. you normally use the preposition an: Ich bin am Meer aufgewachsen. Don't forget that an can take the accusative (with movement) and the dative (when focusing on location): Ich fahre an den See. Ich liege am See.

Wenn du genug Zeit und Geld hättest ...

16.08

1 Listen to the conversation a few times without looking at the text. Then listen again and read the text. What kind of vacations do Max and Lisa usually take? What do their dream vacations look like?

Lisa and Max are watching the race on the Strandbad (*lido*) at Stralsund. Wally has said that she hopes to finish in under 1 hour 20 minutes. Will she make it?

Lisa	Max, ich hätte gar nicht gedacht, dass es hier an der Ostseeküste so schön ist. Ich könnte mir gut vorstellen, einmal hier Urlaub zu machen.
Max	Ja, das wäre schön. Ich liebe die Küste. Ich bin ja auch am Meer aufgewachsen. Was machst du denn normalerweise, wenn du Urlaub hast?
Lisa	Meistens bin ich ja so beschäftigt und rase von einem Termin zum nächsten. Darum möchte ich mich im Urlaub am liebsten ausruhen und faulenzen. Irgendwo am See liegen und einfach mal nichts tun. Und wie ist das bei dir, Max?
Max	Im Urlaub bin ich ganz gerne aktiv. Du weißt ja, wie sehr ich es liebe zu reisen und neue Städte und Länder zu entdecken. Und ich unternehme auch gern kulturelle Sachen.
Lisa	Also, Max, wenn du genug Zeit und Geld hättest, wohin würdest du dann reisen?
Max	Mmh, wenn ich genug Zeit und Geld hätte, würde ich gern einen anderen Kontinent kennenlernen. Mein Traum wäre es, einmal durch Asien zu reisen, nach Thailand, Vietnam, Laos ... Und wenn ich da wäre, könnte ich ja auch für ein Freiwilligenprojekt arbeiten oder Englisch unterrichten.
Lisa	Du bist ja richtig abenteuerlustig, Max.
Max	Ja, wirklich? Was würdest du denn machen, wenn du Zeit und Geld hättest?
Lisa	Für mich muss es gar nicht so weit sein. Ich war noch nie in Italien, obwohl es ja nicht weit von Wien ist. Ich würde gern einmal eine Tour durch Italien machen.
Max	Lisa, schau mal, ist das nicht Wally? Die Schwimmerin mit der blau-weißen Badekappe?
Lisa	Ja, ich denke schon. Und die Zeit: 1:11,45 Std.
Max	1:11,45 Std? Das hätte ich nie geschafft.

2 Decide if these statements are *true* (richtig) or *false* (falsch). Correct the false statements.

		R	F
a	Lisa sagt, dass sie meistens sehr beschäftigt ist.	R	F
b	Auch im Urlaub ist sie gern aktiv.	R	F
c	Max möchte gern nach Asien reisen, weil er diesen Kontinent kennenlernen möchte.	R	F
d	Er will dort aber nicht arbeiten.	R	F
e	Lisa kennt Italien, aber sie möchte es noch einmal sehen.	R	F

LANGUAGE BUILDER 3

 ## Language discovery 3

Look at these sentences from Conversation 1, what kind of events are they describing?

a Ja, das wäre schön.
b Ich könnte mir gut vorstellen, einmal hier Urlaub zu machen.
c Mein Traum wäre es, einmal durch Asien zu reisen, nach Thailand, Vietnam, Laos ...

Hypothetical situations and the subjunctive

Konjunktiv II (the subjunctive) is a special verb form used to express hypothetical situations and wishes, to offer advice, or to add politeness. It is formed from the Präteritum (*simple past tense*) by adding the appropriate ending and very often an umlaut.

Dann hätte ich mehr Zeit.	*Then I'd have more time.*
An deiner Stelle würde ich mehr reisen.	*In your position I'd travel more.*
Könnte ich Sie etwas fragen?	*Could I ask you something?*

In modern German, Konjunktiv II is normally used with the verbs haben, sein, werden:

	would have	would be	would		would have	would be	would
ich	hätte	wäre	würde	**wir**	hätten	wären	würden
du	hättest	wär(e)st	würdest	**ihr**	hättet	wär(e)t	würdet
Sie	hätten	wären	würden	**Sie**	hätten	wären	würden
er/sie/ es/xier	hätte	wäre	würde	**sie**	hätten	wären	würden

Modal verbs also frequently appear in the Konjunktiv II:

	might, to be allowed	could, would be able to	would have to	should	would want (to)	would like to
ich	dürfte	könnte	müsste	sollte	wollte	möchte
du	düftest	könntest	müsstest	solltest	wolltest	möchtest
er/sie/ es/xier	dürfte	könnte	müsste	sollte	wollte	möchte
wir	dürften	könnten	müssten	sollten	wollten	möchten
ihr	dürftet	könntet	müsstet	solltet	wolltet	möchtet
Sie/sie	dürften	könnten	müssten	sollten	wollten	möchten

> In modern German, especially in speaking, it is common to use würden + infinitive to form the Konjunktiv II: An deiner Stelle würde ich mehr essen.

Language practice 3

1 Match the advice with the problem.

a Ich bin oft so müde.

b Ich weiß nicht, was ich kochen soll.

c Unsere Nachbarn sind abends oft so laut.

d Mein Knie tut seit zwei Wochen weh.

e Die Tickets nach Sevilla sind sehr teuer.

f Wir wissen nicht, was wir am Wochenende machen sollen.

1 Wenn ich Sie wäre, würde ich zum Arzt gehen.

2 Ihr könntet einen Ausflug an die Ostsee machen.

3 Vielleicht solltest du mehr schlafen.

4 An eurer Stelle würde ich mit ihnen reden.

5 Du könntest dir ein paar Foodblogs ansehen.

6 An deiner Stelle würde ich trotzdem fliegen.

2 Put the verbs in italics into the Konjunktiv II.

Example: *Kann* ich Sie etwas fragen? > *Könnte* ich Sie etwas fragen?

a *Können* Sie mir helfen? ....

b Wir *können* uns auch morgen treffen. ....

c Er *muss* regelmäßiger trainieren. ....

d Ich glaube, dass das nichts für mich *ist*. ....

e *Seid* ihr bereit, am Wochenende zu arbeiten? ....

f *Haben* Sie heute Abend Zeit? ....

g *Hast* du Lust, mit uns laufen zu kommen? ....

h *Kannst* du mir einen Kaffee mitbringen? ....

LANGUAGE BUILDER 4

💡 Language discovery 4

Listen to the conversation again and repeat each line in the pauses provided. Look at these sentences from the conversation. Insert the missing verbs. What is special about them?

a Wenn du genug Zeit und Geld ...., wohin .... du dann reisen?

b Wenn ich genug Zeit und Geld ...., ... ich gern einen anderen Kontinent kennenlernen.

c Wenn ich da ...., ... ich für ein Freiwilligenprojekt arbeiten.

Konjunktiv II and 'if' clauses

Konjunktiv II is frequently used in conditional sentences to express unreal, imagined situations. A conditional sentence usually consists of two parts—an 'if' clause starting with wenn setting out the condition and a main clause describing its hyrethetical consequence.

Condition	Consequences
Wenn ich mehr Geld hätte,	würde ich eine Städtereise nach Paris machen.
Wenn es wärmer wäre,	würde ich schwimmen gehen.

Remember: in the wenn clause the verb goes to the end and the main clause starts with the appropriate form of werden in the Konjunktiv II.

Language practice 4

1 Put the words in the correct order after the comma.

a Wenn Peter mehr Zeit hätte, er / mehr Bücher / würde / lesen

b Wenn Inka mehr Zeit hätte, mehr Sport / machen / würde / sie

c Wenn Jinjin reicher wäre, kaufen / ein neues Auto / sie / würde

d Wenn Enrico reicher wäre, würde / er / Lautsprecher / kaufen / eine neue Gitarre und

e Wenn Ria und Paul eine Traumreise machen könnten, sie / nach / Kenia / fliegen / würden

f Wenn Noura eine Traumreise machen könnte, Dubai / gerne / würde / sie / besuchen

2 Answer these questions for yourself.

a Was würden Sie machen, wenn Sie mehr Zeit hätten?

b Was würden Sie tun, wenn Sie reicher wären?

c Wohin würden Sie fahren, wenn Sie eine Traumreise machen könnten?

3 Now play Conversation 2 again and play Max's role. Speak in the pauses provided and try not to refer to the text.

SKILL BUILDER

1 Find the odd one out.

a Strand Küste Wald Meer

b Berg Gegend Gebirge Erhebung

c Landschaft Fluss See Kanal

d bergig flach gebirgig hügelig

e Freiwilligenarbeit Strandurlaub
Pauschalurlaub Städtereise

f sonnig wolkig langweilig windig

 2 Complete these facts about Germany with the correct adjective endings.

> In Europa ist Deutschland nach Frankreich, Spanien und Schweden das viertgrößt....... Land – mit 357.588 Quadratkilometern. Von der Einwohnerzahl ist es mit knapp 83.5 Millionen Einwohnern der bevölkerungsreichst....... Staat der EU.
>
> Die höchst....... Erhebung bildet die in Bayern gelegene Zugspitze mit 2.962 Metern. Der tiefst....... Punkt an Land liegt mit 3,54 Metern unter Normalhöhennull bei dem Ort Neuendorf-Sachsenbande im Bundesland Schleswig-Holstein. Die längst....... Flüsse sind der Rhein und die Elbe.
>
> In Deutschland herrscht ein gemäßigtes Klima. Die durchschnittlich....... Temperatur liegt im Sommer zwischen 18–19 Grad. Die jüngst....... Winter waren besonders mild, die Sommer besonders heiß. Die wärmst....... Orte liegen im Südwesten – Karlsruhe und Freiburg.

3 Complete these sentences using Konjunktiv II.

Example: Wenn ich mehr Zeit hätte, *würde ich mehr mit meiner Familie unternehmen und auch mehr Sport machen.*

a Wenn ich mehr Zeit hätte, ...

b Wenn ich mehr Geld hätte, ...

c Wenn ich eine Sprache perfekt sprechen könnte, ...

d Wenn ich eine bekannte historische Person sein könnte, ...

e Wenn ich mir meinen Traumjob aussuchen könnte, ...

f Wenn ich eine bekannte Person interviewen dürfte, ...

g Wenn ich eine Traumreise machen könnte, ...

h Wenn ich einen Wunsch frei hätte, ...

4 Talk about your ideal vacation. Use the questions as inspiration.

a Wohin würden Sie fahren?

b Wo würden Sie wohnen?

c Mit wem würden Sie fahren?

d Welche drei Dinge würden Sie auf jeden Fall mitnehmen?

e Was würden Sie unternehmen?

f Wie lange würden Sie bleiben?

5 Listen to geographical descriptions 1–4 and match them with the places a–d.

16.11

a die Nordsee ....

b die Alpen ....

c der Wienerwald ....

d der Zürichsee ....

TEST YOURSELF

 Complete with the correct Konjunktiv II of the verb in parentheses.

Der Lottogewinn

Wenn ich im Lotto gewinnen .... (werden), ... (können)
ich mir meine Träume erfüllen. Ich .... (müssen) nicht mehr arbeiten
und .... (haben) mehr Zeit für meine Familie und Hobbies. Ich ....
(können) mir auch viele Dinge leisten. Zuerst .... (werden) mein Mann und ich
uns ein schönes Haus am Meer kaufen. Das Haus .... (haben) große Fenster
und einen herrlichen Blick auf den Strand. Danach .... (werden) wir unseren
Kindern eine Weltreise schenken. Sie .... (werden) viele Länder besuchen
und neue Kulturen kennenlernen. Außerdem .... (werden) ich meinen Eltern
und Freunden Geld geben. Meine Eltern .... (werden) ein gemütliches Haus
bekommen, und meine Freunde .... (können) sich vielleicht einen Traum
erfüllen. Ich .... (sollen) auch einen Teil des Geldes spenden.
Damit .... (können) ich anderen Menschen helfen. Wenn ich im Lotto
gewinnen .... (werden), ... (sein) mein Leben sehr spannend
und ganz anders als jetzt. Es .... (sein) wunderbar! Was ....
(werden) Sie machen?

Wie geht's weiter? *What happens next?*

Lisa is back in Vienna. Max is still looking for a job and thinks about
doing more writing for his blog. What will he explore next in Berlin?
And will he discover something interesting? Find out in the next unit.

Remember to use **My review** and **My takeaway** to assess your progress and reflect on
your learning experience.

In this lesson you will learn how to:
» Talk about historical events
» Discuss aspects of Berlin's past and present
» Describe diversity in a big city
» Explain some aspects of colonialism
» Write a portrait of your town

Geschichte Berlins und Diversität

My study plan

I plan to work with Unit 17
○ Every day
○ Twice a week
○ Other _____
I plan to study for
○ 5–15 minutes
○ 15–30 minutes
○ 30–45+ minutes

My progress tracker

Day / Date	🎧	🎤	📖	✏️	💬
	○	○	○	○	○
	○	○	○	○	○
	○	○	○	○	○
	○	○	○	○	○
	○	○	○	○	○
	○	○	○	○	○
	○	○	○	○	○

My goals

What do you want to be able to do or say in German when you complete this unit?

Done
1 .... ○
2 .... ○
3 .... ○

My review

SELF CHECK

	I can ...
●	... talk about historical events.
●	... discuss aspects of Berlin's past and present.
●	... describe diversity in a big city.
●	... explain some aspects of colonialism.
●	... write a portrait of my own town.

CULTURE POINT 1

Deutsche Geschichte nach 1945

Nach dem Ende des Zweiten Weltkrieges (*World War II*) 1945 wurde Deutschland in vier Besatzungszonen (*occupied areas*) geteilt. 1949 wurde aus den westlichen Besatzungszonen, also der amerikanischen, britischen und französischen Zone, die Bundesrepublik Deutschland (*Federal Republic of Germany*) gegründet (*founded*). Gleichzeitig wurde

die sowjetische Besatzungszone zur Deutschen Demokratischen Republik (*German Democratic Republic*). Meistens benutzte man die Abkürzungen (*abbreviations*) BRD und DDR oder sprach von West- und Ostdeutschland. Berlin war immer noch in zwei Teile geteilt: Ost-Berlin war Teil der DDR und West-Berlin gehörte zur BRD.

Weil es im Westen mehr Freiheiten und Möglichkeiten gab, verließen (*left*) viele Menschen die DDR. Aus diesem Grund entschied die Regierung (*government*) dort, eine Mauer zwischen West-Berlin und Ost-Berlin zu bauen und die Grenzen zwischen der DDR und der BRD zu schließen. Die Bürger:innen waren mit der Situation in der DDR unzufrieden und 1989 gab es viele friedliche Demonstrationen gegen die Regierung. Diese Proteste führten zur Öffnung der Grenzen und zum Mauerfall (*Fall of the Wall*) am 9. November 1989. Das war auch das Ende der DDR und Deutschland wurde am 3. Oktober 1990 offiziell wiedervereinigt (*reunited*).

Am selben Tag wurde Berlin auch Hauptstadt des wiedervereinigten Deutschlands. Neun Jahre später zog das Parlament von Bonn nach Berlin um. Seitdem ist Berlin auch wieder das wirkliche politische Zentrum von Deutschland.

 Die Stasi, kurz für Staatssicherheitsdienst (*secret service*) in der DDR, spionierte die Menschen in der DDR aus. Das ehemalige (*former*) Stasi-Gefängnis (*prison*) in Hohenschönhausen ist heute eine Gedenkstätte (*memorial*) und ein Museum. Hier können Sie mehr über die Stasi erfahren:
Wann wurde Hohenschönhausen zum Stasi-Gefängnis? Wie viele Menschen haben hier im Gefängnis gesessen? Was hatten die Menschen, die hier im Gefängnis waren, getan? Würde es Sie interessieren, eine Führung in der Gedenkstätte zu machen?

VOCABULARY BUILDER 1

17.01

Look at the words and phrases and complete the missing English words and expressions. Then listen and try to imitate the pronunciation of the speakers.

GESCHICHTE	*HISTORY*
die Ära (Ären)	....
die Alliierten (-n)	*allies*
die Armee (-n)	....
die Besatzungszone (-n)	*occupied area*
der Erste / Zweite Weltkrieg	*the First / Second World* ....
der Frieden (-)	*peace*
das Jahrtausend (-e)	*millennium*
das Jahrzehnt (-e), das Jahrhundert (-e)	*decade, century*
die Jubiläumsfeier (-n)	*anniversary celebration*
der Krieg (-e)	*war*
die Luftbrücke (-n)	*airlift*
die Mauer (-n)	....
das Opfer (-)	*victim*
die Teilung (-en)	*division*
der Waffenstillstand (-"e)	*ceasefire / truce*
der Wiederaufbau (no plural)	*rebuilding / reconstruction*
die Wiedervereinigung (-en)	*reunification*
der Zeitraum (-"e)	*period*
die Zerstörung (-en)	*destruction*

AKTIVITÄTEN	*ACTIVITIES*
besetzen	*to occupy*
erklären	*to declare*
gründen	*to found*
kämpfen	*to fight*
leiden	*to suffer*
teilen	*to divide*
verteidigen	*to defend*
wieder/aufbauen	*to rebuild / reconstruct*

ADJEKTIVE	*ADJECTIVES*
bedeutend	*significant*
friedlich	*peaceful*
historisch	....
mächtig	*powerful*
unabhängig	*independent*

Vocabulary practice 1

Complete with the best word from the box.

Krieg	deutsche Geschichte	Besatzungszonen
Frieden	Berliner Mauer	Zeitraum

a .... : das Jahrzehnt, das Jahrhundert, das Jahrtausend

b .... : amerikanisch, britisch, französisch, sowjetisch

c .... : kämpfen, besetzten, verteidigen, leiden

d .... : Bau, Fall, Öffnung

e .... : Besatzungszonen, Teilung, Wiedervereinigung, Demokratie

f .... : Waffenstillstand, friedlich, Wiederaufbau

Pronunciation practice

To express the years and centuries in German:

- Up to 2000 you say the number of the two digits first, followed by Hundert and then the remaining digits as you already know them, e.g. 1517 > fünfzehnhundertsiebzehn.
- From the year 2000 you say zweitausend and then the relevant year: e.g. 2021 > zweitausendeinundzwanzig.

1 Listen to these years and repeat them in the pauses.

a	1884	c	1945	e	1989
b	1918	d	1961	f	2006

2 Say the following years. Check the pronunciation with the audio.

a	1871	c	1933	e	1990
b	1919	d	1949	f	2028

CONVERSATION 1

Die Berliner Luftbrücke

1 Listen to the conversation a few times without looking at the text. Then listen again and read the text. Which historical events does Wally mention in her conversation with Max?

Max often goes for a walk or a run in Tempelhofer Feld and knows that it used to be part of the Tempelhof Flughafen (*airport*). He noticed that you can visit the building, so he asks Wally about the history of the airport.

Max	Was ist eigentlich am Flughafen Tempelhof so besonders?
Wally	Die Geschichte des Flughafens ist sehr interessant. Er hat eine bedeutende Rolle in der Geschichte der Stadt gespielt, vor allem während der Berlin-Blockade 1948/49.
Max	Was ist denn damals passiert?
Wally	Du weißt wahrscheinlich, dass Berlin nach dem Zweiten Weltkrieg in der sowjetischen Zone lag und nur ein Teil Berlins den westlichen Alliierten gehörte. Zwischen beiden Seiten gab es damals viele Konflikte. Deshalb hat die Sowjetunion 1948 auch Transporte nach West-Berlin blockiert. Aber wegen des Flughafens konnten die westlichen Alliierten Berlin trotz der Blockade noch erreichen.
Max	Also wurden alle Lebensmittel mit dem Flugzeug nach Berlin gebracht?
Wally	Genau. Das nannte man die Luftbrücke. Sie hat vielen Menschen in Berlin das Leben gerettet.
Max	Und das war 1948? Lange vor dem Bau der Mauer?
Wally	So ist es. Die wurde dann 1961 gebaut. Und dann war Berlin in zwei Teile getrennt – Ost-Berlin und West-Berlin – bis zum Fall der Mauer 1989.
Max	Und warum hat man den Flughafen trotz seiner Bedeutung dann geschlossen?
Wally	Er war zwischen 1975 und 1990 schon einmal geschlossen. Endgültig dann aber 2008 aufgrund des Baus eines neuen Berliner Flughafens, nämlich des Flughafens Berlin Brandenburg International. Das war wirklich das Ende einer Ära. Wenn du mehr über Deutschlands Geschichte erfahren möchtest, solltest du mal ins Deutsche Historische Museum gehen. Das ist wirklich interessant.
Max	Das klingt gut. Danke für den Tipp!

2 Match the dates with the correct events.

a 1948/1949	**1** Bau der Mauer
b 1961	**2** Tempelhof wird für immer geschlossen
c 1989	**3** Tempelhof ist für eine Zeit geschlossen
d 1975–2000	**4** Berlin-Blockade
e 2008	**5** Fall der Mauer

LANGUAGE BUILDER 1

 Language discovery 1

Complete these sentences from Conversation 1. Can you identify what these structures express? How would you translate the sentences?

a Die Geschichte .... Flughafens ist sehr interessant.

b Er hat eine bedeutende Rolle in der Geschichte .... Stadt gespielt.

c Und das war 1948? Lange vor dem Bau .... Mauer?

d Das war wirklich das Ende .... Ära.

The genitive case

The genitive case is used to express a sense of ownership and possession. It can roughly be translated as of the or of a. Here is the genitive case with the definite and indefinite article and a possessive:

Nominative		Genitive	
(m) der Flughafen	des Flughafen**s**	eines Flughafen**s**	unseres Flughafen**s**
(n) das Land	des Land**es**	eines Land**es**	unseres Land**es**
(f) die Geschichte	der Geschichte	einer Geschichte	unserer Geschichte
(pl) die Museen	der Museen		unserer Museen

Note that masculine and neuter nouns in the genitive add -s (-es is usually added to one-syllable nouns: des Mann**es**, eines Kind**es**). Feminine nouns or nouns in the plural do not change.

> When using the genitive with names of people, cities, countries, etc. you start with the 'owner' of the object and add an s to them: Wallys Wohnung (*Wally's apartment*), Berlins Geschichte (*the history of Berlin*), Deutschlands Nationalmannschaft (*the national team of Germany*).
> Note that, unlike in English, there is no apostrophe used in German. However, if the name ends in -s, -ss, -ß, -z, -tz, or -x you use an apostrophe instead of s: Max' Eltern (*Max's parents*).

Language practice 1

Complete with correct genitive forms with the definite article. Don't forget to add the endings to the noun in the genitive when needed.

a Wegen .... Schwierigkeiten zwischen den Alliierten mussten viele Menschen leiden.

b Der Bau .... Mauer fand 1961 statt.

c Die Geschichte .... Mauerbau .... ist interessant.

d Wegen .... Teilung konnten sich die Menschen nicht leicht besuchen.

e Durch das Ende .... Kalten Krieg .... ergaben sich neue Möglichkeiten für Berlin.

f Nach dem Umzug .... Parlament .... wurde die Stadt wieder das politische Zentrum.

LANGUAGE BUILDER 2

💡 Language discovery 2

17.05

Listen to the conversation again and repeat each line in the pauses. Complete the three sentences from the conversation. What case follows these prepositions?

a Er hat eine bedeutende Rolle in der Geschichte der Stadt gespielt, vor allem .... der Berlin-Blockade 1948/49.

b Aber .... des Flughafens konnten die westlichen Alliierten .... der Blockade Berlin noch erreichen.

c .... des Baus eines neuen Berliner Flughafens wurde Tempelhof geschlossen.

Prepositions and the genitive

There are a few prepositions in German that are followed by the genitive case. Here is a list of the more common ones and their meaning.

anstatt	*instead of*	innerhalb	*inside of, within*
aufgrund	*due to*	trotz	*despite of*
außerhalb	*outside of*	während	*during*
bezüglich	*concerning, with regard to*	wegen	*because of*

Remember that adjectives with articles always end in **-en** in the genitive: eines neuen Flughafens; des kleinen Kindes; einer bekannten Schauspielerin; der schönen Parks.

Language practice 2

1 Match the sentence halves.

  a Trotz des Regens   **1** kaufe ich nur wenig ein.

  b Während der Pause im Theater   **2** gehen wir spazieren.

  c Wegen der hohen Preise   **3** esse ich ein Stück Kuchen.

  d Anstatt einer Kugel Eis   **4** trinken viele Zuschauer:innen etwas.

  e Aufgrund der niedrigen Temperaturen   **5** werden wir uns bald bei Ihnen melden.

  f Bezüglich Ihrer Frage   **6** ziehe ich meine Winterjacke an.

> In modern German the genitive is often replaced by von + dative:
>
> Das ist das Handy meines Bruders. > Das ist das Handy von meinem Bruder.
> Kennst du den Namen des Cafés? > Kennst du den Namen von dem Café?

17.06

2 Listen to Conversation 2 again and play Wally's role. Her lines are longer, so you may need to use the book for reference.

CULTURE POINT 2

Die deutsche Kolonialgeschichte

Im Vergleich zu anderen Ländern ist Deutschlands Kolonialgeschichte sehr kurz. Deutschland hatte Kolonien in Afrika, Ozeanien und Ostasien, zum Beispiel in Deutsch-Südwestafrika, Togo, Kamerun und Neuguinea. Zeitweise war Deutschland aber die viertgrößte Kolonialmacht (*colonial power*). Während dieser Zeit verursachten die Deutschen großes Leid (*suffering*) in den Kolonien. Viele Menschen wurden von den Deutschen ermordet (*murdered*).

Die Auswirkungen (*effects*) dieser Zeit kann man auch heute noch spüren (*feel*). Man findet heute in Deutschland immer noch Orte, die nach deutschen Kolonisatoren benannt (*named after*) sind. In deutschen Museen gibt es Ausstellungsstücke (*exhibits*), die in den Kolonien gestohlen (*stolen*) wurden. Menschen in den ehemaligen Kolonien warten immer noch auf Entschädigungen (*reparations*).

Manche Orte wurden umbenannt, Ausstellungsstücke wurden zurückgegeben und Deutschland hat den Völkermord (*genocide*) anerkannt (*acknowledged*) und sich offiziell bei Namibia entschuldigt, aber die Dekolonialisierung ist erst am Anfang.

 Das Deutsche Historische Museum hat eine Ausstellung zur deutschen Kolonialgeschichte. Warum gibt es eine neue Ausstellung? Welche Bereiche gibt es in der Ausstellung? Welche Kolonien stehen im Mittelpunkt? Hat Ihr Land eine Kolonialgeschichte? Wie geht es mit dieser Geschichte um?

VOCABULARY BUILDER 2

Look at the words and phrases and complete the missing English words and expressions. Then listen and try to imitate the pronunciation of the speakers.

KOLONIALISMUS	COLONIALISM
die Ausbeutung (-en)	*exploitation*
die Diskriminierung (-en)	*discrimination*
der/die Einheimische (-n)	*local / indigenous population*
die Gewalt (singular only)	*violence*

der Handel (no plural)	trade
die Kolonie (-n), die Kolonialmacht (-¨e)	...................., colonial power
die Reparationen (plural only)	....
die Unabhängigkeit -(en)	independence

AKTIVITÄTEN	**ACTIVITIES**
auf/klären	to explain, clarify
entdecken	to discover
entschädigen	to compensate / make amends
ermorden	to murder
erorbern, befreien	to conquer, to liberate
schweigen	to remain silent
thematisieren	to make a topic of discussion
unterdrücken	to suppress
versklaven	to enslave

MULTIKULTURALISMUS	**MULTICULTURALISM**
der Einwanderer (-) / die Einwanderin (-nen)	immigrant
die Einbürgerung (-en)	naturalization
der Flüchtling (-e)	refugee
die Integration (-en)	....
die Parallelgesellschaft (-en)	.... society
die doppelte Staatsbürgerschaft (-en)	dual citizenship
diskriminieren	to ....
sich integrieren	to ....
willkommen heißen	to welcome
divers	....

NÜTZLICHE AUSDRÜCKE	**USEFUL EXPRESSIONS**
Ich bin ganz baff.	I am stunned.
mit etwas / jemandem um/gehen	to deal with something / someone
grausam	awful, cruel

Vocabulary practice 2

Complete the text with a word from the box.

> willkommen   Integration   Flüchtlinge   doppelte Staatsbürgerschaft
> divers   Einwanderer:innen   Parallelgesellschaften

In Berlin leben viele .... Daher ist die Bevölkerung Berlins sehr ....
Viele der Einwander:innen sind als .... nach Deutschland gekommen. Die
Berliner:innen haben sie .... geheißen und ihnen bei der .... geholfen.
Daher gibt es meistens keine .... Viele haben heute auch die ....

Multikulturelles Berlin

17.08

1 Listen to the conversation a few times without looking at the text. Then listen again and read the text. Which former German colony do they talk about? Which country is that today?

After visiting the Deutsche Historische Museum and its Dauerausstellung (*permanent exhibition*) on Germany's colonial history, Max meets up with Aylin for a drink.

Max   Ich bin noch ganz baff. Ich hatte gar nicht gewusst, dass Deutschland so viele Kolonien hatte.

Aylin   Ich weiß auch viel zu wenig über diesen Zeitraum in der deutschen Geschichte. In der Schule wurde das nicht viel thematisiert.

Max   Ich glaube, das ist leider überall so. Darüber wird meistens geschwiegen. Deshalb wird der Umgang mit der Kolonialgeschichte auch von vielen kritisiert. Die Ausstellung versucht das zu ändern.

Aylin   Wie ist die Ausstellung denn?

Max   Wirklich interessant. Ich habe mich vor allem über die Geschichte der größten deutschen Kolonie, Deutsch-Südwestafrika, informiert. Das ist das heutige Namibia. Es wurde 1884 von Deutschland kolonialisiert.

Aylin   Und warum?

Max   Es gab verschiedene Gründe, vor allem ging es um Handel, aber auch um Macht. Daher wurden die Einheimischen dort unterdrückt und versklavt. Durch die Gewalt der deutschen Armee wurden daher auch viele Menschen ermordet.

Aylin   Das ist wirklich grausam.

Max   Ja, ich bin wirklich froh, dass diese Zeit vorbei ist. Heute leben so viele verschiedene Kulturen friedlich in Berlin zusammen. Die Stadt ist so divers und multikulturell. Deine Familie ist ein gutes Beispiel.

Aylin   Das stimmt, aber wir dürfen die Vergangenheit nicht vergessen.

Max   Es wird auch immer noch diskutiert, wie man die Menschen in Namibia entschädigen kann. Es wird zum Beispiel über Reparationen gesprochen.

2 True (richtig) or false (falsch)? Correct the false statements.

   a Max hat schon lange gewusst, dass Deutschland viele Kolonien hatte.   R   F

   b Aylin hat in der Schule viel über Kolonialismus gelernt.   R   F

   c Die Ausstellung will, dass mehr Menschen über Kolonialismus sprechen.   R   F

   d Deutschland hatte noch größere Kolonien als das heutige Namibia.   R   F

   e Max denkt, dass die Situation in Berlin jetzt positiv ist.   R   F

   f Die Menschen in Namibia wurden von Deutschland schon entschädigt.   R   F

Language discovery 3

Complete these sentences from Conversation 2. Which verb is used in all of them?

a In der Schule .... das nicht viel thematisiert.

b Daruber .... meistens geschwiegen.

c Es .... 1884 von Deutschland kolonialisiert.

The passive voice

To focus on the action rather than the person carrying out the action, use the passive voice. This is a lot more common in German than in English.

Die Kolonie wurde gegründet.   *The colony was founded.*

Viele Menschen werden diskriminiert.   *Many people are being discriminated against.*

The passive is formed with the verb werden in the appropriate tense and the past participle of the main verb that expresses the action. You are already familiar with the past participle forms through the present perfect tense. Here is werden in the passive, in three main tenses:

	Present	Past	Perfect		Present	Past	Perfect
ich	werde	wurde	bin worden	**wir**	werden	wurden	sind worden
du	wirst	wurdest	bist worden	**ihr**	werdet	wurdet	seid worden
er, sie, es, xier	wird	wurde	ist worden	**Sie, sie**	werden	wurden	sind worden

In the present and past tense, werden is in second position in a main clause and the past participle goes to the end:

Present tense: Die Ausstellung <u>wird</u> heute eröffnet.

Past simple: Die Ausstellung <u>wurde</u> gestern eröffnet.

In a subordinating clause, both verbs go to the end, with werden coming last:

Ich denke, dass die Ausstellung heute <u>eröffnet wird</u>.

I think that the exhibition is opening today.

When using the perfect, the order is different. The past participle of werden in the passive is worden, and it comes last or in second position:

Main clause: Die Ausstellung <u>ist</u> gestern eröffnet <u>worden</u>.

Subordinating clause: Ich denke, dass die Ausstellung gestern eröffnet <u>worden</u> <u>ist</u>.

> Don't confuse the passive voice with the future tense. Both use werden, but the passive voice takes the past participle while the future tense takes the infinitive of the main verb:
> Passive: Eine Geschichte wird erzählt.   *A story is being told.*
> Future: Ich werde eine Geschichte erzählen.   *I will tell a story.*

Language practice 3

1 Complete with the appropriate form of werden.

a Present

1 Die Kinder .... jeden Tag von der Schule abgeholt.

2 Ich .... nicht gerne angerufen.

3 Wir .... immer herzlich willkommen geheißen

b Past

1 Du .... vor 20 Jahren geboren.

2 Gestern .... ein Wolf im Wald gesehen.

3 .... ihr schon zu der Party von Pascal eingeladen?

LANGUAGE BUILDER 4

💡 Language discovery 4

17.09

Listen to Conversation 2 again and repeat each line in the pauses provided. Then identify the missing preposition. Choose from either von or durch.

a Deshalb wird der Umgang mit Kolonialgeschichte auch .... vielen kritisiert.

b .... die Gewalt der deutschen Armee wurden daher auch viele Menschen ermordet.

Adding the agent in the passive voice

The focus in the passive voice is on the action, and the person carrying out the action (the agent) can often be omitted entirely. But when you want to include the agent, use the preposition von + dative. Note that von + dem is usually shortened to vom.

Der Kuchen wurde vom Bäcker gebacken.   *The cake was baked by the baker.*

Use durch + accusative to give the means by which something is done:

Viele Häuser wurden durch den Sturm zerstört.   *Many houses were destroyed by the storm.*

Unser Leben wurde durch die Pandemie verändert.   *Our lives were changed by the pandemic.*

Language practice 4

1 Durch or von? Choose the correct preposition.

a Die Post wird .... der Briefträgerin gebracht.

b Das Essen wurde .... einer 3-Sterne-Köchin gekocht.

c Alex wurde .... durch einen Unfall verletzt.

d Die Blumen werden .... den Regen bewässert.

e Die Grammatik wird .... den Lehrer:innen erklärt.

f Die Stadt wurde .... eine Flut überschwemmt.

2 Now play Conversation 2 again and play Max's role. Speak in the pauses provided and try not to refer to the text.

17.10

SKILL BUILDER

1 Complete using the correct genitive form and definite article.

a Wie war der Name .... Hotel .... ?
b Was sind die Öffnungszeiten .... Museum .... ?
c Fast die Hälfte .... Besucher Berlin .... kommen aus dem Ausland.
d Wer war noch einmal der Autor .... Buch .... ?
e Die Geschichte .... Berliner Mauer ist sehr interessant.
f Seit 1990 ist Berlin wieder die Hauptstadt .... Bundesrepublik.

2 Reorder the sentences and start with the underlined word.

a wird – von Millionen Besuchern – <u>Das Schloss Schönbrunn in Wien</u> – besichtigt
b wurde – gebaut – <u>Es</u> – ab 1696 – als Jagdschloss
c <u>Zwischen 1743 und1749</u> – umgebaut – das Schloss – wurde – zum ersten Mal
d <u>Es</u> – von Kaiserin Sisi – bewohnt – wurde – zum Beispiel
e aufgenommen – 1996 – wurde – <u>Es</u> – in die Liste des Weltkulturerbes der UNESCO
f schon – im 18. Jahrhundert – wurde – eröffnet – <u>Der Tiergarten Schönbrunn</u>
g gehalten – <u>Hier</u> – werden – viele Tiere aus aller Welt
f viele interessante Details – werden – <u>Während der Fütterungen</u> – erzählt – über die Tiere

3 Listen to a podcast on diversity in Berlin and answer the questions.

17.11

Here are a few words to help you:

die Vielfalt (singular only)	*variety*	küren	*to choose/select somebody for something*
das Gotteshaus (-"er)	*place of worship*	der Ruf (-e)	*reputation*
die Behinderung (-en)	*disability*	schwul	*gay (for men)*
barrierefrei	*accessible*	lesbisch	*gay (for women)*

a Warum ist Berlin vor allem bei jungen Menschen sehr beliebt?
b Wie beschreibt der Podcast das Essen in Berlin?
c Was ist besonders an dem *House of One*?
d Wie hat die EU-Kommission Berlin genannt?
e Was ist der besondere Ruf von Berlin?
f Was passiert am Christopher Street Day?

4 Talk about the history of your home town. Here are a few questions to help you.

   a Wann wurde die Stadt gegründet? Von wem wurde sie gegründet?

   b Welche besonderen Ereignisse gab es in der Geschichte der Stadt? Was ist passiert?

   c Was kann man in der Stadt besichtigen? Was würden Sie empfehlen?

   d Wer lebt heute in der Stadt? Wie divers und multikulturell ist die Stadt?

   e Gibt es typische Spezialitäten aus Ihrer Stadt? Was sollte man essen und trinken?

5 Here are three reviews about the exhibition at the Deutsche Historische Museum. Match the headings with the reviews. Here are a few words to help you:

das Kapitel (-) *chapter*   enttäuschend *disappointing*   schockierend *shocking*

   a Wichtiges Thema, aber es gibt noch viel zu verbessern

   b Keine Ausstellung zum Entspannen

   c Alle sollten diese Ausstellung sehen!

 Marion_Gesch   ···

Eine wirklich interessante und wichtige Ausstellung! Wir wissen alle viel zu wenig über dieses Kapitel der deutschen Geschichte. Was die Kolonialmacht damals getan hat, ist wirklich schlimm. Wir müssen die Menschen über diese Zeit aufklären. Leider wird das Thema in der Schule zu wenig behandelt. Ich werde mit meinen Kindern in die Ausstellung gehen, wenn sie alt genug sind. Ich hoffe, dass viele Eltern dieses Thema mit ihren Kindern besprechen.

 Alex_2005   ···

Ich finde es wichtig, dass die deutsche Kolonialgeschichte endlich auch im Museum thematisiert wird. So kann man mehr Menschen über diese dunkle Seite unserer Geschichte informieren. Ich fand die Ausstellung aber leider sehr enttäuschend. Es wurden einfach zu viele Stereotypen über schwarze Menschen reproduziert. Die Geschichte wird aus der Sicht der Deutschen gezeigt und ist daher nicht dekolonialisiert.

 DHM_Fan879   ···

Auf so eine Ausstellung habe ich lange gewartet. Endlich kann man sich auch über dieses Kapitel unserer Geschichte informieren, ohne langweilige Bücher oder Artikel zu lesen. Ich fand die Ausstellung insgesamt sehr gut und realistisch. Was dort passiert ist, ist wirklich schockierend. Es gibt auch einen interessanten Film zu diesem Thema: „Der vermessene Mensch" von Lars Kraume.

6 Identify which person in exercise 5 fits the description best.

   a Diese Person geht gern in Ausstellungen, um sich über Geschichte zu informieren.

   b Diese Person denkt, dass kleine Kinder die Ausstellung noch nicht sehen sollen.

   c Diese Person findet, dass die Ausstellung die Geschichte realistisch darstellt.

   d Diese Person ist der Meinung, dass die Ausstellung die Besucher:innen nicht richtig informiert.

   e Diese Person glaubt, wir müssen alle mehr über den Kolonialismus lernen.

7 Answer these questions. Start your sentence with a genitive preposition.

Example: Was machen Sie während der Ferien? > *Während der Ferien relaxe ich.*

a Was tun Sie trotz des heißen Wetters?

b Was machen Sie wegen der Kälte?

c Was machen Sie während des Urlaubs?

d Was möchten Sie anstatt eines Nachtisches?

e Was kaufen Sie aufgrund der niedrigen Preise?

f Was machen Sie trotz der vielen Arbeit?

g Was tun Sie wegen des Klimawandels?

TEST YOURSELF

Translate these sentences about the history of Switzerland into German.

a The history of Switzerland is interesting.

b In the 16th century, the Reformation was introduced in Zurich by Ulrich Zwingli.

c During the Napoleonic Wars (Napoleonischen Kriege), Switzerland was occupied by France.

d Modern Switzerland was founded in 1848.

e Because of its neutrality (Neutralität), Switzerland did not participate in World War II.

f German is only one of the official languages in Switzerland.

g Bern is the seat (Sitz) of the parliament.

h Many laws are being decided through referendums (Referenden).

Wie geht's weiter? *What happens next?*

Max is learning more about Berlin and Germany every day. What will he find out next? And will he find a way to stay in Berlin for longer? Will he see Lisa again soon? Find out more in Unit 18.

Remember to use **My review** and **My takeaway** to assess your progress and reflect on your learning experience.

In this lesson you will learn how to:

» Describe what you do for the environment
» Talk about the importance of recycling
» Discuss some of the issues around climate change
» Make suggestions

Umwelt und Nachhaltigkeit

My study plan

I plan to work with Unit 18

○ Every day
○ Twice a week
○ Other _____

I plan to study for

○ 5–15 minutes
○ 15–30 minutes
○ 30–45+ minutes

My progress tracker

Day / Date	🎧	🎤	📖	✏️	💬
	○	○	○	○	○
	○	○	○	○	○
	○	○	○	○	○
	○	○	○	○	○
	○	○	○	○	○
	○	○	○	○	○
	○	○	○	○	○

My goals

What do you want to be able to do or say in German when you complete this unit?

	Done
1	○
2	○
3	○

My review

SELF CHECK

	I can ...
○	... describe what I do for the environment.
○	... say how important recycling is in my town/country.
○	... discuss some of the issues around climate change.
○	... make suggestions.

CULTURE POINT 1

Recycling in Deutschland

Mülltrennung (*separation of waste*) und Recycling haben eine lange Tradition in Deutschland und begannen Ende der 1970er Jahre. Mittlerweile gibt es in Deutschland ein einheitliches System. Man sammelt den Müll in verschiedenfarbigen Tonnen (*bins*). Zum

Beispiel ist die blaue Tonne meistens für Zeitungen und Papier und die schwarze Tonne für den Restmüll (*general, nonrecyclable trash/rubbish*). Flaschen und Gläser kommen in den Altglascontainer (*bottle bank*). Die Recyclingquote für Hausmüll liegt bei etwa 70 Prozent.

Um Müll zu reduzieren, gibt es in Deutschland ein Pfandsystem für Flaschen (*bottle deposit scheme*). Das heißt, wenn man eine Flasche kauft, bezahlt man Pfand, beispielsweise 25 Cent. Bringt man die Flasche zurück, bekommt man die 25 Cent wieder. Dieses System gilt nicht nur für Glasflaschen, sondern auch für Kunststoffflaschen (*plastic bottles*), Getränkedosen oder Joghurtgläser. Werfen Sie also keine Flaschen weg!

Als eine der grünsten und ökologischsten Städte in Deutschland gilt Freiburg im Breisgau, das sich selbst Green City nennt. Freiburg ist Vorreiter (*pioneer*) in Sachen Solarenergie. Auf allen gewerblichen (*nonresidential*) Gebäuden gibt es Solaranlagen, Freiburger:innen fahren mehr Fahrrad als Auto und mit Dietenbach entsteht ein neuer Stadtteil, der klimaneutral sein soll.

 Was wissen Sie über Umweltschutz? Machen Sie den Test.
Wie viele Antworten waren richtig?
Was haben Sie nicht gewusst?
Welche Informationen haben Sie überrascht?

18.01

VOCABULARY BUILDER 1

Look at the words and phrases and complete the missing English words and expressions. Then listen and try to imitate the pronunciation of the speakers.

UMWELT	*ENVIRONMENT*
der Abfall (-"e) / der Müll (no plural)	*waste / trash / rubbish*
der Biomüll (no plural)	*organic waste*
die Energiesparlampe (-n)	*energy-saving lamp*
der Essensrest (-e)	*leftovers, leftover food*
das Gerät (-e)	*device, equipment*
der Klimawandel (no plural)	*climate change*
die Solarenergie (-n), die Solaranlage (-n)	*................ power, solar system*
die Tonne (-n)	*trashcan / bin*
die Umweltverschmutzung (no plural)	*environmental pollution*
die Verpackung (-en)	*package / packaging*
das Verpackungsmaterial (-ien)	*packaging material*
der Wasserhahn (-"e)	*faucet / tap*

AKTIVITÄTEN	*ACTIVITIES*
ab/holen	*to collect, pick up*
aus/schalten, aus/machen	*to switch off, turn off*
klar/kommen	*to cope, manage*
vermeiden	*to avoid*
zu/drehen	*to close, turn off*
den Müll trennen	*to separate the ....*

VERBEN IM KONJUNKTIV II	*VERBS IN THE SUBJUNCTIVE II*
wir täten	*we would do*
ich wünschte	*I'd wish*

NÜTZLICHE AUSDRÜCKE	*USEFUL EXPRESSIONS*
staatlich	*state, public*
verwundert	*astonished / surprised*
die Subvention (-en)	*subsidy*
die Subventionshilfe (-n)	*subsidy, grant aid*
die Unterstützung (-en)	*support*
etwas laufen lassen	*to leave something running / on*

> Remember, to switch something on, you say einschalten; to switch something off use ausschalten. To turn on a faucet / tap you would use aufdrehen, and to turn it off zudrehen. Remember that all these verbs are separable verbs, so you will need to split them up when you use them in a main clause.

Vocabulary practice 1

Complete these sentences about the environment with a verb from the box.

trinke	fahre	laufen	zudrehen	auszumachen
	vermeiden	kaufen	trennen	

a Wenn du dir die Zähne putzt, solltest du den Wasserhahn ....

b Im Supermarkt versuche ich immer lokale Produkte zu ....

c Wir .... den Müll schon seit vielen Jahren.

d Den Laptop oder den Fernseher lasse ich nie auf Stand-by ....

e Wenn ich aus dem Zimmer gehe, vergesse ich nicht, das Licht ....

f Ich .... kein Wasser aus Plastikflaschen.

g Statt mit dem Auto .... ich jetzt öfter mit dem Fahrrad oder öffentlichen Verkehrsmitteln.

h Ich gehe oft auf dem Markt einkaufen. Für Obst und Gemüse, aber auch für Lebensmittel gibt es keine Verpackung. So .... wir Plastik.

Pronunciation practice

18.02

1 Nouns relating to the environment are often compound nouns. Listen to these words and repeat them in the pauses.

Klima, Klimawandel, Klimaaktivist
Umwelt, Umweltschutz, Umweltverschmutzung
Verpackung, Verpackunsgsmüll, Verpackungsmaterialien
Wasser, Wasserhahn, Wasserflasche
Solarauto, Solarenergie, Solaranlage

18.03

2 How would you pronounce these words? Listen to the audio to check.

Klimadebatte   Verpackungsindustrie   Solarflugzeug
Umweltbewegung   Wasserverbrauch

CONVERSATION 1

Ich wünschte, wir täten alle mehr

18.04

1 Listen to the conversation a few times without looking at the text. Then listen again and read the text. Can you name at least three things Fabian and his family do for the environment?

> Max is visiting Fabian and Nuri. Nuri is busy working on a school project on the environment, and Max and Fabian start talking.

Max	Das finde ich ja toll, dass sich die Kinder in der Schule schon so früh mit der Umwelt beschäftigen.
Fabian	Du hast ja wahrscheinlich bemerkt, dass Umweltfragen in Deutschland sehr wichtig sind.
Max	Recycling gibt es ja auch in den USA, aber es ist nicht so systematisch wie hier oder in Österreich.
Fabian	Bist du denn am Anfang gut klargekommen?
Max	Ich war schon ein wenig verwundert, aber ich habe ja schnell gelernt: Zeitungen und Papier kommen in die blaue Tonne. Der Biomüll, die Essensreste kommen in die braune Tonne. Und alles wird dann meistens alle zwei Wochen abgeholt.
Fabian	Siehst du, da bist du ja schnell ein Müll-Experte geworden. (lacht)
Max	Aber ihr als Familie tut ja auch viel für die Umwelt, oder?
Fabian	Ja, wir benutzen Energiesparlampen und lassen die Geräte nie auf Stand-by laufen. Beim Zähneputzen drehe ich den Wasserhahn zu. Da passt Nuri immer auf!
Max	Und ihr kauft ja auch viel auf dem Markt ein.
Fabian	Ja, wir versuchen, so viele regionale Produkte wie möglich zu kaufen. So vermeiden wir Plastik. Und wir kaufen auch nur Pfandflaschen.
Max	Und wie ist das bei dir in der Elektrofirma?
Fabian	Wie du weißt, installieren wir ja auch Solaranlagen. Es wäre gut, wenn es mehr staatliche Subventionshilfen für Solarenergie gäbe.
Max	Ja, ich denke, vielen Leuten ist immer noch nicht klar, was der Klimawandel wirklich bedeutet. Ich wünschte, wir täten alle mehr.

2 Complete the sentences.

Example: Am Anfang war Max über die Mülltrennung *ein wenig verwundert*.

a In die blaue Tonne kommen ....

b Die braune Tonne ist für ....

c Beim Zähneputzen drehen Fabian und Nuri ....

d Wenn man auf dem Markt einkauft, ...

e Fabian wünscht, es gäbe mehr ....

LANGUAGE BUILDER 1

 Language discovery 1

Look at these compound nouns from Conversation 1. Which letter is used to join the nouns together?

a die Essensreste   **b** die Subventionshilfe

Linking compound nouns

As you have probably realized compound nouns, nouns that consist of two or more elements, are an important feature in German. When joining two nouns together an extra -s is often inserted to make the pronunciation easier. This normally happens with:

Nouns ending in **-heit, -ing, -ion, -keit, -ling, -schaft, -tät,** or **-ung**	Infinitives used as nouns
die Verpackung + das Material: das Verpackung**s**material (*packaging material*)	das Essen + der Rest: der Essen**s**rest (*leftover food*)
die Mannschaft + der Sport: der Mannschaft**s**sport (*team sport*)	das Leben + das Mittel: das Leben**s**mittel (*food*)

Note that nouns ending in -e usually add an -n when joining with another noun:

die Sonne + die Energie: die Sonnenenergie (*solar power*)

die Tasche + das Messer: das Taschenmesser (*pocket knife*)

> Don't forget that the last noun defines the gender: der Pfand + die Flasche: die Pfandflasche.

Language practice 1

Join these nouns together and add the missing -s or -n. Include the article.

Example: die Zeitung + der Artikel > *der Zeitungsartikel*

a die Öffnung + die Zeiten: ....

b der Liebling + das Land: ....

c die Wirtschaft + das Klima: ....

d die Schönheit + die Creme: ....

e die Arbeit + die Zeit: ....

f die Familie + der Urlaub: ....

g die Woche + die Karte: ....

h die Sonne + der Schein: ....

i das Auge + die Farbe: ....

j das Leben + der Lauf: ....

k die Universität + das Ranking: ....

💡 Language discovery 2

18.05

Listen to the conversation again and repeat each line in the pauses provided. What do these sentences from the conversation express? What verb form is normally used to express this? Can you rephrase the sentences using a verb form you already know?

a Es wäre gut, wenn es mehr staatliche Subventionshilfen für Solarenergie gäbe.
b Ich wünschte, wir täten alle mehr.

Konjunktiv II

You have learned that Konjuktiv II—with the exception of haben, sein, and the modal verbs—is normally formed with würden + the main verb. However, it is also possible to construct Konjunktiv II with any verb:

	Regular verbs		Irregular verbs		Mixed verbs	
	infinitive stem + -te endings		past stem + endings (+ umlaut)		past stem + -te endings (+ umlaut)	
ich	brauch**te**	kauf**te**	gäb**e**	ging**e**	däch**te**	wüss**te**
du	brauch**test**	kauf**test**	gäb**est**	ging**st**	däch**test**	wüss**test**
er/sie/ es/xier	brauch**te**	kauf**te**	gäb**e**	ging**e**	däch**te**	wüss**te**
wir	brauch**ten**	kauf**ten**	gäb**en**	ging**en**	däch**ten**	wüss**ten**
ihr	brauch**tet**	kauf**tet**	gäb**t**	ging**t**	däch**tet**	wüss**tet**
Sie/sie	brauch**ten**	kauf**ten**	gäb**en**	ging**en**	däch**ten**	wüss**ten**

For irregular and mixed verbs, you add an umlaut whenever possible. There is no extra umlaut for regular verbs. Here are a few examples:

Tina denkt, wir brauchten mehr Zeit.　　*Tina thinks we would need more time.*

Ich ginge gern mehr aus.　　*I would like to go out more.*

Ich wüsste gern, wie alt er ist.　　*I would like to know how old he is.*

Although these forms are less frequently used than würden + infinitive, you will still find them in conversations, in more formal TV and radio programs and podcasts, and especially articles and news reports.

Language practice 2

1 Rewrite these sentences using the Konjunktiv II forms of the verbs in italics.

Example: Es wäre gut, wenn wir mehr Strom *sparen würden.*
> *Es wäre gut, wenn wir mehr Strom sparten.*

a Es würde helfen, wenn Leute weniger Wasser aus Plastikflaschen *trinken würden*.

b Es wäre auch gut, wenn wir mehr Produkte aus der Region *kaufen würden*.

c Wir würden Ressourcen sparen, wenn wir kaputte Sachen *reparieren würden*.

d Wir könnten die Kohlenstoffdioxid (CO_2)-Emissionen reduzieren, wenn wir weniger Fleisch *essen würden*.

e Ich fände es gut, wenn man mehr Geld in alternative Energien *investieren würde*.

f Ich wünschte mir, man *würde* weniger Fast Fashion *herstellen*.

g Wenn es doch nur ein besseres öffentliche Verkehrsnetz *geben würde*, würden mehr Leute Bus und Bahn benutzen.

18.06

Now play the conversation again and play Max's role. Speak in the pauses provided and try not to refer to the text.

CULTURE POINT 2

Klimawandel und Umweltschutz

Nach der Atomkatastrophe von Fukushima im Jahre 2011 beschloss die damalige deutsche Bundesregierung einen Ausstieg (*phasing out*) aus der Atomenergie. Die letzten beiden Kernkraftwerke (*nuclear power plants*) wurden 2023 abgeschaltet. Diese Transformation – weg von Öl, Kohle, Gas und Atomkraft hin zu erneuerbaren Energien wie Wasser- und

Solarkraft, Windenergie und Erdwärme (*geothermal energy*) – nennt man offiziell die Energiewende *(energy transformation)*. Ziel ist es, den Anteil der erneuerbaren Energien bis 2030 auf 80 Prozent zu steigern. Im Jahre 2050 soll der gesamte Strom aus erneuerbaren Energiequellen kommen.

Mittlerweile ist der Klimawandel aber auch in Deutschland angekommen. In den letzten Jahren gab es in vielen Teilen in Deutschland immer wieder Extremwetter (*extreme weather*). 2021 starben bei extremem Hochwasser (*flooding*) mehr als 180 Menschen.

Für den Schutz der Umwelt setzen sich in Deutschland viele Organisationen ein. Die Partei Die Grünen – eine Partei zum Schutz der Umwelt – wurde bereits 1979 gegründet. Andere bekannte Umweltorganisationen sind NABU, Greenpeace, der Deutsche Alpenverein und BUND – Freunde der Erde. Sehr viele Ehrenamtliche (*volunteers*) engagieren sich für diese Organisationen.

 Finden Sie mehr Informationen über den größten deutschen Umweltverband, NABU. Was bedeutet der Name NABU? Können Sie fünf Beispiele finden, wofür sich NABU engagiert? Gibt es ähnliche Organisationen auch in Ihrem Land?

VOCABULARY BUILDER 2

18.07

Look at the words and phrases and complete the missing English words and expressions. Then listen and try to imitate the pronunciation of the speakers.

DER KLIMAWANDEL	CLIMATE CHANGE
der Anstieg des Meeresspiegels	*rise in sea level*
der Ausstoß (-"e)	*emission*
die Auswirkung (-en)	*impact / effect*
der Brennstoff (-e)	*fuel*
die Dürre (-n)	*drought*
die Einwegverpackung (-en)	*disposable packaging*
die Erderwärmung (singular only)	*global* ....
die Flut (-en) / die Überschwemmung (-en)	*flood*
der Gletscherschwund (singular only)	*glacial retreat*
die Hitzewelle (-n)	*heat wave*
die Katastrophe (-n)	....
die Nachhaltigkeit (singular only)	*sustainability*
der Orkan (-e), der Wirbelsturm (-"e)	*hurricane, tornado*
das Reparaturgeschäft (-e)	*repair shop*
das Treibhaus (-"er)	*greenhouse*
der Waldbrand (-"e)	*wildfire*
die Wetterdaten (plural)	.... *data*
erneuerbar	*renewable*
klimaneutral	*carbon neutral*

AKTIVIVITÄTEN	ACTIVITIES
Druck aus/üben	*to put pressure on*
erreichen	*to reach*
sanieren	*to renovate, to restore*
verringern	*to reduce*
zu/nehmen	*to increase*

Vocabulary practice 2

1 Choose the best word to complete the sentence.

    a Benzin ist ein Treibhausgas / Brennstoff.

    b Der Anstieg des Meeresspiegels ist ein gutes Beispiel für Erderwärmung / Extremwetter.

    c Wenn nicht genug Regen fällt, kann es Hochwasser / eine Dürre geben.

    d Höhere Temperaturen haben Auswirkungen / Ausstöße auf die Menschen.

Es geht nur gemeinsam!

18.08

1 Listen to the conversation a few times without looking at the text. Then listen again and read the text. Who is affected by climate change in Berlin and Brandenburg? What does Silke Rau think needs to happen?

Max has become very interested in environmental issues and decides to interview Silke Rau, an Expertin (*expert*) on this topic from Berlin, for his blog.

Max   Ich wollte zuerst fragen, ob der Klimawandel Berlin schon erreicht hat?

Silke Rau   Ja, auf jeden Fall. In den letzten Jahren hat das Extremwetter hier und in Brandenburg deutlich zugenommen. Das heißt: Hitzewellen, Dürre und Starkregen.

Max   Könnten Sie beschreiben, was das für Auswirkungen hat?

Silke Rau   Die hohen Temperaturen im Sommer haben natürlich Auswirkungen auf die Gesundheit, vor allem auf ältere Menschen. Und für Brandenburg ist die Landwirtschaft sehr wichtig. Wenn es nicht genug Wasser gibt, wäre das natürlich eine Katastrophe.

Max   Und tut Berlin etwas dagegen?

Silke Rau   Berlin will bis 2045 klimaneutral werden. Wir müssen vor allem versuchen, den Ausstoß von CO_2 zu verringern. Das geht natürlich nur, wenn wir mehr in erneuerbare Energien investieren, Häuser sanieren und generell versuchen, nachhaltiger zu leben.

Max   Mein Eindruck ist, dass es hier in Berlin viele Initiativen gibt.

Silke Rau   Ja, sicherlich. Man findet hier viele Urban Gardening Projekte, Zero Waste Shops, kleine Reparaturgeschäfte, Secondhand-Kaufhäuser ... Und auch junge Startup-Unternehmen, die umweltfreundliche Produkte entwickeln.

Max   Hätten Sie dafür ein Beispiel?

Silke Rau   Ja, es gibt zum Beispiel eine Reihe von Firmen, die versuchen, etwas gegen die Einwegverpackungen, zum Beispiel To-go-Becher, zu unternehmen.

Max   Könnten Sie mir noch sagen, wie Sie die Zukunft sehen?

Silke Rau   Viele sagen: Es ist fünf vor zwölf. Ich denke, wir müssen viel Druck auf die Politik ausüben. Wenn alle Länder zusammenarbeiten, können wir viel machen. Aber es geht nur gemeinsam!

> Es ist fünf vor zwölf is a common proverb in German and means *It is almost too late* (lit. *It is five to twelve [i.e. midnight]*).

2 Complete the sentences.

a Das Extremwetter hat in Berlin und Brandenburg ....

b Im Sommer gibt es Hitzewellen und ....

c Bis 2045 will ....

d Wichtig ist es, den ....

e Viele Firmen versuchen, ...

f Silke glaubt, wir können noch viel machen. Aber es ....

LANGUAGE BUILDER 3

 ## Language discovery 3

Look at these questions from Conversation 2. Complete with the missing word. When do you normally use these words? What do you notice about the word order?

a Ich wollte zuerst fragen, ... der Klimawandel Berlin schon erreicht hat?

b Könnten Sie beschreiben, ... das für Auswirkungen hat?

c Könnten Sie mir noch sagen, ... Sie die Zukunft sehen?

Indirect questions

Indirect questions are a more polite way of asking for information. They are normally introduced by phrases like Könnten Sie mir sagen, ... (*Could you tell me, ...*); Könnte ich Sie fragen, ... (*Could I ask you, ...*); Wissen Sie, ...? (*Do you know, ...?*). Compare these types of questions:

Direct question: Wie sehen Sie die Zukunft?

Indirect question: Könnten Sie mir sagen, wie Sie die Zukunft sehen?

In indirect questions, the question becomes a subordinate clause: the question word stays at the beginning, but the main verb goes to the end.

Wissen Sie, wo man hier gut essen gehen kann?
Do you know where there is a good place to eat?

For yes/no questions, use ob (*if/whether*).

Weißt du, ob Nuri kommt?   *Do you know if Nuri is coming?*

Language practice 3

Rephrase more politely using indirect questions.

Example: Wo ist der nächste Supermarkt? > *Könnten Sie mir sagen, wo der nächste Supermarkt ist?*

a Kann man hier in der Nähe gut essen gehen? **d** Wie weit ist es bis zum nächsten Glascontainer?

b Wo gibt es hier ein gutes Fitnessstudio?

c Was kann man hier abends unternehmen? **e** Wie oft wird der Müll abgeholt?

f Gibt es hier einen Park in der Nachbarschaft?

g Kann man hier noch spät einkaufen?

h Fährt hier ein Nachtbus?

LANGUAGE BUILDER 4

18.09

💡 Language discovery 4

Listen to the conversation again and repeat each line in the pauses provided. Here are three examples from the last units containing Konjunktiv II structures. What is the function of Konjunktiv II in these sentences?

Könnten Sie mir helfen?

Hättest du Lust, mit uns laufen zu kommen?

Könnten Sie mir sagen, wie Sie die Zukunft sehen?

Konjunktiv II—Overview

You have seen that Konjunktiv II in German is used in a number of contexts:

1 to add a tone politeness: Könntest du bitte kommen?

2 to offer advice: An deiner Stelle ginge ich zum Arzt.

3 to express wishes: Wenn er nur pünktlicher wäre.

4 to express hypothetical situations / ideas: Es gäbe verschiedene Optionen.

5 in hypothetical conditional sentences: Wenn ich mehr Zeit hätte, würde ich mehr reisen.

Remember that, with the exception of haben, sein and the modal verbs, würden + the main verb is commonly used, but you can also use the forms you've learned in this unit.

Language practice 4

1 Complete with words from the box. Which context (1–5 above) applies?

solltest	~~würde~~	ginge	täten
könnte	hätte	hätte	würde

Example: An deiner Stelle *würde* ich nicht so viel Krafttraining machen. (2 = to offer advice)

a Ich .... gern zwei Eintrittskarten für die Ausstellung. (......)

b Du .... dich mehr bewegen. (......)

c Nina, ... ich dich etwas fragen? (......)

d Wenn ich mehr Zeit ...., ... ich öfter ins Fitnessstudio. (......)

e Der Kurs .... dich 1000 Euro kosten. (......)

f Wenn die Politiker:innen doch nur mehr für den Klimaschutz .... (......)

2 Now play Conversation 2 again and play Silke's role. Silke's exchanges are a bit more complex than usual, so you may need to refer to the text more often.

18.10

SKILL BUILDER

1 Match the words with the definitions.

a	der Umweltschutz	**1**	Zum Beispiel CO_2 oder Methan.
b	der Klimawandel	**2**	Man tut etwas für die Umwelt.
c	das Extremwetter	**3**	Zum Beispiel ein Kaffeebecher, den man nur einmal benutzt.
d	klimaneutral	**4**	Man bekommt Geld zurück, wenn man sie zurückbringt.
e	der Müll	**5**	Ein anderes Wort für Abfall.
f	die Treibhausgase	**6**	Ein Produkt oder ein Service erhöht nicht das CO_2.
g	die Pfandflasche	**7**	Fährt mit einer Batterie, ohne Benzin.
h	die Einwegverpackung	**8**	Zum Beispiel Hitzewellen oder Starkregen.
i	das Elektroauto	**9**	Das Wetter und die Temperaturen ändern sich.

2 Listen to the interview with Milena Garcia, owner of a Zero Waste Shop. Decide if the sentences are *true* (**richtig**) or *false* (**falsch**).

18.11

a Milena wollte einen Zero Waste Shop gründen, nachdem sie in einem Supermarkt gearbeitet hatte.   R   F

b Kund:innen bringen ihre eigenen Behälter mit; man kann aber auch Behälter mieten.   R   F

c Der Shop verkauft nur Lebensmittel.   R   F

d Man kann auch Medikamente unverpackt kaufen.   R   F

e Ein Vorteil ist, dass man selbst entscheiden kann, wie viel man kaufen möchte.   R   F

f Bei Milena kaufen vor allem junge Leute ein.   R   F

g Milena sieht Zero Waste Shops als Teil einer Bewegung.   R   F

h Im Moment hat Milenas Geschäft noch keinen Onlineshop.   R   F

> Zero Waste Shops, Urban Gardening Projekte, and To-go-Becher are other examples how English words are used in contemporary German. Sometimes the whole English phrase is used, as with Zero Waste Shops; sometimes English and German words are combined, such as in To-go-Becher.

3 Give advice starting your sentence with **An deiner Stelle...** and use **Konjunktiv II**.

Example: Ich schlafe schlecht. (früher ins Bett gehen)
  An deiner Stelle ginge ich früher ins Bett.

a Ich habe Kopfschmerzen. (eine Kopfschmerztablette nehmen)
b Ich würde gern ein Konzert beim Musikfestival sehen. (die Tickets online bestellen)
c Ich bin oft im Stress. (meditieren)
d Ich habe lange nichts von Tilmann gehört. (ihm eine WhatsApp-Nachricht schreiben)
e Meine Haare sehen uncool aus. (zum Frisör gehen)

f   Ich glaube, Constanze hat Probleme. (mit ihr sprechen)

g   Ich habe manchmal Schmerzen in der Herzgegend. (zum Arzt gehen)

h   Ich habe schon lange vor, Chinesisch zu lernen. (sich bei einem Kurs anmelden)

 4   Read the text and answer the questions.

Das Plastikproblem

 Plastik gibt es eigentlich noch nicht so lange. Doch seitdem wir es in Massen produzieren, hat es fast jeden Aspekt unseres Lebens verändert. Wir verwenden es fast überall in Smartphones, Autos, Spielzeug bis hin zu Kosmetika. Warum eigentlich? Weil Plastik so vielfältig ist. Die globale Kunststoffindustrie ist seit Jahrzehnten stetig gewachsen. Und jedes Jahr wird eine ungeheure Menge davon weggeworfen, wie Plastikflaschen, Plastiktüten oder Verpackungen.

Und das ist jetzt zu einem großen Problem geworden. Missmanagement und falsche Entsorgung (*waste disposal*) haben dazu geführt, dass Millionen Tonnen Plastikmüll in den Flüssen und Ozeanen landen und dabei die Umwelt und am Ende auch uns bedrohen.

Laut einem Bericht der Weltbank (*World Bank*) werden jährlich weltweit 400 Millionen Tonnen Plastik hergestellt. Und wie viel Plastikmüll gibt es? Die Recyclingquote von Plastik liegt weltweit bei nur etwa 15 Prozent. Weitere 15 Prozent des Mülls werden verbrannt. Das heißt also, dass mehr als zwei Drittel des Plastiks, das wir produzieren, als Müll endet. Entweder auf einer Mülldeponie (*waste disposal site, dump*) oder irgendwo in der Natur und – wie wir wissen – zu einem großen Teil auch im Meer.

Deshalb müssen wir schnell handeln: Einwegverpackungen sollten noch teurer werden, bestimmte Formen von Plastikprodukten – wie Mikroplastik in Kosmetik – sollten wir ganz verbieten. Die Recyclingquote muss erhöht werden. Wir brauchen endlich einen Masterplan gegen das Plastikproblem.

a   Wo verwendet man Plastik heutzutage?

b   Warum ist es ein so beliebtes Material?

c   Wie viel Plastik wird jedes Jahr hergestellt?

d   Wie viel Prozent werden weltweit recycelt?

e   Wie viel Plastik endet jedes Jahr als Müll?

f   Wo findet man den Plastikmüll?

g   Was – so der Text – brauchen wir endlich?

5 Talk about your experience regarding climate change and environmental protection. Here are a few questions to help you.

    a Bemerkt man die Auswirkungen der Klimakrise auch in Ihrem Land?
    b Gibt oder gab es zum Beispiel Extremwetter?
    c Gibt es Probleme für die Landwirtschaft?
    d Ist Plastikmüll ein Problem?
    e Gibt es in Ihrem Land Umweltorganisationen wie NABU in Deutschland?
    f Was wissen Sie über diese? Wofür setzen sie sich ein?

TEST YOURSELF

Answer the questions. All the information is in the unit. Use indirect answers as in the example.

Example: Wissen Sie, bis wann Berlin klimaneutral werden möchte?
    Ja, natürlich weiß ich, bis wann Berlin klimaneutral werden möchte. Bis 2045.

a Können Sie mir sagen, ob der Klimawandel schon in Berlin angekommen ist?
b Wissen Sie noch, in welche Tonne Zeitungen und Papier kommen?
c Und wohin kommt der Biomüll?
d Wissen Sie noch, wie oft der Müll in Berlin abgeholt wird?
e Können Sie mir erklären, was Einwegverpackungen sind?
f Können Sie mir ein Beispiel für eine Umweltinitiative in Berlin nennen?
g Wissen Sie, wie viel Plastik jedes Jahr hergestellt wird?
h Wissen Sie, wie viel Prozent davon weltweit recycelt werden?

Wie geht's weiter? *What happens next?*

While Max was writing more blogs, he also continued with his job hunt. Will he be successful next time? And how do Max's and Wally's approaches to news and social media differ? Find out in the next unit.

Remember to use **My review** and **My takeaway** to assess your progress and reflect on your learning experience.

19

In this lesson you will learn how to:

» Describe your social media habits
» Explain how you keep up with the news
» Read and analyze news items
» Understand the media landscape in Germany
» Report what someone else has said

Wie informierst du dich?

My study plan

I plan to work with Unit 19

○ Every day
○ Twice a week
○ Other _____

I plan to study for

○ 5–15 minutes
○ 15–30 minutes
○ 30–45+ minutes

My progress tracker

Day / Date	🎧	🎤	📖	✏️	💬
	○	○	○	○	○
	○	○	○	○	○
	○	○	○	○	○
	○	○	○	○	○
	○	○	○	○	○
	○	○	○	○	○
	○	○	○	○	○

My goals

What do you want to be able to do or say in German when you complete this unit?

Done

1 .... ○
2 .... ○
3 .... ○

My review

SELF CHECK	
	I can ...
○	... describe my social media habits.
○	... explain how I keep up with the news.
○	... read and analyze news items.
○	... understand the media landscape in Germany.
○	... report what someone else has said.

CULTURE POINT 1

Die Medienlandschaft in Deutschland

In Deutschland, Österreich und der Schweiz gibt es sowohl öffentlich-rechtliche (*public*) als auch private Radio- und Fernsehsender (*channels/stations*). Das deutsche System wurde nach britischem Vorbild aufgebaut. Die öffentlich-rechtlichen Sender werden durch den Rundfunkbeitrag (*broadcasting fee*) finanziert, den alle Haushalte monatlich bezahlen müssen. Die privaten Sender finanzieren sich durch Werbeeinnahmen (*advertising revenues*).

ARD und ZDF sind die beiden großen öffentlich-rechtlichen Sender in Deutschland. Außerdem gibt es viele regionale Fernseh- und Radiosender, z.B. rbb (Radio Berlin Brandenburg), WDR (Westdeutscher Rundfunk) und BR (Bayerischer Rundfunk). Alle sollen die Bevölkerung informieren, bilden (*educate*), beraten (*advise*) und unterhalten (*entertain*). Beispiele für Privatsender sind RTL, Sat. 1 und Pro7. Diese kann man kostenlos schauen. Zusätzlich gibt es noch das Pay-TV, vor allem für Sport. Und natürlich kann man auch für einen Streamingdienst bezahlen.

Es gibt auch eine große Auswahl an Zeitschriften (*magazines*) und Zeitungen (*newspapers*). Tageszeitungen (*dailies*) bringen ihren Leser:innen aktuelle Informationen. Bekannte Tageszeitungen sind die *Süddeutsche Zeitung*, *Frankfurter Allgemeine Zeitung*, *Die Welt* und die *Frankfurter Rundschau*. Darüber hinaus gibt es politische Wochenmagazine wie *Der Spiegel* oder *Focus*. Aber man findet auch viele Zeitschriften für spezielle Themen oder Zielgruppen, z.B. Fernsehen, Sport, Reisen, Kochen, Jugendliche, Frauen, Männer.

Die Deutsche Welle ist der Auslandsrundfunk Deutschlands. Neben Programmen in 30 Sprachen bietet er auch Möglichkeiten zum Deutschlernen.

Welche Angebote gibt es für Lerner:innen auf Niveau B1? Was ist „JoJo sucht das Glück"? Browsen Sie die Angebote. Welches finden Sie am interessantesten? Warum? Welche Materialien zum Deutschlernen gibt es?

VOCABULARY BUILDER 1

19.01

Look at the words and phrases and complete the missing English words and expressions. Then listen and try to imitate the pronunciation of the speakers.

NACHRICHTEN	*NEWS*
der Bericht (-e)	*report*
der Klatsch und Tratsch	*gossip*
der Kommentar (-e)	....
der Politiker (-) / die Politikerin (-nen)	....
die Quelle (-n)	*source*
die Schlagzeile (-n)	*headline*
aktuell	*current*
kontrovers	....
live	....
objektiv	....
zuverlässig / verlässlich	*reliable*
MEDIEN	*MEDIA*
das Boulevardblatt (-"er)	*tabloid*
das Fernsehen (singular only)	*television*
der Privatsender (-)	*private channel / station / broadcaster*
das Programm (-e)	*program*
das Radio (-s)	....
die sozialen Medien (mostly plural)	....
einseitig	*one-sided*
erscheinen	*to publish*
senden, aus/strahlen	*to broadcast*
verbreiten	*to spread*
AKTIVITÄTEN	*ACTIVITIES*
auf/passen	*to pay attention*
vertrauen	*to trust*

> Note the difference between das Fernsehen and der Fernseher. Das Fernsehen refers to the medium of television, e.g. Ich schaue viel Fernsehen (*I watch a lot of TV*). Der Fernseher is the television set, e.g. Unser neuer Fernseher ist ein Flachbildschirmfernseher (*Our new TV is a flat-screen television*).

Vocabulary practice 1

Match the words with the definitions.

a der Bericht
b das Boulevardblatt
c der Kommentar
d die Quelle
e der öffentlich-rechtliche Sender
f die Schlagzeile
g die Werbung

1 steht über dem Artikel
2 wo die Informationen herkommen
3 man soll etwas kaufen, ein Auto, Schmuck, etc.
4 ein anderes Wort für Artikel
5 die subjektive Meinung eines Journalisten/einer Journalistin
6 berichtet viel über Klatsch und Tratsch
7 kein Privatsender

Pronunciation practice 1

19.02

1 **A vowel or umlaut is short before a double s but long before an ß. Listen and repeat.**

verlässlich	hässlich	Süßigkeit
muss	saß	groß
aufpassen	Fußabdruck	
Wasser	Straße	

19.03

2 **How would you pronounce these words? Say them out loud. Listen to the audio to check.**

Hasskommentar	süß	Passwort
Spaß	zuverlässig	begrüßen

CONVERSATION 1

Sind diese Informationen zuverlässig?

19.04

1 **Listen to the conversation a few times without looking at the text. Then listen again and read the text. What are Wally's sources to keep up to date with the news?**

Max has noticed that Wally gets a Tageszeitung (*daily paper*) delivered every day but Sunday, and that she watches the news at 8 p.m. every day of the week. He is intrigued and asks her about this Gewohnheit (*habit*).

Max   Wally, warum bezahlst du eigentlich immer noch für ein Zeitungsabonnement? Heutzutage kann man sich doch ganz leicht im Internet über das informieren, was in der Welt passiert.

Wally	Ach, ich finde, wir verbringen viel zu viel Zeit am Handy und im Internet. Ich lese lieber Zeitung. Die *Berliner Zeitung* hat alles, was ich brauche. Sie berichtet über Ereignisse in Berlin, Deutschland und der ganzen Welt. Man hat das Gefühl, sie ist immer dort, wo etwas passiert.
Max	Aber das geht im Internet auch. Und die Informationen, die man dort bekommt, sind viel aktueller.
Wally	Und wie weißt du, dass die Informationen, die du dort findest, auch zuverlässig sind?
Max	Da muss man etwas aufpassen. Ich benutze aber nur Webseiten, deren Informationen verlässlich sind. Bei den Nachrichten, die du bekommst, weißt du doch auch nicht, ob sie zuverlässig sind, oder?
Wally	Ich finde schon. Ich schaue ja immer die Tagesschau in der ARD. Das ist ein öffentlich-rechtlicher Sender, dem ich vertraue. Und bei der *Berliner Zeitung* gibt es einen Journalisten, den ich kenne. Ich weiß, dass sie nur verlässliche Quellen benutzen.
Max	Und findest du die Artikel auch objektiv?
Wally	Ja, die ARD und auch die *Berliner Zeitung* sind politisch unabhängig. Es gibt da oft kontroverse Berichte und Interviews mit Politikern und Politikerinnen, die unterschiedliche Meinungen haben.
Max	Das ist gut. Vor allem bei den sozialen Medien ist das nicht immer so. Da werden vom Algorithmus oft nur bestimmte Artikel ausgewählt.
Wally	Vielleicht sind gute Zeitungen also doch besser.

2 **Decide if these statements are *true* (richtig) or *false* (falsch). Correct the false ones.**

a	Wally hat ein kostenloses Zeitungsabonnement.	R	F
b	In der *Berliner Zeitung* stehen nur lokale Nachrichten.	R	F
c	Max findet, dass Berichte in Zeitungen nicht ganz aktuell sind.	R	F
d	Es gibt im Internet und in Zeitungen Informationen, die nicht verlässlich sind.	R	F
e	Die ARD ist ein privater Sender.	R	F
f	Bei sozialen Medien entscheiden oft Algorithmen, was man liest.	R	F

LANGUAGE BUILDER 1

 Language discovery 1

Complete the sentences from Conversation 1.

a Und die Informationen, ... man dort bekommt, sind viel aktueller.

b Das ist ein öffentlich-rechtlicher Sender, ... ich vertraue.

c Und bei der *Berliner Zeitung* gibt es einen Journalisten, ... ich kenne.

What do the missing words remind you of? What do they refer to in the sentence?

Relative clauses

Relative clauses provide more information about a noun or phrase mentioned in the main clause. They are introduced by a relative pronoun. In English these are *who(m)*, *that*, *which* and *whose*. In German they are often similar to the definitive articles: der, die, das.

Das ist eine Serie, die aus Deutschland kommt.	*This is a series which comes from Germany.*
Das ZDF ist ein öffentlich-rechtlicher Sender, den viele Menschen schauen.	*The ZDF is a public broadcaster that is watched by many people.*
Hier gibt es ein neues Café, das ich mag.	*There is a new café here, which I like.*

As with all subordinating clauses in German, the main verb in the relative clause goes to the end. The form of the relative pronoun depends on three things:

1 the gender of the noun it refers to (masculine, feminine or neuter)

2 the number of the noun it refers to (singular or plural)

3 the case required by the relative clause (e.g. if the pronoun is the subject of the relative clause it will be in the nominative, but if it is the direct object of the relative clause it will be in the accusative; it can also be in the dative or genitive).

Note that only the genitive and the dative plural forms differ from the definite articles.

	Masculine singular	Feminine singular	Neuter singular	Masculine, feminine, neuter plural
Nominative	der	die	das	die
Accusative	den	die	das	die
Dative	dem	der	dem	denen
Genitive	dessen	deren	dessen	deren

> The relative clause usually follows straight after the noun or phrase it refers to and can therefore be inserted into the main clause.
> Die *Süddeutsche Zeitung*, die täglich erscheint, ist eine bekannte Zeitung in Deutschland.
> *The* Süddeutsche Zeitung*, which is published daily, is a well-known daily newspaper in Germany.*

Language practice 1

Complete with the correct relative pronoun.

a Ein Boulevardblatt ist eine Zeitung, ... viel über Klatsch und Tratsch berichtet.

b Im Fernsehen gibt es oft Sendungen, ... sehr informativ sind.

c Der *Stern* ist ein Magazin, ... meine Eltern gerne lesen.

d Den Kommentar, ... ich gelesen habe, finde ich sehr gut.

e Das öffentlich-rechtliche Fernsehen ist die Quelle, ... ich vertraue.

f Die *Bild* ist eine Zeitung, ... Schlagzeilen oft sehr lustig sind.

LANGUAGE BUILDER 2

19.05

💡 Language discovery 2

Listen to the conversation again and repeat each line in the pauses provided. Match these clauses. What kind of word does the second part of the sentence begin with?

a Heutzutage kann man sich doch ganz leicht im Internet über das informieren,

b Die *Berliner Zeitung* hat alles,

c Man hat das Gefühl, sie ist immer dort,

1 wo etwas passiert.

2 was in der Welt passiert.

3 was ich brauche.

More relative pronouns

When the relative pronoun refers to quantities such as alles, nichts, vieles, etwas, and das, or when it refers back to the whole clause, use the relative pronoun was:

Werbung ist etwas, was mich ärgert.

Advertising is something that annoys me.

In diesem Boulevardblatt steht nichts, was mich interessiert.

In this tabloid there is nothing that interests me.

Heute gab es nur gute Nachrichten, was mich gefreut hat.

Today, there was only good news, which made me happy.

When the relative pronoun refers to a place or words indicating a place such as da, dort, and hier, use the relative pronoun wo:

Das ist das Haus, wo wir früher gewohnt haben.

This is the house where we used to live.

Die Journalistin war genau dort, wo es passierte.

The journalist was right there where it happened.

> Unlike in English you always have to use a relative pronoun in German:
> Das ist etwas, was mich interessiert. *That's something (which) I am interested in.*

Language practice 2

1 Match these clauses.

a In den Boulevardblättern steht vieles,

b Viele Journalist:innen sind immer dort,

1 wo etwas passiert.

2 was man wissen muss.

c Die Tagesschau kommt aus Hamburg,
d In diesem Podcast gibt es immer etwas,
e Nicht alle Quellen sind verlässlich,
f Die Sendung war nicht sehr objektiv,

3 was mich interessiert.
4 was mich geärgert hat.
5 was ich nicht glaube.
6 wo die TV-Studios sind.

2 Now listen to Conversation 1 again and play Wally's role. Speak in the pauses provided and try not to refer to the text.

19.06

CULTURE POINT 2

Die Medienlandschaft in Deutschland

Das moderne Leben spielt sich heutzutage im Internet ab. In Deutschland ist das nicht anders. Viele Dinge, z.B. Termine buchen oder Tickets kaufen, kann man oft nur online erledigen. Es gibt aber immer noch eine Minderheit, die das Internet nicht nutzt oder keinen Internetanschluss (*internet connection*) hat. Das betrifft vor allem ältere Menschen. Auf dem Land (*in the countryside*) muss das schnelle Internet noch ausgebaut werden. Kostenloses

WLAN (*Wi-Fi*) im öffentlichen Raum (*in public spaces*) findet man in Deutschland seltener als in anderen westlichen Ländern.

Die meisten Deutschen benutzen ihr Handy (*cell phone*) bzw. Smartphone, um das Internet zu nutzen. Durchschnittlich gehören die Deutschen aber zu den Schlusslichtern (*bottom of the pile*), was die Dauer der täglichen Internetnutzung angeht (*to concern*). Je jünger man ist, desto mehr Zeit verbringt man im Internet. Das Internet wird vor allem zur Kommunikation genutzt. Onlinespiele und soziale Medien sind besonders bei jungen Menschen beliebt. Diese Gruppe benutzt auch eher Künstliche Intelligenz (*artificial intelligence*), aber die Nutzung ist hier bisher noch auf niedrigem Niveau.

Dieser Trend bestätigt sich auch, wenn man auf die Beliebtheit der einzelnen Apps schaut. Messengerdienste (*instant messaging platforms*) und soziale Medien sowie Videoanbieter und Browser liegen hier auf den vorderen Plätzen.

 Nicht alle Menschen finden es gut, dass wir mittlerweile so abhängig von unseren Smartphones sind. Lesen Sie dazu das Manifest der Radikalen Anti Smartphone Front. Versuchen Sie, das Manifest auf Deutsch zu lesen. Es gibt aber auch eine englische Übersetzung. Was leidet unter der ständigen Nutzung des Smartphones? Welche gesundheitlichen und gesellschaftlichen Folgen kann das haben?

VOCABULARY BUILDER 2

Look at the words and phrases and complete the missing English words and expressions. Then listen and try to imitate the pronunciation of the speakers.

INTERNET UND SOZIALE MEDIEN	INTERNET AND SOCIAL MEDIA
das Benutzerkonto (-konten)	account
der Benutzername (-n)	username
die Nachricht (-en)	message
der Nutzer (-) / die Nutzerin (-nen)	user
das Passwort (-"er)	....
benutzerfreundlich	user ....
der Beitrag (-"e)	post
das gefällt mir	I like it
der Kommentar, der (Hass-) Kommentar (-e)	comment, (hate) post
das Profil (-e), der Trend (-s)	........................,.........................
unterhaltsam	entertaining
sich an/melden	to register / sign up
sich ein/loggen, sich aus/loggen	to log ....,.........................
herunter/laden, down/loaden	to ....
hoch/laden	to ....
schicken	to send
erhalten / bekommen	to receive
aktualisieren	to update
blockieren	to ....
erstellen, folgen	to create, to follow
liken	to like
löschen	to delete
posten	to ....
teilen	to share
sich vernetzen	to network
die Daumen drücken	to keep one's fingers crossed

> When talking about social media, a lot of words used in German are the same as in English, but they have been integrated into the German grammar by adding -en to the infinitive of the verb—e.g. posten, liken—and they form the past participle like regular verbs: gepostet, gelikt.
> Emre hat meinen Post gelikt.
> *Emre liked my post.*

Vocabulary practice 2

Complete the sentences with a word from the box.

aktualisiere	Beiträge	blockiere	Trend
Follower:innen	Hasskommentare	like	
poste	Profil	sozialen Medien	

Gleich morgens checke ich alle meine .... Ich will wissen, was für neue .... gepostet wurden. Gibt es vielleicht einen neuen .... ? Dann .... ich die Posts, die mir gefallen. Ich .... natürlich auch mehrmals täglich mein eigenes .... Ich .... zwischen fünf- und achtmal am Tag. Ich hoffe immer, dass ich neue .... bekomme. Manchmal .... ich aber auch eine:n Benutzer:in, wenn er/sie .... schreibt.

CONVERSATION 2

Eine schöne Überraschung!

19.08

Listen to the conversation a few times without looking at the text. Then listen again and read the text. What kind of job is Lisa talking about?

Lisa has been told about a job by her record label that might be something for Max. She is very excited and wants to tell him immediately, so she calls him.

Max   Hallo, Lisa! Das ist ja eine schöne Überraschung!

Lisa   Hallo, Max! Du, ich muss dir unbedingt etwas erzählen.

Max   Du bist ja total aufgeregt, Lisa. Ist etwas passiert?

Lisa   Nein, alles gut. Meine Managerin hat mir gerade erzählt, dass sie im Label eine Stelle als Social Media Content Creator ausschreiben würden.

Max   Wow, das klingt echt cool! Aber ich weiß nicht, ob ich das wirklich kann.

Lisa   Aber du kennst dich doch total gut mit sozialen Medien aus und du interessierst dich für Musik. Das ist doch die perfekte Kombination!

Max   Meinst du? Was muss man denn in dem Job machen?

Lisa   Also, Monika, meine Managerin, hat gesagt, dass es bereits ein Team von zwei Mitarbeiter:innen gebe. Das Team sei dafür verantwortlich, die Musiker:innen des Labels dabei zu unterstützen, ständig neue, unterhaltsame und informative Beiträge auf allen Kanälen der sozialen Medien zu posten. Die Beiträge sollten mehr Likes bekommen und das Label wolle auch mehr Follower:innen für die Profile der Musiker:innen gewinnen.

Max   Neue Beiträge kann ich ja tatsächlich gut erstellen. Aber wo ist die Stelle denn?

Lisa   Monika meinte, man könne die meiste Zeit im Homeoffice arbeiten, aber müsse auch ein bis zwei Tage im Büro arbeiten. Also, das würde bedeuten, dass du nach Wien ziehen müsstest.

Max   Naja, das könnte doch ganz schön sein... Kannst du mir die ganzen Informationen schicken?

Lisa   Klar, mach' ich! Ich drücke dir die Daumen!

2 Decide if these statements are *true* (richtig) or *false* (falsch). Correct the false ones.

a	Max hatte schon auf Lisas Anruf gewartet.	R	F
b	Lisa ruft an, weil etwas Schlimmes passiert ist.	R	F
c	Max ist sich am Anfang nicht sicher, ob er für die Stelle geeignet ist.	R	F
d	Das Label hat schon andere Social Media Content Creators.	R	F
e	In dem Job kann man viel von zu Hause arbeiten.	R	F

LANGUAGE BUILDER 3

Language discovery 3

Look at these two sentences from Conversation 2. Notice the underlined verbs and state what is significant about the context in which they appear.

a Meine Managerin hat gesagt, dass es bereits ein Team von zwei Mitarbeiter:innen <u>gebe</u>.

b Monika meinte, man <u>könne</u> die meiste Zeit im Homeoffice arbeiten, aber <u>müsse</u> auch ein bis zwei Tage im Büro in Wien arbeiten.

Indirect speech—Konjunktiv I

To report what someone has said with indirect/ reported speech, Konjunktiv I is often used:

Andy sagt, er verbringe viel Zeit im Internet. *Andy says he spends a lot of time online.*

Rita erwähnte, sie poste mehrmals täglich neue Beiträge. *Rita mentioned that she posts something new several times a day.*

When it is clear that you are reporting what someone has said you do not need to signal it with a verb like sagen or meinen.

Suki sagt, sie schicke selten Nachrichten in den sozialen Medien. Aber sie like viele Beiträge. *Suki says she rarely sends messages on social media. But (that) she likes a lot of posts.*

Per sagte, er könne sich nicht einloggen. Er habe sein Passwort vergessen. *Per said that he could not log in. He had forgotten his password.*

The Konjunktiv I is formed by adding the appropriate endings to the stem of a verb, regardless of whether the verb is regular or irregular. The only exception is sein:

	benutz-en	hab-en	sein (!)		benutz-en	hab-en	sein (!)
ich	benutz-**e**	hab-**e**	sei	wir	benutz-**en**	hab-**en**	seien
du	benutz-**est**	hab-**est**	sei(e)st	ihr	benutz-**et**	hab-**et**	seiet
Sie	benutz-**en**	hab-**en**	seien	Sie	benutz-**en**	hab-**en**	seien
er/sie/es/xier	benutz-**e**	hab-**e**	sei	sie	benutz-**en**	hab-**en**	seien

To talk about the past, use the Konjunktiv I form of haben or sein and the past participle of the main verb:

Olivia sagte, sie habe etwas Neues gepostet. *Olivia said she had posted something new.*

Rico sagte, er habe ein neues Profil in den sozialen Medien erstellt. *Rico said he had created a new profile on social media.*

Language practice 3

Complete with the correct Konjunktiv I form of the verb in parentheses. In some sentences you need to use the past tense.

a Angela sagt, dass sie sich immer .... (aus/loggen)

b Herr Peters sagt, dass niemand in seiner Familie ein Profil in den sozialen Medien .... (haben)

c Die Lehrerin erzählt, dass ihr im Unterricht viel im Internet .... (sein)

d Er meint, ich .... (sollen) mich besser vernetzen.

e Du sagst, du .... (haben) einen neuen Beitrag .... (posten)

f Cem hat gesagt, die Zahl seiner Follower:innen .... (sein) seit der letzten Woche .... (steigen)

> You can choose to introduce indirect speech with dass or without, but this affects the word order. With dass the conjugated verb goes to the end; without, it is in second position.
>
> Simona sagt, dass sie viele Follower:innen habe.
> *Simona says that she has many followers.*
> Simona sagt, sie habe viele Follower:innen.
> *Simona says she has many followers.*

LANGUAGE BUILDER 4

💡 Language discovery 4

19.09

Listen to the conversation again and repeat each line in the pauses provided. Look at these three sentences from Conversation 2. They are all in indirect speech. Identify the verb forms used.

a Meine Managerin hat mir gerade erzählt, dass sie im Label eine Stelle als Social Media Content Creator ausschreiben würden.

b Monika hat gesagt, die Beiträge sollten mehr Likes bekommen.

Using **Konjunktiv II** in indirect speech

In the Konjunktiv I, forms for the first-person singular (for most verbs), as well as the first- and third-person plural, are the same as those for the present tense (ich benutze, wir benutzen, sie benutzen) or perfect tense (ich habe benutzt, wir haben benutzt, sie haben benutzt). They are therefore indistinguishable from each other. To ensure that it is still clear that this is indirect speech, you can use Konjunktiv II instead:

Viele sagen, sie würden zu viel Zeit im Internet verbringen.	*Many people say they spend too much time online.*
Meine Eltern sagen, wir dürften keine sozialen Medien benutzen.	*My parents say we are not allowed to use social media.*
Maria hat gesagt, ich hätte sie blockiert	*Maria said I had blocked her.*

> Don't worry too much about using Konjunktiv I and II for indirect speech yourself at this stage. While they are often found in formal texts and in the media, it is common to use the regular present or past tense form of the verb or würde in everyday situations when it is clear from the context that you are reporting what someone else has said.

Language practice 4

1 Decide whether it is better to use Konjunktiv I or Konjunktiv II to clearly indicate it is indirect speech. Use the verbs provided in parentheses.

a Mein Lehrer sagt, man .... (müssen) aufpassen, was man im Internet herunterlädt.

b Viele Politiker:innen sagen, dass sie keine Zeit .... (haben), ihre Profile zu aktualisieren.

c Ingo hat gesagt, dass ich zu viele Bilder hochgeladen .... (haben).

d Meine Freunde denken, ich .... (sollen) nicht alle Beiträge liken.

e Frieda sagt, dass sie dir bei Instagram .... (folgen). Stimmt das?

f Die Benutzer:innen finden, dass wir zu viele Filter .... (benutzen).

19.10

2 Now listen to Conversation 2 again and play Max's role. Speak in the pauses provided and try not to refer to the text.

Pronunciation practice 2

19.11

When you use the Konjunktiv II for indirect speech and in any other context, the correct pronunciation of würde is important. This is to ensure that it is not confused with wurde, used for the past tense of the passive. Listen and repeat.

wurde   würde
Ein Hasskommentar wurde gepostet.
Ich würde nie einen Hasskommentar posten.
Die Sendung wurde live ausgestrahlt.
Sie würden die Sendung gerne schauen.
Der Post wurde von vielen gelikt.
Würdest du diesen Post liken?

SKILL BUILDER

1 **Form relative clauses. Start all sentences with** Das ist Herr Hoffmann, …

   Example: Er kommt aus Stuttgart. > *Das ist Herr Hoffmann, der aus Stuttgart kommt.*

   a Er arbeitet als Blogger. ....

   b Seine Freundin ist auch Bloggerin. ....

   c Sein Sohn studiert in den USA. ....

   d Er fährt einen roten Porsche. ....

   e Er trägt meistens italienische Anzüge. ....

   f Man sieht ihn auf vielen Partys. ....

   g Von ihm bekomme ich noch 500 €. ....

2 **Describe these athletes using a relative clause. Here are some useful words:**

Gewichte heben (*to lift weights*)	boxen
American Football spielen	Gymnastik machen

   Example: Udo ist der Mann, der Judo macht.

   a Alexander   **c** Annika   **e** Angelo   **g** Erkan
   b Ole   **d** Franka   **f** Britta   **h** Sabine

     a   b   c d   e   f g   h

19.12

3 **Listen to the message Lisa received from her manager. Help her tell Max about it using indirect speech.**

   a Meine Managerin hat gesagt, dass die Stelle ....

   b Sie erwarten, dass der oder die Kandidat:in ....

   c Die Person, ...

   d Sie ....

e Sie suchen jemanden, der fließend Deutsch und Englisch spricht, weil sie ....

f Die Person ....

g Ein Interesse für Musik ....

h Sie ....

4 **Read the short news items and match them with a suitable headline. There are two more headlines than news items.**

1 Gutes Wetter

2 Weniger Menschen arbeitslos

3 Es bleibt regnerisch

4 Erwarteter Sieg

5 Überraschender Sieg

6 Souveräner Sieg

7 Arbeitslosenquote gestiegen

8 Ganz Österreich feiert

a ....

Heute wird es sonnig und es gibt nur wenig Wolken. Die Temperaturen liegen bei 25 Grad. In der Nacht kühlt es auf angenehme 14 Grad ab. Auch in den nächsten Tagen bleibt es trocken.

b ....

Österreich ist Weltmeister. In einem spannenden Finale gewannen die österreichischen Damen gegen die Gastgeberinnen aus der Schweiz, die als Favoritinnen ins Finale gegangen waren.

c ....

Am Ende war es ein klarer Sieg. Die Schweiz hat den Nationencup der Männer im alpinen Skifahren mit mehr als 1000 Punkten Vorsprung vor den Österreichern gewonnen. Deutschland kam unter die Top Ten.

d ....

Wie von den Meinungsforscher:innen prognostiziert, haben die Oppositionsparteien am Sonntag die Nationalratswahlen gewonnen. Gemeinsam werden sie mehr als die Hälfte der Sitze im Parlament haben.

e ....

Der 26. Oktober 1955 war der Tag, an dem die Alliierten Österreich nach dem Zweiten Weltkrieg verlassen haben. Deshalb ist dies der österreichische Nationalfeiertag. Die Menschen müssen nicht arbeiten und die Geschäfte bleiben geschlossen. Auch dieses Jahr wieder.

f ....

Die Arbeitslosenquote ist im Mai von 5,4% auf 5,0% zurückgegangen. Ein Grund für diese positive Veränderung ist das gute Wetter. Restaurants und Kneipen, aber auch Baufirmen haben daher mehr Mitarbeitende eingestellt.

TEST YOURSELF

You are in Berlin and meet Jeremy, an American influencer, who you follow on social media. You talk to him and translate for your friend Lara, who only speaks German. Use indirect speech.

Jeremy	Sie
I have heard a lot about Berlin and always wanted to visit it. It is such a diverse and creative city.	Jeremy meint, er habe viel über Berlin gehört und wollte es ....
	I follow you on Instagram, but I haven't seen any posts from you about Berlin yet. You haven't updated your profile for two weeks. Why is that?
	Ich habe Jeremy gesagt, ... Ich habe ihn dann gefragt, warum ....?
I needed a break. It is really hard to constantly create new posts. I hope Berlin will inspire me. I already have lots of new ideas for posts.	Jeremy sagte, ...
	And where are you going now?
I am going to this really trendy bar in Kreuzberg now. You can find out more about it on my Instagram later.	Ich habe Jeremy gefragt, ... Er meinte, ...

Wie geht's weiter? *What happens next?*

Max really needs to find a paid job, so he has applied for the job at Lisa's record label as well as for a few other jobs in Berlin. Will he get any of them? And if so, where will he go? It is almost a year since Max arrived in Berlin and it is time for him to make some big decisions. Find out what happens next in Unit 20.

Remember to use **My review** and **My takeaway** to assess your progress and reflect on your learning experience.

20

In this lesson you will learn how to:
» Evaluate some contemporary issues in society
» Express attitudes and preferences
» Discuss stereotypes
» Talk about past events in your life
» Reflect on your German language learning journey

Die große Entscheidung

My study plan

I plan to work with Unit 20
○ Every day
○ Twice a week
○ Other _____

I plan to study for
○ 5–15 minutes
○ 15–30 minutes
○ 30–45+ minutes

My progress tracker

Day / Date	🎧	🎤	📖	✏️	💬
	○	○	○	○	○
	○	○	○	○	○
	○	○	○	○	○
	○	○	○	○	○
	○	○	○	○	○
	○	○	○	○	○
	○	○	○	○	○

My goals

What do you want to be able to do or say in German when you complete this unit?

Done

1 .... ○

2 .... ○

3 .... ○

My review

SELF CHECK	
○	I can ...
○	... evaluate some contemporary issues in society.
○	... express attitudes and preferences.
○	... discuss stereotypes.
○	... talk about some past events in my life.
○	... reflect on my German language learning journey.

CULTURE POINT 1

Das politische System

Deutschland ist eine parlamentarische Demokratie. Das Parlament – der Bundestag – wird normalerweise alle vier Jahre von den Bürgerinnen und Bürgern (*citizens*) gewählt. Der Bundestag wählt dann den Bundeskanzler/die Bundeskanzlerin (lit. *federal chancellor*), der/die Regierung bildet und die Minister:innen benennt. Die Mitglieder des Bundestages heißen Abgeordnete.

Deutschland hat ein Verhältniswahlrecht (*system of proportional representation*). Das heißt, dass alle Parteien, die mehr als 5 Prozent der Wählerstimmen (*votes*) erhalten, in den Bundestag einziehen. Seit der ersten Bundestagswahl 1947 hatte keine Partei die absolute Mehrheit und deshalb gab es seitdem nur Koalitionsregierungen (*coalition governments*) zwischen verschiedenen Parteien. Das bedeutet auch, dass die jeweiligen Regierungspartner Kompromisse finden müssen und bislang sorgte dies für eine große Stabilität des politischen Systems.

Auch Österreich ist eine parlamentarische Demokratie. Hier heißt das Parlament Nationalrat, der alle fünf Jahre gewählt wird und 183 Abgeordnete hat. Die Aufgaben des Bundeskanzlers/der Bundeskanzlerin sind ähnlich wie in Deutschland. In beiden Ländern ist das Staatsoberhaupt (*head of state*) der/die Bundespräsident/in, der/die aber vor allem repräsentative Aufgaben hat.

Im Schweizer Parlament sitzen 246 Abgeordnete. Diese wählen das Kollegium (die Regierung), das aus sieben Mitgliedern besteht. In der Schweiz wird sehr viel Wert auf direkte Demokratie gelegt: Das Volk kann durch Volksabstimmungen (*referenda*) bei vielen Themen mitbestimmen.

Hier finden Sie mehr Informationen über den Deutschen Bundestag. Klicken Sie auf „Sitzverteilung" und finden Sie heraus:
Wie viele Abgeordnete gibt es insgesamt?
Welche Partei hat die meisten Sitze?
Gibt es mehr Frauen oder Männer im Parlament?
Und aus welchem Bundesland kommen die meisten Abgeordneten?

Try to read the text on the website in German. However, if you get stuck, just switch to the English version of the site.

VOCABULARY BUILDER 1

Look at the words and phrases and complete the missing English words and expressions. Then listen and try to imitate the pronunciation of the speakers.

EIGENSCHAFTEN UND STEREOTYPE	*CHARACTERISTICS AND STEREOTYPES*
arbeitsam	*hardworking*
(in)direkt	....
diszipliniert	....
(un)ehrlich	*(dis)honest*
humorvoll, humorlos	*having, lacking a sense of humor*
(in)korrekt	*(in)* ....
lebenslustig	*fun-loving*
locker	*laid-back*
(un)organisiert	*(dis)* ....
reiselustig	*fond of traveling*
(in)tolerant	*(in)* ....
verrückt	*crazy*
verschlossen, gesellig	*reserved, outgoing / sociable*
weltoffen, engstirnig	*open-minded, narrow-minded*

MODERNE GESELLSCHAFT	*MODERN SOCIETY*
die Demokratie (-n)	....
die Herausforderung (-en)	*challenge*
die Meinungsfreiheit (no plural)	*freedom of speech*
die Polarisierung (-en)	*polarization*
der Populismus (no plural)	....
die Toleranz (no plural)	....
die Zivilgesellschaft (-en)	*civil society*
die Zuverlässigkeit (-en)	*reliability*

> To make an adjective or noun negative, you often add the prefix un- in German: freundlich > unfreundlich, ehrlich > unehrlich. For some words you add in-: direkt > indirekt, tolerant > intolerant.

NÜTZLICHE AUSDRÜCKE	*USEFUL EXPRESSIONS*
ergehen	*to fare, to go (well/badly)*
erkunden	*to explore, find out*
halten	*to last*
wählen	*to vote*
eher	*rather*
die Freundschaft	....
im Kopf haben	*to have in mind*

Vocabulary practice 1

Complete with the best adjective.

a Die Leute sind fleißig und arbeiten viel. Sie sind a _ b _ _ t _ _ _.

b Sie steht jeden Morgen um sieben Uhr auf. Sie ist d _ _ z _ _ _ _ _ _ _ _ t.

c Sie lachen gern und machen Witze. Sie sind _ _ _ _ _voll.

d Vorausplanen ist eine ihrer Stärken. Sie sind gut o _ g _ _ _ _ _ _ _ t.

e Er spricht nicht gern über sich und ist nicht offen. Er ist v e r _ _ _ _ _ _ _ e n.

f Man nennt die Deutschen auch die Reiseweltmeister. Sie sind _ _ _ _ _ l _ _ _ i g.

g Sie sagen, was sie denken. Sie sind e _ _ l _ _ _.

h Sie lassen die Meinung von anderen nicht gelten. Sie sind _ _ t o _ _ _ _ _ _.

i Sie interessieren sich für andere Kulturen und Perspektiven. Sie sind w _ _ t _ f _ _ _.

j Sie genießen das Leben. Sie sind _ _ _ _ _ _ l _ _ _ i g.

Pronunciation practice

20.02

1 If two consonants appear together, then the vowel that precedes the consonants is pronounced short. Listen and repeat.

humorvoll	verrückt	Gesellschaft
kommen	interessieren	

20.03

2 When a vowel is followed by the letter h, the vowel is pronounced long. Listen and repeat.

wahr	eher	wohnen
ehrlich	Lohn	Wahl

3 How would you pronounce these words? Listen to the audio to check.

20.04

verschlossen	Erfahrung	kennenlernen
willkommen	unehrlich	
wählen	Kompromisse	

CONVERSATION 1

Stereotype und Realität

20.05

Listen to the conversation a few times without looking at the text. Then listen again and read the text. What did Nabi think about Germans before she came to Berlin?

Max runs into Nabi, Wally's old friend, while going for walk at Tempelhofer Feld. Nabi is originally from Korea but has been living in Berlin for more than 25 years.

Nabi   Max, jetzt bist du fast ein Jahr in Berlin, oder? Wie ist es dir ergangen?

Max   Ich hatte wirklich eine wunderbare Zeit, Nabi. Am Anfang habe ich Berlin entdeckt und dann habe ich auch ein paar Reisen gemacht.

Nabi   Und was waren deine Eindrücke?

Max   Ich war überrascht, wie unterschiedlich und vielfältig Deutschland ist, nicht nur die Landschaften, sondern auch die Städte, die Menschen, das Essen. Wie war das denn für dich, als du nach Deutschland kamst?

Nabi   Ich hatte natürlich ein paar Stereotype im Kopf. Ich dachte zum Beispiel, die Menschen seien sehr diszipliniert, arbeitsam, korrekt und auch ein wenig humorlos.

Max   Und wie hast du die Deutschen dann tatsächlich erlebt?

Nabi   Bevor ich nach Berlin zog, war ich schon ein paar Mal in Deutschland gewesen. Und ich hatte vorher auch einen Sprachkurs besucht. Ich wusste also, dass die meisten Deutschen freundlich und locker sind. Aber am Anfang fand ich es schwer, Leute kennenzulernen. Wenn man sich aber erst einmal kennengelernt hat und mag, dann halten Freundschaften oft ein Leben lang. Was magst du an Berlin?

Max   Hier in Berlin mag ich die Offenheit der Leute. Ich mag auch die Zuverlässigkeit und überhaupt das Gefühl von Toleranz und Freiheit.

Nabi   Ja, da stimme ich dir zu. Deutschland hat sich in den 25 Jahren, die ich hier bin, stark verändert. Es ist viel offener geworden und bunter. Aber wie in anderen Ländern auch, gibt es eine gewisse Polarisierung in der Gesellschaft.

Max   Ja, die Welt wandelt sich und wir stehen vor großen Herausforderungen. Aber es gibt ja keine einfachen Antworten.

2 Answer the questions.

     a Was hat Max am Anfang gemacht?

     b Was hat ihn überrascht, als er durch Deutschland reiste?

     c Was war am Anfang schwer für Nabi?

     d Was mag Max an Berlin?

     e Wie hat sich – glaubt Nabi – Deutschland verändert?

LANGUAGE BUILDER 1

💡 Language discovery 1

Look at Conversation 1 again. Find the corresponding nouns in the text. What do you notice about how they are formed?

a offen: ....

b zuverlässig: ....

c frei: ....

Word formation: nouns

By adding the suffixes -heit and -keit you can transform many adjectives into nouns. Note that these nouns are all feminine.

offen > die Offenheit	*openness*
frei > die Freiheit	*liberty, freedom*
freundlich > die Freundlichkeit	*friendliness*
zuverlässig > die Zuverlässigkeit	*reliability*

The ending -heit is more common, but adjectives ending in -lich or -ig usually take -keit.

Language practice 1

Which suffix works: -heit or -keit?

a offen > die Offen...........

b frei > die Frei...........

c freundlich > die Freundlich.........

d krank > die ....

e zuverlässig > die ....

f gesund > die ....

g bunt > die ....

h direkt > die ....

i verrückt > die ....

j ehrlich > die ....

k berühmt > die ....

l pünktlich > die ....

m persönlich > die ....

n wahr > die ....

LANGUAGE BUILDER 2

20.06

💡 Language discovery 2

Listen to the conversation again and repeat in the pauses. In these two sentences from the conversation, Nabi refers to events in the past that happened at an earlier time. She uses the past perfect tense. Identify how to form this tense.

a Bevor ich nach Berlin zog, war ich schon ein paar Mal in Deutschland gewesen.

b Und ich hatte vorher auch einen Sprachkurs besucht.

The past perfect tense

The past perfect tense (Plusquamperfekt) is used to refer to events that took place prior to another event or moment in the past. It is often used with nachdem (*after*):

Als wir zum Bahnhof kamen, war der Zug schon abgefahren.	*When we got to the station, the train had already left.*
Er wollte Spanisch lernen, nachdem er durch Mexiko gereist war.	*He wanted to learn Spanish after he had traveled through Mexico.*

The past perfect tense is formed just like the present perfect tense (see Unit 8), but haben and sein are in the simple past. Verbs which take sein in the present perfect tense, such as gehen, fahren, or reisen, do so in the past perfect tense, too.

ich	hatte gekauft	war gereist	wir	hatten gekauft	waren gereist
du	hattest gekauft	warst gereist	ihr	hattet gekauft	wart gereist
Sie	hatten gekauft	waren gereist	Sie	hatten gekauft	waren gereist
er/sie/es/xier	hatte gekauft	war gereist	sie	hatten gekauft	waren gereist

Language practice 2

1 Complete these sentences with the appropriate form of hatten or waren.

a Er erzählte mir, wohin er letztes Wochenende gefahren ....

b Wir mussten uns beeilen, denn wir .... zu spät aufgestanden.

c Sie war gestresst, weil sie acht Stunden am Bildschirm gearbeitet ....

d Er konnte sich in Peking gut verständigen, weil er Chinesisch gelernt ....

e Ich musste den Termin absagen, da ich krank gewesen ....

f Die Menschen waren überrascht, denn so etwas .... noch nie passiert.

20.07

2 Now listen to Conversation 1 again and play Max's role. Speak in the pauses provided and try not to refer to the text.

CULTURE POINT 2

Deutschsprachige Literatur

Der international bekannteste deutschsprachige Autor ist wohl immer noch Johann Wolfgang von Goethe. 1749 in Frankfurt am Main geboren, wurde er durch Werke wie *Die Leiden des jungen Werther*, *Wilhelm Meisters Lehrjahre* oder dem Theaterstück *Faust* weltberühmt. Er interessierte sich aber nicht nur für Literatur, sondern schrieb auch

über naturwissenschaftliche Themen, wie zum Beispiel Botanik und Mineralogie. Das deutsche Kulturinstitut, das Goethe Institut, ist nach ihm benannt.

Seit 1902 gab es mehr als ein Dutzend (*dozen*) deutschsprachiger Schriftsteller:innen, die den Literaturnobelpreis gewonnen haben. Dazu gehören Thomas Mann (1875–1955) für seinen Roman (*novel*) *Die Buddenbrooks*, Hermann Hesse (1877–1962), Heinrich Böll (1917–1895) und Günter Grass (1927–2015), dessen Roman *Die Blechtrommel* (*The Tin Drum*) ein internationaler Bestseller war. 2004 wurde der Preis an die österreichische Autorin Elfriede Jelinek vergeben, die – oft aus feministischer Perspektive – gesellschaftliche Missstände (*social wrongs*) beschreibt.

Die deutschsprachige Literatur der Gegenwart ist sehr divers. Bekannt sind Julie Zeh, Bernhard Schlink und vor allem Daniel Kehlmann durch sein Buch *Die Vermessung der Welt* (*Measuring the World*). Viele Schriftsteller:innen mit einem Migrationshintergrund wie Abbas Khider, Sharon Dodua Otoo und Saša Stanišić haben die deutsche Literatur um neue Perspektiven bereichert (*enriched*). Wenn Sie aktuelle Literatur kennenlernen möchten: Deutschland hat zwei große Buchmessen (*book fairs*) – die Leipziger und die Frankfurter Buchmesse, die die größte der Welt ist.

Hier berichten Schriftsteller:innen – nicht nur deutschsprachige – welches Wort sie mit Deutschland verbinden.
Welches Wort fällt Jonathan Franzen ein? Was bedeutet es? Woran denkt Richard Ford und was für Beispiele gibt er? Wie fand Julie Zeh Deutschland vor der Wiedervereinigung? Und welches Wort verbinden Sie mit Deutschland?

VOCABULARY BUILDER 2

20.08

Look at the words and phrases and complete the missing English words and expressions. Then listen and try to imitate the pronunciation of the speakers.

VERÄNDERUNGEN	CHANGES
die Abschiedsparty (-s)	farewell ....
an/nehmen	to accept
bereuen	to regret
sich entscheiden	to decide
um/ziehen	to move / relocate
der Umzug (-"e)	move / relocation
unterschreiben	to sign
sich verabschieden	to say ....
verlassen	to leave
vermissen	to .... someone / something
der Vertrag (-"e)	contract
willkommen sein	to be welcome
ziehen nach	to move to
zu/sagen	to confirm / to accept
zu Besuch kommen	to come for a ....
jemandem eine Freude machen	to make someone happy, to please

ADJEKTIVE MIT PRÄPOSITIONEN	ADJECTIVES WITH PREPOSITIONS
dankbar + für	grateful ....
traurig + über	sad ....
verliebt + in (Akk.)	in love with

NÜTZLICHE AUSDRÜCKE	USEFUL EXPRESSIONS
jedenfalls	in any case
ewig	forever, eternal
inspirierend	.... ing
die Lesung (-en)	reading
die Qual der Wahl haben	to be spoiled for choice
Das werde ich nicht schaffen.	I won't manage it.
Wann geht es los?	When does it start?
Ich kümmere mich drum.	I'll take care of it.
Wien ist nicht aus der Welt.	Vienna is not far. (lit. out of this world)

Vocabulary practice 2

1 Match the definitions.

a Ich möchte jemandem etwas Gutes tun.
b Ich akzeptiere das Angebot.
c Es gibt mehrere Angebote.
d Ich erledige das.
e Wir fangen an.
f Ich bin ein Fachmann.
g Das schaffe ich nicht.
h Ich glaube, es war die falsche Entscheidung.
i Dort kommt man leicht hin.
j Wir machen eine Abschiedsparty.

1 Die Qual der Wahl.
2 Es ist nicht aus der Welt.
3 Ich möchte jemandem eine Freude machen.
4 Es geht los.
5 Ich kann es nicht.
6 Ich bereue das.
7 Ich bin ein Experte.
8 Ich kümmere mich drum.
9 Wir feiern, bevor du fährst.
10 Ich nehme das an.

CONVERSATION 2

Die Qual der Wahl?

20.09

1 Listen to the conversation a few times without looking at the text. Then listen again and read the text. What has Max decided to do? What is Wally planning for him?

> Max has had interviews with Berlin Tourism and the record label in Vienna. Both have offered him a job. Max meets Wally at a café to talk about his options.
>
> **Wally** Max, was für großartige Neuigkeiten.
>
> **Max** Eigentlich wollte ich den Job bei Berlin Tourism annehmen und den Vertrag unterschreiben. Dann schrieb mir Monika vom Plattenlabel heute Morgen und Lisa rief mich auch gleich an.
>
> **Wally** Ach, Max. Und jetzt hast du die Qual der Wahl? Aber nicht wirklich, oder?
>
> **Max** Wally, ich glaube, du kennst mich ziemlich gut. Ich habe schon in Wien zugesagt. Aber ich bin auch ein bisschen traurig darüber, Berlin zu verlassen. Ich bin dir sehr dankbar für alles, was du für mich getan hast.
>
> **Wally** Wenn du jetzt nicht nach Wien gehst, dann wirst du es ewig bereuen. Und dann ist da ja noch Lisa... Ich hatte schon in Hamburg bemerkt, dass du in sie verliebt warst.
>
> **Max** Wirklich? Da war mir das selber noch gar nicht klar. Na ja, wahrscheinlich doch. Ich werde dich jedenfalls sehr vermissen – und auch Aylin, Fabian, Nuri und all die anderen Freunde.

Wally	Wien ist ja nicht aus der Welt. Ich komme dich auf jeden Fall besuchen. Und du bist hier auch jederzeit willkommen. Wann geht es denn los in Wien?
Max	Ich soll nächsten Monat anfangen. Das gibt mir genügend Zeit, um alles zu organisieren und mich von allen zu verabschieden.
Wally	Wir sollten auf jeden Fall eine Abschiedsparty für dich organisieren! Da werde ich mich gleich drum kümmern.
Max	Danke, Wally. Das ist eine tolle Idee.
Wally	Gibt es sonst noch etwas, was du gerne machen würdest, bevor du nach Wien ziehst?
Max	Es gibt hier noch so viel zu sehen, das werde ich gar nicht alles schaffen. Aber ich möchte noch zu einer Lesung von Daniel Kehlmann. Und dann sollten wir auf jeden Fall gemeinsam ins Konzert gehen und etwas von deinem Lieblingskomponisten, Beethoven, hören.
Wally	Bist du dir sicher? Damit würdest du mir aber eine große Freude machen, Max!

2 Decide if these statements are *true* (richtig) or *false* (falsch). Correct the false ones.

a	Max hatte den Job bei Berlin Tourism schon angenommen.	R	F
b	Max kann sich nicht entschieden, ob er in Wien arbeiten möchte.	R	F
c	Er ist traurig darüber, Berlin zu verlassen.	R	F
d	Der Job in Wien beginnt in zwei Monaten.	R	F
e	Max möchte noch zu einer Lesung von Daniel Kehlmann.	R	F
f	Max glaubt, er wird es nicht schaffen, noch einmal ins Konzert zu gehen.	R	F

LANGUAGE BUILDER 3

 ### Language discovery 3

Look at this sentence from Conversation 2. What is unusual about the ending of the noun in italics?

Wir sollten etwas von deinem *Lieblingskomponisten*, Beethoven, hören.

Weak nouns: masculine nouns ending in -n, -en

About 10 percent of masculine nouns—called *weak nouns* (schwache Nomen)—add -n or -en to all forms apart from the nominative singular: der/ein Experte, den/einen Experten, dem/einem Experten, des/eines Experten. They often refer to people or animals:

Male people ending in -e	Male professions not ending in -er	Other male people	Names of male animals
der Experte	der Journalist	der Athlet	der Affe
der Junge	der Fotograf	der Herr	der Bär
der Kollege	der Jurist	der Kandidat	der Elefant
der Kunde	der Assistent	der Mensch	der Falke
der Franzose	der Komponist	der Nachbar	der Hase
der Psychologe	(*but not:* der Arzt)	der Student	der Löwe
der Türke		der Tourist	

> **Der Name** is also a weak noun: Wie ist sein Name? Kennst du seinen Namen?
> Remember that there are only weak **masculine** nouns.

Language practice 3

Decide if an ending is needed for these words.

a Hast du noch einmal mit dem Fotograf............. geredet?

b Mario ist Student............. an der Humboldt-Universität in Berlin.

c Hat er dir seinen Name............. gesagt?

d Sie haben den neuen Kollege............. zum Abendessen eingeladen.

e Der Kunde............. wollte unbedingt ein neues Gerät.

f Kennst du einen IT-Experte............., der mir helfen könnte?

g Ich habe selten einen so inspirierenden Mensch............. kennengelernt.

h Kennst du Herr.................... Ismar? Er ist Journalist.................... .

LANGUAGE BUILDER 4

💡 Language discovery 4

20.10

Listen to the conversation again and repeat each line in the pauses provided.
Look at these sentences from the conversation. Which prepositions are missing?

a Aber ich bin auch ein bisschen traurig dar...................., Berlin zu verlassen.

b Ich bin dir sehr dankbar .... alles, was du für mich getan hast

c Ich hatte schon in Hamburg bemerkt, dass du .... sie verliebt warst.

Adjectives and prepositions

Not only verbs but adjectives can also be followed by prepositions:

Ich bin dir sehr dankbar für alles.   *I am very grateful for everything.*

Sie war beeindruckt von Berlin.   *She was impressed by Berlin.*

Here are a few examples:

+ Accusative	+ Dative
bekannt für *(known for)*	abhängig von *(dependent on)*
berühmt für *(famous for)*	begeistert von *(enthusiastic about)*
dankbar für *(grateful for)*	
erstaunt über *(astonished about)*	freundlich zu *(friendly/kind to)*
	interessiert an *(interested in)*
schockiert über *(shocked by)*	nett zu *(nice to)*
stolz auf *(proud of)*	zufrieden mit *(satisfied with)*
traurig über *(sad about)*	
verliebt in *(in love with)*	
verantwortlich für *(responsible for)*	

> Adjectives and prepositions will help you to express an attitude:
> Ich bin beeindruckt von …
> *I am impressed by …*
> Ich bin erstaunt über …
> *I am astonished about …*
> Ich bin schockiert über …
>   *I am shocked by ….*

To form questions, use the same approach as with verbs and prepositions:

- If you ask about an object or idea, use wo(r) + the relevant preposition:
  stolz auf – Worauf bist du stolz?   *What are you proud of?*

- If you ask about a person, use wen (accusative) or wem (dative) + preposition:
  stolz auf + Akk. – Auf wen bist du stolz?   *Who are you proud of?*
  nett zu + Dat. – Zu wem warst du nett?   *Who were you nice to?*

Language practice 4

1 Add the missing prepositions and the correct endings.

   a Wien ist berühmt .... sein........... Oper.

   b Sie ist .... d........... Stadt verliebt.

   c Er war .... d........... Freundlichkeit der Menschen begeistert.

   d Sie sind stolz .... ihr........... drei Kinder.

   e Bist du .... dein........... neuen Job zufrieden?

   f Tom ist sehr .... d........... Geschichte Berlins interessiert.

   g Er ist .... d........... Social-Media-Bereich verantwortlich.

2 Now listen to Conversation 2 again and play Wally's role. Speak in the pauses provided and try not to refer to the text.

20.11

SKILL BUILDER

 1 Change the sentences by replacing the adjective with a noun.

Example: Ahmad mag, dass die Stadt so offen ist. > *Er mag die Offenheit der Stadt.*

a Silvia mag, dass Berlin so bunt ist.
b Florian genießt, dass die Stadt so frei ist.
c Claudio gefällt, dass die Berliner direkt sind.
d Elena gefällt, dass die Leute pünktlich sind.
e Xin mag, dass die Leute zuverlässig sind.
f Akira mag, dass die Berliner leicht verrückt sind.

 2 Read the text and answer the questions.

> Ein Vorurteil ist ein Urteil über Personen oder Dinge, das man ohne wirkliches Wissen (*knowledge*) und oft ohne eigene Erfahrungen gebildet hat. Vorurteile können nützlich sein, weil sie uns helfen, komplexe Dinge einfacher zu sehen und unseren Alltag zu meistern.
>
> Vorurteile sind harmlos, wenn man zum Beispiel sagt, dass die Japaner:innen alle höflich und die Engländer:innen humorvoll sind. Gefährlich werden Vorurteile, wenn sie zur Diskriminierung anderer Menschen führen. Das ist zum Beispiel bei rassistischen Vorurteilen der Fall. Dabei werden Menschen wegen ihrer Herkunft bestimmte negative Eigenschaften zugeschrieben (*attributed*).
>
> Albert Einstein hat einmal gesagt: „Es ist leichter, einen Atomkern zu spalten (*split*) als ein Vorurteil." Es ist einfacher und bequemer, sich an Vorurteile zu hängen als sich eine kritische und rationale Meinung zu bilden. Offenheit und Toleranz sind wichtig, wenn wir etwas gegen die Polarisierung in der Gesellschaft tun wollen.

Decide if these statements are *true* (richtig) or *false* (falsch). Correct the false ones.

a Vorurteile basieren auf solidem Wissen und eigenen Erfahrungen.   R   F
b Sie sind immer negativ.   R   F
c Vorurteile können gefährlich sein.   R   F
d Albert Einstein denkt, dass man Vorurteile leicht abbauen kann.   R   F

3 In the last 12 months, a lot has happened in Max's life. Connect some of the events by using the past perfect tense.

Example: *Bevor Max nach Berlin ging, ... er in Michigan ....*
(studieren) > Bevor Max nach Berlin ging, hatte er in Michigan studiert.

a Nachdem er in Berlin .... , zog er bei Wally ein. (ankommen)

b Nachdem er etwa sechs Monate in Berlin .... , reiste er nach Wien. (leben)

c Bevor er den Karneval in Basel besuchte, ... er Lisa in Wien .... (kennenlernen)

d Nachdem er in Hamburg bei einem Yogakurs .... , musste er zu einer Ärztin. (sein)

e Bevor er und Wally nach Berlin zurückfuhren, ... sie noch Geschenke .... (kaufen)

f Nachdem Max sich bei mehreren Firmen .... , bekam er zwei Angebote. (bewerben)

4 **Write down at least six of your life's events by using the sentences from Exercise 3 to help you.**

20.12

5 **Listen to three people talk about their impressions of Germany and what they see as typically German and answer the questions.**

Interview 1: Magda Zielińska

a Was sind für Magda typisch deutsche Eigenschaften?

b Wie denkt sie über diese Eigenschaften?

c Was – findet sie – gibt es gegenüber den Deutschen?

Interview 2: Zahrif Rahimi

a Wovon ist er beeindruckt?

b Welche zwei Dinge kritisiert er?

Interview 3: Giulia Borelli

a Wann ist sie nach Berlin gezogen?

b Wie – denkt sie – ist Berlin für junge Leute?

c Was ist für sie typisch deutsch?

6 **Now answer these questions for yourself. If possible, give reasons for your reply.**

a Woran sind Sie besonders interessiert?

b Von welcher Person sind Sie beeindruckt?

c Wovon sind Sie begeistert?

d Womit sind Sie in der Stadt, in der Sie leben, zufrieden? Womit nicht?

e Wofür ist Ihre Stadt bekannt?

f Worüber sind Sie manchmal schockiert?

g Worauf oder auf wen sind Sie stolz?

Now that Max has decided to accept the job offer from the record label and move to Vienna, he wants to share the news with his followers and reflects on some highlights during the last 12 months. Complete the text with words from the box.

Initiativen	Monat	Wien	Kaffeehäuser	Elbphilharmonie
Buslinie	Yogakurs	Ausstellung	Schwyzerdütsch	Klimawandel
Touristenführer	Alltag	bunter	Badeschiff	clubben

Max's blog

HOME ABOUT **BLOG** FAQ CONTACT

Hallo Leute,

das ist mein vorläufig letzter Blog aus Berlin. Jetzt war ich ein Jahr hier und ihr habt ja zum großen Teil mitverfolgen können, was ich alles gemacht und erlebt habe.

Meine ersten sechs Monate waren aufregend. Ich habe die Stadt erkundet und Udo, der als .... arbeitet, hat mir viele Tipps gegeben. Ich hoffe, ihr erinnert euch noch an die .... 100 und die vielen Sehenswürdigkeiten. Und dann das .... mitten in Berlin – großartig.

Durch Fabian und Aylin habt ihr auch etwas vom Berliner .... mitbekommen, und dass es nicht so einfach für eine junge Familie in Berlin ist. Zum Glück kann Wally ja helfen.

Ich hoffe, ihr fandet meine Beiträge über .... interessant. Wenn ihr Kunst mögt – die Museen, die Architektur, die alten ...., aber auch der Prater – das war schon beeindruckend.

Der Karneval in Basel war etwas ganz Neues für mich – auch das .... Und ich dachte, mein Deutsch wäre so gut wie perfekt.

Wenn ihr nach Hamburg kommt, müsst ihr den Hafen und die ....
sehen – dort spielt man ja nicht nur Klassik. Aber Vorsicht, falls ihr vorhabt, einen
.... zu machen.

Deutschland beschäftigt sich ja endlich auch mit seiner Kolonialgeschichte – ich
hoffe, ihr fandet die Informationen über die .... im Deutschen Historischen
Museum interessant. Und dass ich euch zeigen konnte, wie der .... auch
Berlin und Brandenburg erreicht hat. Aber auch, dass es viele .... für den
Umweltschutz gibt und dass Berlin .... geworden ist.

Und noch ein Tipp: Wenn ihr gern .... geht, dann seid ihr in Berlin richtig.

So, jetzt ist es Zeit für eine Veränderung. Ich habe einen neuen Job bekommen und
ab nächstem .... arbeite ich für ein Musiklabel in Wien. Aber mein Blog
geht natürlich weiter – also bleibt dabei und folgt mir weiter. Bald gibt es neue und
interessante Geschichten aus Wien.

Servus und bis bald. Max.

Wie geht's weiter? *What happens next?*

Max is moving to Vienna. How will his relationship with Lisa develop?
Will he like his job? Will he travel more and experience new adventures?
And will Wally come to visit him?

This time, you decide what happens next! How do you imagine the
story developing?

Remember to use **My review** and **My takeaway** to assess your progress and reflect on
your learning experience.

Congratulations, you have now completed the third level of your studies! Put your skills
to the test—take the B1 Assessment online at library.teachyourself.com and see how
much you've learned.

Answer key

The German alphabet and pronunciation

LANGUAGE PRACTICE 1 Aachen, Köln, Salzburg, Berlin, Leipzig, Wien, Hamburg, München, Zürich. **2** Peter Brinkmann, Clare Müller, Gediz Yalman, Vivien Timmler. **3** Student's own answer.

First things first

LANGUAGE PRACTICE 1 1 a sieben **b** drei **c** neun **d** zwei **e** zwei **f** drei **g** sechs **h** elf **i** dreizehn **j** fünfzehn **k** neunzehn **l** achtzehn. **2 a** 0 7 7 8 1 5 5 9 6 1 0 **b** 0 7 4 5 8 8 2 3 5 6 6 **c** 0 1 6 0 3 6 5 2 6 7 9 **d** 0 7 5 3 6 6 5 9 1 0 1

WOCHENTAGE / DAYS OF THE WEEK 1 Monday = Montag **2** Tuesday = Dienstag **3** Wednesday = Mittwoch **4** Thursday = Donnerstag **5** Friday = Freitag **6** Saturday = Samstag/Sonnabend **7** Sunday = Sonntag.

MONATE / MONTHS Januar Februar März April Mai Juni Juli August September Oktober November Dezember.

JAHRESZEITEN / SEASON a Frühling **b** Sommer **c** Herbst **d** Winter.

Unit 1

CULTURE POINT 1 QR Code: Student's own answer.

VOCABULARY BUILDER 1 morning, night, problem

VOCABULARY PRACTICE 1 a Guten Morgen. **b** Danke schön. / Vielen Dank. **c** Das tut mir leid. / Entschuldigung. **d** Kein Problem. **e** Hallo. **f** Mein Name ist … / Ich heiße … **g** Tschüss!

CONVERSATION 1 Mein Name ist Max Peterson / ich heiße Rita Hille. **2 a** At some time in the morning. **b** They share the same surname. **c** No. **d** 2b.

LANGUAGE DISCOVERY 1 1 a Sie = you **b** ich = I **c** Ich = I **d** Sie = you. **2** Sie – the formal you – always takes a capital letter.

LANGUAGE PRACTICE 1 a Sie **b** Ich **c** Sie. **d** Ich

LANGUAGE DISCOVERY 2 Sie takes the ending **-en** Ich (I) takes the ending -e.

LANGUAGE PRACTICE 2 1 a -en -e **b** -en, -e **c** -en -e. **2 a** -en -e **b** -en -e.

CULTURE POINT 2 a Normally, you would use **Sie**. **b** You would use **du**. **QR Code:** You normally use **du** at the gym or at a party. / People switch when for instance the older person suggest to a younger person to use **du**. Or when two people like each other.

VOCABULARY BUILDER 2 come, drink, from, Germany, Austria, England, Italy, Morocco, Brazil, India, interesting, loud

VOCABULARY PRACTICE 2 a Deutschland **b** Österreich **c** Polen **d** Indien **e** Marokko **f** China.

CONVERSATION 2 Coffee, Du. **3 a** F **b** R **c** R **d** F **e** R

LANGUAGE DISCOVERY 3 a Was trink*st* du - Kaffee oder Tee? **b** Woher komm*st* du?
c Wie finde*st* du Berlin? – The typical ending is **-st**.

LANGUAGE PRACTICE 3 a heißt **b** kommst **c** wohnst **d** trinkst **e** findest **f** findest **g** bist.

LANGUAGE DISCOVERY 4 The *verb* is in 2nd position.

LANGUAGE PRACTICE 4 1 a Ich heiße Magdalena. **b** Ich trinke Tee mit Zucker. **c** Ich miete
ein Zimmer. **d** Ich bin Blogger. **e** Ich finde Berlin international. **1** Wo wohnst du? **2** Wie heißt du?
3 Was machen Sie? **4** Wie finden Sie Berlin? **5** Was trinkst du? Matching: a-2, b-5, c-1, d-3, e-4

SKILL BUILDER 1 a **2** d **3** c **4** b **2**

Subject	Verb ending						
ich	**- e**	komm**e**	wohn**e**	trink**e**	lieb**e**	find**e**	heiß**e**
du	**- st**	komm**st**	wohn**st**	trink**st**	lieb**st**	finde**st** (!)	heiß**t** (!)
Sie	**- en**	komm**en**	wohn**en**	trink**en**	lieb**en**	find**en**	heiß**en**

3 sein: ich bin, du bist, Sie sind **haben:** ich habe, du hast, Sie haben. **4 a** Wie **b** Wie **c** Woher **d** Wo
e Wie **f** Was **g** Was. **5** chaotisch (N), interessant (P), laut (N), schön (P), langweilig (N), wunderbar (P).
Chaotic, interesting, loud, beautiful, boring, wonderful. **6** miete groß Wally Wally Milch Zucker liebe
chaotisch interessant groß laut

TEST YOURSELF Student's own answer. Here is a sample answer: 1 Ich heiße Magda Nowak.
2 Ich komme aus Warschau. **3** Ich wohne jetzt in Barcelona. **4** Barcelona ist sehr groß und schön, aber
manchmal ein bisschen chaotisch. **5** Ich finde Deutsch interessant und schön.

Unit 2

CULTURE POINT 1 Babbedeggel means driving license (**Führerschein** in standard German).
QR Code: Bairisch is called after a region: Bayern (Bavaria).

VOCABULARY BUILDER 1 partner, friendly, intelligent, a sense of humor

VOCABULARY PRACTICE 1 21 einundzwanzig 75 fünfundsiebzig 53 dreiundfünfzig
41 einundvierzig 97 siebenundneunzig 17 siebzehn 36 sechsunddreißig 18 achtzehn
89 neunundachtzig.

CONVERSATION 1 Wally is cooking a vegetable lasagne and she is making a salad (eine
Gemüselasagne mit Salat). 4 people – Udo, Fabian, Aylin, Nabi. **2 a** Udo **b** Fabian **c** Aylin **d** Nabi

LANGUAGE DISCOVERY 1 a kommt **b** wohnt **c** kommt **d** ist.

LANGUAGE PRACTICE 1 1 a kommt **b** wohnt **c** heißt **d** liebt **e** mietet **f** trinkt **g** schreibt
h findet **i** ist **j** hat.

LANGUAGE DISCOVERY 2 The female forms add an additional -**in** at the end of the noun:
Österreicher**in** Partner**in**

LANGUAGE PRACTICE 2 a Studentin **b** Musikerin **c** Autorin **d** Berlinerin **e** Schweizerin
f Südafrikanerin **g** Freundin.

CULTURE POINT 2 QR Code: Most have a Turkish passport.

VOCABULARY BUILDER 2 Arabic, English, Hindi, Urdu, Spanish, Turkish, doctor, mechanic, IT specialist, to repair

VOCABULARY PRACTICE 2 a 4 **b** 5 **c** 6 **d** 1 **e** 2 **f** 3

CONVERSATION 2 They speak mostly German, but also Turkish. Aylin is a doctor and Fabian is an electrician. **2 a** F **b** R **c** F **d** F

LANGUAGE DISCOVERY 3 a *you* (plural informal) **b** *we* **c** *you* (plural formal) **d** *they*

LANGUAGE PRACTICE 3 1 a she **b** you **c** they **d** she **e** you **f** they **2 Formal: a** en, en **b** en, en **c** en, en **d** en, en **e** en, en **f** en, en **Informal: g** t, en **h** t, en **i** Seid, sind **j** et, en **k** t, en **l** t, en

LANGUAGE DISCOVERY 4 Masculine nouns referring to nationalities end in **-er** or **-e**. Feminine equivalents in **-in**. Languages normally end in **-sch**.

LANGUAGE PRACTICE 4 a Englisch **b** USA, Amerikaner, Englisch **c** Kolumbianerin, Spanisch **d** Ägypter. Arabisch **e** Pole, Polnisch **f** Österreicher, Amerikaner, Deutsch, Englisch **g** Inderin, Hindi

SKILL BUILDER 1 a 01603655677: Nabi **b** 01602656477: Max **c** 01604656315: Aylin **d** 01604646316: Udo **2** Student's own answer **3 a** heißen, heiße **b** kommen, komme **c** kommst, komme **d** machst, arbeite **e** sprecht, sprechen **f** macht, studieren **g** bist, bin **h** sind, bin **4** Student's own answer **5 Sample answers: a** Ich heiße Louise McCloy-Schmidt. **b** Ich komme eigentlich aus Liverpool, in England. **c** Ich wohne jetzt in Berlin. **d** Meine Handynummer ist 07782613499. **e** Ich bin 28 Jahre alt. **f** Ich spreche perfekt Englisch, sehr gut Deutsch und ein bisschen Spanisch. **6**

	Kommt woher?	Beruf	Sprachen
Max	Portland, USA	Blogger	Deutsch, Englisch, Chinesisch
Wally	Hamburg	X	Deutsch, Englisch, Italienisch
Aylin	Berlin	Ärztin	Deutsch und Türkisch
Fabian	Berlin	Elektriker	Deutsch, Türkisch, Englisch
Udo	Berlin	Stadtführer	Berlinerisch

TEST YOURSELF 1 *Er heißt* Roger Federer und ist Schweizer. Er kommt aus Basel. Er spricht fließend Deutsch, Englisch und Französisch. **2** kommt ist heißt haben sind wohnen.

Unit 3

CULTURE POINT 1 QR Code: The museums are: **Altes Museum**, **Neues Museum**, **Alte Nationalgalerie**, **Bode-Museum**, **Pergamonmusuem**. In German it is called **Büste der Nofretete**. It is found at Neues Museum.

VOCABULARY BUILDER 1 café, club, gym / fitness studio, hotel, museum, opera (house), restaurant

VOCABULARY PRACTICE 1 a Wie geht es Ihnen? **b** Wie geht es dir? **c** Wie geht es dir? **d** Wie geht es Ihnen?

CONVERSATION 1 1 The tour ends at the Alexanderplatz. **2 a** 5 **b** 4 **c** 2 **d** 6 **e** 1 **f** 3

LANGUAGE DISCOVERY 1 a der **b** das **c** die

LANGUAGE PRACTICE 1 1 a der **b** Der **c** Die **d** Die **e** das **f** das **2 a** ein **b** ein **c** eine **d** eine **e** eine **f** ein

LANGUAGE DISCOVERY 2 1 a Telefonnummer **b** Automechanikerin **c** Stadtführer **d** Glaskuppel **2** Student's own answer

LANGUAGE PRACTICE 2 a das Fitnessstudio **b** die Hausnummer **c** der Biergarten **d** der Automechaniker **e** die Altbauwohnung **f** die Buslinie **g** die U-Bahnstation.

CULTURE POINT 2 QR code: The wall was about 160 kilometres long. The info markers provide information in several languages on the division of Germany and the construction and fall of the Berlin Wall. There are 14 sections and they are between 7 and 14 kilometers long. You can walk or cycle.

VOCABULARY BUILDER 2 tourists, new, left, right, problem

VOCABULARY PRACTICE 2 a 3 **b** 2 **c** 1

CONVERSATION 2 Max wants to see something that is related to German history and the Wall. Udo advises him to use his cell phone for directions. **2 a** F **b** R **c** F **d** R

LANGUAGE DISCOVERY 3 Udo is using the Imperative form. In these structures, the verb is in first position and - in the three examples — they do not have endings.

LANGUAGE PRACTICE 3 a 5 **b** 4 **c** 6 **d** 2 **e** 1 **f** 3

LANGUAGE DISCOVERY 4 An -**e** is added when the noun following the article is feminine, in this case **Passion**. **Eindruck** ist masculine and **Handy** is neuter, so they don't take an -**e**. **a** Mein **b** Meine **c** mein.

LANGUAGE PRACTICE 4 a dein, Mein **b** deine, Meine **c** deine, meine **d** deine, meine **e** Ihr, mein **f** Ihr, mein **g** Ihre, Meine.

SKILL BUILDER 1 a Fernsehturm **b** Bundestag **c** Glaskuppel **d** Reichstag **e** Tiergarten **f** Alexanderplatz **g** Staatsoper **h** Pergamonmusuem **i** U-Bahnstation **j** Mauermuseum **k** Friedrichstraße. Other combinations may also be possible. **2 a** der **b** die **c** die **d** das **e** die. **3 a** Machen Sie Pilates. **b** Gehen Sie joggen. **c** Besuchen Sie ein Wellnesscenter. **d** Arbeiten Sie nicht so viel. **e** Gehen Sie zu einem Tanzkurs. **f** Finden Sie ein neues Hobby. **g** Denken Sie positiv. **5 a** R **b** F **c** F **d** R
6 a 3 **b** 1 **c** 4 **d** 2

TEST YOURSELF Hallo, wie geht es Ihnen? / Vielen Dank. Mir geht es sehr gut. / OK. Dann gehen Sie links und geradeaus. / Ja, und dann nehmen Sie die zweite Straße links. / Das Restaurant heißt Istanbul. / Es ist sehr nett und nicht so teuer. / Ja, bis später.

Unit 4

CULTURE POINT 1 Kale with sausage (Grünkohl mit Pinkel) and donuts (Berliner). Grünkohl mit Pinkel can be mostly found in North Germany. Berliner can be found everywhere, but they are called differently in other regions. **QR Code:** Krapfen is mostly used in Austria and Bavaria. Kräppel is used in the area between Mainz and Erfurt. Faschingskrapfen is used in Austria. Pfannkuchen is used in East Germany.

VOCABULARY BUILDER 1 hamburger, veggieburger, sauce, mayonnaise, ketchup, orange, mineral water, vegan

VOCABULARY PRACTICE 1 a 4,79 €: Kaffee, **b** 1,39 €: Bananen **c** 7,89 €: Burger **d** 6,99 €: Veggieburger **e** 2,45 €: Ketchup **f** 0,77 €: Mineralwasser

CONVERSATION 1 He orders Currywurst classic. He pays 12,70 Euro. **2 a** F **b** R **c** F **d** R

LANGUAGE DISCOVERY 1 a einen **b** eine. The change is for the masculine article which changes from **ein** to **einen**.

LANGUAGE PRACTICE 1 1 a eine **b** eine **c** einen **d** einen **e** einen **f** einen **g** eine **h** eine **2 a** die **b** die **c** den **d** den **e** den **f** den **g** das **h** die

LANGUAGE DISCOVERY 2 The vowel changes in the **du**- and **er**-, **sie**-, **es**-, **xier**- form in comparison to the infinitive.

LANGUAGE PRACTICE 2 a nimmst **b** sprichst **c** läuft **d** sieht **e** fährt **f** liest

CULTURE POINT 2 Lena invented the curry sauce by accident when she came home carrying bottles of ketchup and curry powder. When she dropped her purchases, the ketchup and curry powder got mixed up. She quite liked the taste and then made further improvements to the recipe. In the alternative version, Herta Heuwer invented the currywurst out of boredom in Berlin in 1949. **QR code:** Student's own answer. -

VOCABULARY BUILDER 2 soup, lamb, fish, salad, rice, apple, red, gluten, free

VOCABULARY PRACTICE 2

vegan	vegetarisch	nicht-vegetarisch
die Bohne, der Salat. die Kartoffel, der Reis	der Feta, der Käse	das Fleisch, das Hähnchen, das Schweinefleisch, die Boulette, der Fisch

Depending on the ingredients, *Pizza* could be all three. The same applies to *Kuchen* (cake).

CONVERSATION 2 Wally orders a vegetarian dish. They pay by card. **2 a** Max **b** Wally **c** Max **d** Wally

LANGUAGE DISCOVERY 3 If the singular form ends in **-e**, you normally add **-n**.

LANGUAGE PRACTICE 3 1 die Tomate – die Tomaten die Vorspeise – die Vorspeisen die Sprache – die Sprachen die Kneipe – die Kneipen die Buslinie – die Buslinien die U-Bahn – die U-Bahnen die Station – die Stationen der Salat – die Salate der Fisch – die Fische das Problem – die Probleme das Geschäft – die Geschäfte das Restaurant – die Restaurants das Hotel – die Hotels der Park – die Parks.

LANGUAGE DISCOVERY 4 Nicht and **kein/keinen**.

LANGUAGE PRACTICE 4 1 a Er isst nicht gerne Fleisch. **b** Die Suppe schmeckt nicht gut. **c** Die Bouletten sind nicht vegetarisch. **d** Sie ist nicht satt. **e** Xier kommt nicht aus Kanada. **f** Wir bestellen nicht. **2 a** Nein, ich nehme keinen Nachtisch. **b** Nein, ich möchte kein Bier. **c** Nein, ich trinke keinen Kaffee. **d** Nein, ich habe keinen Hunger. **e** Nein, ich habe heute keine Zeit. **f** Nein, das ist kein Witz.

SKILL BUILDER 1 a Wein **b** Gemüse **c** Orangensaft **d** Käse **e** Hauptgericht **f** Rechnung. **2 a** N **b** A **c** A **d** N **e** A **f** N **3 a** Ich möchte ein Mineralwasser und einen Orangensaft. **b** Ich nehme einen Veggieburger und Pommes. **c** Können wir bitte bestellen? **d** Ich möchte eine Tomatensuppe als Vorspeise, bitte. **e** Ich nehme die Pizza, bitte. **f** Ich möchte einen Kaffee und ein Stück Kuchen. **g** Ich möchte ein Bier, bitte. **h** Ich möchte ein Bier, alkoholfrei. **i** Was macht das zusammen? **4**

Eduarda isst und trinkt gerne:	Eduarda isst und trinkt nicht gerne:
Fisch, Salat, Orangensaft, Mocktails, Pancake/ Pfannkuchen	Lammfleisch, Cola

5 a Xin Weng **b** Viktor B **c** Susi Klose **d** Xin Weng **e** Susi Klose

6 Ufa-Fabrik Tomatensuppe Kürbissuppe Hauptgericht Kartoffeln Bohnen Fladenpizza Feta

TEST YOURSELF Ich möchte bitte bestellen. / Ich möchte einen Salat mit Feta als Vorspeise. / Ich nehme das Hähnchen mit Reis. / Ich möchte ein Glas Weißwein und ein Mineralwasser. / Ja, sehr gut. / Ich nehme ein Stück Apfelkuchen und einen Tee. Und die Rechnung, bitte. / Mit Karte, bitte.

Unit 5

CULTURE POINT 1 QR Code: There are nearly 90,000 sport clubs. was invented in Germany. Bayern Munich is the world's largest football club. And a **Sportmuffel** is someone who does not like doing sports, a 'couch potato'.

VOCABULARY BUILDER 1 to swim, to shop, Pilates, yoga, basketball, beer, concert

VOCABULARY PRACTICE 1 a kocht **b** hört **c** malt **d** reisen **e** trifft **f** liest **g** spielen **h** shoppen

CONVERSATION 1 She goes twice a week. Music and singing. He offers to go with her to the opera. **2 a** W+M **b** M **c** M **d** W **e** W **f** M **g** W **h** M

LANGUAGE DISCOVERY 1 a in den **b** in die **c** ins

LANGUAGE PRACTICE 1 1 a ins Restaurant. **b** in den Park. **c** in den Club. **d** ins Fitnessstudio. **2** Student's own answer.

LANGUAGE DISCOVERY 2 You use **gern/gerne** in combinations with a verb/an activity. You use **mögen** with a noun.

LANGUAGE PRACTICE 2 1 a Ich trinke gern Kaffee. **b** Ich spiele gern Schach. **c** Ich sehe gern Musikfilme. **d** Wir spielen gern Computerspiele. **e** Anita macht gern Yoga. **f** Ich lese gern Krimis von Henning Mankell. **g** Wir spielen gern Tennis. **h** Corinna reist gern. **2** Student's own answer.

CULTURE POINT 2 QR Code: The zoo is open from 9.00 to 18.00. For a child you can buy a day ticket from 7,50 €, for an adult from 16 €. (All times and prices refer to time of first print.) The answers about the project will vary.

VOCABULARY BUILDER 2 up, school

VOCABULARY PRACTICE 2 1 a acht Uhr fünfundvierzig **b** vierzehn Uhr dreißig **c** siebzehn Uhr zwanzig **d** einundzwanzig Uhr **e** vier Uhr siebzehn **f** achtzehn Uhr **2 a** Es ist halb vier. **b** Es ist zwanzig nach neun. **c** Es ist Viertel vor zwölf. **d** Es ist Viertel nach sieben.

CONVERSATION 2 At 6. At around 7.30. At 17.00. **2 a** F **b** F **c** R **d** F **e** R

LANGUAGE DISCOVERY 3 a auf **b** an **c** an **d** ein. The prefix of these verbs splits up and goes to the end of the sentence/clause.

LANGUAGE PRACTICE 3 1 b **2** h **3** e **4** c **5** a **6** g **7** d **8** f

LANGUAGE DISCOVERY 4 a Gegen halb acht gehe (V) ich (S) in die Werkstatt. **b** Dann rufe (V) ich (S) Kund:innen an. **c** Ich (S) arbeite (V) gern im Büro. **d** Am Wochenende treffen (V) wir (S) oft Freunde.

LANGUAGE PRACTICE 4 1 a Sie steht um 8 Uhr auf. **b** Dann trinkt sie einen Tee. **c** Ihre Arbeit fängt um 9 Uhr an. **d** Um 13 Uhr trifft sie eine Freundin. **e** Sie gehen in ein Café. **f** Um 18 Uhr macht sie Yoga. **g** Dann kocht sie etwas zu Hause. **h** Danach spielt sie Computerspiele.

SKILL BUILDER 1 nie, selten, manchmal, regelmäßig, oft, immer. **2 a** Es ist 22 Uhr elf. / Es 22 Uhr und elf Minuten. **b** Es ist 17 Uhr 34. / Es ist 17 Uhr und 34 Minuten. **c** Es ist fünf Uhr. **d** Es ist 11 Uhr 15. / Es ist Viertel nach elf. Es ist 15 nach 11. **e** Es ist 15 Uhr 45. / Es ist Viertel vor vier. Es ist 15 (Minuten) vor vier. **f** Es ist neun Uhr 30. / Es ist halb zehn. Es ist 30 Minuten nach neun. Es ist 30 Minuten vor neun. **3 a** Ich trinke gern Wein. / Ich trinke nicht gern Wein. **b** Ich gehe gern ins Theater. / Ich gehe nicht gern ins Theater. **c** Ich mache gern Yoga. / Ich mache nicht gern Yoga. **d** Ich sehe gern Musikfilme. / Ich sehe nicht gern Musikfilme. **e** Ich trinke gern Pfefferminztee. / Ich trinke nicht gern Pfefferminztee. **f** Ich gehe gern in die Oper. / Ich gehe nicht gern in die Oper. **g** Ich esse gern Fleisch. / Ich esse nicht gern Fleisch. **4 a** ins **b** in die **c** in die **d** in den **e** ins **f** in den **5 Sample answers: a** Ich stehe um halb 8 auf. **b** Am Morgen trinke ich meistens einen Kaffee, manchmal aber auch einen Tee. **c** Meine Arbeit fängt normalerweise um 9 Uhr an. **d** In der Mittagspause esse ich etwas. Manchmal kaufe ich ein oder gehe ein bisschen spazieren. **e** Ich habe um 18 Uhr Feierabend. **f** Am Abend treffe ich gern Freunde, koche oder sehe eine Serie.

TEST YOURSELF Ich stehe um halb 10 auf. Um zehn Uhr frühstücke ich. Dann mache ich mich fertig. Ich fange um 11 Uhr mit meinem Blog an. In der Mittagspause sehe ich fern. Dann schreibe ich bis 16 Uhr weiter. Um 17 Uhr kaufe ich immer ein. Vor dem Abendessen gehe ich manchmal ins Fitnessstudio. Manchmal gehe ich auch in den Park und jogge. Dann koche ich Abendessen. Ich esse oft Pasta. Nach dem Abendessen surfe ich im Internet. Um 23 Uhr höre ich auf. Dann gehe ich ins Bett.

Unit 6

CULTURE POINT 1 QR code: Boys: 1 Noah 2 Matteo 3 Elias 4 Leon 5. Paul.
Girls: 1 Emilia 2 Emma 3 Sophia 4 Hannah, 5 Mia. (All names refer to time of first print). Student's own answer.

VOCABULARY BUILDER 1 uncle, cousin, parents, brother, creative

VOCABULARY PRACTICE 1 a Vater **b** Mutter **c** die Schwester **d** die Mutter **e** der Cousin **f** der Bruder **g** die Oma / Omi / Großmutter **h** die Enkelkinder

CONVERSATION 1 1 Aylin has two siblings Max is an only child. **2 a** 4 **b** 5 **c** 1 **d** 6 **e** 3 **f** 2

LANGUAGE DISCOVERY 1 a Meine **b** Unsere **c** Sein **d** Ihr. My = mein(e) his = sein(e) her = ihr(e) our = unser(e)

LANGUAGE PRACTICE 1 1 a Ihr **b** ihre **c** Meine **d** sein **e** Ihr **f** Meine **g** ihr **h** sein **i** Unsere

LANGUAGE DISCOVERY 2 There are two verbs. The first verb is in second position and the second verb goes to the end.

LANGUAGE PRACTICE 2 können: a kann **b** Kannst **c** können **d** Können **e** kann
müssen: f muss **g** Musst **h** muss **i** müsst **j** Müssen.

SPEAKING PRACTICE Student's own answer.

CULTURE POINT 2 QR code: Student's own answer.

VOCABULARY BUILDER 2 study, part-time, software

VOCABULARY PRACTICE 2 1 Student's own answer.

CONVERSATION 2 He says the work is interesting and the atmosphere at work is good. Wally teaches and sometimes sings in a choir. She is also doing volunteering work at a home for refugees. **2 a** F **b** R **c** F **d** R **e** F

LANGUAGE DISCOVERY 3 a im **b** in der **c** im. They differ because of the different gender of the noun they are referring to.

LANGUAGE PRACTICE 3 1a P, **b** M **2a** P, **b** M **3a** M, **b** P **4a** P, **b** M **5a** M, **b** P

LANGUAGE DISCOVERY 4 2 a war **b** hatte **c** war. He is talking about his old job.

LANGUAGE PRACTICE 4 1 a waren **b** warst **c** war **d** waren **e** wart **f** hatte **g** hatte **h** hattest **i** hatten **j** hattet

SKILL BUILDER 1 a2 **b**7 **c**5 **d**1 **e**3 **f**4 **g**6 **2 a**7 **b**3 **c**6 **d**2 **e**8 **f**1 **g**5 **h**4 **3** hatte war war waren hatte waren hatten hatte war waren hatten warst **4 a** muss, kann **b** musst, kannst **c** müsst, könnt **d** muss, kann **e** müssen, können **f** müssen, können.

TEST YOURSELF 1 a Udo: Alexanderplatz, Berlinerisch. **b Aylin:** verheiratet, zweisprachig. **c Fabian:** Elektriker, Zoo **d Hakan:** Arbeitsatmosphäre, kreativ. **e Wally:** Opernsängerin, Musik. **2** Sample answer: Max kommt aus Portland. Portland ist in den USA. Seine Mutter ist Deutsche. Sein Vater ist Amerikaner. Max ist Einzelkind. Er spricht fließend Englisch und Deutsch und ein bisschen Chinesisch. Er isst gern Currywurst. Er findet Geschichte interessant, hört gern neue Musik und geht auch gern ins Kino und schaut Serien. Im Moment arbeitet er als Blogger. In den USA hatte er verschiedene Jobs.

Unit 7

CULTURE POINT 1 QR Code: There is a 48h Vienna City Card. The card offers a number of benefits, including reduced entry prices at museums and sights and 20% off consumption at participating restaurants. You can buy it online or for instance at tourist offices in Vienna. Student's own answer. (Information is correct at the time of printing.)

VOCABULARY BUILDER 1 bus, e-scooter, underground/subway train

VOCABULARY PRACTICE 1 a das Auto **b** das Fahrrad **c** das Schiff **d** der Zug **e** der E-Scooter **f** die U-Bahn **g** die Straßenbahn, die/das Tram **h** der Bus **i** das Flugzeug **j** das Motorrad / der (Motor-)Roller

CONVERSATION 1 Because it's much cheaper going by public transport. **2 a** F **b** R **c** F **d** F **e** R.

LANGUAGE DISCOVERY 1 a dem **b** dem **c** der **d** den In the nominative, masculine articles are **der**, feminine **die** and neuter **das**. In the accusative the pattern it is: **den, die, das**. Here, masculine and neuter articles are **dem**, and the feminine one is **der**. You may remember these endings from the previous unit, following **in** when the focus is on position. Here, the articles follow another preposition: **mit**.

LANGUAGE PRACTICE 1 a dem **b** der **c** der **d** dem **e** dem **f** den

LANGUAGE DISCOVERY 2 zum, **zur** correspond to *to* **vom** to *from*. These prepositions require the dative.

LANGUAGE PRACTICE 2 1 a zum **b** zur **c** vom, zum **d** zum. **2 a** seit **b** gegenüber **c** aus **d** nach **e** mit **f** beim.

CULTURE POINT 2 Klimt lived from 1862 to 1918. His father worked as an engraver and goldsmith. The family was poor. During his 'Golden Phase' he used gold leaf. Students' own answers.

VOCABULARY BUILDER 2 Parking space, traffic, traditional

VOCABULARY PRACTICE 2

Auto	Bus, U-Bahn	Fahrrad, E-Roller etc.
Autobahn, Parkplatzprobleme, Baustelle, Parkplatz, Parkschein	Haltestelle, umsteigen, Tageskarte, Monatskarte, Bahnhof, öffentlicher Nahverkehr, Straßenbahn, U-Bahnstation, Wochenkarte	man tut etwas für die Gesundheit. Radfahrweg. Fahrradabstellplatz

CONVERSATION 2 He said it's easy to get from A to B and it's not expensive. The Klimt Villa is further away. **2 a** Der Zug hatte ein bisschen Verspätung. **b** Er fährt meistens mit dem Fahrrad. **c** Es gibt zu viele Baustellen, Staus und mit dem Parken ist es schwierig. **d** Gustav Klimt. **e** Er kann ein Fahrrad oder einen Scooter ausleihen.

LANGUAGE DISCOVERY 3 1 a deiner **b** meinem **c** seiner. **2** They are in the dative case because they follow the preposition **mit** and **von**.

LANGUAGE PRACTICE 3 a 3 **b** 5 **c** 4 **d** 1 **e** 6 **f** 2

LANGUAGE DISCOVERY 4 a nach **b** in **c** zu **d** zur. They mean *to* and *into*.

LANGUAGE PRACTICE 4 1 a in **b** zum **c** Mit, nach **d** ins **e** zum

SKILL BUILDER 1 a Flugzeug **b** Verspätung **c** Umwelt **d** Fahrkarte **e** Ermäßigung **2 a** dem, zur **b** der, zur **c** dem **d** dem **e** der **3 a** 3 **b** 2 **c** 1 **d** 3 **4 a** The Palace of Versailles. **b** You can see modern art, but also Art Noveau (Jugendtil). **c** It has a special charm. **d** Mozart **5 a** Wiener Seccession **b** Prater und „Wurstelprater" **c** Stephansdom **d** Schloss Schönbrunn.

TEST YOURSELF Student's own answer.

Unit 8

CULTURE POINT 1 QR Code: A family of five is going on a walk in the countryside. They are well-dressed and try to protect their faces from the sun as it is a warm day. However, there are some clouds coming, so the weather might be changing. In the background you can see a building that looks like a church. Maybe the family are on their way back from church.

VOCABULARY BUILDER 1 to switch **off**, to switch **off**, breakout room, chat, camera, microphone.

VOCABULARY PRACTICE 1 a singt und tanzt **b** staubsaugt **c** packt ... aus **d** verkauft etwas **e** putzt **f** frühstückt

CONVERSATION 1 On Saturday. On Saturday and Sunday. **2**

	eingekauft	fotografiert	gekocht	geputzt	gearbeitet
Wally	X			X	X
Fabian			X		
Nuri		X			

LANGUAGE DISCOVERY 1 a hat **b** habe **c** hast. The verb „haben" is used in all sentences. The present perfect tense is formed with two verbs (haben + gemacht, geschmeckt, geputzt). The simple past is made up of only one verb.

LANGUAGE PRACTICE 1 a gespielt **b** gekauft **c** geheiratet **d** getanzt **e** gedauert **f** gemietet

LANGUAGE DISCOVERY 2 a Dann habe ich <u>eingekauft</u>. **b** Abends habe ich auf Nuri <u>aufgepasst</u>. **c** Hast du schon viel <u>besichtigt</u>?

In the first two examples 'ge' goes between the prefix and the main verb. In the last example there is no 'ge' in front.

LANGUAGE PRACTICE 2 a ausgemacht **b** reserviert **c** entfernt **d** studiert **e** eingekauft **f** verkauft **g** aufgeräumt **h** ausgepackt

CULTURE POINT 2 Traditionally, a glass of water is served with coffee because it's meant to cleanse the palate. The face-down coffee spoon on top of the glass is a sign that the glass has been freshly filled up. When referring to cream, people use traditionally 'Obers' or 'Schlagobers'. 'Wiener Schnitzel' originated in Italy.

VOCABULARY BUILDER 2 come, love, skate

VOCABULARY PRACTICE 2 a fahren **b** laufen **c** reiten **d** skaten **e** fliegen

CONVERSATION 2 Her experience in the choir. She composes her own music. **2 a** An *Einspänner* (espresso with whipped cream) **b** She got up early. **c** Nigeria **d** She went to church. **e** The label discovered her songs on YouTube. **f** Max.

LANGUAGE DISCOVERY 3 a Ich habe schon viel Kaffee <u>getrunken</u> und viel Torte <u>gegessen</u>. **b** Ich habe schlecht <u>geschlafen</u>. **c** Ein Label hat mich <u>angerufen</u>. The past participles end in **-en**.

LANGUAGE PRACTICE 3 a5 **b**8 **c**6 **d**2 **e**7 **f**1 **g**3 **h**4

LANGUAGE DISCOVERY 4 a bin **b** ist **c** sind. The verb 'sein' is used to form the present perfect.

LANGUAGE PRACTICE 4 1 a bist **b** hat **c** haben **d** sind **e** ist **f** habt **g** bin **h** ist

SKILL BUILDER 1 habe hat ist ist sind ist hat haben **2 a** Café Hawelka **b** Café Central **c** Café Landtmann **d** Café Hawelka **e** Den Stephansplatz und den Stephansdom **f** Café Landtmann **g** Café Central **h** Café Central **3** Max: ... ist schon ins Zentrum gegangen; hat Fotos von Wien gemacht; hat ein Sandwich gegessen; ist ins MueumsQuartier gefahren; hat eine Ausstellung über moderne Architektur gesehen. / muss noch einkaufen (gehen); muss für Gustav kochen; muss später seine Eltern anrufen. **4 a** geflogen **b** gerannt **c** gelaufen **d** gekommen **e** gefahren **f** gegangen **g** geblieben **5** Student's own answer.

TEST YOURSELF a Zum Frühstück habe ich Tee getrunken und ein Croissant gegessen. **b** Ich bin mit der U-Bahn zur Arbeit gefahren. **c** Ich habe bis 17 Uhr gearbeitet. **d** Ich habe eine Freundin getroffen.

e Wir sind ins Fitnesscenter gegangen. **f** Zu Hause habe ich einen Salat gemacht. **g** Ich habe meine Schwester angerufen. **h** Ich habe eine Serie und die Nachrichten angeschaut. **i** Um 23 bin ich ins Bett gegangen. **j** Ich habe noch ein bisschen gelesen und dann geschlafen.

Unit 9

CULTURE POINT 1 The most expensive city is Munich. The cities with the highest rents are usually the major cities of a region / Bundesland. The answers for the other questions will vary.

VOCABULARY BUILDER 1 bungalow, balcony, kitchen

VOCABULARY PRACTICE 1 1a Schlafzimmer **b** Kinderzimmer **c** Küche **d** Badezimmer/Bad **e** Wohnzimmer **f** Balkon **g** Arbeitszimmer **h** Esszimmer **2** Student's own answer.

CONVERSATION 1 One flatmate – Marion – is a student and is doing a master in statistics. The other flatmate Ron is a musician. Yes, she likes the area a lot. **2 a** F **b** R **c** F **d** F **e** R **f** R

LANGUAGE DISCOVERY 1 a sehr = very **b** ziemlich = quite **c** wirklich = really

LANGUAGE PRACTICE 1 a3 **b**1 **c**2 **d**3

LANGUAGE DISCOVERY 2 a kleinen **b** schöne, große **c** gemütliches The masculine form ends in **-en**, the feminine in **-e** and the neuter in **-es**.

LANGUAGE PRACTICE 2 1 a neue gemütliches großes ruhiges nettes helle **b** schönes großen moderne guten nettes italienisches **c** neue viele interessante kleinen

CULTURE POINT 2 The museum was founded by the artist himself, Friedensreich Hundertwasser. You can see different aspects of his oeuvre, including paintings, printed graphics, tapestries. architectural designs and also his commitment to ecological causes. The answers to the other questions will vary.

VOCABULARY BUILDER 2 apartment, hostel, hotel, double, free, to book, washing machine, winter garden/conservatory

VOCABULARY PRACTICE 2 a On-site parking √ Good breakfast √ Free Wi-Fi √ Mini Bar √ Family rooms X Air conditioning X Pets allowed X Free bike rental √ Fitness facilities √ Good links to public transportation √ **b** Guests can use public transport for free. **c** Tramline 2 goes directly to the main station and the trade fair center. They rated the hotel 9.2.

CONVERSATION 2 The three options are a hostel, a hotel or a tiny house. He decides to take the hotel. **2 a** No **b** There are no single rooms available. **c** 1.2 km **d** In a loft bed. **e** You can use the swimming pool. **f** He is going to book the accommodation.

LANGUAGE DISCOVERY 3 a billiger **b** zentraler **c** teurer, komfortabler

LANGUAGE PRACTICE 3 a länger **b** billiger **c** interessanter **d** teurer **e** ruhiger, langweiliger **f** wärmer **g** freundlicher

LANGUAGE DISCOVERY 4 a Und es ist auch am teuersten und liegt am weitesten vom Zentrum entfernt. **b** Dann nimm doch am besten das Budget Hotel. The word you use is **am**.

LANGUAGE PRACTICE 4 1 a Hamburg ist größer als München. Berlin ist am größten. **b** Hanna ist netter als Ria nett. Xia ist am nettesten. **c** Die Elbe ist länger als die Donau. Der Rhein ist am längsten. **d** Mit der Vespa ist es schneller als mit dem Bus. Mit der U-Bahn ist es am schnellsten. **e** Pasta schmeckt besser als Salat. Pizza schmeckt am besten. **f** Ungarisch ist komplizierter als Portugiesisch. Chinesisch ist am kompliziertesten. **g** Das 3-Sterne-Hotel ist komfortabler als das 2-Sterne-Hotel. Das Luxus-Hotel ist am komfortabelsten. **h** Das Taschenbuch kostet weniger als das Hardcover. Das E-Book kostet am wenigsten.

SKILL BUILDER

1

klein	kleiner	am kleinsten
langweilig	langweiliger	am langweiligsten
alt	älter	am ältesten
zentral	zentraler	am zentralsten
groß	größer	am größten
gut	besser	am besten
viel	mehr	am meisten
gern	lieber	am liebsten

2 a Hypothek **b** Keller **c** Wohngemeinschaft **d** Aufenthalt **e** Hochbett **f** zentral **3 a** Unser Stadtteil ist wirklich nett. **b** Der lokale Park ist besonders schön. **c** Man kann hier relativ gut einkaufen. **d** Ich gehe ungefaehr 15 Minuten bis zur U-Bahnstation. **e** Da hast du absolut recht. **4 a** interessantes **b** gute **c** neues **d** starken **e** jüngere **f** schnelleren **g** nette **h** schönes. Student's own answer.

TEST YOURSELF a Ich habe eine kleine Wohnung im Zentrum von Wien. **b** Sie haben eine große Küche. **c** Wir teilen die Miete. **d** Der Supermarkt ist um die Ecke. **e** Ich brauche einen neuen Kühlschrank und einen neuen Schreibtisch. **f** Was ist dein Lieblingsort. **g** Ich möchte ein Einzelzimmer, bitte. **h** Hast du die Unterkunft gebucht. **i** Das Hostel ist viel billiger als das Hotel. **j** Er findet die Menschen in Berlin freundlicher als in Wien.

Unit 10

CULTURE POINT 1 QR Code: The Carnival starts on the Monday after Ash Wednesday, so the exact date depends on when Easter takes place. The **Morgestreich** marks the start of the Carnival. At 4.00 a.m. thousands of costumed pipers and drummers march through the Basel's center which turns into a sea of illuminated lanterns. The **Schnitzelbanks** are satirical rhyming songs. The oldest document about the Carnival dates back to 1376.

VOCABULARY BUILDER 1 shoe, green, red, gray, pink, dark, blue

VOCABULARY PRACTICE 1 a R **b** F **c** R **d** F

CONVERSATION 1 In Basel, the spectators do not dress up. **2 a** F **b** M + F **c** M + F **d** M **e** F

LANGUAGE DISCOVERY 1 a Ich ziehe gern **etwas** Bequemes an. I like to wear something comfortable. **b** Aber zur Fasnacht will ich **etwas** Anderes, **etwas** Buntes anziehen. For carnival, however, I like to wear something different, something more colorful.

LANGUAGE PRACTICE 1 a Modisches **b** Schwarzes **c** Sportliches **d** Wichtiges **e** Besonderes **f** Interessantes

LANGUAGE DISCOVERY 2 a schwarzen **b** weißen **c** roten

LANGUAGE PRACTICE 2 a Stephanie: einer weißen Bluse, einer schwarzen Hose, eleganten Schuhen, einer bequemen Jeans. **b Siggi:** einem modischen T-Shirt, einer coolen Mütze. **c Tom:** einem blauen Hemd, einer dunkelblauen Krawatte einem alten Hemd, bequemen Schuhen. **d Florbella:** einem warmen Pullover, warmen Stiefeln, leichten Sommerschuhen.

CULTURE POINT 2 Student's own answer.

VOCABULARY BUILDER 2 second-hand, produce, urban

VOCABULARY PRACTICE 2 a4 **b**3 **c**1 **d**5 **e**2

CONVERSATION 2 No, but he likes a particular brand. It has to be comfortable and the quality must be good. **2 a** 72 Stunden / 3 Tage **b** Er mag elegante Designs mit einem modernen Twist. **c** Sie haben beide in Basel studiert. **d** Max findet Markenkleidung ist nicht so wichtig für ihn. Er findet sie auch oft zu teuer. **e** Er geht gern in Secondhandläden. **f** Felix schreibt oft über nachhaltige Mode und Fair Fashion.

LANGUAGE DISCOVERY 3 The **masculine** forms are different. They are **-en** in the accusative: Wir hatten ein**en** toll**en** Morgen.

LANGUAGE PRACTICE 3 a modischer **b** farbige **c** schöne **d** eleganter **e** coole **f** bequeme, schicke

LANGUAGE DISCOVERY 4 a toller **b** junges **c** elegante, modernen

LANGUAGE PRACTICE 4 1 a lila **b** rosa **c** teuren **d** schwarzen **e** prima

SKILL BUILDER 1 a3 **b**4 **c**5 **d**1 **e**2 **2 a** der Gürtel **b** das Hemd **c** die Krawatte **d** der Schal **e** der Anzug **3 a** schönes, reiches **b** interessante, vielen **c** tolle, viele **d** großen, fantastischen **e** lustige, interessanten **f** schöne, schwierige. **4** Student's own answer **5 a** Frederike **b** Lou **c** Carla. **6** Fasnacht Tage dunkel Laternen Fashionblogger Zwiebelkuchen Fasnächtler:innen Modelabels Erlebnis Blog. **7 a** F **b** R **c** F **d** R

TEST YOURSELF Students' own answers.

Unit 11

CULTURE POINT 1 QR Code: Event types include concerts, lunch-time/tea-time concerts, film and film music, readings, lectures, presentations and workshops. Different genres include Orchestra concerts, Chamber music, Opera, Choir, Contemporary music, Jazz, World music. Rock, Pop, Singer-Songwriter, Electronic. Then student's own answer.

VOCABULARY BUILDER 1 fitness, earring, link

VOCABULARY PRACTICE 1 a Geburtstagsparty **b** Hochzeit **c** Einladung **d** Grillparty.

CONVERSATION 1 Wally wants to show Max lots of attractions in Hamburg, including the Elbphilharmonie. Because Fabian is fan of the football club FC St. Pauli they can buy something related to the club. **2 a** R **b** F Sie hat Karten für eine Gala. **c** R **d** R **e** F Sie möchten vorher etwas essen.

LANGUAGE DISCOVERY 1 a dir **b** ihm **c** ihr **d** ihnen. Meaning: *(to you)*: **dir** *(informal)* *(to him)*: **ihm** *(to her)*: **ihr** *(to them)*: **ihnen**.

LANGUAGE PRACTICE 1 **a** ihr **b** ihm **c** ihnen **d** ihr **e** ihm **f** ihr **g** ihnen **h** ihnen

LANGUAGE DISCOVERY 2 **a** dem **b** der **c** dem **d** den

LANGUAGE PRACTICE 2 **a** Hast du dem Verkäufer (IO) schon das Geld (DO) gegeben? **b** Kannst du mir (IO) bitte eine Flasche Olivenöl (DO) mitbringen? **c** Sie haben ihrem Sohn (IO) einen E-Scooter (DO) gekauft. **d** Leroy hat seinen Freunden (IO) seine neue Wohnung (DO) gezeigt. **e** Wally möchte ihrer Schwiegertochter (IO) eine Halskette (DO) schenken. **f** Kann Opa uns (IO) eine Geschichte (DO) vorlesen? **g** Der Guide empfiehlt den Tourist:innen (IO) ein Restaurant (DI)

CULTURE POINT 2 **QR Code:** It was founded in 1703. You can find a variety of goods, from second-hand goods to fruits, meat and of course fish. The **Fischauktionshalle** offers brunch with live music. In the summer the opening hours are from 5 a.m. to 9:30 and in winter from 7.30 a.m. to 9:30. (Information is correct at the time of print.)

VOCABULARY BUILDER 2 gel, bike, handbag, coffee machine, cable, perfume, me

VOCABULARY PRACTICE 2

Schmuck	Kleidung	Körperpflege / Kosmetika	Elektronisches	Anderes
Halskette, Ohrring	Hemd, Hose, Jacke, Schal	*Handcreme,* Duschgel, Bürste Kamm, Parfüm, Shampoo, Zahnpasta	Bohrmaschine, Fön, Kaffeemaschine, Ladekabel, Laptop, Tablet	Fahrradhelm Fitnessuhr, Handyhülle Handtasche, Pflanze Regenschirm, Trinkbecher

CONVERSATION 2 Max says that Wally is about 70 years old and that she is still very active. Max does not like the first perfume. **2 a** Max denkt, Wally ist etwa um die 70 (Jahre alt). **b** Es muss etwas Besonderes sein. **c** Er ist bisschen zu süßlich. **d** Sie sagt, es ist erdig, aber auch exotisch. **e** Die Kasse ist vorne rechts.

LANGUAGE DISCOVERY 3 These verbs are followed by the dative case.

LANGUAGE PRACTICE 3 **a**5 **b**1 **c**8 **d**6 **e**7 **f**4 **g**3 **h**2

LANGUAGE DISCOVERY 4 **b** The preposition **mit**. **c** The verb **gratulieren**. **d** The verb **helfen**. **e** The preposition **nach**.

LANGUAGE PRACTICE 4 **1 a** zur **b** im **c** meinem **d** der **e** meinen **f** einem. **2 a** dir **b** mir **c** ihm **d** dir **e** Ihnen **f** mir.

SKILL BUILDER 1 a Schmuck **b** Regenschirm **c** Schmuck **d** Fahrradhelm **e** Handtasche **f** herzlich. **2 a** Moritz muss länger arbeiten und kann keine Geschenke für Lea und Ahmed kaufen. **b** Ich soll die Geschenke kaufen. **c** Für Lea soll ich ein Adidas-Shirt holen. **d** Für Ahmed soll ich einen Gutschein für ein Computerspiel kaufen. **e** Moritz hat schon eine Flasche Prosecco gekauft. **f** Vor dem Hauptbahnhof um Viertel vor acht. **3 a** Pierre schenkt seiner Mutter ein Bild. **b** Sie haben ihren Freunden eine Flasche Champagner geschenkt. **c** Wir kaufen unserem Sohn ein neues Handy. **d** Hast du deiner Schwester ein Geschenk zum Geburtstag gekauft? **e** Können Sie uns ein Hotel in Hamburg empfehlen. **f** Kannst du mir helfen? **4 a** R **b** F Sie liegt an der Elbe. **c** F Ein Besuch ist kostenlos **d** R **e** F Es gibt verschiedene Musik, zum Beispiel klassische Musik, Jazz, Elektro- oder Popmusik.

TEST YOURSELF Sie: Guten Tag. Können Sie mir helfen. / Ich suche ein Buch über Berlin. Können Sie mir etwas empfehlen? / Nein, es tut mir leid. Es gefällt mir nicht. / Das ist interessant. Es gefällt mir. Was kostet es? / Vielen Dank. Wo ist die Kasse, bitte?

Unit 12

CULTURE POINT 1 QR Code: Women eat healthier than men. 81 percent of female respondents eat fruit and vegetables every day. This applies to only 63 percent of man. The majority buy vegetarian or vegan food out of curiosity and concern for animal welfare. This is followed by taste and concern for the climate and environment. The most popular regional products are eggs, vegetables, bread and meat.

VOCABULARY BUILDER 1 active, at the computer, unfit, think, cook for, energy, sport, problem, back

VOCABULARY PRACTICE 1

gesund	ungesund
aktiv sein, oft Sport treiben, sich gesund ernähren, Obst und Gemüse essen, viel Wasser trinken, schwimmen, Yoga machen, positiv denken, im Park spazieren gehen	zu lange vor dem Bildschirm sitzen, Fastfood essen, acht Stunden ohne Pause am Computer arbeiten, regelmäßig Alkohol trinken, viele Süßigkeiten essen

CONVERSATION 1 Wally had back pain. Max wants to come along to a yoga session with Wally. **2 a** Sie ernährt sich gesund. Sie isst viel Obst und Gemüse und kocht meistens selbst. Sie trinkt viel Wasser und Tee. **b** Sie hat ihr empfohlen, schwimmen zu gehen und Yoga zu machen. **c** Sie versucht, aktiv zu leben und positiv zu denken. **d** Manchmal hat er Rückenschmerzen, weil er zu lange am Computer sitzt. **e** Er glaubt, er muss mehr Sport machen. **f** Er schwimmt nicht besonders gern.

LANGUAGE DISCOVERY 1 They are placed in last position. **a** Ich glaube, <u>dass</u> ich mich gesund **ernähre**. **b** Du weißt ja, <u>dass</u> ich regelmäßig Sport **treibe**. **c** Meine Orthopädin hat mir gesagt, <u>dass</u> ich viel **schwimmen soll**.

LANGUAGE PRACTICE 1 a Jakob glaubt, dass er zu viele Süßigkeiten isst. **b** Ich denke, dass Fitnessstudios oft zu teuer sind. **c** Marlene findet, dass zu viel Sport nicht gut ist. **d** Ganja meint, dass Kaffee gut für die Gesundheit ist. **e** Nicolas findet, dass er topfit ist. **f** Kazim glaubt, dass er mehr Sport machen muss. **g** Ines denkt, dass sie genug für ihre Gesundheit tut.

LANGUAGE DISCOVERY 2 a und **b** wenn **c** weil

LANGUAGE PRACTICE 2 a3 **b**7 **c**2 **d**6 **e**4 **f**1 **g**5

CULTURE POINT 2 Health insurance in Germany is mandatory so that every resident has equal access to healthcare, regardless of their income or health status. it is funded through social security contributions deducted from employees' salaries. Less than 0,1% of the population in Germany is uninsured. (All information correct at time of printing.)

VOCABULARY BUILDER 2 hair, nose, lip, arm, hand, finger, foot, earache, tablet/pill

VOCABULARY PRACTICE 2 1 a Magenschmerzen/Bauchschmerzen **b** Zähne **c** Hand **d** Auge **e** Halsschmerzen **f** Bein.

CONVERSATION 2 No. She does not think it is serious. She prescribes an ointment, painkillers and 10 massages. **2 a** F Er hat Schulter-und Rückenschmerzen. **2 b** R **c** R **d** F Max soll die Tabletten zweimal am Tag nehmen. **e** F In den nächsten sieben Tag darf er keinen Sport machen. **f** R

LANGUAGE DISCOVERY 3 a May I have a look? **b** May I / Am I allowed to go to the gym or to do exercise? **c** In the next seven days you must not do any exercise.

LANGUAGE PRACTICE 3 1b 2h 3d 4g 5c 6a 7e 8f

LANGUAGE DISCOVERY 4 a darf **b** will **c** müssen **d** soll

LANGUAGE PRACTICE 4 1 a soll **b** will **c** wollen **d** Darfst **e** darf **f** dürfen **g** muss

SKILL BUILDER 1 Julia: Gemüse, Fleisch, besser, Fitnessstudio, dass. **Michael:** Probleme, soll, Außerdem, sitze, will **Lydia:** treibe, rauche, Alkohol Salat, krank, will. **2 a** Ich gehe gern ins Fitnesscenter, wenn ich Zeit habe. **b** Ich bin topfit, weil ich dreimal pro Woche Sport mache. **c** Ich habe Herzprobleme, weil ich Stress habe. **d** Ich glaube, dass Berlin eine interessante Stadt ist. **e** Ich bin mehr gejoggt, als ich jünger war. **f** Meine Augen tun weh, weil ich 10 Stunden an meinem Laptop gearbeitet habe. **3 a** It combines sport, philosophy and the harmony of body and soul. **b** About 5000 years. **c** About 2,5 million. **d** It strengthens the cardiovascular system, the back and other parts of the body and reduces stress. **e** They should start with a professional yoga teacher. **4 Sie:** Ich habe Halsschmerzen. / Seit zwei Tagen. / Ja, natürlich, danke. / Ja, hier tut es weh. / Soll ich sonst noch etwas machen? / Vielen Dank.

TEST YOURSELF Wien: a Öffis **b** Ringstraße **c** Gustav Klimt **d** Chor **e** Wohngemeinschaft **f** Prater. **Basel: a** Fasnacht **b** drei, 72 **c** verkleiden **d** Magisches **e** Mehlsuppe, Zwiebelkuchen. **Hamburg: a** Elbe **b** Fischbrötchen **c** Elbphilharmonie **d** Parfüm **e** geistig **f** aktiver, gesünder.

Unit 13

CULTURE POINT 1 QR Code: J. F. Kennedy sagte: Ich bin ein Berliner. Das Lieblingstier der Berliner ist der Hund. Berlin hat mehr Brücken. Es gibt 1000 „Spätis".

VOCABULARY BUILDER 1 concentrate, see

VOCABULARY PRACTICE 1 1 a trocknet ... ab **b** cremt ... ein **c** zieht ... an **d** kämmt **e** schminkt.

CONVERSATION 1 Rainer is back from his night shift. He said that it is really quiet in the morning. Max is going to have breakfast. **2 a** F Max rasiert sich nicht oft im Fitnessstudio. **b** F Er muss sich noch erholen. **c** F Er langweilt sich oft. **d** R **e** R **f** F Rainer geht trainieren, aber Max geht frühstücken.

LANGUAGE DISCOVERY 1 a mich **b** mich **c** mich **d** uns

LANGUAGE PRACTICE 1 a euch **b** mich **c** sich **d** sich **e** dich **f** uns

LANGUAGE DISCOVERY 2 a mir **b** mir

LANGUAGE PRACTICE 2 a sich **b** mir **c** dir **d** dir **e** mich, mir **f** mich, dir, mich **g** dir

SPEAKING PRACTICE Student's own answer.

CULTURE POINT 2 Das Waschcafé liegt in der Nähe des Ostkreuzes. Man kann im Laden sitzen, aber auch vor dem Laden. Für Kinder gibt es eine Ecke mit Spielzeug (toys). Es gibt Pastagerichte, Bagels, Ciabatta. Die Gerichte serviert man mit Salat. Außerdem gibt es Frühstück und zum Kaffee auch Kuchen. Then students' own answers.

VOCABULARY BUILDER 2 inform, love

VOCABULARY PRACTICE 2

an	auf	bei	für
sich erinnern, sich gewöhnen	sich einigen, sich konzentrieren	sich bedanken, sich entschuldigen	sich bedanken, sich entschuldigen, sich einsetzen, sich entscheiden

in	mit	über	um
sich verlieben	sich unterhalten	sich ärgern, sich äußern, sich informieren, sich beschweren, sich unterhalten	sich kümmern

CONVERSATION 2 He likes Berlin and finds it interesting and got used to the lifestyle. Another reason is that Lisa will come to Berlin with her band and he wants to meet her again. **2 a** F Er denkt, dass er nicht den Rest seines Lebens nur bloggen kann. **b** F Er ist sich nicht sicher. **c** R **d** R **e** R

LANGUAGE DISCOVERY 3 **a** an **b** auf **c** um

LANGUAGE PRACTICE 3 **1 a** mit **b** über **c** bei **d** für **e** auf **f** um **g** an **h** mit

LANGUAGE DISCOVERY 4 **a** Worüber **b** Wofür. They are formed with Wo + (r) + preposition.

LANGUAGE PRACTICE 4 **1 a** Worüber **b** Worauf **c** Worum **d** Worauf **e** Worüber **f** Wofür

SKILL BUILDER **1 a** 2 **b** 2 **c** 1 **d** 1 **2 a** wen **b** wen **c** wem **d** wem **e** wen **f** wem **3 a** mich erholen **b** wünscht sich **c** mir ... überlegen **d** sich konzentrieren **e** mich ... umziehen **4 a** über **b** an **c** bei / für **d** für **e** auf **5 a** Ich interessiere mich für Fußball. **b** Ich bedanke mich für die Hilfe. **c** Ich äußere mich über die politische Situation. **d** Ich konzentriere mich auf die Arbeit. **e** Ich gebe mir Mühe mit der Aufgabe. **f** Ich entschuldige mich für den Lärm. **g** Ich informiere mich über die Schweiz. **h** Wir haben uns auf einen Kompromiss geeinigt. **i** Ich ärgere mich über den vielen Verkehr. **j** Ich freue mich auf die Ferien. **6** Student's own answer.

TEST YOURSELF **a** Worauf wartet Alberto? **b** Auf wen wartet er? **c** Bei wem bedankt sich Angela? **d** Wofür bedankt sie sich? **e** Worüber informiert sich Herr Schneider? **f** Worauf konzentriert sich Benjamin? **g** Für wen setzt sich xier ein? **h** Um wen kümmert sich Freddie?

Unit 14

CULTURE POINT 1 **QR Code:** Es gibt beispielsweise die folgenden Themen/Bereiche: Berufe für Soziales (social work), Berufe im Gesundheitswesen (health service), Berufe mit Sport (sport), Berufe mit IT (IT), Berufe mit Kindern (children), Berufe mit Gaming (gaming), Berufe mit Marketing and Werbung (marketing and advertising), Berufe mit Sprachen (languages), Berufe mit Technik (technology). The student's own answer.

VOCABULARY BUILDER 1 designer, programmer

VOCABULARY PRACTICE 1

1

Positiv	Negative
Man kann viel reisen. Die Kolleg:innen sind freundlich. Wir helfen uns gegenseitig. Ich arbeite gern mit Patient:innen. Ich habe flexible Arbeitszeiten. Man kann zwei Tage im Homeoffice arbeiten. Ich kann kreativ sein.	*Es kann sehr stressig sein.* Die Arbeitszeiten sind lang. Das Gehalt ist nicht so hoch. Ich muss oft länger arbeiten. Die Arbeitsatmosphäre ist nicht besonders gut.

CONVERSATION 1 1 Aylin wanted to become an actress and Max a basketball player. In two days Max will have a job interview. **2 a** Sie arbeitet dort seit 8 Jahren. **b** Sie arbeitet gern mit Patienten. Die Kolleg:innen sind freundlich und alle helfen sich gegenseitig. **c** Das Problem sind die Arbeitszeiten. Sie arbeitet oft länger als sie sollte. **d** Sie konnte nicht gut schauspielern. **e** Er hat noch nicht erzählt, dass er übermorgen ein Vorstellungsgespräch hat.

LANGUAGE DISCOVERY 1 a wollte **b** konnte **c** sollte **d** konnte. The ending used here is **-te**.

LANGUAGE PRACTICE 1 a wollte, wollte **b** konnte, konnte **c** Durftet **d** Musstest **e** sollte, konnte

LANGUAGE DISCOVERY 2 a Als ich in Kind war (subordinate), wollte ich Basketballprofi werden (main). **b** Wenn man als Ärztin arbeitet (subordinate), ist das bestimmt eine gute Eigenschaft (main). **c** Obwohl ich nur eine Teilzeitstelle habe (subordinate), arbeite ich oft länger (main). The main clause starts with the verb (followed by the subject).

LANGUAGE PRACTICE 2 1 a 5 **b** 4 **c** 1 **d** 6 **e** 2 **f** 7 **g** 3 **2 a** ..., esse ich ein Sandwich. **b** ..., arbeite ich im Homeoffice. **c** ..., ist Svetlana mit ihrem Beruf zufrieden. **d** ..., arbeitet Ronny gern als Altenpfleger. **e** ..., wollte ich Eisverkäufer werden. **f** ..., findet Andreas keinen Job. **3** Student's own answers.

CULTURE POINT 2 Man nennt diese Unternehmen auch KMU. Mehr als 99% gehören zum Mittelstand. Eine Firma, die zum Mittelstand gehört, hat weniger als 500 Beschäftigte. Mehr als 800.000 Menschen mit Migrationshintergrund besitzen eine eigene Firma.

VOCABULARY BUILDER 2 customer service, university, flexible, communicative

VOCABULARY PRACTICE 2 1 a 1 **b** 2 **c** 2 **d** 2

CONVERSATION 2 Celine Großmann, the founder of the company is doing the interview. Max is asked the following questions: Can you talk about yourself and your career? Why did you apply for the job? What are your strengths? What are your weaknesses? **2 a** F Celine hat das Start-Up-Unternehmen gegründet. **b** F Er hat an der University of Michigan Marketing studiert. **c** R **d** F Max meint, dass er kommunikativ ist, aber auch gut im Team arbeitet. **e** R

LANGUAGE DISCOVERY 3 All three verbs here take the ending **-te**.

LANGUAGE PRACTICE 3 1 a wohnte **b** spielte **c** studierte **d** Interessiertest **e** postete **f** regnete **g** verabredeten **h** diskutierten.

LANGUAGE DISCOVERY 4 a ... wuchs ... auf **b** fand.

LANGUAGE PRACTICE 4 1 stand trank aß ging fuhr schrieb hatten sprach dauerte traf gingen aßen las ging.

SKILL BUILDER 1 a Kundenservise **b** das Gehalt **c** die Hochschule **d** den Fokus verlieren **e** teilweise **2 Answers will vary. Here are some sample answers:** Als Kind wollte ich Krankenschwester werden.

Als Kind konnte ich gut singen und laufen, aber ich konnte nicht gut malen. Ich durfte als Kind viel tun, aber ich durfte das Handy nicht so lange benutzen. Als Kind sollte ich immer um 7 Uhr zu Hause sein. Ich sollte auch nicht so viele Süßigkeiten essen, aber manchmal habe ich doch viel Schokolade und viele Bonbons gegessen. Ich musste als Kind im Haushalt helfen, zum Beispiel mein Zimmer aufräumen oder Blumen gießen. Ich musste aber zum Beispiel nicht staubsaugen. **3 a** als **b** obwohl **c** bevor **d** weil **e** wenn **f** obwohl **4 a** Als sie ein Kind war, wollte Ronja Astronautin werden. **b** Obwohl die Arbeit körperlich anstrengend ist, ist Zac gern Kfz-Mechatroniker. **c** Bevor sie um 17.00 Feierabend hat, hat sie noch ein Meeting um 16.00 Uhr. **d** Weil sie immer etwas Neues lernt, mag Yasmin ihren Job. **e** Wenn man als Designer arbeitet, muss man sehr kreativ sein. **f** Obwohl er sehr nervös war, blieb Ole im Bewerbungsgespräch ganz ruhig. **5**

a bekommen – bekam	**e** helfen – half	**i** kommen – kam	**m** sitzen – saß
b bewerben – bewarb	**f** fahren – fuhr	**j** stehen – stand	**n** trinken – trank
c bleiben – blieb	**g** finden – fand	**k** schreiben – schrieb	**o** wachsen– wuchs
d essen – aß	**h** gehen – ging	**l** tragen – trug	

6 a Sie hat sich um die Stelle als Jugendcamp-Leiterin beworben. **b** Rita (Schüller) stellt die Fragen. Sie ist Gründerin und Leiterin von Youthcamps. **c** Sie hat einen BA in Soziologie in Kiel gemacht. **d** Sie will nächstes Jahr einen Master machen und die Erfahrung als Jugendcamp-Leiterin ist dafür nützlich. Außerdem will sie auch in der Zukunft mit jungen Menschen arbeiten. **e** Selima ist geduldig, kreativ und hat viele Ideen für Aktivitäten. Ihr Bachelor-Studium hat sie gut auf die Arbeit vorbereitet. **f** Sie kann zu perfektionistisch sein und dann dauert die Arbeit zu lange.

TEST YOURSELF wollte, war, wuchs, begann, spezialisierte, schrieb, arbeitete, machte, ging, wollte, reiste, schrieb.

Unit 15

CULTURE POINT 1 QR Code: **a** 3 **b** 1 **c** 4 **d** 2 The other answer will vary.

VOCABULARY BUILDER 1 album, gig, reaction, clubbing, emotional

VOCABULARY PRACTICE 1 a Piotr **b** Gabriel **c** Marie, Matze **d** Marie

CONVERSATION 1 She said that they were very emotional because there were so many friends in the audience. The next days she would like to stay in Berlin to see an old friend from school and to get to know the music and club scene in Berlin. **2 a** auf Tour zu sein und live vor Publikum zu spielen. **b** das Album vor der Tournee fertigzustellen. **c** waren sehr positiv. **d** die Berliner Club-und Musikszene kennenlernen. **e** bei der Probe zu sein.

LANGUAGE DISCOVERY 1 a sehen **b** sein, spielen **c** zeigen. The verbs are all in the infinitive.

LANGUAGE PRACTICE 1 a 3 **b** 4 **c** 5 **d** 1 **e** 2

LANGUAGE DISCOVERY 2 Um ... zu corresponds to the English *in order to*; **um** is placed at the beginning of the clause and **zu** + infinitive at the end.

LANGUAGE PRACTICE 2 1 a um eine Ausstellung über Pop-Art zu sehen. **b** um sich besser verteidigen zu können. **c** um in einem Orchester zu spielen. **d** um seinen Flug nicht zu verpassen. **e** um eine Serie auf Netflix zu schauen. **f** um Ausstellungen zu sehen und clubben zu gehen.

2 Student's own answer. Here are some samples: **a** Ja, ich habe große Lust, für ein paar Tage nach Berlin zu fahren. Ich liebe Berlin. **b** Es tut mir leid, aber ich habe keine Lust, einen Salsa-Kurs zu machen. Ich tanze wirklich nicht gern. **c** Ich habe leider keine Zeit, am Wochenende zu einem Konzert zu gehen. Wir fahren dieses Wochenende weg. **d** Ja, Ende April passt mir gut. Da habe ich Zeit. **e** Ja, natürlich ist es möglich, uns nächste Woche zu treffen. An welchen Tag hast du gedacht. **f** Ja, ich habe heute Abend auch Lust, etwas zusammen zu kochen. Wollen wir chinesisch kochen?

CULTURE POINT 2 QR code: Student's own answers.

VOCABULARY BUILDER 3 impressionism, museum, ticket price, video installation, art, modern art, art, music, atmospheric, not

VOCABULARY PRACTICE 3

Positiv	Negativ
Ich liebe zeitgenössische Kunst. Ich mag die Bilder von van Gogh. Ich bevorzuge Fotografien.	Das ist mir zu traditionell. Ich interessiere mich nicht für Malerei. Abstrakte Kunst gefällt mir nicht wirklich. Museen sind nicht mein Ding. Videoinstallationen sind mir zu langweilig.

CONVERSATION 2 The concert went well and was sold out and they played four encores. Wally and Lisa talk about music and art and their preferences. **2 a** F Max hat viel über Lisa erzählt. **b** F Wally bevorzugt traditionelle Musik. **c** R **d** R **e** F Sie sagt, sie kann bis Mittwoch bleiben. **f** R

LANGUAGE DISCOVERY 3 a Interessierst **b** Beschäftigst.

LANGUAGE PRACTICE 3 Student's own answer. Here are some sample answers: **a** Nein, ich interessiere mich nicht für Fußball. Ich finde, Fußball ist langweilig. **b** Ja, ich interessiere mich sehr für Musik. Ich höre gern Jazz, Rock und vor allem Popmusik. **c** Ja, ich beschäftige mich sehr mit sozialen Medien. Ich benutze verschiedene soziale Netzwerke und poste selbst auch viel. **d** Nein, ich begeistere mich nicht für Mode. Markenkleidung ist nicht wichtig für mich. **e** Als ich jünger war, habe ich mich mehr mit Kunst beschäftigt. Jetzt gehe ich nur noch manchmal ins Museum oder in eine Ausstellung. **f** Ja, ich ärgere mich manchmal über zu hohe Ticketpreise. Viele Sachen sind sehr teuer geworden. **g** Ja, ich interessiere mich für Kunst und informiere mich oft über neue Ausstellungen.

LANGUAGE DISCOVERY 4 In all three sentences the verb **werden** is used to form the future tense.

LANGUAGE PRACTICE 4 1 a Er wird nachher ins Fitnesscenter gehen. **b** Naomi wird nächste Woche ihre Prüfung schreiben. **c** Wir werden im September umziehen. **d** Das Museum wird in 15 Minuten öffnen. **e** Wann wird Tim seinen neuen Job anfangen? **f** Ich werde ein neues Handy kaufen müssen.

SKILL BUILDER 1 Sample answers: a um ein paar Freunde zu treffen. **b** um bessere Berufschancen zu haben. **c** um einen Spaziergang zu machen. **d** um eine Serie zu schauen. **e** um dort drei Wochen Urlaub zu machen. **f** um gesünder zu leben. **2 a** wird **b** werde **c** wird **d** werden **e** Wirst **3**

	Mag am liebsten:	Warum:	Zusätzliche Info:
Marlene	Musik	Es gibt viele interessante neue Bands und Musiker:innen.	Spielt selbst Gitarre und arbeitet manchmal als DJ.

Mirja	Kunst	Liebt die Romantiker seit ihrer Kindheit.	Lieblingsmaler: Caspar David Friedrich
Lars	Sport	Ist gern aktiv und an der frischen Luft.	Geht manchmal ins Theater oder in den Comedyclub.

4 a Ding **b** Spaß, entdecken **c** die Natur darstellt **d** ganz ehrlich **5 Student's own answers.**

TEST YOURSELF 1 a3 **b**1 **c**4 **d** **2 Sample summary:** The history of electronic dance music started in Berlin after the Fall of the Wall. Young artists from East and West Berlin started to organise raves and techno parties in derelict buildings. The first well-known clubs were E-Werk, Tresor and Ufo. However, techno music was not invented in Berlin but a few years earlier in Detroit. The originator of German techno music was the band Kraftwerk. Their album *Autobahn* was an international hit and inspired musician world-wide. You can find the best techno clubs nowadays between Alexanderplatz and Revaler Straße. One of the most well-known clubs is *Berghain*. Other popular places are *Tresor* and *Kater Blau*. What makes clubbing so special in Berlin is that there is no closing time for clubs on the weekends. There is also no dress code.

Unit 16

CULTURE POINT 1 QR Code: Berge gibt es im Schwarzwald, am Bodensee, im Allgäu, im Elbsandsteingebirge, im Harz und in der Eifel. Gut schwimmen gehen kann man vor allem in der Ostsee und Nordsee. Aber auch im Spreewald, im Allgäu, im Bodensee und in der Eifel. Ideal zum Wandern sind der Schwarzwald, das Allgäu, das Elbsandsteingebirge, der Harz, die Lüneburger Heide und die Eifel. The last question will vary.

VOCABULARY BUILDER 1 field, cliff, sandy, sunny, day

VOCABULARY PRACTICE 1 Bild 1: a der Baum **b** das Gebirge **c** der Berg. **Bild 2: d** der Wald **e** der See **f** der Strand.

CONVERSATION 1 Lisa said she realised how different/varied the landscapes are. Wally specifically likes the chalk cliffs and the long, sandy beaches. **2 a**4 **b**3 **c**7 **d**1 **e**5 **f**2 **g**6

LANGUAGE DISCOVERY 1 a bergig **b** waldig **c** sonnig. The adjective forms for these nouns all end in **-ig**.

LANGUAGE PRACTICE 1 a hügelig **b** waldig **c** wolkig **d** fleißig **e** durstig **f** salzig **g** sonnig **h** vielfältig

LANGUAGE DISCOVERY 2 a höchste **b** vielen schönen **c** waldreichste **d** größte, deutsche

LANGUAGE PRACTICE 2 1 a deutsche **b** kleine **c** höchste **d** letzten **e** bekannteste, meisten **f** polnischen **g** sandigen, warme **h** größte

CULTURE POINT 2 QR Code: Die Festspiele finden von Mitte Juni bis Ende August statt. Sie finden in dem Ort Ralswiek statt, direkt am Wasser. Die Karten kosten zwischen 20-50 Euro (at time of print). The play may vary.

VOCABULARY BUILDER 2 camping, continent, party, round, city, wellness, world, sunbathe

VOCABULARY PRACTICE 2 a Wellnessurlaub **b** Pauschalurlaub **c** Partyurlaub **d** Heimaturlaub **e** Abenteuerurlaub

CONVERSATION 2 Lisa möchte sich am liebsten ausruhen und faulenzen, zum Beispiel irgendwo am See liegen und nichts tun. Max reist gern und entdeckt neue Städte und Länder. Er interessiert sich auch für Kultur. Sein Traumurlaub wäre es, durch Asien zu reisen. Er würde dann auch gern für ein Freiwilligenprojekt arbeiten oder Englisch unterrichten. Lisa würde gern eine Tour durch Italien machen. **2 a** R **b** F Im Urlaub möchte sich Lisa ausruhen und nichts tun. **c** R **d** F Er würde dann gern für ein Freiwilligenprojekt arbeiten oder Englisch unterrichten. **e** F Sie war noch nie in Italien.

LANGUAGE DISCOVERY 3 The verb form indicates that something is not real but rather hypothetical or a wish.

LANGUAGE PRACTICE 3 1 a3 **b**6 **c**5 **d**1 **e**6 **f**2 **2 a** Könnten Sie mir helfen? **b** Wir könnten uns auch morgen treffen. **c** Er müsste regelmäßiger trainieren. **d** Ich glaube, dass das nichts für mich wäre. **e** Wäret ihr bereit, am Wochenende zu arbeiten? **f** Hätten Sie heute Abend Zeit? **g** Hättest du Lust, mit uns laufen zu kommen? **h** Könntest du mir einen Kaffee mitbringen?

LANGUAGE DISCOVERY 4 a hättest würdest **b** hätte, würde **c** wäre, würde All missing verbs are in the *Konjunktiv II* form.

LANGUAGE PRACTICE 4 1 a würde er mehr Bücher lesen. **b** würde sie mehr Sport machen. **c** würde sie ein neues Auto kaufen. **d** würde er eine neue Gitarre und Lautsprecher kaufen. **e** würden sie nach Kenia fliegen. **f** würde sie gerne Dubai besuchen. **2 Student's own answer. Here are some sample answers:** Wenn ich mehr Zeit hätte, würde ich ein neues Instrument lernen. Wenn ich reicher wäre, würde ich mir wahrscheinlich eine schöne Wohnung oder ein schönes Haus kaufen. Ich würde auch mehr Geld spenden. Wenn ich eine Traumreise machen könnte, würde ich eine Weltreise machen und verschiedene Länder besuchen.

SKILL BUILDER 1 a Wald **b** Gegend **c** Landschaft **d** flach **e** Freiwilligenarbeit **f** langweilig **2** viertgrößte bevölkerungsreichste höchste tiefste längsten durchschnittliche jüngsten wärmsten. **3** Student's own answers. **4** Student's own answer. Here is a sample answer: Mein Traumurlaub? Nun, am liebsten würde ich eine Reise nach Südamerika unternehmen. Ich würde mit meiner besten Freundin Rita zuerst nach Buenos Aires fliegen. Wir würden zuerst einen Tangokurs machen und die Kultur und das Essen genießen. Dann würden wir weiter in den Süden nach Patagonien fahren. Die Landschaft und die Natur dort sollen fantastisch sein. Dann würden wir auch den Norden des Landes besuchen. Wir würden vier Wochen bleiben und in Hotels, aber auch mal im Zelt übernachten. Ich würde natürlich mein Handy mitnehmen, mein Spanischbuch und mein Mückenspray. (*mosquito repellent*) **5 a**4 **b**1 **c**3 **d**2

TEST YOURSELF würde könnte müsste hätte könnte würden hätte würden würden würde würden könnten sollte könnte würde wäre wäre würden.

Unit 17

CULTURE POINT 1 QR Code: 1951 übernahm die Stasi das Gefängnis. Insgesamt saßen hier rund 11.000 Menschen im Gefängnis. Die Menschen, die hier im Gefängnis waren, waren Kritikerinnen und Kritiker der SED-Regierung. Zum Beispiel Leute, die am Aufstand von 1953 beteiligt waren. Später auch Personen, die aus der DDR flüchten wollten, auch Schriftstellerinnen und Schriftsteller oder Bürgerrechtlerinnen und Bürgerrechtler (*civil rights activists*).

VOCABULARY BUILDER 1 era, army, war, wall, historic(al)

VOCABULARY PRACTICE 1 a Zeitraum **b** Besatzungszonen **c** Krieg **d** Berliner Mauer **e** Deutsche Geschichte **f** Frieden

CONVERSATION 1 The Berlin Blockade in 1948; separation of Berlin in different zones/sectors; the air lift; the building of the Berlin Wall in 1961; the Fall of the Wall in 1989. **2 a**4 **b**1 **c**5 **d**3 **e**2

LANGUAGE DISCOVERY 1 a des **b** der **c** der **d** einer. The structures express a sense of ownership and possession. Translation: **a** The history of the airport is very interesting. **b** It played a significant role in the history of the city. **c** And it was in 1948? Long before the building of the Wall? **d** It was really the end of an era.

LANGUAGE PRACTICE 1 a der **b** der **c** des Mauerbaus **d** der **e** des Kalten Krieges **f** des Parlaments

LANGUAGE DISCOVERY 2 a während **b** wegen, trotz **c** Aufgrund. These prepositions are followed by the genitive.

LANGUAGE PRACTICE 2 1 a2 **b**4 **c**1 **d**3 **e**6 **f**5

CULTURE POINT 2 QR Code: Es gab viele Diskussionen zur deutschen Kolonialgeschichte und Kontroversen, wie man die Geschichte zeigen soll. Jetzt gibt es die Bereiche „Wirtschaft und Welthandel", „Koloniale Räume und Gesellschaften", „Herrschaft und Gewalt" sowie „Widerstand, Selbstbehauptung und Völkermord". Im Mittelpunkt stehen die ehemaligen deutschen Kolonien in Afrika. Es gibt aber auch ein Kapitel über die deutsche Handelskolonie Kiautschou.

VOCABULARY BUILDER 2 colony, reparation, integration, parallel, discriminate against, integrate, divers

VOCABULARY PRACTICE 2 a Einwanderer:innen **b** divers **c** Flüchtlinge **d** willkommen **e** Integration **f** Parallelgesellschaften **g** deutsche Staatsangehörigkeit.

CONVERSATION 2 They talk about the biggest former colony, Deutsch-Südwestafrika (German Southwest Africa), today's Namibia. **2 a** F Max hat nicht gewusst, dass Deutschland viele Kolonien hatte. **b** F In der Schule von Aylin wurde das nicht viel thematisiert. **c** R **d** F Deutsch-Südwestafrika, das heutige Namibia, war die größte deutsche Kolonie. **e** R **f** F Man diskutiert darüber, wie man die Menschen in Namibia entschädigen kann.

LANGUAGE DISCOVERY 3 a wurde **b** wurde **c** wurde. The verb **werden** is used in all three sentences.

LANGUAGE PRACTICE 3 1 a werden **b** werde **c** werden **d** wurdest **e** wurde **f** Wurdet

LANGUAGE DISCOVERY 4 a von **b** Durch

LANGUAGE PRACTICE 4 a von **b** von **c** durch **d** durch **e** von **f** durch

SKILL BUILDER 1 a des Hotels **b** des Museums **c** der ... Berlins **d** des Buches **e** der **f** der **2 a** Das Schloss Schönbrunn in Wien wird von Millionen Besuchern besichtigt. **b** Es wurde ab 1696 als Jagdschloss gebaut. **c** Zwischen 1743–1749 wurde das Schloss zum ersten Mal umgebaut. **d** Es wurde zum Beispiel von Kaiserin Sisi bewohnt. **e** Es wurde 1996 in die Liste des Weltkulturerbes der UNESCO aufgenommen. **f** Der Tiergarten Schönbrunn wurde schon im 18. Jahrhundert eröffnet. **g** Hier werden viele Tiere aus aller Welt gehalten. **h** Während der Fütterungen werden viele interessante Details über die Tiere erzählt. **3 a** Berlin ist beliebt, weil es Vielfalt bietet. **b** Es gibt Restaurants und

Imbisse mit Gerichten aus aller Welt. **c** Im House of One gibt es eine Kirche, eine Moschee und eine Synagoge. **d** Sie hat Berlin eine „Barrierefreie Stadt" genannt. **e** Berlin gilt als eine der tolerantesten Stadte der Welt. **f** Dort kommen etwa 750.000 Menschen zusammen, um zu feiern und für die Rechte von schwulen, lesbischen und queeren Menschen zu demonstrieren. **4** Student's own answer. **5 a** Alex_2005 **b** DHM_Fan879 **c** Marion_Gesch **6 a** DHM_Fan879 **b** Marion_Gesch **c** DHM_Fan879 **d** Alex_2005 **e** Marion_Gesch. **7** Student's own answer. Here are some sample answers: **a** Trotz des heißen Wetters fahre ich mit dem Fahrrad. **b** Wegen der Kälte trage ich heute meinen dicken Wintermantel. **c** Während des Urlaubs möchte viel von dem Land kennenlernen. **d** Anstatt eines Nachtisches trinke ich einen Espresso. **e** Aufgrund der niedrigen Preise habe ich mehr eingekauft. **f** Trotz der vielen Arbeit treffe ich meine Freunde. **g** Wegen des Klimawandels fahre ich weniger Auto.

TEST YOURSELF a Die Geschichte der Schweiz ist interessant. **b** Im 16. Jahrhundert wurde die Reformation von Ulrich Zwingli in Zürich eingeführt. **c** Während der Napoleonischen Kriege wurde die Schweiz von Frankreich besetzt. **d** Die moderne Schweiz wurde 1848 gegründet. **e** Wegen/Aufgrund ihrer Neutralität nahm die Schweiz nicht am 2 Weltkrieg teil. **f** Deutsch ist eine der offiziellen Sprachen in der Schweiz. **g** Bern ist der Sitz des Parlaments. **h** Viele Gesetzte in der Schweiz werden durch Referenden entschieden

Unit 18

CULTURE POINT 1 QR Code: All answers are provided in the online test.

VOCABULARY BUILDER 1 solar, trash/rubbish

VOCABULARY PRACTICE 1 a zudrehen **b** kaufen **c** trennen **d** laufen **e** auszumachen **f** trinke **g** fahre **h** vermeiden.

CONVERSATION 1 They use energy-saving bulbs, they don't have their devices in standby mode, they close the faucet when brushing their teeth, they buy regional products and buy mineral water in returnable bottles. **2 a** … Zeitungen und Papier. **b** … Biomüll, zum Beispiel Essensreste. **c** … den Wasserhahn zu. **d** …, vermeidet man Plastikmüll. **d** … mehr Subventionshilfen für Solarenergie.

LANGUAGE DISCOVERY 1 The letter -s Is used to join these nouns together.

LANGUAGE PRACTICE 1 1 a die Öffnungszeiten **b** das Lieblingsland **c** das Wirtschaftklima **d** die Schönheitscreme **e** die Arbeitszeit **f** der Familienurlaub **g** die Wochenkarte **h** der Sonnenschein **i** die Augenfarbe **j** der Lebenslauf **k** das Universtätsranking.

LANGUAGE DISCOVERY 2 The sentences express wishes. The **Konjunktiv II** form is normally used to express this. **a** Es würde gut sein, wenn es mehr staatliche Subventionshilfen für Solarenergie geben würde. **b** Ich würde wünschen, wir würden alle mehr tun.

LANGUAGE PRACTICE 2 1 a Es würde helfen, wenn Leute weniger Wasser aus Plastikflaschen trinken würden. **b** Es wäre auch gut, wenn wir mehr Produkte aus der Region kauften. **c** Wir würden Ressourcen sparen, wenn wir kaputte Sachen reparierten. **d** Wir könnten die CO_2-Emissionen reduzieren, wenn wir weniger Fleisch äßen. **e** Ich fände es gut, wenn man mehr Geld in alternative Energien investierte. **f** Ich wünschte mir, man stellte weniger Fast Fashion her. **g** Wenn es doch nur ein besseres öffentliches Verkehrsnetz gäbe, würden mehr Leute Bus und Bahn benutzen. **2 Student's own answer.**

CULTURE POINT 2 QR Code: NABU bedeutet Naturschutzbund. Nabu engagiert sich zum Beispiel für Artenvielfalt, den Schutz intakter Lebensräume, gute Luft, sauberes Wasser, gesunde Böden und den schonenden Umgang mit endlichen Ressourcen.

VOCABULARY BUILDER 2 warming, catastrophe, weather

VOCABULARY PRACTICE 2 1 a Brennstoff **b** Erderwärmung **c** eine Dürre **d** Auswirkungen

CONVERSATION 2 Higher temperature have an effect on health, especially on elder people. Silke thinks we need to put more pressure on politicians and all countries need to work together. **2 a** ... hat deutlich zugenommen. **b** ... teilweise Dürre und auch deutlich mehr Starkregen. **c** ... Berlin klimaneutral werden. **d** ... den Ausstoß von CO_2 zu verringern. **e** ... etwas gegen die Einwegverpackungen zu unternehmen. **f** ... es geht nur gemeinsam.

LANGUAGE DISCOVERY 3 a ob **b** was **c** wie

LANGUAGE PRACTICE 3 a Können Sie mir sagen, ob man hier in der Nähe gut essen gehen kann? **b** Wissen Sie, wo es hier ein gutes Fitnessstudio gibt? **c** Wissen Sie, was man hier abends unternehmen kann? **d** Können Sie mir sagen, wie weit es bis zum nächsten Glascontainer ist? **e** Wissen Sie, wie oft der Müll abgeholt wird? **f** Entschuldigung, könnte ich Sie fragen, ob es hier einen Park in der Nachbarschaft gibt? **g** Entschuldigung, könnte ich Sie fragen, ob man hier noch spät einkaufen kann? **h** Wissen Sie, ob hier ein Nachtbus fährt?

LANGUAGE DISCOVERY 4 In the sentences, the main function is to add a tone of politeness.

LANGUAGE PRACTICE 4 a hätte (*1 = to add a tone politeness*) **b** solltest (*2 = to offer advice*) **c** könnte (*1 = to add a tone politeness*) **d** hätte, ginge (*5 = within hypothetical conditional sentences*) **e** würde (*4 = to express hypothetical situations / ideas*) **f** täten (*3 = to express wishes*).

SKILL BUILDER 1 a 2 **b** 9 **c** 8 **d** 6 **e** 5 **f** 1 **g** 4 **h** 3 **i** 7 **2 a** F **b** R **c** F **d** F **e** R **f** F **g** R **h** R **3 a** An deiner Stelle nähme ich eine Kopfschmerztablette. **b** An deiner Stelle bestellte ich Tickets online. **c** An deiner Stelle meditierte ich. **d** An deiner Stelle schrieb ich ihm eine WhatsApp-Nachricht. **e** An deiner Stelle ginge ich zum Frisör. **f** An deiner Stelle spräche ich mit ihr. **g** An deiner Stelle ginge ich zum Arzt. **h** An deiner Stelle meldete ich mich bei einem Kurs an. **4 a** Man verwendet es fast überall, zum Beispiel in Smartphones, Autos, Spielzeug, Kosmetika. **b** Es ist so beliebt, weil es so vielfältig ist. **c** Weltweit werden 400.000 Tonnen hergestellt. **d** Nur etwa 15% werden weltweit recycelt. **e** Mehr als zwei Drittel endet als Müll. **f** Wir finden den Plastikmüll auf einer Mülldeponie oder irgendwo in der Natur, zu einem großen Teil auch im Meer. **g** Wir brauchen einen Masterplan gegen das Plastikproblem. **5** Student's own answers.

TEST YOURSELF Sample answers: **a** Natürlich weiß ich, dass der Klimawandel schon in Berlin angekommen ist. Es gibt in den letzten Jahren mehr Extremwetter, was Auswirkungen auf die Gesundheit, aber auch auf die Landwirtschaft hat. **b** Natürlich weiß ich, in welche Tonne Zeitungen und Papier kommen. Sie kommen in die blaue Tonne. **c** Und ich kann Ihnen auch sagen, wohin der Biomüll kommt. Er kommt in die braune Tonne. **d** Ich weiß, wie oft der Müll abgeholt wird. Man holt ihn alle 14 Tage ab. **e** Und ich kann Ihnen auch erklären, was Einwegverpackungen sind. Das sind Verpackungen, die man nur einmal benutzt. **f** Ja, natürlich kann ich Ihnen ein paar Initiativen nennen. Es gibt Urban Gardening Projekte, Zer0-Waste-Shops, kleine Reparaturgeschäfte, Secondhand-Kaufhäuser und Startup-Unternehmen, die umweltfreundliche Produkte herstellen. **g** Ich kann Ihnen auch sagen, wie viel Plastik jedes Jahr hergestellt wird. Etwa 400.000 Tonnen weltweit. **h** Und ich weiß auch, wie viel Prozent davon weltweit recycelt wird. Nämlich weltweit nur etwa 15 Prozent.

Unit 19

CULTURE POINT 1 QR Code: Man kann Deutsch mit Kursen, Nachrichten oder mit Musik lernen und vertiefen. Außerdem gibt es Beiträge zu Wortschatz, Gesellschaft und dem Leben in Deutschland. „JoJo sucht das Glück" ist eine Telenovella mit Übungen. Student's own answer.

VOCABULARY BUILDER 1 commentary, politician, controversial, live, objective, radio, social media

VOCABULARY PRACTICE 1 a4 **b**6 **c**5 **d**2 **e**7 **f**1 **g**3

CONVERSATION 1 Wally reads the *Berliner Zeitung*. And she watches the news, the *Tagesschau*. **2 a** F **b** F **c** R **d** R **e** F **f** R

LANGUAGE DISCOVERY 1 a die **b** dem **c** den. The missing words are similar to definite articles. They refer to a noun in the previous clause.

LANGUAGE PRACTICE 1 a die **b** die **c** das **d** den **e** der **f** deren

LANGUAGE DISCOVERY 2 a2 **b**3 **c**1 So far, you used **wo** and **was** primarily as question words but they can also act as relative pronouns.

LANGUAGE PRACTICE 2 1 a5 **b**1 **c**6 **d**3 **e**2 **f**4

CULTURE POINT 2 Freundschaften und Beziehungen in der realen Welt leiden unter der ständigen Nutzung des Smartphones. Das kann gesundheitliche Folgen haben, wie zum Beispiel Magersucht. Der ständige Gebrauch von Smartphones führt auch zur Polarisierung und zu weniger Toleranz in der Gesellschaft.

VOCABULARY BUILDER 2 password, friendly, profile, trend, in, to log out, download, upload, block, post

VOCABULARY PRACTICE 2 sozialen Medien Beiträge Trend like aktualisiere Profil poste Follower:innen blockiere Hasskommentare

CONVERSATION 2 Lisa is talking about the job of a Social Media Content Creator at her label. **2 a** F Max sagt, es ist eine schöne Überraschung. **b** F Sie ruft an, weil ihr Label eine neue Stelle ausschreiben möchte. **c** R **d** R **e** R

LANGUAGE DISCOVERY 3 The context in which the verbs appear is indirect / reported speech. Find out more in the section.

LANGUAGE PRACTICE 3 a auslogge **b** habe **c** seiet **d** solle **e** habest, gepostet **f** seien, gestiegen.

LANGUAGE DISCOVERY 4 a ausschreiben (infinitive), würden (Konjunktiv II) **b** sollten (Konjunktiv II), bekommen (infinitive)

LANGUAGE PRACTICE 4 1 a müsse (Konjunktiv I) **b** hätten (Konjunktiv II. Konjunktiv I, *haben*, would be identical with the present tense form) **c** hätte (Konjunktiv II. Konjunktiv I, *habe*, would be identical with the present tense form). **d** solle (Konjunktiv I) **e** folge (Konjunktiv I) **f** benutzten (Konjunktiv II. Konjunktiv I, *benutzen*, would be identical with the present tense form).

SKILL BUILDER 1 Das ist Herr Hoffmann, ... **a** der als Blogger arbeitet. **b** dessen Freundin auch Bloggerin ist. **c** dessen Sohn in den USA studiert. **d** der einen roten Porsche fährt. **e** der meistens italienische Anzüge trägt. **f** den man auf vielen Partys sieht. **g** von dem ich noch 500 € bekomme. **2 Sample answers: a** Alexander ist der Mann, der Gewichte hebt. **b** Ole ist die Person, die Fahrrad fährt. **c** Annika ist die Frau, die Basketball spielt. **d** Franka ist die Frau, die läuft. **e** Angelo ist der Mann, der American Football spielt. **f** Britta ist die Frau, die Tennis spielt. **h** Erkan ist der Mann, der boxt. **i** Sabine ist die Frau, die Gymnastik macht. **3 Suggested answers: a** … Teilzeit sei. **b** … attraktive und lustige Videos und Bilder erstelle. **c** … solle diese auf unsere Kanäle in den sozialen Medien hochladen. **d** … müsse auch mit den Musiker:innen sprechen, um neue Inhalte zu entwickeln. **e** … internationale Follower:innen hätten / haben. **f** … brauche ein Studium im Bereich Marketing und Erfahrung mit sozialen Medien. **g** … sei von Vorteil. **h** … freue sich auf die Bewerbung von Max. **4 a**1 **b**5 **c**6 **d**4 **e**8 **f**2 Not used: 3, 4, 7

TEST YOURSELF

Suggested answers:

Sie	*Jeremy meint, er habe viel über Berlin gehört* und *wollte* es immer besuchen. Es sei so eine diverse und kreative Stadt.
Sie	*Ich habe Jeremy gesagt,* dass ich ihm auf Instagram folge. Ich habe noch keine Post von ihm über Berlin gesehen. *Ich habe ihn dann gefragt, warum das so sei.*
Sie	*Jeremy sagte*, er habe eine Pause gebraucht. Es sei wirklich hart / schwierig, immer neue Posts zu kreieren / zu schreiben. Er hoffe, dass Berlin ihn inspiriere. Er habe schon viele neue Ideen für Posts.
Sie	*Ich habe Jeremy gefragt*, wohin er jetzt gehe. *Er meinte*, er gehe zu dieser trendigen Bar / Szene-Bar in Kreuzberg. Er sagte, wir könnten später mehr auf seinem Instagram herausfinden.

Unit 20

CULTURE POINT 1 QR Code: Details will depend on the most recent election results.

VOCABULARY BUILDER 1 (in)direct, disciplined, (in)correct, (dis)organized, (in)tolerant, democracy, populism, tolerance, friendship

VOCABULARY PRACTICE 1 a arbeitsam **b** diszipliniert **c** humorvoll **d** organisiert **e** verschlossen **f** reiselustig **g** ehrlich **h** intolerant **i** weltoffen **j** lebenslustig

CONVERSATION 1 Before Nabi came to Germany she thought that Germans are disciplined, hard-working, correct/uptight and a bit humourless. **2 a** Am Anfang hat Max Berlin entdeckt. **b** Ihn hat überrascht, wie unterschiedlich und vielfältig Deutschland ist, nicht nur die Landschaften, die Städte, aber auch die Menschen, das Essen. **c** Am Anfang fand sie es schwer, Leute kennenzulernen. **d** Er mag die Offenheit der Leute, die Zuverlässigkeit und das Gefühl von Toleranz und Freiheit. **e** Sie glaubt, Deutschland ist viel offener und bunter geworden.

LANGUAGE DISCOVERY 1 a Offenheit **b** Zuverlässigkeit **c** Freiheit. You add -**heit** or **keit**.

LANGUAGE PRACTICE 1 a Offenheit **b** Freiheit **c** Freundlichkeit **d** Krankheit **e** Zuverlässigkeit **f** Gesundheit **g** Buntheit **h** Direktheit **i** Verrücktheit **j** Ehrlichkeit **k** Berühmtheit **l** Pünktlichkeit **m** Persönlichkeit **n** Wahrheit

LANGUAGE DISCOVERY 2 It is formed with the past tense of haben or sein + the past participle: **a** *war … gewesen.* **b** *hatte … besucht.*

LANGUAGE PRACTICE 2 a war **b** waren **c** hatte **d** hatte **e** war **f** war

CULTURE POINT 2 **QR Code:** Für Jonathan Frentzen ist es das Wort Gründlichkeit. Es bedeutet *thoroughness* auf Englisch. Für Richard Ford ist es das Wort Kultur. Als Beispiele nennt er: Musik, Wissenschaft, Romane, Gedichte, Literaturkritik, Theater. Für Julie Zeh ist es Liebe. Vor der Wiedervereinigung fand sie Deutschland blöd (silly, stupid). Jetzt hat sie im Osten von Deutschland ihre Heimat gefunden und sieht sich als Deutsche und Europäerin.

VOCABULARY BUILDER 2 party, goodbye, to miss, visit, for, about, inspiring

VOCABULARY PRACTICE 2 **a**3 **b**10 **c**1 **d**8 **e**4 **f**7 **g**5 **h**6 **i**2 **j**9

CONVERSATION 2 Max wants to take the job in Vienna and Wally is going to organise a farewell party for him. **2 a** F Max hatte den Job bei Berlin Tourism noch nicht angenommen. **b** F Er hat sich entschieden, in Wien zu arbeiten. **c** R **d** F Der Job in Wien beginnt nächsten Monat. **e** R **f** F Max will auf jeden Fall noch einmal mit Wally ins Konzert gehen.

LANGUAGE DISCOVERY 3 The noun takes an **-n** although it is the singular: Lieblingskomponisten.

LANGUAGE PRACTICE 3 **a** Fotografen **b** Student **c** Namen **d** Kollegen **e** Kunde **f** IT-Experten **g** Menschen **h** Herrn, Journalist

LANGUAGE DISCOVERY 4 **a** darüber **b** für **c** in

LANGUAGE PRACTICE 4 **1 a** für seine **b** in die **c** von der **d** auf ihre **e** mit deinem **f** an der **g** für den

SKILL BUILDER 1 a Sie mag die Buntheit der Stadt. **b** Florian genießt die Freiheit der Stadt. **c** Claudio gefällt die Direktheit der Berliner. **d** Elena gefällt die Pünktlichkeit der Leute **e** Xin mag die Zuverlässigkeit der Leute. **f** Akira mag die leichte Verrücktheit der Berliner. **2 a** F Vorurteile basieren auf keinem soliden Wissen. Oft werden sie ohne eigene Erfahrungen gebildet. **b** F Sie können nützlich sein, weil sie uns helfen, komplexe Dinge einfacher zu sehen und unseren Alltag zu meistern. **c** R **d** F Er hat gesagt: „Es ist leichter, einen Atomkern zu spalten als ein Vorurteil." **3 a** ankommen war **b** gelebt hatte **c** hatte ... kennengelernt **d** gewesen war **e** hatten ... gekauft **f** beworben hatte **4** Student's own answer. **5 Interview 1: a** Typisch deutsche Eigenschaften für Magda sind, dass die Leute pünktlich und zuverlässig sind. Sie findet die Menschen auch direkt und ehrlich. **b** Sie mag diese Eigenschaften. **c** Sie meint, dass es viele Vorurteil gegenüber den Deutschen gibt. **Interview 2: a** Zahrif hat beeindruckt, dass Deutschland 2015 so viele Flüchtlinge aufgenommen hat. **b** Er kritisiert. dass man in Deutschland oft zu bürokratisch ist. Man sollte auch mehr an die Zukunft denken und mehr in die Infrastruktur investieren. **Interview 3: a** Sie ist nach ihrem Studium nach Deutschland gezogen. **b** Sie sagt, für junge Leute bietet die Stadt sehr viel – es gibt viele Freizeitangebote und Arbeitsmöglichkeiten. **c** Typisch deutsch ist für sie, dass sich die Leute sehr um die Umwelt kümmern. Typisch deutsch ist für sie auch, dass die Geschäfte sonntags geschlossen sind. **6** Student's own answers. Here are a few sample answers: **a** Ich bin besonders an Reisen interessiert. **b** Ich bin besonders von Amal Clooney beeindruckt. **c** Ich bin von allem begeistert, was mit Mode zu tun hat. **d** Ich bin damit zufrieden, dass die Stadt, in der ich lebe, weltoffen und tolerant ist. Ich bin aber nicht mit der Luftqualität zufrieden. **e** Meine Stadt ist für ihren schonen Hafen bekannt. **f** Manchmal bin ich darüber schockiert, was Leute alles wegwerfen. **g** Ich bin auf meine Eltern stolz.

TEST YOURSELF Touristenführer Buslinie Badeschiff Alltag Wien Kaffeehäuser Schwyzerdütsch Elbphilharmonie Yogakurs Ausstellung Klimawandel Initiativen bunter clubben Monat

Index of grammatical topics